Essential GCSE ICT

for OCR

Stephen Doyle

OXFORD

UNIVERSITY PRESS

OXFORD
UNIVERSITY PRESS

Great Clarendon Street, Oxford OX2 6DP

Oxford University Press is a department of the University of Oxford.
It furthers the University's objective of excellence in research,
scholarship, and education by publishing worldwide in

Oxford   New York

Auckland   Cape Town   Dar es Salaam   Hong Kong   Karachi
Kuala Lumpur   Madrid   Melbourne   Mexico City   Nairobi
New Delhi   Shanghai   Taipei   Toronto

With offices in
Argentina   Austria   Brazil   Chile   Czech Republic   France   Greece
Guatemala   Hungary   Italy   Japan   Poland   Portugal   Singapore
South Korea   Switzerland   Thailand   Turkey   Ukraine   Vietnam

Oxford is a registered trade mark of Oxford University Press
in the UK and in certain other countries

British Library Cataloguing in Publication Data

Data available

ISBN 978-1-85008-545-4

10 9 8 7 6 5 4 3 2

Printed in Malaysia by Vivar Printing Sdn Bhd.

Paper used in the production of this book is a natural, recyclable product
made from wood grown in sustainable forests. The manufacturing process
conforms to the environmental regulations of the country of origin.

Editor:	Geoff Tuttle
Project development:	Adrian Moss (Instructional Design Ltd) with Rick Jackman (Jackman Publishing Solutions Ltd)
Concept design:	Patricia Briggs
Layout artist:	GreenGate Publishing Services
Illustrations:	GreenGate Publishing Services
Cover design:	Jumpto! www.jumpto.co.uk
Cover image:	Courtesy of Chris Harvey/Fotolia.com

Contents

Introduction to the OCR GCSE

What the book covers

This book covers both the GCSE and the GCSE (Short course) in ICT.

To obtain a GCSE (Short course) in ICT you need to study Unit B061 and Unit B062.

To obtain a GCSE in ICT you need to study Unit B061, Unit B062, Unit B063 and either Unit B064 or Unit B065.

Units

The specification for GCSE ICT is arranged in units. You are required to take four units for the GCSE and two units for the GCSE Short course. The units are as follows:

- **Unit B061**: ICT in today's world
- **Unit B062**: Practical applications in ICT
- **Unit B063**: Written
- **Unit B064**: Creative use of ICT OR
- **Unit B065**: Coding a solution

The way the book is organized

The book covers the content needed for all the units. This means that if you are taking the GCSE you will need to cover all the material in this book. It you are taking the GCSE (Short course) you will only need to cover some of the material in this book.

The book is organized in topics:

- Topics 1 to 9 cover the material for the Unit B061 examination.
- Topics 10 to 20 cover the material for the Unit B063 examination

Unit B061: ICT in today's world

- GCSE course 20%
- GCSE Short course 40%
- External examination (written paper or computer-based test): 1 hour

In this unit you will study a range of ICT systems as used in the home, at school and in society. You will need to be aware of current and emerging technologies and the impact that these advances have on yourselves and others.

Unit B062: Practical applications in ICT

- GCSE course 30%
- GCSE Short course 60%
- Controlled assessment

In this unit you will study a range of everyday software applications. You need to develop your skills in using common software and be able to apply them to solve problems. For controlled assessment you will need to manipulate and process data/ information effectively and efficiently and to present the results in a format suitable for purpose and audience.

Unit B063: ICT in context

This is unit is only taken by students who are doing the GCSE course and not the GCSE Short course.

- GCSE course 20%
- External examination (written paper or computer-based test): 1 hour

In this unit you will study a range of ICT systems in a business or organizational context. You must also be aware of current and emerging technologies and their impact on yourself and on others.

The question paper is based on pre-release material that relates to a specific business or organization. You will be given this pre-release material prior to the examination and you will need to study and do some research on it before taking the examination. You will need to remember the work you have done as you are not allowed to take any preparatory work into the examination with you.

This unit is not stand-alone as it will also build on the knowledge and understanding you gained in Units B061 and B062.

Unit B064: Creative use of ICT OR Unit B065 Coding a solution

One of these units is only taken by students who are doing the GCSE course and not the GCSE Short course.

Unit B064: Creative use of ICT

- GCSE course 30%
- Controlled assessment

For this unit, you have to solve a problem by creating and developing a multimedia solution with appropriate creative elements.

Unit B065: Coding a solution

- GCSE course 30%
- Controlled assessment

For this unit, you have to identify a potential coded solution to a problem and solve it using basic programming techniques.

The organization of Unit B061: ICT in today's world

The material for unit B061 is divided into topics:

Topic 1 ICT systems
Topic 2 Exchanging information
Topic 3 Presenting information
Topic 4 Manipulating data
Topic 5 Keeping data safe and secure
Topic 6 Legal, social, ethical and environmental issues when using ICT
Topic 7 Using ICT systems
Topic 8 Monitoring, measurement and control technology
Topic 9 ICT and modern living

The organization of Unit B063: ICT in context

Topic 10 ICT systems
Topic 11 Networks
Topic 12 Information knowledge based systems (IKBS) and expert systems
Topic 13 Project planning
Topic 14 Exchanging information
Topic 15 Presenting information
Topic 16 Manipulating data
Topic 17 Legal, social, ethical and environmental issues when using ICT in businesses and organizations
Topic 18 Managing data/keeping data safe and secure when using ICT
Topic 19 Current and emerging technologies
Topic 20 The Examination for Unit B063: ICT in context

Note: You may notice that some of the titles of the topics are the same for Units B061 and B063. In Unit B063 you have to study the material as applicable to business and organizations. In the examination for Unit B063 you will have to have knowledge of both these units.

The controlled assessment units

In this section you will be looking at what you have to do for the controlled assessment units. Controlled assessment involves completing coursework in a supervised environment. The controlled assessment is worth 60% of the total mark for ICT for both the full and short courses.

The tasks are all set by OCR but you do have a choice with some of them which you will see later.

The controlled assessment units you need to take

If you are taking the GCSE Short course you only take the unit:

- **Unit B062**: Practical applications in ICT

If you are taking the GCSE course you take two units:

- **Unit B062**: Practical applications in ICT

and one of the following two units:

- **Unit B064**: Creative use of ICT
- **Unit B065**: Coding a solution

Unit B062: Practical applications in ICT

For this unit you are required to use common applications software to manipulate and process data and other information effectively and efficiently, and present information in a format suitable for purpose and audience.

You will be given a choice of set tasks from which you have to choose. The tasks are set out in controlled assessment material that is produced by OCR and given to your school or college. You will be given your own copy of this material. You will also be given your own copy of the controlled assessment mark scheme. This is very useful as it gives further information on what you need to do to get a good mark. You should keep referring to both of these documents to check that what you are producing is appropriate.

Unit B064: Creative use of ICT

The assessment for this unit consists of a controlled assessment, in which you will complete one task from a choice of tasks. This is practical work so you will be using computers and popular applications software to create material and/or a product.

You will be given a paper outlining the controlled assessment material that you will need to read very carefully. This will give you the tasks and also show you the controlled assessment mark scheme. This will show exactly how your work is to be marked and you should keep referring to this through your work on the assessment.

There is example specimen material showing a typical controlled assessment with its corresponding mark scheme on the OCR website.

Unit B065: Coding a solution

The assessment for this unit consists of a controlled assessment. You will be given a task and you will need to complete the task by coding a solution using programming code.

The controlled assessment material will outline exactly what you have to do. You will need to read this very carefully and keep referring back to it to check that you have produced exactly what is required. You must also keep referring to the marking criteria, which you can use to gauge how well you are doing.

There is example specimen material showing a typical controlled assessment with its corresponding mark scheme on the OCR website.

Introduction to the features in the student book

The philosophy behind the student book

This student book has been based on extensive research from schools and colleges on the different ways ICT is taught and this book has been developed with all the findings in mind. As this is a new specification, many students and teachers/lecturers will be finding their way and the aim of the book is to provide a depth of coverage for the material for the units for the course.

This book builds on the material your students will have covered at Key Stage 3 and seeks to cover the material needed for the OCR GCSE and OCR GCSE Short course in ICT.

This book should be used by the teacher/lecturer in conjunction with the teacher support materials. Of course this book can be used stand-alone, but if you are a teacher then there are many resources in the teacher support materials to help your students succeed and maximize their marks. The Teacher's Resource Guide DVD-ROM contains the following non-digital resources: Answers to the Questions, Worksheets, Activities, Case studies and Multiple-choice questions.

The Teacher's Resource Guide DVD-ROM also includes a wealth of digital materials such as PowerPoint presentations, Multiple-choice questions and Matching questions. These will all help your students consolidate their understanding of the topics.

The structure of the student book

There are two units for the GCSE short course and four units for the GCSE course. The student book covers all four units.

Units B061 and B063 are assessed by examination and Units B062 and either B064 or B065 are assessed by controlled assessment.

The material for Units B061 and B063 is divided into topics with each topic being further divided up into double-page spreads. This allows division of each topic into bite-size easily digested chunks of material. There is a consistent page design in each of these units.

The material for the controlled assessment units (i.e., Units B062 and B064/B065) is dealt with briefly and further information can be found on the OCR website.

Topic introduction pages

The first page of each topic consists of an introduction to the material in the topic and includes the following features:

Topic introduction: just a couple of paragraphs introducing students to the subject matter in the topic.

Key concepts: this lists the key concepts covered in the topic. These key concepts are identical to those in the GCSE OCR specification.

Contents: the contents lists the spreads used to cover the topic and each spread covers key concepts.

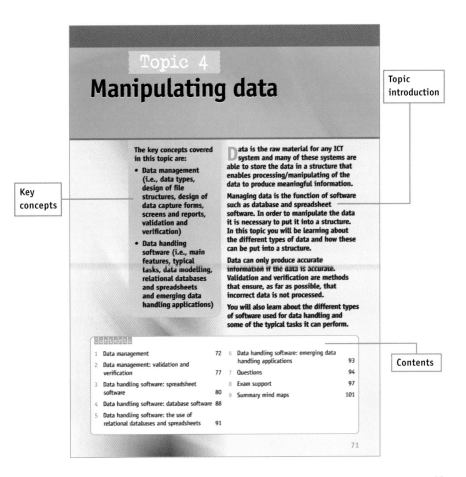

Introduction to the features in the student book *continued*

Topic spreads

You will find out

Photographs   Questions   Extension activity

Examples

Some of the topics covering Unit B063 (i.e. Topics 10 to 19) contain examples. These examples explain the material in the topics in a context. They enable you to learn using a real-life situation and prepare you for studying ICT in relation to a context.

Questions and Extension activities

Questions are usually included at the end of each content spread and are used to consolidate learning. Some **Extension activities** are also included within the content spreads. This allows you to look at the spreads and then practise the questions. The answers to all the questions are available in the teacher support materials, which are available separately on DVD-ROM and complement the student text.

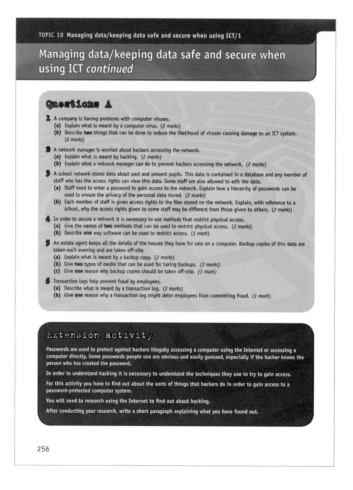

Questions spreads

Examination style questions: are designed to be similar to GCSE examination questions and have marks to give you the opportunity to understand how answers are marked. The answers to the questions are included on the Teacher's Resource Guide DVD-ROM.

Test yourself: consists of a series of statements with a blank space in which to insert the missing word or words that appear in a list. Students can either write the missing words as a list or they can write the complete sentence with the missing word inserted. The answers to these are available on the Teacher's Resource Guide DVD-ROM.

Activities: offer interesting things for you to do that will help add to and reinforce the material in the spreads and give you practice with ICT skills.

Case study spreads

Case studies: real-life case studies are included in some of the topics that relate directly to the material in the topic. Case studies give a context in which you can answer the examination questions. Often examination questions on ICT ask not only for a definition or explanation but also an example. Case studies build up your knowledge of how the theory you learn about is used in practice.

Case study questions: will give you practice at answering questions that relate to real-life situations. The questions have been carefully constructed to be similar to the examination questions you could be asked and relate directly to the case study and other material contained in the content spreads. If your teacher has the Teacher's Resource Guide, they will have the answers to these case study questions.

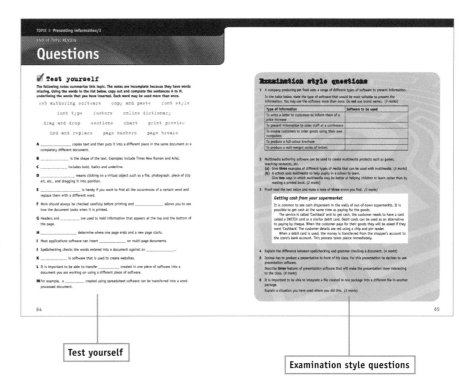

Test yourself

Examination style questions

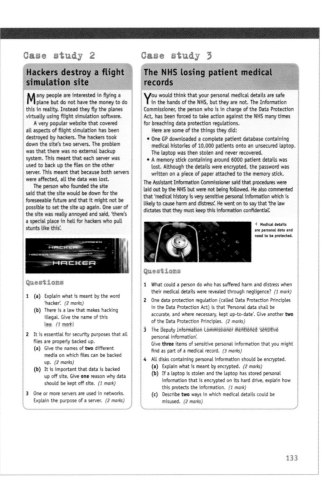

Exam support

Worked example: is an important feature because it gives you an insight into how the examination questions are marked. At GCSE, you can have the knowledge but still fail to get a good mark because you have failed to communicate what you know effectively. It is essential that you understand just what is expected of you when answering questions for GCSE.

Student answers: you can see an examination question with examples of two different student answers. For each student answer there is a corresponding sample Examiner's comment.

Examiner's comment: offers you an insight into how examiners mark student answers. The main thing here is to be able to see the mistakes that can be made and ensure that you do not make similar mistakes. By analysing the way answers are marked, you will soon be able to get more marks for the questions that you answer by not making common mistakes.

Examiner's answers: offers some of the many possible answers and an indication of how the marks are distributed between the answers. It should be borne in mind that there are many possible correct answers to some questions and that any mark scheme relies on the experience of the markers to interpret the mark scheme and to give credit for answers that do not appear in the mark scheme.

Summary mind maps

Mind maps are great fun to produce and a very good way of revising. They are included at the end of each topic to summarize the material contained in the topic. Sometimes there will be only one mind map and other times there will be several – it all depends on how the material in the topic is broken down.

As well as using these mind maps to help you revise, you should produce your own.

Why not produce them using the computer? There are many good pieces of mind-mapping software.

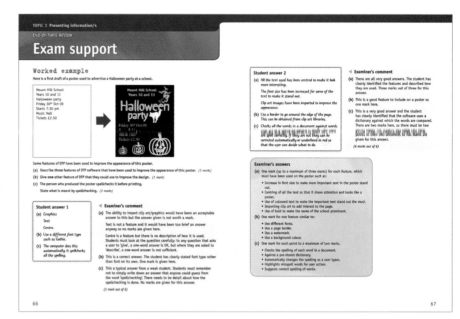

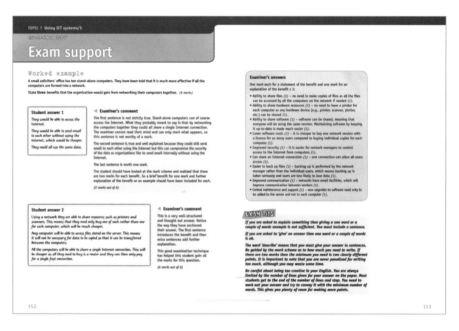

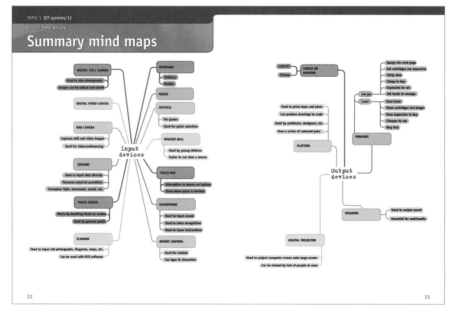

Topic 1

ICT systems

The key concepts covered in this topic are:

- **The main components of a computer system**
- **Common applications where microprocessor technology is used**
- **Differences between hardware and software**
- **Different types of software**
- **The appropriate use of input, output, storage and communication devices**
- **The advantages and disadvantages of a variety of input, output, storage and communication devices**
- **User interfaces**
- **Different types of commonly used software and their uses**
- **Advantages and disadvantages of different software**
- **The different file types used to support software**

All ICT systems consist of two main parts: the hardware and the software.

Hardware refers to those items of an ICT system that you can touch. This means that hardware means components such as printers, keyboards, memory, storage devices, etc. Even the storage media is classed as hardware. This means that a CD is hardware but if it has a program on it then the program itself is classed as software. It is hard to separate the program (i.e., the software) from the hardware that is used to store it.

Software is the programs that are necessary to get the hardware to do a useful job. In this topic you will be looking at the purposes of different types of software.

In this topic you will also be looking at ICT systems and their components.

Contents

Systems

You will find out

▷ **About the main components of a computer system**

▷ **About common applications where microprocessor technology is used**

▷ **About the differences between hardware and software**

▷ **About different types of software**

Computer systems consist of hardware and software and these are used together with procedures and sometimes people to create systems. All ICT systems consist of microprocessors, which are the brains of the system, but microprocessors are also present in other devices such as washing machines, cameras, children's toys, etc. In fact most of the electrical or battery-controlled devices you use in the home have microprocessors in them to help control their operation.

▲ The power supply for a desktop computer.

The main components of a computer system

The main components of a computer system are:

- **Central processing unit (CPU)** – microprocessor (one or more) processes the raw data and turns it into information.
- **Main/internal memory** – are chips inside the computer where data is held and can be accessed immediately by the computer. Some program instructions are stored here along with the data the computer is currently working on.
- **Input devices** – these are those devices that are under the control of the computer (either wired or wireless) and are used to input data (e.g., commands/ instructions, raw data) for processing. Input devices can include a keyboard, mouse, joystick, stylus, etc.
- **Output devices** – these are the devices that give the results of processing the data by the computer. Output devices can range from screens and printers to motors and robot arms.
- **Secondary/backing storage** – this is any storage that is not classed as memory. It is used to hold programs and data. Secondary/backing storage devices include magnetic hard drives, optical drives (CD or DVD), flash/pen drives, etc.
- **Power supplies** – when used with mains power (230V) the power needs to be lowered and changed from AC to DC and this is the purpose of the power supply. Laptops need power supplies to power them when they are plugged in or to charge the batteries so that they can be used away from mains power.

What is hardware?

Hardware are the physical components that make up the ICT system. If you can touch it, then it is hardware. Hardware includes input devices (keyboards, mouse, scanner, etc.) storage (memory, hard drive, etc.) the processor and the output devices (screen, printer, plotter, etc.). Also included in hardware are the communication devices needed to send data across networks.

Examples of hardware

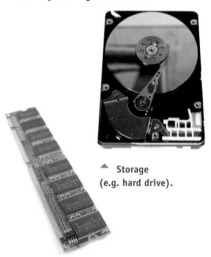

▲ Storage (e.g. hard drive).

▲ Memory chips.

▲ Mouse.

▲ Keyboard.

How many pieces of hardware can you name?

There are many different pieces of hardware that make up or can be used with computer systems. How many of them can you name? Produce a list and it is ok to use the names of the examples given in this topic. About 20 different names would be a good score.

Microprocessor technology

Modern computer systems consist of many different pieces of hardware but the most important is the microprocessor.

Microprocessors are computers, usually on a single chip, that are put into electronic devices to check, regulate and control something. A microprocessor performs all the processing that is needed. It does all the calculations and decides what to do next. You can find microprocessors in washing machines, cars, sewing machines, central heating controls, children's toys, etc.

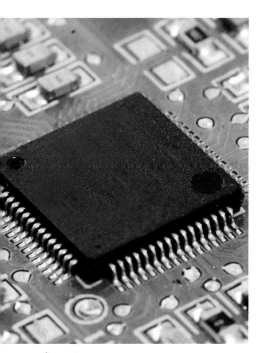

▲ A microprocessor.

Applications for microprocessors

Microprocessors are the brains of many devices and make them more intelligent. Any device that can be controlled can have a microprocessor in it. Microprocessor technology can be used in many different places for lots of different things such as:

- Microprocessors in the home:
  - Washing machines – used to control valves to let the water in, motors to turn the drum, pumps to pump the water out, heaters to heat the water up and so on.
  - Children's toys – use microprocessors to control lights, motors, speakers, etc.
  - Heating systems – control the time the heating comes on, keep the temperature constant by turning the heating on/off, etc. Modern heating systems can control the individual temperatures of each room from a central place.
  - Alarm systems – can detect the presence of an intruder and some systems will even contact the police.
- Microprocessors in everyday life:
  - Traffic lights – keep the traffic moving freely and they can adjust the time the lights are on green depending on the traffic flow from each direction.
  - Mobile phones – use microprocessors to control their many functions. For example, they control messages coming into the phone.
  - Used in cars – many parts of cars are microprocessor controlled. Examples include airbags, ABS braking systems, which help stop the car skidding when braking hard.
- Microprocessors in the workplace:
  - Computers, communications and videoconferencing, which all contain microprocessors, enable many people to work from home.
  - Robots in factories and warehouses all contain microprocessors and are used for assembling components, spray painting, packing, etc.
  - Process control – microprocessors control valves to allow liquids into large vessels for fermenting, reacting, cooking, etc.

Software

Computer hardware is useless without the software, as it is the software that instructs the hardware what to do. Software is the general name given to all the programs that can be run on computer hardware. They all give the hardware instructions and can be divided into two main categories: operating systems and applications software.

Operating systems software and applications software will be looked at in detail later in this topic.

Examples of software include:

- Operating system software (e.g. Windows, Linux, Mac OS)
- Word-processing
- Database
- Spreadsheet
- Presentation
- Web design
- Web browser
- Graphics
- Photo editing.

When asked to name types of software, do not use brand names. So, for example, you should use word-processing rather than saying Word.

Hardware the parts of the computer that you can touch and handle.

Microprocessor the brain of the computer consisting of millions of tiny circuits on a silicon chip. It processes the input data to produce information.

Software the actual programs (i.e. instructions) that allow the hardware to do a useful job.

Systems *continued*

Types of computer

Personal computers (PCs)

Personal computers or PCs for short are the computers you are most likely to use at home, school or work. They include desktop computers, laptops, notebooks and PDAs.

Mainframe computers

Mainframe computers are large, powerful computers capable of supporting a large number of terminals. Mainframe computers contain a number of processors, which means they can perform many tasks at the same time. Mainframe computers are found in banks, airlines, government departments, the NHS, etc.

Supercomputers

Supercomputers are the most powerful computers you can get. They contain many processors, which enables them to make many billions of calculations per second. They are used for the most complicated of tasks such as predicting climate change, producing weather forecasts, etc.

▲ **Mainframe computer with console.**

Embedded computers

Embedded computers act as the brain of many electronic/electrical devices. They are microprocessors that act as small computers and they are connected directly to the devices to control them in some way. Embedded computers have a program stored on chips that gives them the instructions on what to do.

Any electrical/electronic device that can be controlled in some way probably has an embedded computer in it. Embedded computers can be found in:

- children's toys
- dishwashers, tumble driers and washing machines
- burglar alarms
- cameras
- mobile phones
- toasters
- heating systems.

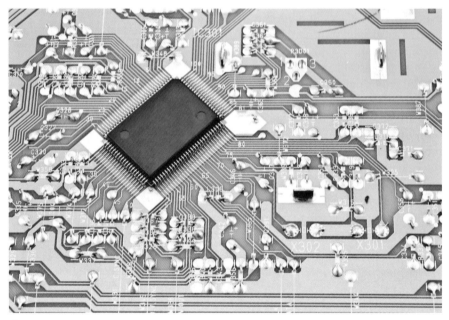

▲ **Embedded computers are used to control many electronic/electrical devices.**

Questions A

1 Computer systems consist of a number of components.

Explain the purpose of each of the following components:
  (a) Central processing unit (CPU) (*1 mark*)
  (b) Internal/main memory (*1 mark*)
  (c) Backing storage (*1 mark*)
  (d) Power supply (*1 mark*)

2 A computer system consists of both hardware and software.
  (a) Explain the difference between hardware and software. (*2 marks*)
  (b) Give **two** examples of hardware and **two** examples of software.
    (*2 marks*)

Hardware: input devices

You will find out

▷ **About the appropriate use of input, output, storage and communication devices**

▷ **About the advantages and disadvantages of a variety of input, output, storage and communication devices**

▷ **About user interfaces**

Input devices are used to enter data into the computer ready for processing. Some input devices, such as a mouse and joystick, supply data in the form of instructions. Other input devices, such as the keyboard, enable the entry of text. In this section you will learn about a whole range of input devices, each suitable for entering a certain type of data.

Input devices

In this section you will be looking at the huge range of input devices each with their advantages and disadvantages.

Keyboard

Keyboards are the most popular input device. Using a keyboard:

- is the most popular way of inputting data as most computer systems come with one
- is a slow method of input for large amounts of data
- is inaccurate as it is easy to make mistakes
- needs typing skills so it is hard for beginners to use.

▲ This keyboard for a cash dispenser has raised dots on the keys so that it can be used by blind or partially sighted users as well as other users.

Special keyboards for the disabled

Braille keyboards make it easy for blind users to input data into the computer.

For those users who have failing vision, there are also keyboards that have large coloured keys that are easier to see. Each key is about one inch square.

▲ A large-keyed, colour-coded keyboard for the visually impaired.

Mouse

This is called a mouse because its shape looks like a mouse and it has a tail in the form of the wire. Many mice do not have wires as they are used wirelessly. The main points about a mouse are:

- Mice are input devices because they are used to issue instructions by making selections.
- When the mouse is moved, a pointer or cursor moves on the screen mirroring the movement of the mouse.

- Selections can be made by pressing the mouse buttons.
- A scroll wheel can be used for scrolling through long documents.
- A mouse may also be used for drawing lines, sizing graphic objects such as pictures or clip art.

Joystick/video game controller

Most of you have used a joystick or video game controller. Here are some facts about them:

- They are ideal for quick movement and selection.
- This means they are an ideal input peripheral for playing games.
- They can be used to move a cursor on the screen.
- Joysticks are useful for the disabled because they can be operated by the foot, mouth, etc.

Tracker ball

This is a bit like an upside down mouse. The 'mouse' part is stationary and you move the 'ball' part with your fingers and this moves the cursor on the screen in the same way as a mouse does. Their main use is for people who are disabled or very young children who find it hard to use a mouse.

▲ A tracker ball is an alternative to a mouse.

Hardware: input devices *continued*

Touch pad

Touch pads are seen on most laptop computers and are used where there is no smooth surface on which to use a mouse or where there is no space.

Most people would prefer to use a mouse if there is room as it takes longer to do tasks using a touch pad.

▼ **Touch pads are used as an alternative to a mouse where there is not much space for a mouse to be used.**

Microphone

A microphone allows sound to be converted into data. Special software called voice recognition software is used to interpret the sounds into words.

Here is what a microphone allows you to do:

- You can tell the computer what to do (i.e., you can issue instructions).
- You can dictate letters and other documents directly into your word-processor or email package. This is called voice recognition.
- You will need a microphone if you want to send voice mail or take part in videoconferencing.
- You can issue instructions verbally to your computer instead of typing them in.
- You can use the Internet for Internet phone calls, which are much cheaper than normal calls.

Remote controls

Remote controls are input devices as they issue instructions to ICT systems.

▼ **Remote controls are input devices and are used to issue commands as well as allow characters to be typed.**

Scanners

Here are some important points about scanners:

- They are used to scan in photographs and other images to put into documents or webpages.
- They can also be used to scan text into a word-processing or other package. This saves having to re-type the text. To be able to recognize the characters, special software called optical character recognition software is needed.

▼ **Scanners are useful for converting old photographs so that they can be stored on the computer and used for websites, presentations, documents, etc.**

Digital still camera

A digital camera looks like an ordinary camera except there is no film and there is usually a screen on which to view the picture (called an image) when taken.

Here are some facts about digital cameras:

- Digital cameras have memory cards where they store the image.
- The more memory a camera has, the more pictures you can store.
- There are no developing fees as with an ordinary camera.
- If the picture is not suitable (as viewed on the screen) then it can be taken again.
- You can transfer the pictures to your computer where you can store and edit them.

Digital cameras produce an image made up of millions of dots called pixels. The greater the number of dots in the same space, the clearer the picture will appear. This is called the resolution of the image. High resolution images use more dots and take up more storage space on the storage media.

Most mobile phones are capable of taking digital photographs.

KEY WORDS

Input the act of entering data into an ICT system.

Input device the hardware device such as a keyboard or a scanner used to feed the input data into an ICT system.

Voice recognition the ability of a computer to 'understand' spoken words by comparing them with stored data.

Scanner a hardware device used to scan pictures or text into a computer system.

"I HAVE TO STAY HOME TONIGHT AND HELP MY DAD WITH HIS NEW CAMERA PHONE. WE NEED TO DELETE 750 PICTURES OF HIS HAND."

Digital video camera

Digital video cameras look the same as ordinary video cameras except that they store the image digitally. Here are some other facts:

- Most digital video cameras can capture still as well as moving images.
- Images may be stored and edited on the computer.
- You can use video in websites.

Web cameras

A web camera (webcam) is simply a digital camera that is used to capture still images and video images (i.e., moving images). These images can then be transmitted to a computer where they are stored in a suitable graphics format. If required, pictures can be used on a website.

▷ Webcams are good fun because you can see the person you are talking to.

Webcams are often included with complete computer set ups with the camera in these systems placed on top of the screen. Such a system allows videoconferencing.

Webcams are not, however, restricted to the tops of computers. There are webcams everywhere. Here are some uses:

- To check the weather in ski resorts and other holiday destinations.
- To allow parents to check on their children in nurseries.
- To allow bar owners to check that staff are not giving free drinks to friends.
- To allow people to check on their home while they are away.

Sensors

Sensors are able to sense quantities such as temperature, pressure and amount of light. The signals picked up by the sensors can be sent to and then analysed by the computer.

Here is some information about sensors:

- Sensors can be connected to the computer directly.
- Sensors can record data over time and then the data can be transferred to the computer (this is called data logging).
- Sensors can be found in lots of devices such as burglar alarms, central heating systems, washing machines, etc. As well as sensing, they are also used to control the device in some way.

Touch screen (touch sensitive screen)

To operate a touch screen you simply touch the item on the screen to make

a selection. Touch screens are ideal input devices in some situations. Here are some facts about touch screens:

- Touch screens are easy for the general public to use.
- They are used in restaurants and shops because the staff need little training to use them.
- They are ideal for public information systems such as tourism displays, timetable information, etc.

▲ Many mobile phones have touch screen interfaces.

▲ Sat navs use touch screens.

▲ Computerised ticket dispensers at train stations make use of touch screens.

KEY WORDS

Digital camera a camera that takes a picture and stores it digitally.

Web camera (webcam) a digital camera used to capture still and video images.

Sensors devices that measure physical quantities such as temperature, pressure, etc.

Touch screen a special type of screen that is sensitive to touch. A selection is made from a menu on the screen by touching part of it.

Hardware: input devices *continued*

Magnetic strip readers

Magnetic strip readers are able to read data stored in magnetic strips on plastic cards.

Magnetic strip readers are used for:

- reading data off credit/debit cards (as an alternative to chip and pin)
- reading loyalty card details
- access control to rooms
- access to computers.

▲ Data is stored as a magnetic pattern in the strip on the card.

MIDI (Musical Instrument Digital Interface) instruments

MIDI is an interface, which means a way of connecting and getting two devices to communicate with each other. MIDI can send signals to electronic devices such as keyboards, music synthesizers, guitars and drum machines. These devices can also send the signals back to the computer hardware so that the signals can be stored and modified in some way. For example, the sound from a drum might be too loud in a recording. Using MIDI you could save the sound from the drum and make it softer whilst keeping the loudness of the other instruments the same.

Chip and pin

Most credit/debit cards are chip and pin, which means there is a small chip on the card containing encrypted data that only the reader in the store can read. This means that when you enter your PIN (personal identification number), the store can be sure that you are the correct owner of the card. Chip and pin has reduced card fraud when a card is being used in ordinary stores.

▲ Most credit/debit cards are chip and pin to help prevent fraud.

▲ A chip and pin reader: the customer inserts their card then enters their PIN.

Bar code readers

Bar code reading involves using a series of light and dark bars of differing widths to enter a code that is usually printed underneath the bar code. Using the code, the system can determine from a product database the country of origin, the manufacturer, the name of the product, the price and other information about the product.

ISBN 978-1-85008-280-4

▲ Bar code.

Suitable applications for bar code recognition include:

- recording of goods in supermarkets
- warehouse stock control systems
- parcel tracking systems
- linking books to borrowers in libraries
- luggage labelling at airports.

Advantages of bar code input

- Faster – scanners are sophisticated and can read bar codes at different angles.
- More accurate – compared to typing in long codes manually.
- Low printing costs – can be printed on labels.

Disadvantages of bar code input

- Can only be used for the input of numbers.
- Expensive – the laser scanners in supermarkets are expensive, although hand-held scanners are relatively cheap.

Questions B

1 Tick **one** box in each row to show which item is most suitable for each of the tasks shown.

Task	Touch pad	Scanner	Digital camera
Inputting a drawing on paper into a computer			
Controlling the cursor on a laptop computer			
Taking a photograph to be edited and stored on a computer			

2 Most computer screens are output devices but some screens act as both input and output devices.
   (a) Give the name of a screen that acts as both an input and output device. (*1 mark*)
   (b) Give the name of a device where the screen can be used for both input and output. (*1 mark*)

3 Here is a diagram showing some devices used with a computer:
   (a) Give the name of an input device shown in the diagram. (*1 mark*)
   (b) Give the name of an output device shown in the diagram. (*1 mark*)

4 (a) Explain the purpose of an input device. (*1 mark*)
   (b) Give the names of **two** input devices that would be used by a desktop computer. (*2 marks*)
   (c) Give the name of an input device that would be found on a laptop computer that you would not find on a desktop computer. (*1 mark*)

5 Laptop computers enable people to do work or keep in touch when they are travelling.

   Give the name of **two** input devices normally used with a laptop computer. (*2 marks*)

6 The image on the right shows an input device being used.
   (a) Give the name of this input device. (*1 mark*)
   (b) Explain how this device is used. (3 marks)
   (c) Give **two** applications where this reader could be used. (*2 marks*)

7 Web cameras are popular input devices used with personal computers.
   (a) Explain what is meant by a webcam. (*2 marks*)
   (b) Explain **two** different users for webcams. (*2 marks*)

Hardware: output devices

Once data has been entered into the computer and has been processed, the resulting information is output. Output devices are those parts of an ICT system that produce the information in the most appropriate form for the user. There are many output devices, with a screen/VDU and a printer being the most popular.

Output devices

In this section you will cover the main output devices and learn about their appropriate uses.

Screen or monitor

Screens are sometimes called monitors. Here are some facts about screens:

- They come in lots of sizes.
- They are usually in colour.
- They are useful for enquiries (when is the next train to...?, do you have a holiday on this date....?).

TFT/LCD screens

Both desktop and laptop computers use TFT/LCD (thin film transistor/ liquid crystal display) flat panel display screens. The advantages of TFT/LCD screens are:

- They are light – hence their use in laptop computers.
- They are cheaper to run – because they consume less power.

- In the case of desktop computer systems – they do not take up very much desk space.

Plasma screens

Plasma screens are large flat panel screens and are generally available in larger sizes compared to TFT/LCD screens. They have the following uses in ICT:

- in reception areas
- in videoconferencing systems
- for presentations to a large audience.

Printers

There are many different types of printer but the main ones are laser printers and ink-jet printers. Both types of printer produce hard copy. This means they produce output on paper.

Laser printers

Laser printers are the type of printer mostly used by businesses and organizations mainly because of their high speed. Most laser printers print in black and white, although you can buy colour laser printers but they are relatively expensive.

Advantages of laser printers:

- Supplies last longer – the toner cartridge lasts longer than ink-jet cartridges.
- High printing speed – essential to have high speed if lots of people on a network are using the one printer.
- Very reliable – fewer problems compared to ink-jet printers.
- No wet pages that smudge – ink-jet pages can smudge but there is no such problem with a laser printer.

Disadvantages of laser printers:

- More expensive to buy – but they are cheaper to run.
- Colour lasers are very expensive to buy.
- Power consumption is high.

Ink-jet printers

Ink-jet printers are popular with home users because they are cheap to buy. They are expensive to run, because of the high cost of the ink cartridges. They work by spraying ink onto the paper and can produce very high quality colour or black and white printouts.

Advantages of ink-jet printers:

- High quality print – ideal for printing photographs, brochures or just simple text.
- Quietness of operation – this is important in an office as telephone calls or conversations with colleagues can be conducted while it is printing.
- Cheap to buy – ink-jet printers are very cheap.

Disadvantages of ink-jet printers:

- High cost of the ink cartridges – this is ok for low volume work but for large volumes it is much cheaper to use a colour laser printer.
- Ink smudges – when the printouts are removed the paper can get damp, which tends to smudge the ink.
- Need special paper – thick glossy paper is needed for high quality printouts.

▼ Laser printers are ideal for use in offices.

Other output devices

Speakers

Speakers are used to output sound and are an important component of multimedia systems.

Digital projectors

Digital projectors are used to project what is on a computer screen onto a large screen. They are used when there is an audience that needs to view what is on the screen and are therefore used with presentations. They are also used with electronic whiteboards in classrooms.

Plotters

Plotters are used to output diagrams such as maps and plans. They produce accurately scaled diagrams and can print on much larger paper than a printer can print on. They use pens to draw lines with each pen drawing a different colour.

Actuators

Computers can issue signals to control devices based on the data they receive from sensors. They can, for example, turn a motor on or off, they can turn a heater on or off, etc.

Devices that respond to a signal from a computer are called actuators. Examples of things that can be controlled by a computer include:

- lights
- motors
- pumps
- buzzers
- heaters.

Head/ear phones

These allow people to listen to sound and not disturb others as they do so. They are particularly popular for use in public places and can be used to: access websites where there is sound, watch and listen to video or just listen to music.

Questions C

1 Tick **one** box in each row to show whether the component is an input or output device. (*10 marks*)

Component	Input	Output
Ear phones		
Webcam		
Microphone		
Speaker		
Ink-jet printer		
Digital projector		
Chip and pin reader		
Actuator		
Plotter		
Monitor/screen		

2 Ink-jet printers are very popular with home computer users.
   (a) Give **two** advantages of ink-jet printers compared to other types of printer. (*2 marks*)
   (b) Give **two** disadvantages of ink-jet printers compared to other types of printer. (*2 marks*)

3 The manager of an office is buying a printer for the office. They are looking to buy one of the following types of printer:
   Laser printer
   Ink-jet printer

Discuss the relative advantages and disadvantages of each of these types of printer. (*4 marks*)

Extension activity

For this activity you have to research the range of printers that are available.

Two types of printer have been discussed in this section (i.e. laser printers and ink-jet printers) but there are others as well.

Produce a document showing a diagram of each printer along with at least two advantages and disadvantages.

When you have completed you document you should print a copy out.

▶ Ear phones are output devices.

Hardware: storage

▷ **About storage devices and their appropriate use**

In this section you will learn about the different types of backing storage and the need to keep backup copies of programs and data should the originals be damaged or lost.

▾ Hard disks store data as a magnetic pattern.

Backups and the reasons for taking them

Backups are copies of data and program files kept for security reasons. Should the originals be destroyed then the backups can be used.

Backing/secondary storage devices and media

Memory (ROM and RAM) is an expensive component of a computer and the RAM loses its contents when the power is switched off. Backing or secondary storage is used for the storage of programs and data that are not needed immediately by the computer. They are also used for storing backups of programs and data in case the originals are damaged or destroyed.

Flash drive/memory stick/pen drive/USB drive

Flash drives, memory sticks, pen drives and USB drives are all names for the same things and are ideal storage for photographs, music and other data files. These are the portable small stick-like devices that you insert into the USB port/slot and use for storing

work on. These are a very useful backing storage device and probably the way you transfer your work between home and school or college. They consist of printed circuit boards enclosed in a plastic case.

The main advantages are:

- small and lightweight – easy to put on your key ring or in your pocket and can be used with any computer
- large storage capacity (up to 30 GB)
- no moving parts, so they are very reliable
- not subject to scratches like optical media.

Flash/pen drives are the most popular portable storage media. Their portability is their main advantage and you simply plug them into the USB port where they are recognized automatically.

The main disadvantages are:

- their small size means they are easily stolen
- they are often left in the computer by mistake and lost
- they do not have as high a transfer rate as magnetic hard disk drives.

Magnetic hard disk drives

Magnetic disk drives are the main form of backing/secondary storage on a computer. Hard drives consist of a series of disks with a magnetic coating and a series of read/write heads that put the data onto or record it off each surface.

Magnetic hard drives have the advantages of:

- a very high transfer rate (quick to put data on and to read it off)
- a very high storage capacity.

You can buy additional hard drives for backup purposes. These hard drives are called portable hard drives and may be removed each night and stored safely.

Magnetic tape drives

Magnetic tape is still used for backing up large amounts of data quickly.

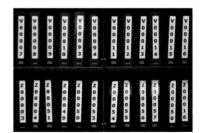
▲ Magnetic tape is still used for taking backups.

Optical disks include CDs and DVDs and are used to store digital data as a binary pattern on the disks.

Optical drives

Optical disks are flat circular disks on which data is stored as a series of bumps. The way the bumps reflect laser beam light is used to read the data off the disk. CD/DVD drives read the data off the disk or in some cases store the data onto the disk.

CD-ROM (Compact Disk-Read Only Memory)

CD-ROMs are used mainly for the distribution of software. Although most home computers are equipped with DVD drives, a lot more computers, especially those used in businesses, still only have CD drives. You can read a CD using a DVD drive but you cannot read a DVD with a CD drive. This is why software is still being sold on CD rather than DVD.
    With CD-ROM:

- data is read only
- data is stored as an optical pattern
- there is a large storage capacity (600 MB)
- they are used for the distribution of software.

DVD-ROM (Digital Versatile Disk-Read Only Memory)

DVDs have a much higher storage capacity than CDs and are ideal for the storage of multimedia files such as MP3, digital images and video clips.

DVD-ROM is used for the distribution of movies where you can only read the data off the disk. A DVD-ROM drive can also be used for reading data off a CD.

CD-R (CD-Recordable)

CD-R allows data to be stored on a CD, but only once. It is ideal for the backing up of data or for storing digital music.

CD-RW (CD-Rewriteable)

A CD-RW disk allows data to be stored on the disk over and over again – just like a hard disk. You can treat a CD-RW like a hard drive but the transfer rate is less and the time taken to locate a file is greater. The media is not as robust as a hard drive.

DVD-RAM (Digital Versatile Disk – Random Access Memory)

DVD-RAM drives allow repeated storage and erasure of data so they act a bit like a hard drive but the disks cannot be used with all DVD drives.

DVD-R (DVD-Recordable)

DVD-R allows data to be stored on a DVD, but only once. It is ideal for backing up data, for storing digital music or a film.

DVD+RW (Digital Versatile Disk+Read/Write)

A DVD+RW drive can be used to write to as well as read data from a DVD. DVD–RW are sometimes called DVD burners because they are able to be written to and not just read from. Typical storage capacities are:

- 4.7 GB for the older DVD drives
- 8.5 GB for the latest DVD drives.

Flash memory, card drives and memory cards

Memory cards are the thin cards you see in digital cameras. They are ideal storage media for photographs but can also be used for storing other types of data.

A CD-R disk being used with a laptop.

Hardware: storage *continued*

Solid state drives

A solid state drive is use to store data and it is used in a similar way to a hard drive except, unlike a hard drive, there are no moving parts. They have the advantage over a hard drive that they are very robust so not easily damaged. Data is also transferred between the drive and computer and vice versa faster compared to a hard drive.

Online storage

Online backup companies are companies who charge a fee for you to store your backup data on their computers. The Internet is used to transfer the files to and from their storage devices.

Backing up data

Backup copies of data and programs need to be taken on a regular basis. Backup copies should be stored on removable media or devices. This is so that they can be removed away from the computer and, if possible, the building. The chances are that if a thief steals the computer, they will also steal any media or devices they see. There is also a chance that the building could be destroyed by fire, earthquake, etc.

Home computer users often use flash drives or portable hard drives for backing up their important data such as family photographs.

Questions D

1 Which **three** of the following are backing storage devices? *(3 marks)*
   RAM
   Hard drive
   CD-RW drive
   ROM
   Plotter
   Speaker
   Keyboard
   Flash drive

2 Give the meaning of the following abbreviations.
   (a) DVD-R *(1 mark)*
   (b) DVD-RW *(1 mark)*

3 Backups of programs and data should be taken on a regular basis.
   (a) Explain what is meant by a backup. *(2 marks)*
   (b) Give **one** reason why backups should be taken on a regular basis. *(1 mark)*
   (c) Give **one** example of backing storage suitable for the taking of backup copies and explain why it is suitable. *(3 marks)*

Extension activity

Everyone who uses a computer needs to store their data and programs somewhere.

For this activity you have to find out about the backing storage devices that are available for computer users. Use the Internet to find out:

- **Types of storage devices and their storage capacity.**
- **The main advantages and disadvantages of each device.**
- **The cost of the storage device.**
- **The media they need if applicable.**

A good place to look for information is the website of the large online stores who sell computer equipment such as **PC World**.

Hardware: communication devices and user interfaces

You will find out

▷ **About communication devices and their appropriate uses**

▷ **About user interfaces**

Most computers are connected to a network. For example, PCs at home are often connected to the Internet. If you use a computer in school, then it is probably networked. Networking computers bring many benefits and there are a number of hardware devices that are needed for networking. For example, data needs to be prepared for being sent out and received over communication channels such as telephone cables. A device called a modem is needed for this. These communication devices will be discussed here.

There needs to be a way for a user to interact with the hardware and this is done using a human-machine interface. Human-machine interfaces are often referred to as user interfaces and there are many different ones to choose from. Some of the main ones are covered in this section.

Using communication devices to access the Internet

There are a number of communication devices that can be used to access the Internet.

Modem

Modems are devices that enable a communication link to be set up between the computer and a medium such as a wire or cable that is used to carry the data. There are two types of modem.

Dialup modem

This is a slower more old-fashioned modem. When you log onto the Internet using a dialup modem it dials the number of your Internet service provider. You are then asked for your user-ID or screen name and a password. On providing this, you are connected to the Internet.

Broadband modem

Broadband modems are the latest modems and offer connection to the Internet using a broadband link. Broadband is much faster than dialup and allows you to:

- download files at high speed
- watch online video
- use web cameras
- listen to online radio
- watch TV programmes
- surf the Internet very quickly.

Routers

A router is a device that enables a network to be connected to the Internet. They are frequently used in homes where several computers need to share a single Internet connection. Wireless routers are very popular and allow wireless connection to the Internet by any computers in range of the router.

▲ A broadband modem.

▼ A wireless router allows several computers to access the Internet wirelessly.

Hubs

Hubs are simple devices used to join computers in a network so they are able to share files and an Internet connection.

15

Hardware: communication devices and user interfaces *continued*

Network interface card (NIC)

If you intend to connect a computer to a network using a cable, then you will need a network interface card (NIC). Almost all computers have these already built in when you buy them. As you can see from the picture, they consist of a circuit board and a socket into which the network cable (often called an Ethernet cable) is plugged.

Network interface cards prepare the data for sending over the network.

User interfaces

User interfaces are the means by which the user interacts with a computer. For example, the user may interact with the computer by keying in and moving the mouse to click on menu items on the screen. User interfaces are often referred to as human–computer interfaces and they are important because having a good one means the computer is easier to use. User interfaces are being developed all the time and many of the new interfaces are making more use of touch screens and voice recognition.

The features and uses of different types of user interface

An interface is where two things meet, so a user interface in ICT is the point where the human user meets or interacts with the ICT system. This is commonly called the user interface or sometimes the human–computer interface (HCI).

User interfaces have seen huge changes over the years and are being developed all the time so that ICT systems are made as easy to use as possible. In this section you will be looking at the range of user interfaces used by ICT systems and their relative strengths and weaknesses.

The different user interfaces and their features

When you turn on the computer you see a user interface. The cursors, prompts, icons, menus, etc., allow you to get things done with your computer. They are all part of the user interface. A user interface can make your computer either hard or easy to use. You will probably have experienced software that is frustrating to use.

There are many different types of user interface and here are some of them:

- **Command line/driven interface** – here you have to type in a series of commands. This type of interface is very hard to use.
- **Menu-driven interface** – here you are presented with a list of things to do and you have to choose one of them by typing in either a number or a letter. These are easy to use but are limited in the sorts of things you can do with them.
- **Graphical user interface (GUI)** – these are very easy to use and have all the features such as windows, icons, menus, pointers, etc.

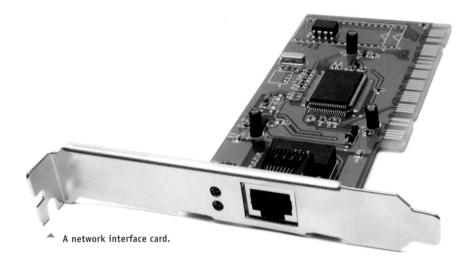

▲ A network interface card.

▲ A cable provides the connection to the Internet.

16

List Employee No, Surname
For Job = "Production"

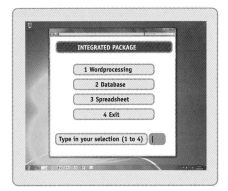

▲ Command line interface.

▲ Menu-driven interface

▲ The icons (small pictures) representing folders in a GUI.

Graphical user interfaces (GUI) and WIMP

Graphical user interfaces (GUIs) are very popular because they are easy to use. Instead of typing in commands, you enter them by pointing at and clicking on objects on the screen. Microsoft Windows and Macintosh operating systems use graphical user interfaces. The main features of a GUI include:

Windows – the screen is divided into areas called windows. Windows are useful if you need to work on several tasks.

Icons – these are small pictures used to represent commands, files or windows. By moving the pointer and clicking, you can carry out a command or open a window. You can also position any icon anywhere on your desktop.

Menus – menus allow a user to make selections from a list. Menus can be pop-up or pull-down and this means they do not clutter the desktop whilst they are not being used.

Pointers – this is the little arrow that appears when using Windows. The pointer changes shape in different applications. It changes to an 'I' shape when using word-processing software. A mouse can be used to move the pointer around the screen.

Notice that the first letter of each feature in the above list spells out the term WIMP (i.e., Windows, Icons, Menus, Pointers).

Other types of user interface

There are many new ways of interacting with a computer and many of these ways replicate the way humans communicate with each other.

Direct neural interface

A direct neural interface is a direct connection between the brain of a human and a device. This type of interface is very important as it can be used to repair damaged hearing, sight or movement. In some of these interfaces, electrodes are implanted into the person's brain and a computer is used to process the signals and provide the person with sight, hearing or movement that they would not have without the system.

Voice driven interfaces

We are used to communicating with each other using voice, so it makes sense to communicate with ICT devices such as computers, mobile phones, MP3 players, etc., in a similar way. Voice driven applications, also called voice recognition, can be used to:

• issue commands to the software
• enter data into the software.

Voice driven is a popular interface because manufacturers are trying to make devices small, but if there is a small keyboard, then it makes the device harder to use.

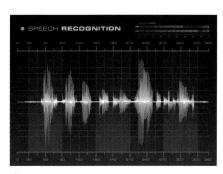

▲ Many interfaces use speech/voice recognition.

Software: systems software

You will find out

▷ **About systems software and their uses**

▷ **About programming software and their uses**

▷ **About the advantages and disadvantages of different software applications**

▷ **About the different file types used to support software**

In order for ICT hardware to do a useful job it needs two types of software: systems software and applications software. The applications software performs a particular job or application but the operating system software is needed to control the hardware directly. Both these two types of software are essential components of any ICT system. Any software has to interact with the user and this is through the user interface. The main aim is to make this interface as easy to use as possible. In this section you will be looking at the functions of the operating system.

Systems software

Systems software is software that operates the computer hardware directly and also provides the means of running the applications software such as word-processing, payroll, web browser, etc.

Systems software consists of the following parts:

- operating system
- utility software
- drivers.

The functions of an operating system

Operating systems are programs that control the hardware directly. The operating system supplies the step-by-step instructions that tell the computer hardware what to do.

Operating systems have the following functions:

- Manage and control any devices such as printers, scanners, webcams, etc., that are attached to the computer.
- Provide a user interface that makes it easy for the user to load programs, search for files, copy files, etc.
- Hide the complexity of the hardware from the user.
- Deal with any errors that occur while the computer is working on tasks.
- Provide the interface between the application packages being run and the hardware.

▼ **Burning CDs or DVDs is performed using a utility program.**

- Handle the storage of data by keeping track of all the files and directories/folders on the disk drives.
- Maximize the use of computer memory by the operating system deciding where in the memory the program instructions are placed.
- Organize resources (e.g., processing time and memory) when the computer user is running several programs at the same time.
- Handle the saving of data by keeping track of all the files and directories/folders on the disk drives.

Utilities

Utility programs are provided as part of the system software and they help the user with everyday tasks such as:

- file maintenance tasks such as creating new folders, copying files, renaming files, deleting files
- compressing files so that they take up less storage space or can be transferred quickly over the Internet
- installing and uninstalling software
- compacting files on the hard drive so they can be found faster
- checking for and removing viruses
- format a disk ready for use
- burn CDs and DVDs.

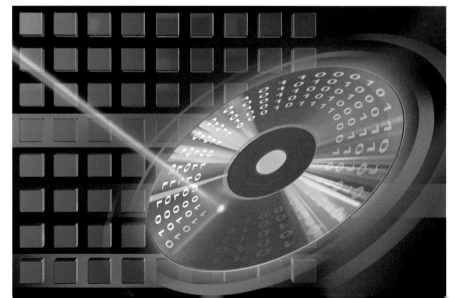

▲ Many files are zipped (i.e. compressed) before being transferred using the Internet.

Drivers

Drivers are software used to supply instructions to the hardware on how to operate equipment that may be connected to the computer such as printers, scanners, external hard drives, etc.

Most operating systems are able to recognize when new hardware, such as a flash drive, camera, portable hard drive, etc., has been attached to the computer and automatically load the driver software needed to control it.

KEY WORDS

Driver a short specially written program that understands the operation of the device it controls/operates. For example, driver software can operate/control a printer or scanner. Driver software is needed so as to allow the systems or applications software to control the device properly.

Operating system software that controls the hardware of a computer and is used to run the applications software. Operating systems control the handling of input, output, etc.

Systems software any computer software that manages and controls the hardware thus allowing the applications software to do a useful job. Systems software consists of a group of programs.

Utility software part of the systems software that performs a specific task such as creating a new folder, copying files, etc.

Questions F

1 Choose **three** tasks from the list below that are carried out by all operating systems. (*3 marks*)

Renaming a file

Deciding where to store data on a hard disk drive

Underlining text in a word-processing package

Cropping a picture

Loading a file from the disk drive.

2 (a) Give **three** tasks (other than those in Q1) performed by an operating system. (*3 marks*)
  (b) Some printers come with driver software. Give **one** purpose of driver software. (*1 mark*)

3 Write down the name of the piece of system software that carries out each of the following by matching the name to the correct description. (*3 marks*)

Utility

Driver

Operating system

	Description	Name
(a)	Deals with errors that occur when the computer is working on tasks	
(b)	Software that is sometimes needed when a new piece of hardware is attached to the computer	
(c)	Software used to copy, delete and rename files	

Extension activity

Some applications software is very specialist and likely to be used by only a few people.

Write down the names of as many types of application software as you can find and for each one, explain the task it performs. To give you the idea, the first one has been done for you.

Name of software	Specialist task it performs
Payroll	Working out wages, dealing with tax, dealing with National Insurance, etc.

Software: applications software

You will find out

▷ **About applications software and their uses**

▷ **About how to select and use software applications to meet needs and solve problems**

Applications software is software designed to do a particular job or application. You will have used many different types of applications software in your Key Stage 3 study and also at home. Basically applications software covers the software other than the systems software that we use to get a job done.

In this section you will learn about the tasks that are suited for particular pieces of software.

How to select and use software applications to meet needs and solve problems

In order to select the right software you need to consider the requirements of the task. Generally the more complex the task is then the more likely you will need more specialist software. For example, a simple poster can easily be created in word-processing software but the graphic capabilities of the software are very limited. A better solution would be to use specialist DTP software.

Over the GCSE course you will be using a lot of different software and you will understand the strengths and weaknesses of each piece of software.

Word-processing software

Word-processing packages are used to produce documents containing text such as:

- letters
- reports
- memos
- essays.

Word-processing software is also used to prepare text for other packages such as DTP or web design software. The idea is that that the text is prepared and edited using the word-processing software and then saved and imported into the other package for further arrangement. Word-processing software is perfect for processing text but less good for creating posters, diagrams and complex newsletters.

Before starting to word-process a document you need to think about the layout of the page.

Once text has been entered, you can start thinking about adding structure to certain text and making some text stand out. This is called formatting text.

To add further structure to the document you can format blocks of text to make paragraphs, sections, etc.

KEY WORDS

Bullet point a block or paragraph of text that has a symbol placed in front to make the section of text stand out.

Footer text placed at the bottom of a page.

Header text placed at the top of a page.

Templates files that hold standardized document layouts. Templates hold the design of the document so that only the variable information needs to be added.

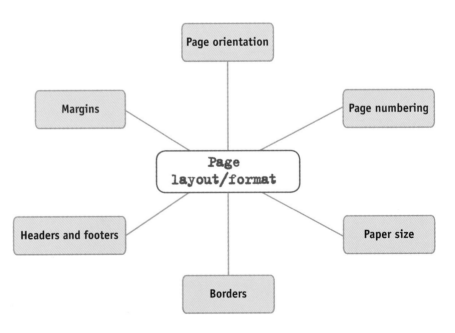

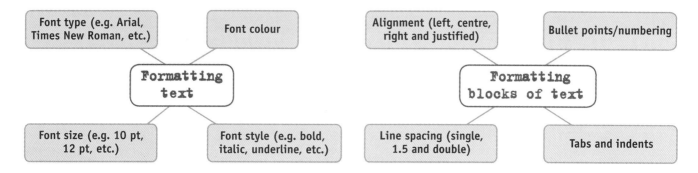

DTP software

Desktop publishing software, commonly called DTP software, is used to produce posters, brochures, magazines, newsletters, etc. It is ideal where the page design is quite complex and involves lots of graphics. For very simple documents it is possible to use word-processing software.

Spreadsheet software

Spreadsheet software is used to manipulate numbers and text arranged in cells. Formulas are used to relate one cell with other cells. Once a formula has been entered, then if one value of a cell, on which the formula is based, changes, then the formula will automatically perform the calculation with the new value.

Spreadsheets are ideal for:

- budgets
- cash flow forecasts
- accounts (e.g., profit and loss, end of year accounts, etc.)
- creating and using models
- performing statistical analysis on data
- producing graphs and charts from sets of data.

The basic features of spreadsheet software are shown in the diagram below:

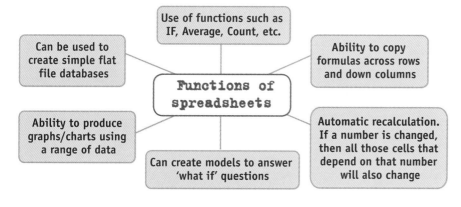

Database management software

Database software is used where a store of data needs to be kept and where the information needs to be extracted from this store in lots of different ways.

Simple databases can be created using spreadsheet software but these have limited use. More complex and useful databases are created in specialist database software and these are called relational databases.

Web authoring software

You can create simple websites in lots of different software such as word-processing software. However, it is better to use specialist web design software because there are lots of effects you can use.

Presentation software

You will already be familiar with presentation software such as PowerPoint for producing slide presentations. Presentation software can also be used for:

- creating self-running presentations
- creating interactive presentations where the user can decide what to do next

- creating multimedia quizzes
- creating teaching material.

Proprietary and open source software

Open source software is software where the licence to use the software allows users to use, change and improve the software freely, if they so wish.

Proprietary software is software that is neither free nor open source. This means that the user pays for the software and is not free to alter it in any way. Most of the software you use is proprietary software.

Multimedia software

Multimedia means many media such as text, audio, still images, animation, video and interactivity. Usually multimedia means more media than just text and graphics, so this means that a normal book or magazine would not be considered multimedia.

Multimedia software is software that can be used to create multimedia products such as games, educational materials, training material, interactive books, etc.

Slideshow software

Slideshow software is used to present digital images and allow the sharing of these with friends and family in an interesting way. For example, you can set your photos to a soundtrack, you can record your own narrations (i.e., you talking explaining what each photo shows) and you can add text captions to the photos.

Software: applications software *continued*

Photo-editing software

This software is used to improve the appearance of digital photographs and is a very popular piece of software for home users. You can do all sorts of things to improve a digital image such as:

- crop the image so that only part of an image is used
- remove unwanted parts of an image
- remove red eye
- alter the colours in an image
- change the size of an image.

Video-editing software

Like digital still images, digital video images are easily edited. For example, you can remove blurred sections or where the camera was moved too fast. You can alter the brightness, colours and contrast and you can even add a soundtrack to the video. There are many special effects that can be used to add further interest.

Graphics manipulation software

Graphics software is any software that can be used to create, edit and manage graphics images, which can include line diagrams, drawings, clip art and digital photographic images. General purpose graphics software generally deals only with 2D images, whereas special graphics modelling software or CAD (computer-aided design) software deals with 2D and 3D graphics.

Gaming software

Software used to play games is a popular type of software and this software is very sophisticated and expensive to produce. Games software includes simulation software (playing football, racing cars, etc.), traditional games such as chess, Scrabble and educational games that make learning fun.

Communications software

Communications software is any software that allows two or more people to communicate with each other and would include:

- Social networking software – to enable you to create profiles, send messages to other site users, etc.
- Chat software – to enable you to conduct real-time conversations with others.
- Instant messaging – to enable private conversations to be conducted with others.
- Web browsers – this software is used to access the Internet and its facilities such as search, email, file attachments, file transfer, etc.

▲ Graphics manipulation software can be used to produce eye-catching graphics like this.

Extension activity

Make a list of all the different types of applications software you use at school or college and produce lists of the tasks you have used them for.

Questions G

1. Which type of software, from the list, would be best used for the following tasks? *(7 marks)*

    Database
    Word-processing
    Spreadsheet
    Web design
    DTP

    (a) Creating a website.
    (b) Creating a model showing the money coming into and going out of your bank account.
    (c) Writing a letter to be posted.
    (d) Creating bar charts to show the sales of goods in a sports shop.
    (e) Adding up lots of columns of numbers.
    (f) Producing a high-quality glossy brochure.
    (g) Storing the personal details of all the pupils in a school.

2. Which one of the following types of applications software is often used for creating financial models? *(1 mark)*

	Tick **one box only**
Desktop publishing	☐
Database	☐
Spreadsheet	☐

Software: programming software

People need to create software and the people who do this are called programmers. Programmers create the step-step-by step instructions that are given to the computer to tell it how to work or what to do. There are many different computer languages a programmer can use to program a computer. Computer programming is quite difficult and it is easy to make mistakes and these are called bugs. Programs need to be tested thoroughly. In this section you will learn about some aspects of computer programming.

When you want to carry out a task in ICT there are usually different types of software to choose from. You therefore have to decide which software to choose. This section also covers the advantages and disadvantages of different software applications.

Software used to create computer programs

A program is a set of instructions that a computer can understand. Computers ultimately need instructions in binary (i.e., codes of 0s and 1s) but this makes it difficult or almost impossible for programmers to program in. Instead a programming language is used and there are a number of different ones to choose from such as:

- Basic
- C++
- Visual Basic
- JAVA
- FORTRAN
- COBOL.

Instructions in a programming language are fairly easy to understand and use and include such instructions as PRINT, GOTO, READ, etc. In order for the computer to understand these commands, software is needed to turn them into binary code.

Compilers

Compilers are programs that change the instructions written in programming languages such as Basic into binary (0s and 1s). A compiler converts the whole of a program written in the programming language into binary in one go. The program is then stored in binary and when it is run, it runs much faster.

Interpreters

Like compilers, interpreters convert program language instructions into the machine code (i.e., the binary code that the hardware can understand directly) but the way they do it is different. Interpreters are programs that take each program instruction written in the programming language and turn it into the binary code. They then move onto the next programming instruction and then turn it into binary. The process is repeated until all the instructions have been turned into binary. This process is being done as the program is run, which slows it down.

Debuggers

It is easy to make mistakes when you write a program. Mistakes in programs are called bugs and these 'bugs' can be difficult to find. Luckily help is available in the form of a piece of software called a debugger. A debugger is a program that is used to test and remove the mistakes (i.e., bugs) from another program.

▲ Debuggers are software used to test and check programs for bugs.

Linkers

Linkers are programs that are usually part of the compiler and they take care of the linking between the code the programmer writes and other resources and libraries to make up the whole program file that can be executed (i.e., run).

Editors

Editors allow you to write the program instructions and change them.

Software: programming software *continued*

The advantages and disadvantages of different software applications

Sometimes it is possible to use different types of software to produce a product. For example, a brochure could be created using word-processing software or DTP software. A simple database (called a flat file database) can be created using spreadsheet software but for a more complex database, specialist database management software should be used. Specialist database management software is capable of producing a relational database that allows data to be stored more efficiently.

Activity

Advantages and disadvantages of different software applications

By now you will have experience in using lots of different types of software. You should have experience of the advantages and disadvantages of each type of software when compared with each other.

For this activity you have to use your own experiences and also do some research, if necessary, to draw the following mind maps:

1 Mind maps showing the advantages and disadvantages in using word-processing or DTP software to produce a school magazine.
2 Mind maps showing the advantages and disadvantages in using spreadsheet or database management software to store a list of your friends' names and addresses and other brief details.
3 Mind maps showing the advantages and disadvantages in using word-processing or graphics software to produce a simple diagram.

Questions H

1 Programmers write software in a computer language.
   (a) Give the name of **one** computer language. (*1 mark*)
   (b) Explain what is meant by a computer program. (*2 mark*)
   (c) Computer programs often contain bugs. What is meant by a bug? (*1 mark*)

2 A school is holding a Halloween disco. Posters need to be produced to put around the school.
   (a) Write down the names of **two** different types of application software that could be used to produce the poster. (*2 marks*)
   (b) Write down which **one** of the two pieces of software named in part (a) you would choose and write down **two** reasons for your choice. (*3 marks*)

3 Which three of the following tasks are carried out by all operating systems?
   A Transferring data to a printer
   B Allocating storage space on a disk
   C Positioning text in a word-processing document
   D Finding a database record
   E Accepting keyboard input
   F Adding colour to a drawing on screen

   Write the correct letters in the spaces below.

   1..........................
   2.........................
   3.......................... (*3 marks*)

File types used to support software

You will find out

▷ **About the different file types used to support software**

You may have noticed that different file types are used with different software. If, for example, you try to open a file created using spreadsheet software with word-processing software, it does not show the correct data.

File types for images

There are lots of different file types used for images and here are the main ones.

GIF (Graphical Interchange Format) files

Along with JPEG, it is one of the two main file formats for images used on the Internet. GIF files are small in size because the original file is compressed by removing any irrelevant data in the file.

The main disadvantage with GIF files is that only 256 colours are used even though an actual image can contain 16 million colours. This means that GIF images do not look quite the same as the original image.

GIF files are good for:

- images on the web
- photographs on the web.

JPEG (Joint Photographic Expert Group) files

With GIF, it is the main file format for images on the web. JPEG is ideal for photographs and many digital cameras automatically create files with this file format. Like GIF, JPEG compresses the original image. There is a slight distortion when the image is converted to a JPEG file. This is noticeable at the edges of the image. JPEG files use 16 million colours, which is why they are ideal for photographic images.

PNG (Portable Network Graphics) files

PNG files use compression that creates a compressed image without any loss in image quality. It uses 16 million colours but the resulting file size is slightly larger than GIF or JPEG files.

When you create a graphic using the software Macromedia Fireworks, you create it in this file format. You can then choose to save the file in different file formats depending on the use to which the graphic is to be put.

TIF (Tagged Image Format) files

TIF is a bitmapped image format and is ideally suited to scanned images, images with continuous colours and photographs. TIFs are widely used and can be easily modified and can have any number of colours.

PSD (PhotoShop Document) files

PhotoShop is a popular piece of software used for creating and modifying images. PSD file format produces very high quality images but as there is no compression, the file sizes are large. This means that if you used PSD files with the Internet, they would take a while to upload.

BMP (bitmap) files

This file format saves the image as a map of pixels. It supports millions of colours but because of the very large file size, the time taken to load the file from the Internet is large.

Pictures created using the package Windows Paint are saved as bmp files.

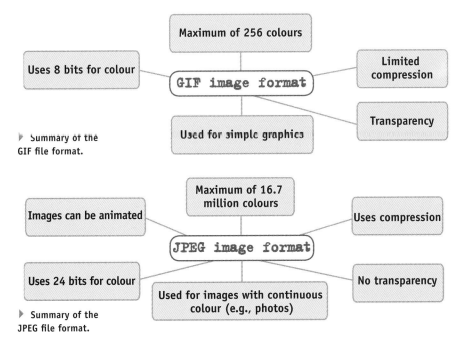

▶ Summary of the GIF file format.

▶ Summary of the JPEG file format.

File types used to support software *continued*

File types for audio

There are a huge number of different file types for audio (i.e. sound) but here are the main ones:

- **WAV** – this is the standard file type used by Windows when storing sound. Sound stored in this format is CD quality and this means that the file sizes are quite large.
- **MIDI** – this is the file type used when electronic musical instruments, computers, and other equipment need to work with each other.
- **MP3** – this is the most popular file type for downloading and storing music. This file type uses compression, which means you can store lots of tracks on your portable player.

File types for video

File types for video include the following:

- **WMV** – this is the file type used by the Windows media player.
- **MPEG-4** – this file type is used with portable media players such as iPods, mobile phones, PSPs and also to store video on DVD.
- **Flash (.swf)** – files in this format can be created using the software Flash.
- **QuickTime (.mov)** – files in this format can be played back using the QuickTime player.

Document files

Document file types are all those file types used for the production of documents using software such as word-processing, DTP, web authoring software, etc. The main file types for document files are:

- **Portable document format (PDF)** – this file type is very popular because the file can be read by almost any computer, as the software used to view it can be obtained free.
- **.doc (.docx)** – this is the popular file format that the word-processing package Microsoft Word uses to save its documents in.
- **HTML** – used for storing text and images in webpages/websites.

Executable files

Executable files are files that can be run on their own without any other applications software. They represent program files as opposed to data files.

You can spot an executable file in a list of files because it has a .exe after the file name like this: 'EssentialICT.exe'.

Questions I

1 Images can be stored as a variety of different file types.
  (a) Give the name of **two** file types used for images. (*2 marks*)
  (b) A digital photograph is stored as a bitmap. Explain what this means. (*2 marks*)

2 Put a tick in all of the boxes that represent file types. (*5 marks*)

Item	Tick if item is a correct file type
CPU	☐
JPEG	☐
MP3	☐
OCR	☐
MICR	☐
WAV	☐
GIF	☐
BMP	☐

3 John looks at the files on a CD and notices one file with .exe after the filename. He remembers that this is an executable file.
  (a) Explain what is meant by an executable file. (*1 mark*)
  (b) He notices another file containing documentation with a .doc after the file name. Give the name of the software he would need to use in order to view the documentation on this file. (*1 mark*)

Extension activity

Produce a mind map showing the different file types that can be used for the following:

- images
- audio
- video.

END-OF-TOPIC REVIEW

Questions

 Test yourself

The following notes summarize this topic. The notes are incomplete because they have words missing. Using the words in the list below, copy out and complete the sentences A to L, underlining the words that you have inserted. Each word may be used more than once.

input   touch pad

graphical user interface   keyboard   microphone

scanner   programming   joysticks

stylus   digital   mouse   output

A Devices used to get data from the outside world into the computer are called _____ devices.

B The commonest input device, that comes with all computers, is the _____.

C A _____ is used to move a pointer or cursor around the screen and to make selections.

D Where space is restricted, such as when a laptop is being used on your knee, a _____ is used instead of a mouse.

E _____ are used primarily with games software.

F In voice recognition systems a _____ is used as the input device.

G The input device used to scan in text and images is called a _____ .

H Cameras that do not use film and can transfer an image to the computer are called _____ cameras.

I A pen-like device used to draw or write on a tablet is called a _____.

J Printers and plotters are examples of _____ devices.

K A _____ is a type of interface that uses features such as windows, icons, menus, pointers, etc.

L Compilers, interpreters, debuggers and editors are all used with _____ software.

Questions *continued*

Examination style questions

1 Here is a list of devices that may be attached to a computer system:

LCD screen	flash/pen drive
keyboard	microphone
portable hard drive	digital camera
mouse	speakers
touch pad	web camera
laser printer	CD-ROM drive

(a) Write down all the names of the output devices in the list above. *(3 marks)*

(b) List **two** other output devices not in the above list. *(2 marks)*

(c) Give the name of **one** input device that is not included in the list above. *(1 mark)*

(d) Give the name of **one** device in the list above that could be used to back up data and programs. *(1 mark)*

2 (a) Give **two** uses for each of the following input devices in a personal computer *(6 marks)*:
  (i) Mouse
  (ii) Microphone
  (iii) Digital camera

(b) Give the names of **four** output devices and give **one** use for each of them. *(8 marks)*

4 Touch screens can often be seen at tourist information offices.

(a) Describe what a touch screen is and how it works. *(2 marks)*

(b) Give **one** advantage of using a touch screen as an input device for use by the general public. *(1 mark)*

5 Computers need memory and backing storage.

(a) Give **one** difference between memory and backing storage. *(1 mark)*

(b) Give **one** example of what would be stored in memory. *(1 mark)*

(c) Give **one** example of what would be stored in backing storage. *(1 mark)*

6 Data needs to be stored for future use. Here are a number of storage devices/media. For each of these, explain a suitable use and explain clearly why the storage device/media is suited to the application.

(a) Memory card *(2 marks)*

(b) CD-ROM *(2 marks)*

(c) Magnetic hard drive *(2 marks)*

(d) Flash/pen drive *(2 marks)*

3 Copy and complete the table below *(10 marks)*:

Application	Most suitable output device
Alerting the user that an error has occurred by making a beep	
Printing a poster in colour	
Listening to a radio station using the Internet	
Producing a large plan of a house	
Producing a hard copy of a spreadsheet	
Producing a colour picture on paper taken with a digital camera	
Producing a series of invoices with several copies that can be sent to different departments	
Producing a warning when a bar code is read incorrectly	
Listening to messages from a voicemail system	
Displaying the results of a quick search on the availability of a holiday	

7 Which **three** tasks from the list below are carried out by all operating systems? *(3 marks)*

A Underlining text in a word-processing program
B Controlling peripheral devices
C Sorting data into alphabetical order
D Transferring data between memory and a disk
E Managing system security
F Changing the size of a picture

8 Some types of applications software are more suitable than others for carrying out a task.

(a) Here is a list of applications software. Choose the letter of the software that is best used for carrying out the task in the table. *(5 marks)*

A Web design
B Database
C Presentation
D Graphics

Task	Letter
Keeping an organized store of data about pupils in a school	
For developing an e-commerce site	
For creating a logo for a new business	
For editing a digital photograph	
To help explain the benefits of a new product to a group of sales staff in a room	

(b) A company uses a computer and software to model the amount of money coming into and going out of the business. A screenshot of this model is shown below.

Which type of applications software has been used to produce this model? *(1 mark)*

9 It is always best to choose the most suitable software for the job when carrying out a task. Match the best type of applications software A, B, C, D or E to carry out the tasks in the table below. *(4 marks)*

A Database
B DTP
C Word-processing
D Spreadsheet
E Web design

Task	Letter
Producing a personal website	
Typing in, formatting and checking the text for a letter	
Producing a school magazine with lots of graphics and design elements	
A large collection of patient records to be typed in and kept for easy access in a medical practice	

	A	B	C	D	E	F	G	H
1	**Cash Flow Forecast for ABC Products**							
2			Jan	Feb	Mar	Apr	May	June
3	Income							
4		Bank balance from last mor	£1,000	£831	£794	£728	£361	£903
5		Sales	£720	£900	£1,115	£1,200	£2,010	£2,500
6		**Total income**	£1,720	£1,731	£1,909	£1,928	£2,371	£3,403
7								
8	**Expenditure**							
9		Supplies of product	£240	£289	£304	£576	£476	£427
10		Postage	£48	£29	£34	£132	£78	£57
11		Packing	£25	£38	£51	£54	£65	£100
12		Fees	£12	£15	£21	£46	£76	£69
13		Electricity	£24	£26	£31	£28	£33	£32
14		Rent	£140	£140	£140	£140	£140	£140
15		Wages	£400	£400	£600	£600	£600	£600
16		**Total expenditure**	£889	£937	£1,181	£1,567	£1,468	£1,425
17								
18		**End of month balance**	£831	£794	£728	£361	£903	£1,978
19								
20								

END-OF-TOPIC REVIEW

Exam support

Worked example

Web cameras can take live video that can be transferred using the Internet to a computer in the home.

(a) Tick the three applications that are possible using a webcam. *(3 marks)*

	Tick **three** boxes
Watching the evolution of dinosaurs	☐
A parent checking up on their children in a nursery when they are at work	☐
Looking at live video of an erupting volcano in a geography lesson	☐
Watching a movie star constantly wherever they go	☐
Watching the space shuttle taking off as it happens	☐

(b) Give **two** advantages of using a webcam. *(2 marks)*

(c) Give **two** disadvantages of using a webcam. *(2 marks)*

Student answer 1

(a)

	Tick **three** boxes
Watching the evolution of dinosaurs	☑
A parent checking up on their children in a nursery when they are at work	☐
Looking at live video of an erupting volcano in a geography lesson	☐
Watching a movie star constantly wherever they go	☑
Watching the space shuttle taking off as it happens	☑

(b) You can use it to spy on other people.

They are very cheap to buy and many computers have them built into the screen.

(c) They do not produce a very good image.

You cannot store the image produced.

▲ Examiner's comment

(a) Webcams produce live images so you obviously cannot watch the evolution of dinosaurs.

Watching a movie star wherever they go would require a webcam to be present all the time. Clearly this is false.

The last tick is in the correct box.

(b) The first answer is a bit vague and needed further amplification to get the mark. The second answer is ok and gains a mark.

(c) The first answer is correct and gains a mark.

It is possible to save an image produced by a webcam and this is how they are used for security purposes.

(3 marks out of 7)

Student answer 2

(a)

	Tick **three** boxes
Watching the evolution of dinosaurs	☐
A parent checking up on their children in a nursery when they are at work	☑
Looking at live video of an erupting volcano in a geography lesson	☑
Watching a movie star constantly wherever they go	☐
Watching the space shuttle taking off as it happens	☑

(b) *You can look at famous sites throughout the world using live or almost live pictures.*

They can be used for surveillance by the police and MI5 as they are extremely small.

(c) *They can be used to make secret films of people without their knowledge which is morally wrong.*

Webcams can encourage online flirting with people who are married, which could destroy a marriage.

▲ Examiner's comment

(a) All the ticks are in the correct places so all three marks are given here.

(b) Both of these are advantages of webcams, so full marks for this part.

(c) Both of these are valid answers and so full marks are awarded.

(7 marks out of 7)

Examiner's answers

(a) One mark for each correctly placed tick.

	Tick **three** boxes
Watching the evolution of dinosaurs	☐
A parent checking up on their children in a nursery when they are at work	☑
Looking at live video of an erupting volcano in a geography lesson	☑
Watching a movie star constantly wherever they go	☐
Watching the space shuttle taking off as it happens	☑

(b) One mark for each of two advantages such as:

A webcam can watch a bar to check that staff are not stealing money or drinks.

They can record criminals and be used as evidence.

You can see what the weather is like in a resort you are soon to visit.

They are very cheap to buy.

You can chat with people and see them at the same time.

They are small and so can be hidden easily so people do not know you are looking at them.

Webcams mean that you can have a simple meeting without the need to travel.

People can view things in distant places that it would be hard for them to visit in person.

(c) One mark for each of two disadvantages such as:

The images from webcams are often poor quality.

It can make it easy for others to spy on you without you knowing.

It can invade people's privacy.

Summary mind maps

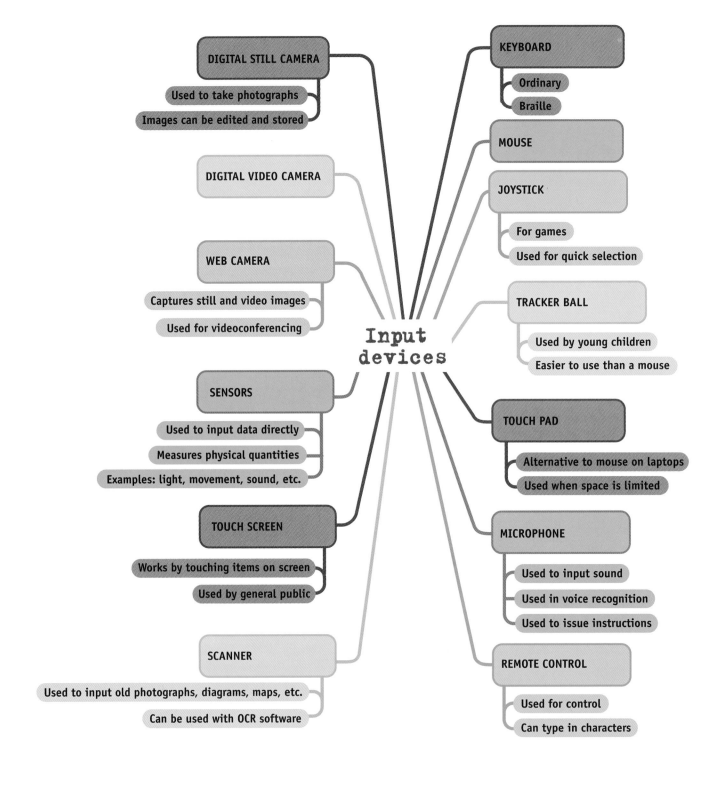

DIGITAL STILL CAMERA

Used to take photographs

Images can be edited and stored

DIGITAL VIDEO CAMERA

WEB CAMERA

Captures still and video images

Used for videoconferencing

SENSORS

Used to input data directly

Measures physical quantities

Examples: light, movement, sound, etc.

TOUCH SCREEN

Works by touching items on screen

Used by general public

SCANNER

Used to input old photographs, diagrams, maps, etc.

Can be used with OCR software

Input devices

KEYBOARD

Ordinary

Braille

MOUSE

JOYSTICK

For games

Used for quick selection

TRACKER BALL

Used by young children

Easier to use than a mouse

TOUCH PAD

Alternative to mouse on laptops

Used when space is limited

MICROPHONE

Used to input sound

Used in voice recognition

Used to issue instructions

REMOTE CONTROL

Used for control

Can type in characters

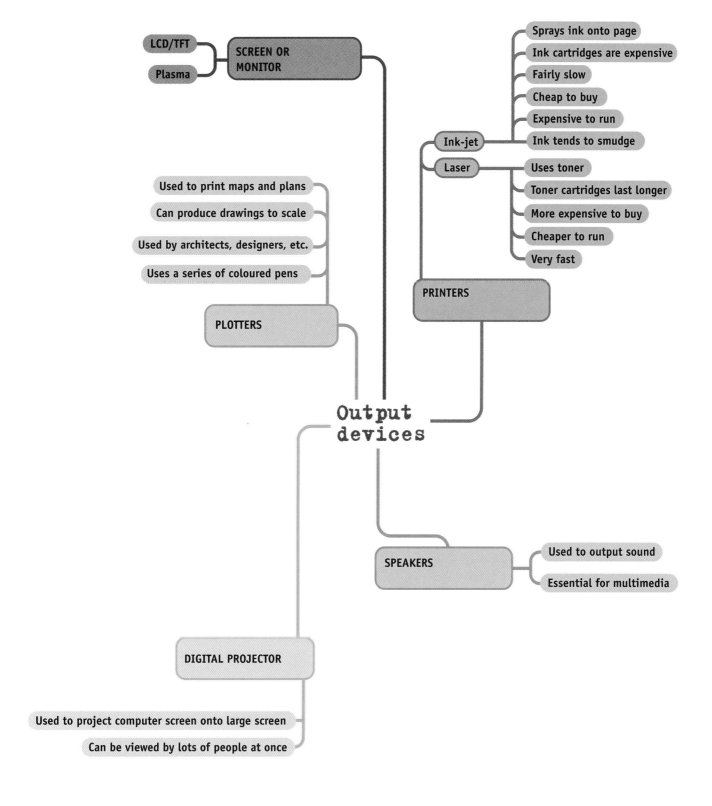

LCD/TFT

Plasma

SCREEN OR MONITOR

Sprays ink onto page

Ink cartridges are expensive

Fairly slow

Cheap to buy

Expensive to run

Ink-jet — Ink tends to smudge

Laser — Uses toner

Toner cartridges last longer

More expensive to buy

Cheaper to run

Very fast

PRINTERS

Used to print maps and plans

Can produce drawings to scale

Used by architects, designers, etc.

Uses a series of coloured pens

PLOTTERS

Output devices

SPEAKERS

Used to output sound

Essential for multimedia

DIGITAL PROJECTOR

Used to project computer screen onto large screen

Can be viewed by lots of people at once

Summary mind maps *continued*

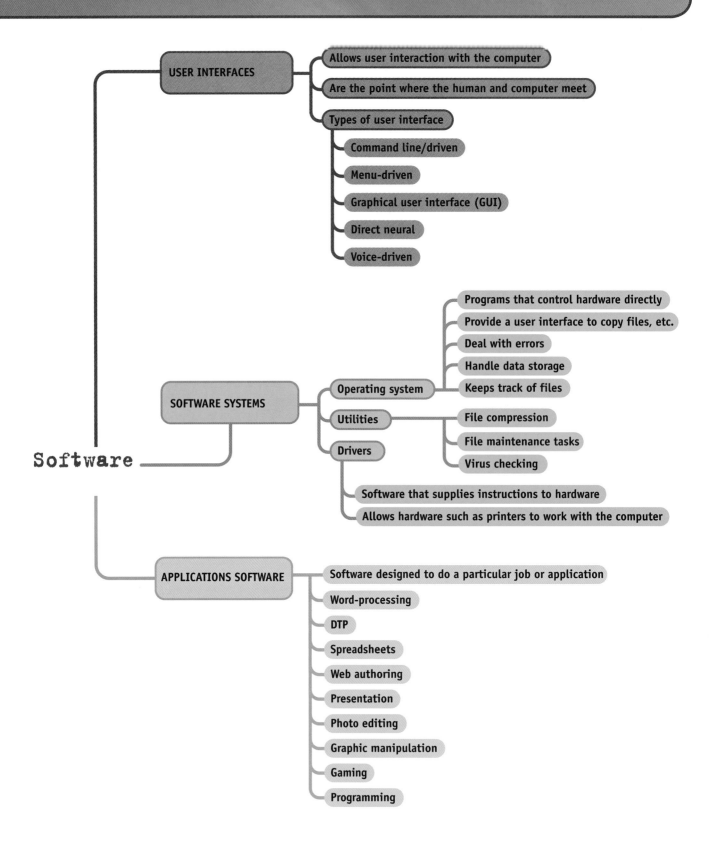

USER INTERFACES
- Allows user interaction with the computer
- Are the point where the human and computer meet
- Types of user interface
  - Command line/driven
  - Menu-driven
  - Graphical user interface (GUI)
  - Direct neural
  - Voice-driven

SOFTWARE SYSTEMS
- Operating system
  - Programs that control hardware directly
  - Provide a user interface to copy files, etc.
  - Deal with errors
  - Handle data storage
  - Keeps track of files
- Utilities
  - File compression
  - File maintenance tasks
  - Virus checking
- Drivers
  - Software that supplies instructions to hardware
  - Allows hardware such as printers to work with the computer

Software

APPLICATIONS SOFTWARE
- Software designed to do a particular job or application
- Word-processing
- DTP
- Spreadsheets
- Web authoring
- Presentation
- Photo editing
- Graphic manipulation
- Gaming
- Programming

Exchanging information

The key concepts covered in this topic are:

- Communication services
- Sharing, exchanging and managing information
- The safe and responsible use of communication services
- Communications software
- The use of the Internet
- Controlling ICT systems remotely
- Monitoring and tracking systems
- Emerging technologies

Communication systems are used for the exchange of data in the form of text, voice, video, images, etc. There has been a huge increase in the number of ways in which it is possible to communicate owing to the widespread use of the Internet.

Communication is a vital part of business and everyday life and in this topic you will be looking at the systems that are used for communication. These systems will cover the use of mobile phones, the use of services available on the Internet, etc.

Communications has brought about systems that are used to monitor our movements and communications over the phone and in this topic you will be looking at these. Communication services can be abused and you have to be careful to take certain precautions when using them.

There are many emerging technologies that offer us huge benefits and these will be looked at here.

Contents

Communication services

There are many different ways of communicating using communication services such as telephones, email, etc. The nature of many of these devices is changing as people demand that they only carry one portable device rather than several. For example, smart mobile phones often incorporate MP3 players, digital cameras, satellite navigation and so on.

In this section you will be looking at communication services and how they allow people to communicate effectively using ICT.

Voice telephones

Telephones are one of the most popular communication devices and, although the land-line phone is still very popular, the growth in the use of mobile phones has meant that these have many more services available. New services for mobile phones are being thought up all the time. Early mobile phones were the equivalent of a telephone that could be used on the move. Nowadays they offer all sorts of new services and have started to blur the difference between a computer or PDA and a mobile phone.

Many mobile phones also act as portable MP3 players, enabling you to play your music on the move. Here are some of the services available through mobile phones:

- send and receive text
- take digital photographs
- take short video clips
- surf the internet
- watch live TV
- send and receive email
- download and listen to music
- download and play games
- send picture messages
- play videos
- GPS (use your mobile phone as a satellite navigation system).

Advantages and disadvantages of mobile phones

Advantages

- You can be contacted in case of an emergency.
- Plans can be changed at the last minute.
- Parents like children to have a mobile phone as they feel it is safer.

Disadvantages

- Many people use their phones when walking along and this has caused accidents.
- Calls can disturb other people in the cinema, theatre, cafes, etc.
- Many people still use hand-held phones when driving, which is dangerous and illegal.
- Long-term use may cause health problems.

SMS (texting)

SMS (short messaging service) or, as most people know it, texting, allows short low-cost messages to be sent between phones. It is also possible to send text messages to phones using a computer or mobile device such as a PDA or palmtop.

"I'm still discovering cool stuff I can do with my smartphone. Today I sent a photo to my mom, bought some music, trimmed my sideburns, blended a smoothie, and neutered my cat!"

"I decided to have the surgery because I need the extra thumb for text messaging."

Fax

Fax is like a long distance photocopier. You put the document in the fax machine at one end and then enter the telephone number of the fax machine to which it is to be sent. The page is scanned, passed along the telephone line and it is printed out on the recipient's fax machine. Documents as well as diagrams/drawings can be sent by fax. It is possible to use a computer with a scanner and a printer as a fax machine.

▲ A fax machine.

Other services

Instant messaging (IM)

Instant messaging is a method of two people using real-time text to conduct a conversation. Some instant message services can make use of webcams that allow the people conducting the text conversation to see each other.

Email

Email is a fast and cheap way of sending messages from one computer to one or more other computers. It has the advantage that you can attach files to an email.

Chat rooms

Chat rooms are virtual meeting places where you can meet and hold conversations with others. They are not without their dangers. Paedophiles have been known to use chat rooms to make contact with children.

Forums

Forums are often called message boards and they allow people to post and respond to messages posted on them. Usually the forum is about a particular subject or interest.

Bulletin boards

A bulletin board is a computer with special software that users can log into. Once logged in, they can upload and download files, read bulletins and messages, etc.

VoIP (Voice over Internet Protocol)/Internet telephone

VoIP enables cheap phone calls to be made using the Internet. It is a technology that allows voice signals to be transferred over the Internet but it can sometimes be unreliable and the quality of the sound can be poor.

Videoconferencing

Videoconferencing allows face-to-face meetings to be conducted without the participants being in the same room or even the same geographical area. You will probably have seen videoconferencing systems used to interview people in distant locations on the TV news. Videoconferencing allows people to hold a 'virtual' meeting. The people at the meeting can see and speak to each other. They are also able to share documents, presentations, etc.

Advantages of using videoconferencing include:

- Less stress as employees do not have to experience delays at airports, accidents, roadworks, etc.
- Improved family life, as less time spent away from home staying in hotels.
- Employees do not have to put in long working hours travelling to and from meetings.
- Saves money as business does not have to spend money on travelling expenses, hotel rooms, meals, etc.
- Improves productivity of employees, as they are not wasting time travelling.
- Meetings can be called at very short notice without too much planning.
- Greener, as there are fewer people flying to meetings. This cuts down on carbon dioxide emissions.
- Roads will not be clogged up with traffic and this will cause less stress and cut down on pollution.

Disadvantages of using videoconferencing include:

- The cost of the equipment, as specialist videoconferencing equipment is expensive.
- Poor image and sound quality.
- People can feel very self-conscious when using videoconferencing and may fail to come across well.
- Although documents and diagrams in digital form can be passed around, an actual product or component cannot be passed around.
- Lack of face-to-face contact may mean a discussion may not be as effective.

Communication services *continued*

Activity

The advantages and disadvantages of email communication compared to making a phone call

Imagine you need to contact someone to give them some information about a holiday you have found that they may want to go on with you. You have a choice of communicating with them by:

- phone
- email.

Produce a list showing the advantages and disadvantages of email communication compared to making a phone call.

Activity

Producing a mind map showing the advantages and disadvantages of different communication methods

For this activity you have to produce one mind map that summarizes all the advantages and disadvantages of all the different methods of communication that have been discussed in this section.

Questions A

1 **(a)** Explain what is meant by the abbreviation VoIP. (*1 mark*)

(b) Describe **one** advantage in a person using VoIP to communicate with others. (*2 marks*)

2 People can communicate using a variety of different devices and services.

Give the names of **three** methods of communication that make use of ICT. (*3 marks*)

3 **(a)** A company has decided to use videoconferencing. Explain what is meant by videoconferencing. (*2 marks*)

(b) Other than a computer, what equipment would the company need to supply to enable videoconferencing? (*2 marks*)

(c) Write down **one** advantage and **one** disadvantage of videoconferencing. (*2 marks*)

4 Emails can be used as a method of communication rather than a phone call or a letter.

(a) Give **two** advantages in using email to communicate rather than by using a letter. (*2 marks*)

(b) Give **two** advantages in using email to communicate with someone rather than by talking to them by phone. (*2 marks*)

Extension activity

Research the features of the latest mobile phones using the Internet. Produce a list of your three most desirable mobile phones and their features.

▶ Videoconferencing allows virtual meetings where delegates are not at the same location.

Sharing, exchanging and managing information, safe and responsible use

Communication services offer methods of sharing, exchanging and managing information and these services are essential to commerce as well as being an essential part of our daily lives. Many people work on projects together and being able to share and exchange information is essential, as many of these people do not work in the same place. In this section you will be looking at the things that can be done to make life easier when sharing and exchanging information with others.

Communication services offer quick and powerful methods of keeping in touch and passing information to each other. This is why services such as email and text messaging are used so much. All these communication services can be misused and they are not without their dangers. In this section you will also be looking at how these services need to be used with caution.

The problems in sharing, exchanging and managing information

One of the problems when sharing and exchanging files with others is that it can make the data less secure. For example, people working remotely might work on the move or in public places on laptops that may be stolen. There are a few other problems that occur when people are working on files that are altered by lots of different people.

In this section you will be looking at the issues concerning the sharing, managing and exchanging of information.

File naming conventions

When many people are working on the same project, such as developing a new website, they often have to share files. It is important to name files carefully. For example, it should be possible to know who created the file from its name. A sensible and logical file naming system should be used by everyone so that files are easily found.

Version control

When working on multiple versions of a file, each version should have a different filename to the previous version. There is always a danger of saving an older version of a file using the same filename and losing work in the process. Saving using different version names helps avoid this. This is called version control.

The secure transfer of data

In order to transfer data, it is often necessary to use the Internet. This exposes the data to the threat from hackers. Hackers may view the data, alter the data or use the data to commit fraud.

In order to transfer data securely it is necessary to encrypt it. Encryption scrambles the data as it is being sent and only the true recipient can unscramble it. You will learn more about the encryption process later.

Secure access to data

It is important to make sure that only people who are authorized to access the ICT system have access to it. There are a number of ways this is done:

- use user-IDs and passwords
- use firewalls that protect against hackers accessing systems using the Internet
- use encryption to store the data so that even if the data were accessed, it could not be understood
- use read/write permissions that allow some staff to view files and other staff to be able to both view and alter (i.e. write) the files.

The responsible and safe use of communication services

The Internet is a great thing and brings tremendous benefits to us all. It is not, however, without its

Sharing, exchanging and managing information, safe and responsible use *continued*

dangers. In this section you will be looking at the dangers lurking in many corners of the Internet. If you are aware of the dangers then at least you can take precautions to ensure that you are not put at risk.

Showing respect towards others

In is important to respect other people who may be different from yourself by:

- not engaging in cyberbullying, which means using the Internet or mobile phones to harass or intimidate another person
- not spreading false rumours about others using chat rooms, social networking sites, etc.
- not using offensive or racially abusive language.

Complying with Data Protection regulations

When working on projects such as creating databases you may be using personal data. If you are using personal data then you have to meet all the requirements of the Data Protection Act. This act controls what you can and cannot do with personal data.

Staying safe

When using communication systems you need to ensure that you use them safely and responsibly. There are a number of things to consider and these are outlined here.

Using appropriate language

When you post messages on a blog or message board or use a chat room it is important to realize that this will be viewed by people of all different ages and backgrounds. You therefore need to ensure:

- you do not use swear words
- you do not use racially offensive words
- you do not use words likely to offend certain groups of people
- that your material can be read by people of all ages
- you do not engage in cyberbullying (i.e. bullying using the Internet, mobile phones, etc.).

Some services, such as chat rooms, message boards, blogs, etc., are moderated. This means that a person is appointed to view the material and remove any inappropriate content. Sometimes the services are regulated automatically, which means that the

computer will pick out inappropriate words. For example, your network software may pick out certain words used in emails sent to your friends. These emails will not reach their destination and will instead be sent to the network manager or head of department for them to read. How embarrassing might that be? Some systems may suspend you from the network service for a certain period. In serious cases you could be suspended from the service permanently.

Disclosure of personal information

You should never ever give out personal information when you are online. You may be chatting to someone who seems genuine but you could be chatting to anyone. If you reveal your personal information or even worse meet them, then you could meet someone who wants to do you harm. There are lots of weird people out there, and they may try to contact you. Parents can use the parental controls provided with the web browser software so their children cannot enter chat rooms, social networking sites, instant message services and other unsuitable websites.

▼ If your project involves personal data then you will need to comply with the Data Protection Act.

Copyright 2000 by Randy Glasbergen.
www.glasbergen.com

"I MET SOMEONE WONDERFUL IN A CHAT ROOM...
AND THEN I FOUND OUT SHE'S A CAT!"

The misuse of images

It is very easy to copy an image off a website or social networking site. Images sent to one person can be passed to others without their permission. It is very easy to misuse an image, so you need to be very careful where you put your images online and what sort of images you send.

Here are some ways in which an image can be misused:

- You may be identified from your image even though there are no other contact details. This can lead to all sorts of personal problems.
- You may encounter stalkers or be pestered by email or worse still they may find where you live and your phone numbers.
- Your image might be posted on an inappropriate website.
- Your image might be edited using image editing software. For example, an innocent image of a person's face could be put on someone else's body. You can imagine what images could be produced.
- Paedophiles use school and athletic club websites to obtain images. Again these images can be edited and put onto pornographic websites.

▲ Social networking sites are great fun but they are not without their dangers.

Questions B

1. (a) When sharing files you need to be careful with file naming conventions. Give **two** reasons why it is important to be careful when naming files. (*2 marks*)

   (b) When sharing and exchanging information with others it is important to be careful about version control. Explain **one** way that getting confused with different versions of the same file can cause problems. (*1 mark*)

2. When sharing and exchanging data with others, it is important to ensure the security of data.

   (a) Describe **two** ways in which the security of data can be put at risk when sharing and exchanging data. (*2 marks*)

   (b) Explain **two** precautions that can be taken to ensure the security of data. (*2 marks*)

3. When working with personal data, the data is often encrypted. In most cases it is encrypted when transferred over the Internet. In some cases it is encrypted when it is stored on portable media and computers such as laptops and other portable devices.

   (a) Explain the meaning of 'encrypted'. (*2 marks*)

   (b) Give **one** reason personal data being transferred using the Internet is often encrypted. (*1 mark*)

   (c) Give **one** reason personal data being stored on portable media and computers is often encrypted. (*1 mark*)

4. Explain **two** ways in which an image posted on a website or social networking site can be misused. (*2 marks*)

5. Personal data should never be disclosed on a network service that anyone can view.

   (a) Give an example of a network service that anyone can view. (*1 mark*)

   (b) Give **two** reasons why this piece of advice is important. (*2 marks*)

Extension activity

Some people get a bit lost with the latest communications technology.

Many people would like to learn a bit more so that they are less ignorant when people start talking about communications devices and media.

For this activity you have to produce a short guide to the technology. Your guide should at least cover the following:

- Texting
- Instant messaging
- Chat rooms
- Forums
- Bulletin boards
- VoIP.

Communications software, the uses of the Internet

▷ **About communications software**

▷ **About the use of the Internet**

Communications software is the software used to provide services on networks and the Internet such as web browsers, email software, messaging and file transfer. In this section you will be looking at all of these along with aspects of the use of the Internet in everyday life.

Communications software

Communications software is software that is used to create the many communication services that are available on computers and portable devices such as PDAs and mobile phones.

Web browser

Web browser software is a program that allows access to webpages stored on the Internet. A web browser allows the user to find information on websites and webpages quickly and it does this by making use of:

- URLs
- key word searches
- links
- menus.

Email software

An email is an electronic message sent from one communication device (computer, telephone, mobile phone, or PDA) to another.

Most web browser software has email software provided as part of it. Email software allows a user to:

- read and write email
- reply to an email
- forward email – send an email that has been sent to you to others
- create an address book – produce a list of the people you need to contact, with their contact details including their email addresses
- send one email to a group of people.

Messaging software

Messaging software is software that allows for written and oral communication between two people using the Internet. In most cases both users will need to have the same messaging software in order to communicate with each other.

Messaging software includes:

- SMS software that allows text messages to be sent and received.
- Instant messaging that allows users to conduct a real-time conversation by typing in messages to each other.
- VoIP, where users are able to make cheap voice calls to each other over the Internet.

File transfer

File transfer software is used to transfer a file of data from one computer to another. File transfer software is available as part of email software and this allows you to

attach files to emails. For example, you could attach a file containing a photograph of yourself obtained from a digital camera, a piece of clip art, a picture that you have scanned in, a long document, etc. Basically, if you can store it as a file, then you can attach it to an email.

The uses of the Internet

The Internet is so useful it is hard to think of how we could cope without it. There are many different uses for the Internet and in this section you will be looking at four uses: for communication, for commerce, for leisure and for information retrieval.

For communication

It is much easier and cheaper for people to contact each other using the many Internet communication services. These services include:

- Email – much cheaper and less time consuming than writing and sending a letter.
- File attachments/file transfer – you can send anything that can be stored as a file (e.g., text, music, video, etc.).
- Text messaging (SMS) – fast and cheap messages can be sent from portable devices such as mobile phones, PDAs, laptops, etc.
- Instant messaging – you can chat by typing in messages.
- Blogs – this is like an online diary where people, who are interested, can find out what you have been doing.
- Social networking sites – these allow you to keep in touch with friends as well as make new friends.

For commerce

Most organizations use websites, sometimes for promotional purposes and sometimes to allow people to order goods or services using the site. This is called e-commerce.

Lots of these websites allow customers to browse online catalogues and add goods to their virtual shopping basket/trolley just like in a real store. When they have selected the goods, they go to the checkout where they have to decide on the payment method. They also have to enter some details such as their name and address and other contact details. The payment is authorized and the ordering process is completed. All that is left is for the customer to wait for delivery of their goods.

▲ On-line shopping is very popular.

For leisure

Many people now spend more time using the Internet than they do watching TV. Here are some of the leisure activities the Internet is used for:

- keeping in touch with friends and family (using VoIP, email, chat rooms, instant messaging, social networking sites, etc.)
- researching places to go, holidays, hobbies, sports, news, etc.
- playing online games with others
- watching videos
- listening to music, listening to the radio, watching old TV programmes, etc.
- shopping.

For information retrieval

The Internet is a huge body of information that is available to everyone. People therefore use the Internet to retrieve the information in their everyday lives such as:

- maps
- information about tax, benefits
- information about illnesses
- information about travel (flight routes, flight times, rail times, accommodation, etc.).

The Internet can also be used when users need to log into their organization's ICT system from a remote location. Once logged in, the user can use the organization's databases to extract the information they need.

Controlling ICT systems remotely, monitoring and tracking systems

In this section you will be looking at how ICT systems can be controlled remotely and how this can be used for convenience as well as for sorting out problems with hardware and software.

ICT systems are able to monitor and track people and vehicles. Many people are worried that all these systems can be used to check up on us and erode our privacy. Other people see these systems as a necessary evil, as they are an important tool in the fight against crime and terrorism. This section covers the different types of monitoring and tracking systems and their applications.

Controlling ICT systems at a distance

ICT systems can be controlled at a distance and there are number of examples, which include:

- **Remote controls** – many computers are used for playing media or watching TV and this may be done with the user not sitting directly in front of the computer. It therefore makes sense to have a remote control just like the one you use with your TV.
- **Help-desks** – if you are experiencing a computer problem then one way of fixing it is to contact a help-desk. As the staff at the help-desk are often in another part of the country or the world, they can use the Internet to take over the running of your computer so they can see if they can fix the problem.
- **Remote access** – many people need to gain access to their organization's computer systems when they are away from the office. They can do this by using the Internet. Once they have entered their user-ID and password, they can then use the computer facilities as if they were using them in the office.

Monitoring and tracking systems

Worker monitoring/logging

Some employers keep a constant check on their employees.

- For example, supermarket checkouts can monitor and log how many goods are put through the checkout each hour by each assistant.
- Internet use is monitored by network managers. They can record what sites are visited and how long an employee spent on them. They can therefore spot employees who are spending too much time browsing the Internet when they are supposed to be working.
- Emails can be read. This means that employers could read work-related emails as well as personal ones that have been sent during work time.

Cookies

Cookies are pieces of text that websites put onto your hard drive when you visit them. Without you knowing, Internet 'cookies' record details of the websites you have visited and how long you spent on them, what pages were looked at, whether you have visited the site before, etc. Many people consider this to be an invasion of their privacy.

Key logging

Key logging is the process of someone recording/monitoring the keys you press when you are using your computer using a key logger, which can either be hardware or software. As it can record keystrokes, someone can record your passwords and banking details. They can then use the information they collect fraudulently.

Call monitoring/recording

Many employers monitor the calls employees make using phones provided by the company in order to detect whether the system is being abused. Mobile phone calls are always recorded by the mobile phone companies and kept for a certain period as part of the fight against terrorists and criminals.

Electronic consumer surveillance

Some supermarkets monitor their shoppers as they walk around the store in order to understand better how shoppers shop. These cameras investigate how best to arrange goods to attract shoppers' attention.

Mobile phone triangulation

Your geographical location can be found if you carry a mobile phone. The mobile phone service locates your phone fairly accurately using a process called triangulation. Some people object to your whereabouts being stored by mobile phone companies.

CCTV cameras

CCTV stands for closed circuit television and these are the cameras you see just about everywhere. Some of these cameras can be used with sophisticated software to actually recognize a person and others can recognize a car registration plate and find the name and address of the registered owner.

Automatic number plate recognition

In an automatic number plate recognition system a digital photograph of a number plate is taken by a CCTV camera and stored. The software then takes the image and uses optical character recognition (OCR) to recognize each character making up the number plate.

Once the number plate is in the system further details can be obtained by using the characters in a search of a database. This system can be used for:

- Recognizing cars picked out by cameras for speeding, illegally travelling in bus lanes or jumping red lights.
- Recognizing cars entering and leaving car parks.
- Recognizing cars entering and leaving the country at ports.
- Recognizing cars that have been used in crimes.
- Identifying cars to check that they have paid road tax and have insurance.

▲ CCTV camera.

▲ Automatic number plate recognition uses cameras like these.

Questions D

1 Employers often monitor the use of the Internet by their staff and they may read their emails and check what they have been looking at.
   (a) Give **one** reason why staff have their Internet use monitored. (*1 mark*)
   (b) Give **one** reason why staff have their email use monitored. (*1 mark*)

2 The police use automatic number plate recognition systems.
   (a) Describe briefly how the automatic number plate recognition system works. (*3 marks*)
   (b) Give **one** advantage in the police using this system. (*1 mark*)
   (c) Give **two** uses by the police of the number plate recognition system. (*2 marks*)

3 CCTV cameras are everywhere and monitor our movements.
   (a) Give **one** advantage in the use of CCTV cameras. (*1 mark*)
   (b) Give **one** disadvantage in the use of CCTV cameras. (*1 mark*)

4 (a) Help-desks sometimes control an ICT system.
       Give **one** reason why help-desks sometimes do this. (*1 mark*)
   (b) Give a different example of a situation where an ICT system is controlled remotely. (*1 mark*)

Extension activity

Snooping

You have been asked to write a short article about the use of ICT for monitoring.

You can find out information in newspapers, on the Internet and by the use of search engines.

Your piece is to be written in a lively style for an audience of 14–18 year olds.

Emerging technologies

▷ **About emerging technologies such as Wi-Fi, Bluetooth, GIS, etc.**

In this section you will be looking at emerging technologies in the field of communication. These are those technologies that are in the process of or have recently become widespread.

Wireless communication (Wi-Fi)

Many computers and other devices are now able to connect to the Internet or communicate with other computers in a local area network wirelessly. With wireless communication, the data travels through the air rather than through cables.

Areas where Wi-Fi can be accessed are called hotspots.

Wireless networks enable people to connect wirelessly to the Internet or to a network set up at home. This means they can work anywhere they can get a radio signal for their network. Many people, especially people who travel a lot, need to access the Internet regularly. There are many public places where the Internet can be accessed wirelessly using a laptop computer or other portable device such as mobile phone or PDA. These places where you can access the Internet using Wi-Fi are called hotspots.

Advantages of wireless communication

- You are not restricted to where you can work.
- You can work whilst on the move.
- Fewer/no trailing wires to trip over.
- It is easier to keep a working area clean if there are not as many wires in the way.
- No costs associated with sinking wires.

KEY WORDS

Hotspot a region where the Internet can be accessed wirelessly.

Wi-Fi a trademark for products that meet certain standards for transmitting data over wireless networks.

Internet service provider (ISP) a company that provides users with an Internet connection.

Bluetooth technology

Bluetooth is a method used to transfer data over short distances from fixed and mobile devices. For example, you could print a document using a laptop and printer even though there were no wires between them. Other applications for Bluetooth include:

- Wireless keyboards and mice avoid clutter on your desk and make the desk easier to clean.
- Wireless headsets allowing you to use a mobile phone legally when driving.
- Sharing data such as voice, music and video wirelessly with others.
- Printing a picture from your camera phone.
- Listening to music using wireless earphones.
- Bluetooth webcams – these are very small and can send a picture using Bluetooth to a computer without using wires. The snag is that it does not produce a really good picture and the range is fairly small.
- Children's games, e.g. Wii, PlayStation and Lego Mindstorms.

Advantages of Bluetooth

- No wires are needed – you can connect several devices such as printers, cameras, mobile phones, PDAs, etc., without using a cable.

Bluetooth allows you to use a mobile phone when you are driving.

Activity

Use the following websites that are geographical information systems or have part of the website that is one.

For each site write a couple of sentences to explain what the GIS does.

- www.energysavingtrust.org.uk
- http://www.gis.rgs.org/whatisgis.html
- http://news.bbc.co.uk/1/hi/technology/7505774.stm

- You can synchronize devices. For example you can ensure that your music collection on your computer and your MP3 player are the same. When you add more music to your computer, it can be added to your MP3 player automatically. This keeps your music collection the same on both devices.
- It is very easy to use. In most cases no new hardware is needed and there is no new software to install.

Disadvantages of Bluetooth

- Can only be used over short distances – uses low power radio signals, which means you can only use it over short distances.
- Relatively small bandwidth – this limits its use. Wireless video is not as clear as the video transferred by wires.
- There are health concerns similar to the use of mobile phones.

▷ If a computer cannot use Bluetooth, you can put this device into the USB port.

Geographical Information Systems (GIS)

A geographical information system, or GIS for short, is an ICT system that is used to capture, manage, analyse and display geographically referenced information.

What can you use a GIS for? Using a GIS you can:

- determine how far it is from one place to another
- see a bird's eye view of your house and its surroundings
- plan the quickest route to school/college
- view the surroundings when you go to a new place or go on holiday
- look at the surrounding area when you are thinking of buying or renting a property.

Examples of GIS

- Satellite navigation systems – you can get navigation instructions as you drive, be directed to the nearest petrol station, locate hotels, etc.
- Google Earth.
- Multimap – useful for maps and aerial views.
- The AA – useful for finding route details from one place/postcode to another.
- The Energy Saving Trust – this site allows you to enter your postcode and it will tell you whether you could use a wind turbine to generate your own electricity.

◁ The AA route planner allows you to get a step-by-step route for any journey.

Advantages of GIS

There are many different advantages in using geographical information systems and here are just some of them:

- They reduce fuel consumption, which is therefore greener because you do not get lost.
- You can arrive at your destination without delay, as you can be warned in advance of roadworks.
- You can save money by choosing the shortest route.
- You can choose a hotel by seeing exactly how far it is from the beach.

Disadvantages of GIS

Some of the disadvantages of GIS include:

- Satellite navigation systems can send you down very small and windy roads.
- Satellite navigation systems are sometimes difficult to use.
- Sometimes the information is out-of-date.
- Satellite navigation systems can cause accidents if people start inputting information into them whilst driving.

Emerging technologies *continued*

Questions E

1 An office is thinking of introducing a wireless network with a wireless connection to the Internet. Give **two** advantages in using a wireless network rather than a wired one. *(2 marks)*

2 A company has a wireless network installed. Give **one** reason why they might be concerned about the security of their data. *(1 mark)*

3 Bluetooth is a method that allows devices to communicate with each other and pass data.
   (a) Give the names of **two** pairs of devices that can communicate using Bluetooth. *(2 marks)*
   (b) Explain **one** advantage in devices communicating using Bluetooth. *(1 mark)*
   (c) Explain **one** disadvantage in devices communicating using Bluetooth. *(1 mark)*

4 Many people make use of geographical information systems (GIS) whilst at home or on the move. Describe **two** different applications for a geographical information system. *(4 marks)*

5 Explain **two** disadvantages of using satellite navigation systems in cars. *(2 marks)*

Extension activity 1

It is useful when you are going on a journey to know how far it is, which is the best route and the likely delays. The AA site provides this information.

Using the Internet, access the following site: http://www.theaa.com/

Type in your home postcode and the postcode of a tourist attraction you would like to visit (you can search for one and get the postcode using the Internet).

Use the AA site to find a route for you.

Write a list of the main features of the site and explain why it might be useful to use this site rather than the information from an in-car satellite navigation system.

Extension activity 2

For this activity you are required to learn more about Bluetooth using the Internet.

Use the following website along with others of your choice: http://www.bluetooth.com

Produce a short magazine article, with some illustrations, which covers all aspects of Bluetooth. You will first need to explain what it is and how many of us use it without really noticing. You can also cover the applications that use Bluetooth.

You will need to collect content for your article and use appropriate design skills to make your article eye-catching and interesting.

Extension activity 3

1 Wi-Fi is a method of wireless communication for computers. Find out about Wi-Fi such as what it is, what its range is and some typical applications for its use.

Produce a short easy-to-read document in your own words on what you have found.

2 Here is a sign containing an icon.

Find out what RSS is and how it is useful.

END-OF-TOPIC REVIEW

Questions

 Test yourself

The following notes summarize this topic. The notes are incomplete because they have words missing. Using the words in the list below, copy out and complete sentences A to I, underlining the words that you have inserted. Each word may be used more than once.

videoconferencing   wireless   web browser

cyberbullying   SMS   Bluetooth   synchronize

website address   geographical information system

A _____ or, as most people know it, texting, allows short low-cost messages to be sent between phones and some other devices.

B Bullying using the Internet and mobile phones is often called _____ .

C _____ allows face-to-face meetings to be conducted without the participants being in the same room or even the same geographical area.

D It is important to check the _____ of any website you are using before you enter any personal or financial information into it, to check that it is the correct site.

E With _____ communication, the data travels through the air rather than through cables.

F _____ software is a program that allows access to webpages stored on the Internet.

G _____ is a method used to transfer data over short distances from fixed and mobile devices.

H A system that is used to capture, manage, analyse and display geographically referenced information is called a _____.

I Bluetooth can be used to _____ the music on your home computer and your portable music player so the tracks stored on each are the same.

Questions *continued*

Examination style questions

1 There are many different ways to meet people using ICT.
   (a) Give the names of **two** ICT facilities that would enable you to meet new friends. *(2 marks)*
   (b) Describe **two** possible dangers in meeting people in real life whom you have communicated with online. *(4 marks)*

2 When emails that contain inappropriate language are sent or received, they are captured by the network. The network manager will then look at them and take further action if needed.
   (a) Explain **one** reason why a network manager might do this. *(2 marks)*
   (b) The use of inappropriate language in a chat room might breach the code of conduct. What action might the organization who supplies the chat room service take? *(1 mark)*

3 Bluetooth is used to transfer data between devices without the need for cables and wires. Describe **two** different applications for Bluetooth. *(2 marks)*

4 A teacher at a school likes students to word-process their homework and submit it to her by email.
   (a) Define what is meant by email. *(2 marks)*
   (b) Give **one** advantage in a student sending their homework to their teacher by email. *(1 mark)*
   (c) In order to send the homework to the teacher the student uses a file attachment.
   Explain what is meant by a file attachment. *(1 mark)*
   (d) When the file attached to the email is large, the email says that the file is being compressed. Give **one** reason why the email package compresses the file before sending. *(1 mark)*

5 A health centre has lots of people working there such as doctors, nurses, midwives, physiotherapists, etc., who work together as a team. They need to pass messages to each other. As the staff work different hours and in different parts of the building, communicating with each other can be difficult.
   (a) Explain **three** advantages of the staff contacting each other by email rather than by phone. *(6 marks)*
   (b) Describe **two** facilities provided by email software that will make it a lot easier to work as a team. *(4 marks)*

6 Data is often encrypted when being stored or sent over the Internet.
   (a) Give the names of **two** items of data a user may send over the Internet that are often encrypted. *(2 marks)*
   (b) What is meant by the term encryption? *(2 marks)*

END-OF-TOPIC REVIEW

Exam support

Worked example

Parents of young children are worried about them using the Internet.

(a) Explain, by giving examples, why their fears are justified. *(4 marks)*

(b) Explain **two** things a parent can do to protect their children from harm when using the Internet. *(2 marks)*

Student answer 1

(a) Their child may reveal a lot about where they live, where they go to school, their phone number.

They may go into a chat room and a stranger might ask them to meet up and this is really dangerous.

(b) They can make sure their child only uses the Internet when they are sitting with them.

They can use a special function of the software called parental controls that will only allow them access to certain parts of the Internet.

◀ Examiner's comment

(a) These are two good answers, but the student should have looked at the marks allocated. It is always a good idea to work on one point is worth one mark unless the question indicates otherwise. Only two marks are given here.

(b) Two good answers get both of the marks. *(4 marks out of 6)*

Student answer 2

(a) They might access inappropriate material such as violent video or pornography by accident.

They may chat to someone in a chat room and arrange to meet them without their parents' knowledge.

The images they send to a stranger could be misused.

They may reveal information in a chat room that could be used by a stalker to harass them.

(b) They can ban the child from using the Internet.

They can tell them that they must not ever go into a chat room.

◀ Examiner's comment

(a) Four points well explained get four marks here.

(b) Banning the child from using the Internet may seriously hinder their education as the Internet for the most part is a good thing. No marks for this answer even though it might be the choice of some parents. The second answer gains a mark.

(5 marks out of 6)

Examiner's answers

(a) One mark for each point to a maximum of four marks.

- They could reveal personal details such as name, address, school, age, phone number, etc., to a stranger.
- They could arrange to meet a stranger without their parents' knowledge.
- They may access unsuitable content (e.g. pornography).
- They may take part in or be a victim of cyberbullying.

(b) One mark for each point to a maximum of two marks.

- Only allow them to access the Internet at home when they are present.
- Do not allow Internet access in a bedroom.
- Set the parental controls so they can only access suitable material and enter certain sites.
- Ask them to report anything they are not happy with to their parents.
- Examine favourites, email, etc., to check there is no abuse.

END-OF-TOPIC REVIEW

Summary mind maps

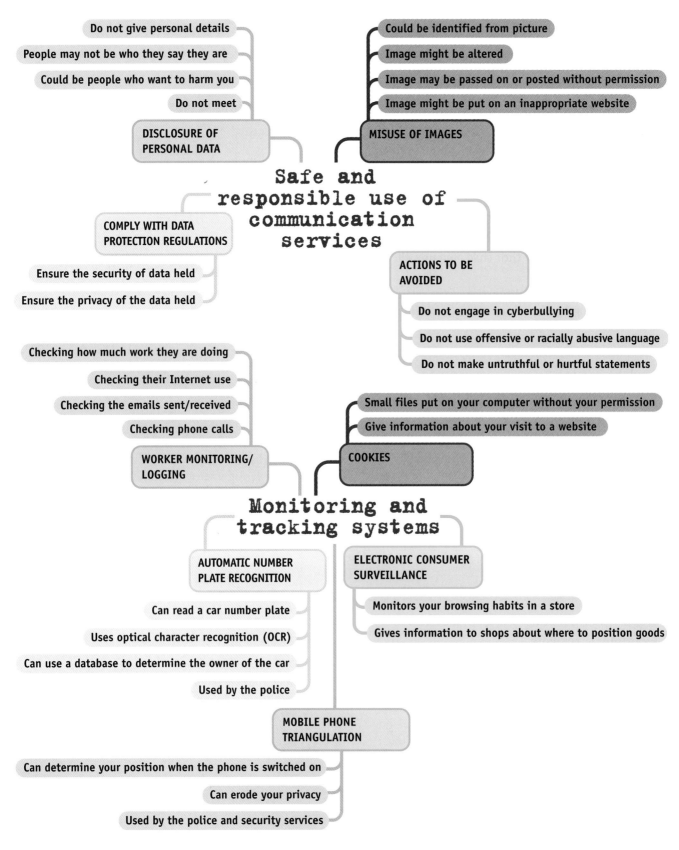

Do not give personal details

People may not be who they say they are

Could be people who want to harm you

Do not meet

DISCLOSURE OF PERSONAL DATA

Could be identified from picture

Image might be altered

Image may be passed on or posted without permission

Image might be put on an inappropriate website

MISUSE OF IMAGES

Safe and responsible use of communication services

COMPLY WITH DATA PROTECTION REGULATIONS

Ensure the security of data held

Ensure the privacy of the data held

ACTIONS TO BE AVOIDED

Do not engage in cyberbullying

Do not use offensive or racially abusive language

Do not make untruthful or hurtful statements

Checking how much work they are doing

Checking their Internet use

Checking the emails sent/received

Checking phone calls

WORKER MONITORING/ LOGGING

Small files put on your computer without your permission

Give information about your visit to a website

COOKIES

Monitoring and tracking systems

AUTOMATIC NUMBER PLATE RECOGNITION

Can read a car number plate

Uses optical character recognition (OCR)

Can use a database to determine the owner of the car

Used by the police

ELECTRONIC CONSUMER SURVEILLANCE

Monitors your browsing habits in a store

Gives information to shops about where to position goods

MOBILE PHONE TRIANGULATION

Can determine your position when the phone is switched on

Can erode your privacy

Used by the police and security services

Topic 3
Presenting information

The key concepts covered in this topic are:

- **The types and purposes of different ways of presenting information**
- **The use of ICT tools and features for presenting information**
- **Integration between and within software applications**

There are lots of different ways of presenting information, each one for a different purpose. For example, if you were a school trying to attract pupils from junior schools, you would create a good website that everyone could access. Another way would be to create a presentation to be given to the parents with children in the last year of the junior school. You might also send them a letter or a newsletter about the school. All these examples are produced using different software.

In this topic you will learn about the presentation of information using different types of software. You will learn about the features of the different pieces of software and how they can be used to present the information efficiently. You will also learn how these ICT tools can be used to produce high quality work. Also covered are the methods of moving objects such as images, tables, graphics from one piece of software to another.

Contents

Types and purposes of different ways of presenting information

You will find out

▷ **About types and purposes of different ways of presenting information**

Presenting material for others is one of the uses of ICT. Presentations can be produced using presentation software or you could present material using a website. It may also be appropriate to send a letter produced using word-processing software or a more complex publication such as a brochure produced using DTP software.

Word-processing software

Word-processing software is ideal for the production and editing of text. You can type text into other software such as desktop publishing software, but it is easier to use word-processing software and then save it as a file that can be imported into other software.

Word-processing software has the following advantages:

- Most people are very familiar with word-processing software so it saves having to learn the editing features of other software such as DTP software.

- You have the facility of mail merge, which means that personalized documents such as letters, invitations, business cards, etc., can be easily created.
- It is very easy to import text from word-processing software into other software such as DTP and web authoring software.

Desktop publishing (DTP) software

DTP is software used for printed page design. The files for the components of documents such as text, photographs, graphics, etc., are usually prepared using different software and then brought into the DTP software so that they can be arranged on the page.

DTP software is ideal for pages where there is a complex page design and where word-processing software would not offer the flexibility of design.

Slideshow/presentation software

Slideshow/presentation software is ideal if you want to present information to a group of people who are all in one place. You can also use self-running presentations where the slides run in a continuous loop. Slideshow/presentation software is ideal because you can choose the most appropriate ways of presenting the material from:

Visual (on screen) presentations
– You will have sat through many of these during your time at school –

some good and some bad. Basically slides are prepared that are then projected onto a large screen so that all the audience can see them. There is another way to show a presentation. You can create a multimedia presentation that allows the user to be in control of which slide or section of the material they would like to view.

Hard copy – You can print out the slides and give them to the audience. Usually these printouts show the slide contents and some space for the viewer to make their own notes.

Multi-sensory – These are presentations that make use of multimedia. For example, you can incorporate text, sound, images, video and interactivity into presentations. This helps people who learn in different ways.

▲ **Many presentations use a data projector as the output device so that a large audience can view the slides.**

Bringing together and organizing different types of information

To present information successfully it needs to come from a number of sources. With paper-based documents you are restricted to text and images but with multimedia material, such as presentations and websites, you can use the full range of multimedia features.

Web authoring software/ website design software

Web authoring software or website design software is used to design and produce websites. Websites are ideal for presenting information because:

- People can find the information by performing searches using a search engine or just browsing.
- People can access them from their own homes using the Internet.
- People can access the information from other countries.
- Other websites can provide links to your website.
- They are a relatively cheap way of showing the information to lots of people.
- You can have a full range of multimedia features.
- It is much easier to keep information up-to-date.

Multimedia authoring software

Multimedia authoring software is used to present information in the form of games, interactive books such as encyclopaedias and teaching/ training materials. They use all the aspects of multimedia such as audio, video, animation and interactivity. There is specialist multimedia authoring software available but it is possible to produce multimedia products using presentation software.

Purposes of information

Material may be created using ICT for different purposes. The purpose of the information determines the best way to present the information.

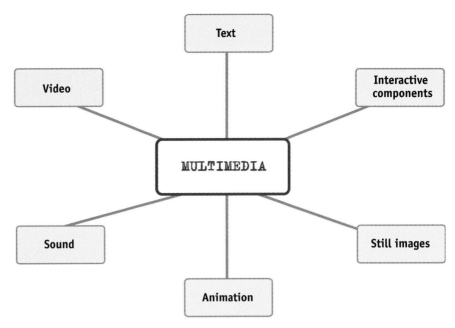

▲ The types of media that can be used in multimedia.

For example, if you need to give the same information to a group of people, then presenting the information on a series of slides may be best.

Once you have decided on the purpose of the information, you can choose the best way to present the information and then pick the most suitable software.

Questions A

1. Presentation software can be used to present information to a large number of people at a sales conference.
   (a) Explain what is meant by presentation software. (*2 marks*)
   (b) Describe **three** features of presentation software that can be used to keep the audience interested in the information being presented. (*3 marks*)

2. A leaflet is to be designed about a new computer game. The main purpose of this leaflet is to encourage gamers to download a free trial version of the game using the Internet.
   There is a choice of software for producing this leaflet:
   - Word-processing software
   - Desktop publishing software
   (a) Give **one** reason why word-processing software might be chosen. (*1 mark*)
   (b) Give **one** reason why DTP software might be chosen. (*1 mark*)
   (c) Explain, giving reasons, which software you would use and what features of the software make its use more appropriate. (*4 marks*)

3. Software used to teach young children Maths and English often uses multimedia features.
   (a) Give the names of **three** multimedia features. (*3 marks*)
   (b) Explain why multimedia features are used to teach young children. (*3 marks*)

Presenting information, and integration between and within software applications

In this section you will be looking at those ICT tools and features that can be used to present information. You will also be looking at the way sections can be transferred between documents that have been created using different software.

Efficiency in using ICT tools

When you present information using ICT you usually want to work as efficiently as possible in order to:

- Ensure that the work is completed in the least possible time – for example, you could use copy and paste to collect text for the document or use photographs off the Internet rather than create your own. You may consider using the software you are most familiar with rather than the most appropriate software for the task.
- Not use valuable resources – for example, you can preview work before printing thus saving paper. You can ensure that in the design of documents you do not go on to a new page for a small amount of text. It is better to try to fit it on the minimum number of pages if it is being printed out.
- Avoid paper altogether – not all information needs to be printed out. Lots of bills, credit card and bank statements are now produced electronically.
- Ensure that you enter data in the best possible way – for example, you could use voice recognition rather than have to type in text. This could be faster as well as help avoid repetitive strain injury (RSI).

Improving the quality of work

It is easy to produce high quality work using ICT. If there are mistakes then the editing features of software

mean that they can be easily corrected. There are also software tools that enable the checking of work.

Ensuring the accuracy of information

When you create your own websites, blogs, multimedia presentations, posters, letters, etc., you need to ensure that the material is accurate. Here are some ways you can do this:

- The more people who look at your work, the more likely they are to spot your mistakes. So use friends and family to read through your material and ask for their comments.
- If you present facts, you should always check these using several reliable sources.
- Use the spelling and grammar checkers provided in the software you are using. Be aware that just because text has been spelling and grammar checked doesn't mean it won't still be incorrect.
- Proof read your work carefully by reading through it slowly to check it makes sense and there is nothing missing.

Limitations of spelling and grammar checkers

Spellcheckers are provided with most software packages used to produce text. The spellchecker checks to see if each word in the document is in its dictionary. If you used the word 'care' instead of 'core', then as both are spelt correctly, the spellchecker will not pick it up. If a word is not spelt correctly, the spellchecker alerts the user and offers some corrections for the user to choose from. Spellcheckers are also able to spot if the same word has been typed in twice.

Grammar checkers can be used to check that:

- sentences end with only one full stop
- there is a capital letter at the beginning of a sentence
- common errors like writing 'you and I' rather than 'you and me' have been avoided.

Here is some text that someone has typed. Can you spot what is wrong?

`I no their are mistakes in my spelling but I will use the spell cheque to cheque them.`

If you look at this sentence, you will see that the words are all spelt correctly. You will also notice that some of the words are the wrong ones. The spellchecker will not pick this up because there are no spelling mistakes. Using the grammar check may pick up some mistakes such as the word 'their'. This should read 'there'.

Type this sentence, then use the spellchecker and then the grammar checker.

Spellchecking and grammar checking will not ensure that your document makes sense. It is therefore important to proof read your document. It is a good idea to get someone else to read through your work, as they might spot mistakes that you have missed.

Activity

Obtain some text for an article off the Internet and copy and paste the text into a word-processed document. Hopefully this document will be accurately spelt and the grammar will be correct.

Make some changes to the spelling and grammar (making a note of what changes you have made). Run the spellchecker first and then the grammar checker. See if both of these can find the errors.

Ensuring the quality of work

In order to ensure that your presentation of information is of a high quality you need to review and modify your work and also to use a number of drafts.

Reviewing and modifying your work

Reviewing your work means you and others looking at your work critically with a view to making comments so that you can make improvements if they are needed.

When you are asked to produce something such as a website, a document (e.g., letter, brochure, poster, booklet, etc.) or a presentation, you will usually have an initial plan of what you intend to do. If you are producing the work for someone else, then the initial plan will be agreed with them.

When producing your own work by making use of ICT you should:

- Work accurately by taking steps not to introduce any errors.
- Check that what you have produced is the same as that outlined in the initial plan.
- Proof read your work to ensure that the text makes sense and that you have not missed any text out.

- Check any diagrams to ensure that they are of an appropriate quality.
- Use the facilities provided by the software (i.e., spellcheckers and grammar checkers) to help eliminate spelling and grammatical errors.
- Check any calculations by performing the calculations manually and comparing the results.
- Check the consistency from one page to another. This means that all the pages in a document or website or slides in a presentation should have a similar design. They should look as though they belong together.
- Seek the opinions of others.

Using drafts

A draft is a piece of work that is not considered to be the final version. It is a working version and it is given to others for their comments. The comments are acted upon and changes are made to give a second draft. The second draft is then given to the same people who reviewed the first draft for their comments. By using a series of drafts all the problems with the first draft are eliminated and the piece of work is completed.

By using drafts you can ensure:

- That the work you have produced is 'fit for purpose'. This means it does what it is supposed to do.
- The meaning is clear. The reviewers will point out things that are not clear.
- The work matches the initial plan. This means that you have done what you set out to do.
- That enough 'eyes' have seen the work to check for accuracy, appearance, ease of use, etc.
- It is suitable for the intended audience. It is a good idea to get some reviews from people who will be your typical audience. So, if you produced a website for young children, it should be shown to them for their comments.

Presenting information, and integration between and within software applications *continued*

The use of ICT tools and features

You will now have experienced using a whole range of software from word-processing software to web design software for presenting information. You may have noticed that this software contains many common features. For example, if as part of a task you have to enter text into the software, you expect to be able to change the font type and size. You will probably expect to be able to cut, copy and paste text. All these are features that are common to most pieces of applications software, and are called generic features of software.

In this section you will be looking at those common features of software that can be used to enter and format text in order to maximize clarity and enhance the presentation of information. You will also be looking at some of the ICT tools, such as copy and paste, that help you complete the task efficiently.

Copy, cut and paste

To cut text or cells in a document or spreadsheet, select them (the selected cells will be highlighted) then right click on the mouse. A menu will appear with a number of options including the following:

- Cut
- Copy
- Paste.

If you click on Cut, the text or cells will now be placed in a temporary storage (called the clipboard) by the computer. You can now move the cursor to another part of your document or worksheet where you want the text or cells to be moved to. Right clicking on the position brings the menu up again where you can choose to paste the contents into position.

When we cut text or cells, they are taken out of the document or worksheet. Suppose we just wanted to use the same text or cells in a different document/worksheet without having to type them in. We can use Copy. Copy is similar to Cut, except that a *copy* of the text/cells is put onto the clipboard. The document from which the text/cells are copied remains unaltered.

Font type and font size

Changing the font type (e.g., Arial, Times New Roman, etc.) alters the appearance of the characters.

Font types are given names and you can change the font by selecting the text and then clicking on the correct part of the formatting toolbar. Notice also that there is a section for altering the font size (i.e., how big the characters appear).

Click here to alter the font size.

Click here to alter the font type (each font is given a name – in this case the font is called Calibri).

▲ Font type is the shape of the letters and can be chosen to suit the purpose of the document.

Drag and drop

Drag and drop means clicking on a virtual object such as a file, photograph, piece of clip art, etc., and dragging it into position. You can drag or drop an object onto a document or you can drag it into a folder or the recycle bin. Drag and drop is a quick way of moving objects.

Undo and redo

Undo is a feature of most software and it erases the last action taken. Redo is the opposite where the last action taken is re-applied. This is one of the most important features of software and most software is able to reverse a whole series of actions. Many people wish that life had an 'undo' button!

Find and replace

Find can be used to quickly find a certain word or phrase in a long document.

Find and replace can be used to search for all the occurrences of a certain word and replace them with a different word.

▲ Here 'find and replace' is looking for all the occurrences of 'email' and replacing them with 'e-mail'.

Zoom

Zoom is found in most software packages and can be used to display a document in more or less detail. This is usually done by altering the % view using the drop down menu.

▲ Document size can be expressed as a percentage of the original size. By altering the percentage you can zoom in and out.

Some software has a small magnifying glass with either a + or – marked on it and when you click on it you either zoom in or zoom out.

▶ **Zoom in and zoom out icons.**

WordArt (or similar)

WordArt is decorative text that you can add to a document. You can create all sorts of text effects such as:

Shadows

Rotated

Stretched

In some packages you can fit the text to certain shapes.

Wizards

Microsoft Office uses Wizards that help you through some of the more complex tasks. For example, you might want to perform a mail merge but you have forgotten the steps you have to take. The Wizard will take you through the steps guiding you through until you have completed the task.

Help

Everyone has been a beginner at using software at some time. It can be frustrating to know what you want to do but not be sure how to do it. This is where online help screens come in. Software packages usually have an online help facility where users can get help supplied by the package rather than have to look through manuals or user guides.

Print and print preview

Software nearly always has a print function so you can get a printout of your work on paper. To save printer and toner/ink most applications software has a print preview feature that is used to check how your work will appear on the page before printing. You should get into the habit of using print preview to save resources.

Page layout

It is very annoying if the headings are inconsistent and the font and font size are changed too often. Always think about what you want to achieve with your document and what will appeal to the readers.

When thinking about the page layout you will need to consider the following:

- position of common items
- page layout
- textual styles
- special features
- paragraph formats
- position of common items.

Page layout is also concerned with the arrangement of the following:

- margins
- headers and footers
- alignment
- page orientation (landscape and portrait)
- pagination
- paper size.

Margins

Margins mark the boundary of the text itself and therefore determine the amount of blank space left at the sides, top and bottom of the page. If you leave insufficient margins, the document will appear cluttered.

Headers and footers

Headers and footers are used to hold information that appears at the top of the page in the case of a header, and at the bottom of each page of the document in the case of a footer. Headers are placed in the top margin whilst footers are placed in the bottom. You can choose whether the text included in the header or footer is included on every page or just some of the pages.

Here are some types of information that are commonly put into headers and footers:

- page numbers
- today's date
- the title of the document
- a company logo (it can be a graphic image)
- the author's name
- the filename of the file that is used to hold the document.

Justifying (aligning) text

Justifying text means aligning (lining up) the text in some way:

- Align left (also called left justified) – this lines the text up with the left margin but leaves the right-hand side ragged. This alignment is the most common and is the one used by a word-processor unless we tell it to use another.
- Align right (also called right justified) – this lines the text up with the right margin but leaves the left-hand margin ragged.
- Centre – this lines text up with the centre of the page.
- Fully justified (also called justified) – this lines text up with both the right and left margins.

Presenting information, and integration between and within software applications *continued*

Orientation

There are two ways in which a page can be printed onto paper. With portrait orientation the height is greater than the width; with landscape orientation the page is turned sideways so that the width of the page is greater than its height. Portrait orientation is much more common and is used for most business documents such as letters, memos and reports; this book is portrait format. However, landscape format can be useful for charts, spreadsheets and notices.

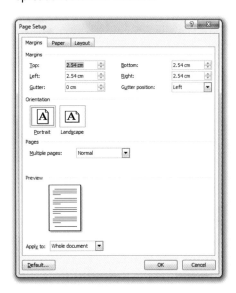

▲ The Page Setup menu allows you to set the page orientation to portrait or landscape.

Page breaks

When you type a page of text or numbers into a document, as a page is filled the software inserts a page break and a new page is started. The software does this automatically. There is a problem with this. For example, you may find that a heading appears at the bottom of a page where the reader is least likely to look. It would be even worse if the heading appeared at the bottom of the page on its own with the text

to which it refers over the page. It is therefore important during the proof reading process to look out for this and correct it. You can make the computer start a new page by inserting what is called a page break.

Page numbering

Pages in documents should always be numbered, as people need to refer to the content of the page by its number. Also if you have a load of unnumbered pages and you drop them, putting them back into order is a difficult task.

Templates

Creating documents from scratch takes time. You have to consider the design of the page as well as the content. Luckily templates help you with the design, leaving you to simply add your own content. A template is a blueprint for the text, graphics and formatting and it ensures that all documents of a particular type look the same. It is common for members of an organization to be given templates, one for each type of document, to ensure a common or corporate style. The template is an electronic file that holds the basic outline of the document. The user needs only to input the variable data, since formatting, font size, etc., will already be included. The main advantage of using templates is consistency of style, irrespective of author.

Most word-processing software has template facilities, so all you need do is 'fill in the blanks'. Each time you want a similar document, simply open the template, fill in the blanks, save the document (under a different name from that of the template) and then print it out.

Text/picture boxes

If you want to put some text that needs to stand out in the middle of a page then you can use a text box. Once the text box has been created you can add a border around it, or give it a colour background or shade the background.

If you want to create an effect like you see with newspapers where the text starts on one page and finishes on another, then you can put the text into two different text boxes and then link them.

> **A simple text box**

Once the text box has been created you can alter the text size and font. You can also make the text italic, bold, etc. You can then start to think about borders, etc.

Activity

Experimenting with background and text colours

Here is an activity to find out which background and text colours work best together.

Produce a text box, type in the text as shown in the box and alter the colours of the text and the background. Produce a table with the combinations of text and background along with a comment about the result for future reference.

> This is a text box that has text of one colour and a background of another.

Obtaining, inserting, resizing, cropping and positioning images

When choosing or designing an image you need to consider the fitness for purpose. Certain images would be too shocking for children yet a shocking image may be needed to get the message across to adults. You will have seen such images in posters and adverts to stop people from drinking and driving. Always ask yourself if the image you intend to use is fit for purpose.

▲ Is the image suitable for the purpose and will it be appropriate for the intended audience?

Obtaining images

When you research images you will often be using other people's images. It is important for you to understand the legislation (i.e. laws) that affects the way you can use other people's images.

There are many methods of obtaining images. For example, you can use:

- your own drawings (produced using software or created on paper and then scanned in)
- sketches (usually scanned in)
- photographs (usually created using a digital camera but could be scanned in from an old photograph)
- photographs on websites that you can copy and paste
- photographs in books, magazines, newspapers, etc.
- the clip art provided with Microsoft Office
- photographs in clip art collections on CD-ROM, the Internet, etc.

Inserting images

Images may be placed in a document such as DTP, word-processing, spreadsheet software, but in the case of web design software the images are usually linked to the document. Images many be inserted using copy/cut and paste or inserted by using Insert Picture.

Resizing images

Images usually need to be re-sized to fit the design of the document. Resizing can be done by clicking on the image and then using the handles (i.e., the small squares at the corners of the image) to alter the size.

Cropping

Cropping means only using part of an image. For example, you might just want a picture of a person's face rather than a picture of their whole body.

Positioning images

Images have to be moved into a suitable position and in some cases you have to work out how you want the text to move around the image. Images can usually be positioned by dragging them.

Manipulation of graphics

Once a graphic has been obtained, it may need adjusting in some way. Graphics software is available that allows you to alter (i.e., manipulate) images. Here are some of the ways that an image can be manipulated:

- It can be resized (i.e., made bigger or smaller).
- It can be rotated through a certain angle.
- It can be mirror imaged (i.e., like reflecting the image in a mirror).
- Part of the image can be cropped (this is just like cutting the part you want out of the picture).

AutoShapes

AutoShapes are shapes that are already stored by the software. You can select the shapes from the various menus and edit them (e.g., resize, rotate, reflect, coloured and combined to make more complex shapes). The AutoShapes can be seen on the Drawing toolbar and include the following:

- lines
- connectors
- basic shapes (e.g., squares, rectangles, triangles, etc.)
- block arrows
- flowchart symbols
- stars and banners.

You can turn any of the boxes used into text boxes, which means you can enter text inside the box. If you then apply a change to the box such as rotate, the text inside the box will also rotate.

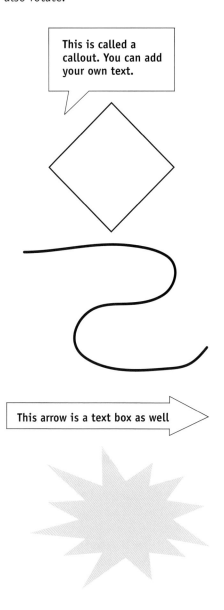

▲ There are lots of AutoShapes and you can add text, fill with colour, change the colour of the lines and so on.

61

Presenting information, and integration between and within software applications *continued*

Wrap text

If you enter text into a spreadsheet cell, the width of the cell will increase to fit in the text. You can instruct the software to wrap the text, which means that the cell width is kept constant and the text overflows automatically onto the next line. Text wrapping occurs in word-processing software where the margins offer a fixed width for the text.

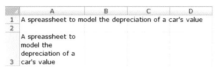

▲ In row 3 the text is wrapped.

Integration between and within software applications

Most computers are networked together, so this allows the sharing and exchanging of information. There are also many occasions when you are working using several pieces of applications software at the same time. This means it is also important to be able to transfer data between applications.

Transferring data within and between applications

Software packages such as web design software or desktop publishing software use files created in lots of different packages. For example, most people would type the text using word-processing software first and then save it as a file. They would then open up the DTP package and import the saved file containing the text into the DTP software. Sometimes the image/text/sound/video file is not in a format that the other package can use. In cases like this you can usually save the file in a file format that is acceptable to the other package. Exporting data means taking some of the data from one file and saving it separately so that it can be used in a completely different software package from the one in which it was created.

Mail merge

A mail merge involves combining a list of, say, names and addresses, with a standard letter, so that a series of similar letters is produced, each addressed to a different person. The list is created either by using the word-processor or by importing data from a database of names and addresses. The letter is typed using the word-processor, with blanks where the data from the list will be inserted.

The steps involved in mail merging are outlined below:

- Create a letter to be sent to different people.
- Create a name and address list for the recipients of the letter.
- Insert the variable fields into the letter.
- Merge the names and address details with the letter to produce the personalized letters.

<<Forename>> <<Surname>>
<<Street>>
<<Town>>
<<Postcode>>

Dear <<Forename>>

As you know you will soon be taking your end of year examinations. For those of you in year 11, these will be your GCSE exams. We will be holding a revision club on Mondays and Wednesdays from 4 p.m. to 6 p.m. A variety of staff will be on hand to help you with your revision questions. You should take advantage of this as it is completely free.

There will be a meeting on Wednesday 3rd May at 4 p.m. in the hall for any of you interested in taking up the offer.

Happy revision and good luck.

▲ Part of a letter, showing the variable fields.

Kerry Jones
3 Grove Street
Liverpool
L7 6TT

Dear Kerry

As you know you will soon be taking your end of year examinations. For those of you in year 11, these will be your GCSE exams. We will be holding a revision club on Mondays and Wednesdays from 4 p.m. to 6 p.m. A variety of staff will be on hand to help you with your revision questions. You should take advantage of this as it is completely free.

There will be a meeting on Wednesday 3rd May at 4 p.m. in the hall for any of you interested in taking up the offer.

Happy revision and good luck.

▲ The letter with the variable information added.

Activity

Fitness of images for purpose

There are lots of reasons why you may not be able to use an image in a document you are preparing. With some simple editing it might still be possible to use the image.

Write down a list of the things that can be wrong in an image. You should assume that the content of the image is suitable.

Integrating sections from one application to another

You often have to use a section from a document created in one piece of software and integrate it into a different document created in another piece of software.

Here are some examples:

- Taking a graph produced in spreadsheet software and incorporating it into a word-processed document.
- Copying text from one file (webpage, PDF document, word-processed document, etc.) and incorporating it into a DTP document.
- Taking data from a spreadsheet and putting it into a table in a word-processed report.
- Creating graphics using drawing software and then importing the file into a word-processed document.
- Creating animation using animation software and then importing the file into web authoring software.

Questions B

1 **(a)** Explain the use of a spellchecker. *(2 marks)*
   (b) Explain why despite the use of a spellchecker a document will still need to be proof read or visually checked. *(1 mark)*

2 To produce good documents that are fit for purpose it is important to produce a number of drafts. Each of these drafts should be reviewed by others.
   (a) Explain what is meant by 'fit for purpose'. *(1 mark)*
   (b) Explain what is meant by a draft. *(1 mark)*
   (c) Explain why draft versions should be reviewed by others. *(2 marks)*

3 One generic feature common to most applications software is text formatting.
   (a) Give **two** examples of text formatting. *(2 marks)*
   (b) A document can be made more attractive by putting artwork (pictures, clip art, photographs, etc.) into it. Describe **two** ways in which artwork can be put into a document. *(2 marks)*

4 Many pieces of software use templates to allow the user to get things done in less time.
   (a) Explain what is meant by a template. *(2 marks)*
   (b) Give the name of a piece of software you have used where the use of the template made things easier for you. *(1 mark)*

Extension activity

Using print screen

Produce a screenshot of the screen in Microsoft Excel by pressing down the Alt key and keeping it down, press the Print Screen key. Nothing happens because the screenshot is stored in the clipboard. Now load the word-processing software, create a new document and then go to Edit and then Paste. The picture of the screen will now appear in the document.

Mark on your diagram (you can do this by hand or by using the drawing tools in the word-processor) the following:

(a) The active cell (sometimes called the cell pointer)

(b) The title bar

(c) The close button

(d) The minimize button

(e) The restore/maximize button

(f) A scroll bar

(g) The formatting toolbar

(h) The column headings

(i) The row headings

Extension activity

Using AutoShapes, images and text boxes to create diagrams

For this activity you are required to produce a diagram that can be included in a book about ICT like this one. This diagram is to be produced using word-processing software.

The purpose of the diagram is to illustrate and explain the different ways of obtaining images for inclusion in a document.

You must use the following in your diagram:

- AutoShapes (for the production of boxes, arrows, etc.)
- Text boxes (you can turn boxes created using AutoShapes into text boxes)
- Images (you can use images to show places where you can get images from).

Your work needs to be printed out on A4-sized paper.

Be sensible in your choice of colour on your diagram.

END-OF-TOPIC REVIEW

Questions

 Test yourself

The following notes summarize this topic. The notes are incomplete because they have words missing. Using the words in the list below, copy out and complete the sentences A to M, underlining the words that you have inserted. Each word may be used more than once.

web authoring software   copy and paste   font style

font type   footers   online dictionary

drag and drop   sections   chart   print preview

find and replace   page numbers   page breaks

A _____ copies text and then puts it into a different place in the same document or a completely different document.

B _____ is the shape of the text. Examples include Times New Roman and Arial.

C _____ includes bold, italics and underline.

D _____ means clicking on a virtual object such as a file, photograph, piece of clip art, etc., and dragging it into position.

E _____ is handy if you want to find all the occurrences of a certain word and replace them with a different word.

F Work should always be checked carefully before printing and _____ allows you to see how the document looks when it is printed.

G Headers and _____ are used to hold information that appears at the top and the bottom of the page.

H _____ determine where one page ends and a new page starts.

I Most applications software can insert _____ on multi-page documents.

J Spellchecking checks the words entered into a document against an _____.

K _____ is software that is used to create websites.

L It is important to be able to transfer _____ created in one piece of software into a document you are working on using a different piece of software.

M For example, a _____ created using spreadsheet software can be transferred into a word-processed document.

Examination style questions

1 A company producing pet food uses a range of different types of software to present information.

In the table below, state the type of software that would be most suitable to present the information. You may use the software more than once. Do **not** use brand names. (*5 marks*)

Type of information	Software to be used
To write a letter to customers to inform them of a price increase	
To present information to sales staff at a conference	
To enable customers to order goods using their own computers	
To produce a full-colour brochure	
To produce a mail-merged series of letters	

2 Multimedia authoring software can be used to create multimedia products such as games, teaching resources, etc.
   (a) Give **three** examples of different types of media that can be used with multimedia. (*3 marks*)
   (b) A school uses multimedia to help pupils in a school to learn.
   Give **two** ways in which multimedia may be better at helping children to learn rather than by reading a printed book. (*2 marks*)

3 Proof read the text below and make a note of **three** errors you find. (*3 marks*)

> ### Getting cash from your supermarket
>
> It is common to see cash dispensers in the walls of out-of-town supermarkts. It is possible to get cash at the same time as paying for the goods.
>
> The service is called 'Cashback' and to get cash, the customer needs to have a card called a SWITCH card or a similar debit card. Debit cards can be used as an alternative to paying by cheque. When the customer pays for their goods they will be asked if they want 'Cashback'. The customer details are red using a chip and pin reader.
>
> When a debit card is used, the money is transferred from the shopper's account to the store's bank account. This process takes plaice immediately.

4 Explain the difference between spellchecking and grammar checking a document. (*4 marks*)

5 Joshua has to produce a presentation in front of his class. For this presentation he decides to use presentation software.

Describe **three** features of presentation software that will make the presentation more interesting to the class. (*6 marks*)

6 It is important to be able to integrate a file created in one package into a different file in another package.

Explain a situation you have used where you did this. (*3 marks*)

Exam support

Worked example

Here is a first draft of a poster used to advertise a Halloween party at a school.

Mount Hill School
Years 10 and 11
Halloween party
Friday 30th Oct 09
Starts 7:30 pm
Music Hall
Tickets £2.50

Some features of DTP have been used to improve the appearance of this poster.

(a) Describe **three** features of DTP software that have been used to improve the appearance of this poster. *(3 marks)*

(b) Give **one** other feature of DTP that they could use to improve the design. *(1 mark)*

(c) The person who produced the poster spellchecks it before printing.

State what is meant by spellchecking. *(2 marks)*

Student answer 1

(a) Graphics

Text

Centre.

(b) Use a different font type such as Gothic.

(c) The computer does this automatically. It spellchecks all the spelling.

◀ **Examiner's comment**

(a) The ability to import clip art/graphics would have been an acceptable answer to this but the answer given is not worth a mark.

Text is not a feature and it would have been too brief an answer anyway so no marks are given here.

Centre is a feature but there is no description of how it is used. Students must look at the question carefully: to any question that asks a user to 'give', a one-word answer is OK, but where they are asked to 'describe', a one-word answer is not sufficient.

(b) This is a correct answer. The student has clearly stated font type rather than font on its own. One mark is given here.

(c) This a typical answer from a weak student. Students must remember not to simply write down an answer that anyone could guess from the word 'spellchecking'. There needs to be detail about how the spellchecking is done. No marks are given for this answer.

(1 mark out of 6)

Student answer 2

(a) All the text used has been centred to make it look more interesting.

The font size has been increased for some of the text to make it stand out.

Clip art images have been imported to improve the appearance.

(b) Use a border to go around the edge of the page. This can be obtained from clip art libraries.

(c) Checks all the words in a document against words that are in a stored dictionary to make sure they are spelt correctly. If they are not they can be corrected automatically or underlined in red so that the user can decide what to do.

◀ **Examiner's comment**

(a) These are all very good answers. The student has clearly identified the features and described how they are used. Three marks out of three for this answer.

(b) This is a good feature to include on a poster so one mark here.

(c) This is a very good answer and the student has clearly identified that the software uses a dictionary against which the words are compared. There are two marks here, so there must be two points made. The student has made two valid points in their two sentences so full marks are given for this answer.

(6 marks out of 6)

Examiner's answers

(a) One mark (up to a maximum of three marks) for each feature, which must have been used on the poster such as:

- Increase in font size to make more important text in the poster stand out.
- Centring of all the text so that it draws attention and looks like a poster.
- Use of coloured text to make the important text stand out the most.
- Importing clip art to add interest to the page.
- Use of bold to make the name of the school prominent.

(b) One mark for one feature similar to:

- Use different fonts.
- Use a page border.
- Use a watermark.
- Use a background colour.

(c) One mark for each point to a maximum of two marks.

- Checks the spelling of each word in a document.
- Against a pre-stored dictionary.
- Automatically changes the spelling as a user types.
- Highlights misspelt words for user action.
- Suggests correct spelling of words.

Summary mind maps

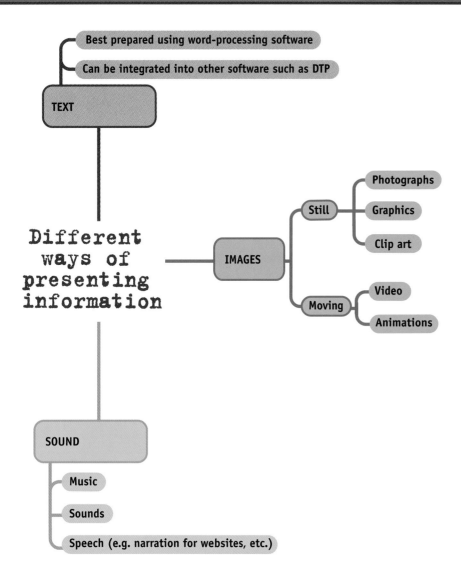

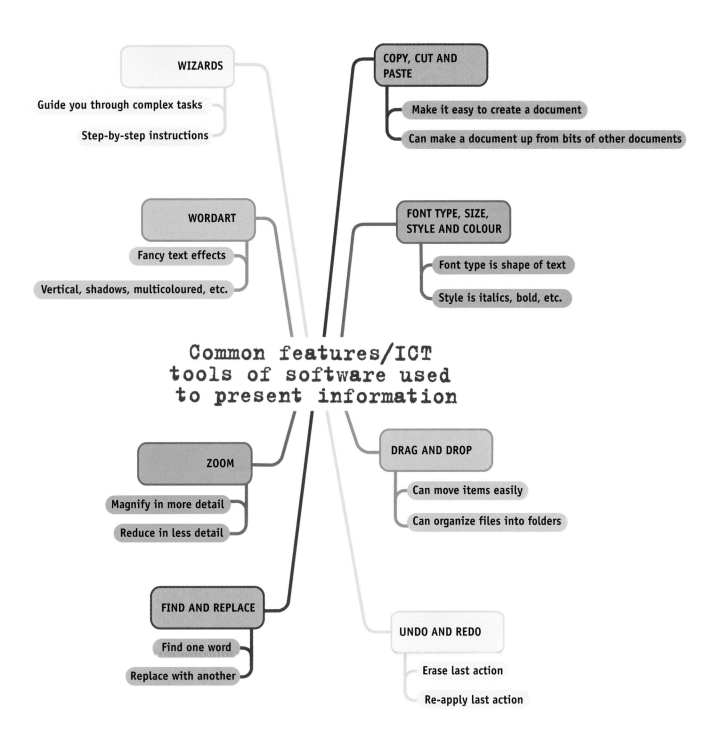

WIZARDS

Guide you through complex tasks

Step-by-step instructions

COPY, CUT AND PASTE

Make it easy to create a document

Can make a document up from bits of other documents

WORDART

Fancy text effects

Vertical, shadows, multicoloured, etc.

FONT TYPE, SIZE, STYLE AND COLOUR

Font type is shape of text

Style is italics, bold, etc.

Common features/ICT tools of software used to present information

ZOOM

Magnify in more detail

Reduce in less detail

DRAG AND DROP

Can move items easily

Can organize files into folders

FIND AND REPLACE

Find one word

Replace with another

UNDO AND REDO

Erase last action

Re-apply last action

Summary mind maps *continued*

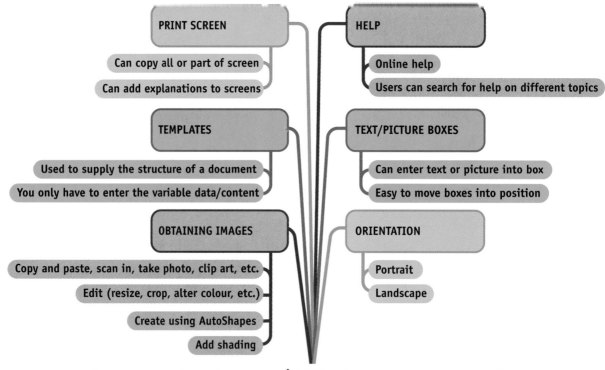

PRINT SCREEN
- Can copy all or part of screen
- Can add explanations to screens

HELP
- Online help
- Users can search for help on different topics

TEMPLATES
- Used to supply the structure of a document
- You only have to enter the variable data/content

TEXT/PICTURE BOXES
- Can enter text or picture into box
- Easy to move boxes into position

OBTAINING IMAGES
- Copy and paste, scan in, take photo, clip art, etc.
- Edit (resize, crop, alter colour, etc.)
- Create using AutoShapes
- Add shading

ORIENTATION
- Portrait
- Landscape

Common features/ICT tools of software used to present information continued

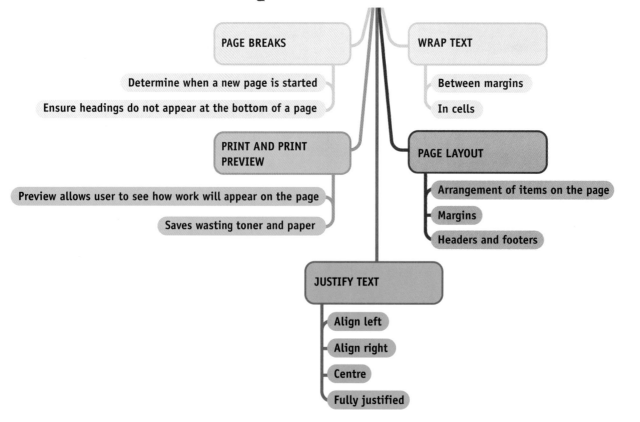

PAGE BREAKS
- Determine when a new page is started
- Ensure headings do not appear at the bottom of a page

WRAP TEXT
- Between margins
- In cells

PRINT AND PRINT PREVIEW
- Preview allows user to see how work will appear on the page
- Saves wasting toner and paper

PAGE LAYOUT
- Arrangement of items on the page
- Margins
- Headers and footers

JUSTIFY TEXT
- Align left
- Align right
- Centre
- Fully justified

Manipulating data

The key concepts covered in this topic are:

- **Data management (i.e., data types, design of file structures, design of data capture forms, screens and reports, validation and verification)**

- **Data handling software (i.e., main features, typical tasks, data modelling, relational databases and spreadsheets and emerging data handling applications)**

Data is the raw material for any ICT system and many of these systems are able to store the data in a structure that enables processing/manipulating of the data to produce meaningful information.

Managing data is the function of software such as database and spreadsheet software. In order to manipulate the data it is necessary to put it into a structure. In this topic you will be learning about the different types of data and how these can be put into a structure.

Data can only produce accurate information if the data is accurate. Validation and verification are methods that ensure, as far as possible, that incorrect data is not processed.

You will also learn about the different types of software used for data handling and some of the typical tasks it can perform.

Contents

Data management

You will find out

▷ About different data types

▷ About the main issues governing the design of file structures

▷ About the main issues governing the design of data capture forms, screens

For data to be managed and manipulated it needs to be input into the computer. The process of entering data is called data capture. In this section you will be looking at methods of data capture and also how to avoid errors during this process.

Data management involves using software to store the data in a structure that allows the processing of that data to produce meaningful information. You normally think of the software to do this as database software but it is possible to hold stores of information and be able to manipulate it using other software such as spreadsheet software.

In this section you will learn about how data can be managed in a way that allows it to be manipulated and output in lots of different ways.

Different data types

Information handling systems have to cope with different types of data and these are summarized here:

Data type	Description
Text	Used for storing names, words and numbers that are not used in calculations (telephone numbers, code numbers, credit card numbers, etc.).
Number	Used for storing numbers that can be used in calculations, such as integers (i.e., whole numbers), numbers to a certain number of decimal places, percentages and fractions.
Date	Used for storing dates.
Time	Used for storing times.
Currency	Used for storing monetary values to two decimal places.
AutoNumber	These are numbers allocated by the computer. It is useful when you want to give each record a unique number (student number, bank account number, etc.).
Boolean	This is used when only one of two choices can be entered for a field (Yes/No, Male/Female, etc.).
Lists	Useful where there are a limited number of choices a user can choose from. The user is presented with a list to choose from. (For example, enter the year 7, 8, 9, 10 or 11.) You can also have radio buttons (i.e., where you mark your choice by filling in a dot) or tick lists where you place a tick in a box.
Picture	Databases often have a picture. It could be of a person, a product, etc. There are also information handling systems that help you organize a large collection of digital images.
Sound	Information handling systems are used to organize music or sounds. You can create playlists and organize the music you like into categories.
Video	Information handling systems can store and organize video collections. These can range from home video selections to huge collections such as YouTube.

The design of file structures

Folders

With any project in ICT it is very important to get organized before you start by thinking about the folder structure you are going to use and about the folders in the folder structure. Being organized by creating a folder tree at the start does take time but you will reap the benefits later on because all the files will be easy to find. It is also much easier to back up the folders and files.

Subfolders

Folders can be arranged into subfolders with each subfolder containing a group of files that have something in common. For example, you could have a folder created for your two practical tasks for the GCSE in ICT. This folder could have two subfolders: one created for one of the practical tasks and the other created for the other practical task. Each subfolder would contain its own group of files.

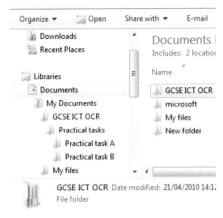

The levels of the different folders.

Filenames

When giving a file a name, always use a name that says something about what the file contains. You can usually use lots of characters for a filename. For example, rather than have a file called 'Intro', it would be better to use a filename such as 'Introduction to my GCSE ICT practical work'. You can see from the name exactly what is in the file.

File types

Different file types are used to hold different types of data. You can tell what type of data the file holds by looking at the file extension (i.e., the letters after the dot). For example, bulldog.bmp would represent an image file as the extension .bmp is a bitmap file.

You do not need to enter the file extension when you save a file – the software you are using adds it automatically.

Paths

Paths are used to point to a specific place in a file/folder structure.

For example: C:\user\docs\Letter. doc shows the path to a file called Letter.doc (a word-processed file) in a subfolder called 'docs' in a folder called 'user' on the 'C' drive (usually the hard drive) of the computer.

Encoding and how it affects data entry and retrieval

Data is often coded when it is collected on input into an ICT system. The reasons for this are:

- Coded data is quicker to type in.
- It takes up less storage space on disk.
- It is easier to check a code using validation checks.
- It is faster to access data that is coded.
- It is quicker to send the data over a network.

There are many examples of encoding data and here are a few:

Sex:
M = Male
F = Female

Date:
19/08/10 = 19 August 2010

Country of origin for cars:
GB = Great Britain
D = Germany
IRL = Ireland
CH = Switzerland

Sizes of clothes:
S = Small
M = Medium
L = Large
XL = Extra large

Airport codes:
LHR = London Heathrow
MAN = Manchester
RHO = Rhodes

All these examples show there is less to type in when data is encoded.

Size labelling in clothes is a form of encoding.

All flights have a code. The codes are shown on the departure board.

This car number plate tells you where the car is from and its year. The arrangement of letters and digits is unique for a particular car.

Data management *continued*

What is data capture?

Data capture is the method by which data from the outside world is entered into the computer so that it is in a form that can be processed by the computer. For example, using a keyboard to enter data written on an application form is a method of data capture. There are lots of different methods of data capture each with advantages and disadvantages.

The ideal method of data capture would be:

- completely accurate
- cheap (i.e., to buy and run the hardware needed)
- automatic (so that wage costs are kept low)
- fast.

Data collection and data capture methods

There are a number of different ways data can be collected and captured by the computer. In many cases the data is first added to paper forms and either the data is typed in from the forms or the forms are read automatically by a machine.

The design of data capture forms and screens

Data capture is the process of collecting data from the outside world and getting it into the computer. Data capture forms are documents, either as hard copy or on a screen, that are used to collect the data. They involve a person filling in the details on a form that can either be on paper or on a computer screen.

Printed data capture forms

Many data capture forms are printed out and then filled in and examples of them include:

- membership forms
- application forms

- order forms
- questionnaires
- census forms.

Some data capture forms capture data by the user shading in boxes. Multiple-choice examination answer sheets and questionnaires can be read automatically by an optical mark reader (OMR) that is able to read the marks made on the sheets.

Important issues when designing data capture forms

Designing forms is not as simple as you might first think. There are a number of things to consider such as:

- Nothing is missed off the form – ensuring all the data you need to collect is on the form.
- Enough space is included – many forms do not leave enough space for the user to write the details.
- Examples given of the data you want – for example, if you want the person to give their date of birth, it is best to give an example like 12/01/89 or DD/MM/YY.
- Clear instructions are given as to how to fill in the form.

KEY WORD

Data capture term for the various methods by which data can be entered into the computer so that it can be processed.

Paper forms

Paper forms are used to collect data from people. For example, you can have order forms, questionnaires, application forms, tax forms, passport forms, etc. The forms are filled in by writing or making marks on the paper. Paper forms can be given to a person to input the details into the computer. Some forms, such as those with marks on them or some where you neatly write numbers and letters, can be read by the computer directly using OMR and optical character recognition (OCR).

Online forms

These are forms that you see on websites where you can fill them in on your own computer.

▼ An online booking form for a holiday company shows a dialogue box.

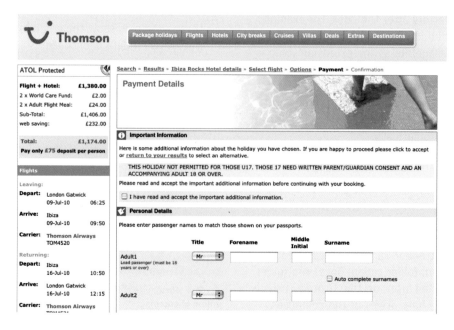

Advantages of electronic forms:

- No paper is used so this method is environmentally friendly.
- Cheap as no wages to pay to enter the data.
- Fast as there is no delay in capturing the data.
- Fewer mistakes as people are likely to enter their personal details correctly.

Disadvantages of electronic forms:

- Not everyone has a computer so paper system cannot be completely replaced.
- People may be put off using them if they do not understand them.
- Need to create a website, which can be expensive.

Chip and pin

Chip and pin is used to capture credit/debit card details when making purchases when you are present with the card.

Advantage of chip and pin:

- Reduces fraud as only the card holder will know the personal identification number (PIN).

Disadvantages of chip and pin:

- Hand-held terminals are needed, which are expensive.
- People forget their PIN, which can be embarrassing.

OMR (optical mark recognition)

Optical mark recognition is used to read data in the form of marks made on a form. This is the method used to read multiple-choice answer sheets and questionnaires.

Advantages of OMR:

- Forms are read automatically.
- Forms are read at high speed.
- Readers are fairly cheap.
- You can adapt the systems to read different documents.

Disadvantages of OMR:

- Some people will not fill in the OMR form properly.
- If forms are folded they cannot be read.
- Damaged forms can jam the reader.

Bar code reading

This method is used to read bar codes on store goods, parcels, library books and cards, luggage, etc.

Advantages of bar coding:

- Use is universal in the case of bar codes in a supermarket.
- Bar codes can be read at a distance, which is useful for large objects.
- Very fast to read the bar code and obtain details such as description, price, etc., from a database.

Disadvantages of bar coding:

- Some bar codes can become damaged so the code has to be input using a keyboard.
- You need shelf labels to tell shoppers the price and this can be confusing.
- Bar code readers can be expensive.

Voice recognition

This uses a microphone and special software to recognize spoken words, numbers and commands.

Advantages of voice recognition:

- Faster – as you can talk quicker than you can type.
- Reduces repetitive strain injury (RSI).
- A good method for disabled people who cannot use their hands.

Disadvantages of voice recognition:

- You need to spend time teaching the system to recognize your voice.
- You cannot use it in a busy office where there is lots of background noise.
- System can make a lot of mistakes so you need to proof read the text carefully.

Biometrics

Biometrics makes use of features of the human body that are unique to a particular person. Usually this is a person's fingerprint or the pattern on the back of the eye (called the retina). Rather than have to log-in to a computer by providing a username and a password, a user can now simply put their finger into a scanner. The system automatically recognizes who it is that is using the computer and gives them the network resources allocated to them.

Advantages of biometrics:

- You do not need anything else such as key, magnetic strip card to gain access to a facility (e.g., room, computer, etc.).
- System is hard to abuse. In school registration systems you cannot register someone else.

Disadvantages of biometrics:

- Some worry about the privacy of data stored – especially fingerprint details.
- The readers are quite expensive.

▲ **Retinal scanning.**

▲ **Fingerprint scanner.**

Data management *continued*

RFID tags

RFID (radio frequency identification) obtains data stored on a tag (a small chip) using radio signals, which means that the reading device and tag do not have to come into contact with each other. This means that the data on the tag can be read from a distance. This system is therefore a wireless system.

Applications of RFID tags:

- Used for stock control in factories.
- Cattle can be tagged so the milking system can identify which cow is being milked and information about yield, etc., can be stored.
- Used for season tickets to car parks.
- Used in libraries as a replacement for bar codes.

Advantages of RFID tags:

- There is no need for the reader and tag to come into contact with each other so you could have a tag on you that could be read without getting it out of your pocket or bag.
- You can store a lot of data on the tags.

Disadvantages of RFID tags:

- The reader and the tags themselves are expensive.

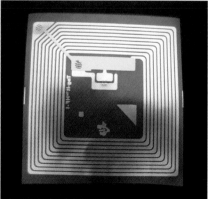

◀ **An RFID tag.**

Questions A

1 (a) Give the name of a biometric method used for the registration of students in a school. *(1 mark)*
  (b) Describe **one** advantage the biometric method has over non-biometric methods. *(2 marks)*

2 OMR is frequently used in schools for school registration systems and also for marking multiple-choice answer sheets.
  (a) Give the meaning of the abbreviation OMR. *(1 mark)*
  (b) Explain how data is captured using OMR. *(2 marks)*
  (c) Give **one** advantage OMR has compared to typing the data in using a keyboard. *(1 mark)*
  (d) Give **one** disadvantage OMR has. *(1 mark)*

3 (a) Explain how RFID is used to capture data. *(1 mark)*
  (b) Give **one** advantage RFID has as a method of data capture. *(1 mark)*

4 Biometric methods are often used for capturing data.
  (a) Explain what the term biometric means. *(1 mark)*
  (b) Give an example of an application that uses a biometric method. *(2 marks)*

5 Voice recognition systems are becoming a popular method of inputting data.
  (a) Give the name of the input device used with a voice recognition system. *(1 mark)*
  (b) Explain how the data is captured using a voice recognition system. *(3 marks)*
  (c) Give **one** advantage of voice recognition. *(1 mark)*
  (d) Give **one** disadvantage of voice recognition. *(1 mark)*

Extension activity

Use the Internet to research biometric methods and their applications.

Produce a document on their advantages and disadvantages.

Data management: validation and verification

You will find out

> **About what validation is and the methods of validation**

> **About what verification is and the methods of verification**

Data is the raw material for computer systems. The way that it is collected is important, because it determines the accuracy of the information produced by the system. If the data is incorrect, then no amount of processing by the computer will turn it into correct information. This section looks at the methods that can be used to ensure that incorrect data is not processed by the computer. It covers the two methods called validation and verification.

This section looks at the methods that can be used to ensure that incorrect data is not processed/manipulated by the computer.

Validation

Validation is a check performed by a computer program during data entry. Validation is the process that ensures that data accepted for processing is sensible and reasonable. For example, a living person's date of birth could not be before 1890 as in 2010 this would make them 120 years old (the current oldest person is 115).

Validation is performed by the computer program being used and consists of a series of checks called **validation checks**.

When a developer develops a solution to an ICT problem, they must create checks to reduce the likelihood of the user entering incorrect information. This is done by restricting the user as to what they can enter, or checking that the data obeys certain rules.

Types of validation check

Validation checks are used to restrict the user as to the data they can enter. There are many different validation checks, each with their own special use including:

- **Data type checks** – these check that data being entered is the same type as the data type specified for the field. This would check to make sure that only numbers are entered into fields specified as numeric.
- **Presence checks** – some database fields have to be filled in, whilst others can be left empty. A presence check would check to make sure that data had been entered into a field. Unless the user fills in data for these fields, the data will not be processed.
- **Range checks** – are performed on numbers. They check that a number being entered is within a certain range. For example, all the students in a college are aged over 14, so a date of birth being entered which would give an age less than this would not be allowed by the range check.

- **Look-up lists** – are very useful and work in the following way. When you enter data, the software looks through a list of data until it finds a match along with other important data. For example, if each product in a shop is given a number, this number can be stored along with the description of the product and its price. If you then input the product number, all the other details for that product are displayed.
- **Format checks** – are performed on codes to make sure that they conform to the correct combinations of characters. For example, a code for car parts may consist of three numbers followed by a single letter. This can be specified for a field to restrict entered data to this format.
- **Check digits** – are added to important numbers such as account numbers, International Standard Book Numbers (ISBNs), article numbers (the numbers under the bar code), etc. These numbers are placed at the end of the block of numbers and are used to check that the numbers have been entered correctly into the computer.

When the large number is entered, the computer performs a calculation using all the numbers to work out this extra number. If the calculation reveals that the extra number (called the check digit) is the same as that calculated by the other numbers, it means that all the numbers have been entered correctly.

Data management: validation and verification *continued*

Parity checks

Parity checks involve checking data after it has been sent through a wire or wirelessly.

Parity checks check that the data has not been corrupted (i.e. altered) in any way.

Restricting the user to a list

One way of helping a user enter correct data is to supply them with a list of items to choose from. Using a list prevents the user from entering data that is not on a list. The only problem with lists is that they are only appropriate when there are only a small number of choices, for a field such as M or F, ranking of 1 to 5, etc.

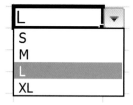

▲ Here the sizes of a shirt are shown as a list from which the user can select.

Verification

Verification means checking that the data being entered into the ICT system perfectly matches the source of the data. For example, if details from an order form were being typed in using a keyboard, then when the user has finished, the data on the form on the screen should be identical to that on the paper form (i.e., the data source). Also if data was sent over a network, the data needs to be checked when it arrives to make sure no errors have been introduced.

▲ Parity checking checks for errors when data is sent over networks.

Here are some methods of verification:

- **Visual check/proof reading** – involves one user carefully reading what they have typed in and comparing it with what is on the data source (order forms, application forms, invoices, etc.) for any errors, which can then be corrected.
- **Double entry of data** – involves using the same data source to enter the details into the ICT system twice and only if the two sets of data are identical will they be accepted for processing. The disadvantage of this is that the cost of data entry is doubled.

  Double entry of data is often used when creating accounts over the Internet. They may ask you to create a password and enter it twice. This ensures there are no mistakes that would prevent you from accessing the account.

Hash and batch totals

When large numbers of input documents are used for data entry, it is necessary to check that all the documents have been input and processed properly. There are two checks that can be performed:

- hash totals
- batch totals.

Hash totals

Hash totals are meaningless totals used for a check. For example, if each survey form is numbered (e.g., 000001, 000002, 000023, etc.) then the total of all the numbers could be calculated and input to compare with the answer the computer calculates. If the hash totals are equal it shows that all the survey forms have been input.

Batch totals

Batch totals are like hash totals except the totals have meaning. For example, adding up all the totals of a batch of invoices could be used to check that all the invoices had been input. The total would be the total amount owed for those invoices processed in the batch. The amounts could be worked out manually and then compared with the answer the computer calculates. Any discrepancies could then be checked.

KEY WORDS

Batch total a meaningful total that is used to check that the computer has input all the data.

Hash total meaningless total of numbers, such as order numbers, used to check that all the data has been entered.

Parity check check to make sure that the data sent is the same as that received when data is transmitted from one computer to another.

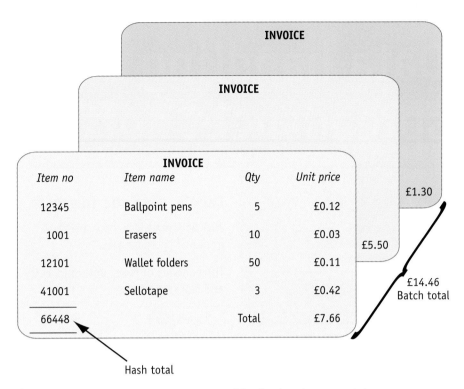

Item no	Item name	Qty	Unit price
12345	Ballpoint pens	5	£0.12
1001	Erasers	10	£0.03
12101	Wallet folders	50	£0.11
41001	Sellotape	3	£0.42
66448		Total	£7.66

£1.30

£5.50

£14.46
Batch total

Hash total

▲ Hash and batch totals are used to make sure all invoices have been processed.

▲ Batch totals have meaning.

Questions B

1 **(a)** What is meant by a check digit? *(3 marks)*
   (b) Give **two** different examples where check digits are used. *(2 marks)*

2 Here are some dates of birth that are to be entered into an ICT system:
   (a) 12/01/3010
   (b) 01/13/2000
   (c) 30/02/1999

Assume that all the dates are in the British format dd/mm/yyyy. For each one, explain why they cannot be valid dates of birth. *(3 marks)*

3 When an employee joins a company they are given an employee code.
   (a) Here is an example of an employee code:
   LLLNNNNNN   where L is a letter of the alphabet and N is a number.
   Explain **one** type of validation that could be used with this field. *(2 marks)*
   (b) Employees are given an annual salary.
   Explain **one** type of validation that could be used with this field. *(2 marks)*

4 A computer manager says, 'data can be valid yet be incorrect'. By giving **one** suitable example, explain what this statement means. *(3 marks)*

5 An online form for ordering DVDs uses a presence check for some of the fields.
   (a) Explain what a presence check is and why some fields have them whilst others don't. *(3 marks)*
   (b) Give **one** field that might have a presence check and **one** field that would not need a presence check. *(2 marks)*

Data handling software: spreadsheet software

You will find out

▷ **About the features of spreadsheet software**

▷ **About the features of modelling software**

You will already be familiar with many features and functions of spreadsheet software. This section seeks to revise some of the basics of spreadsheets but also to let you know what other features are available in spreadsheet software and how they are used.

It is important to bear in mind that you may sometimes have to create spreadsheets for others to use. This means that you need to add titles and labels so that it is clear what the spreadsheet is for and what the data in the rows and columns mean. It is always a good idea to sketch a design of a spreadsheet on paper before you start.

You will, of course, have to develop spreadsheets and build up your practical skills in using some of the techniques and knowledge covered here. This section also covers the use of spreadsheet software for modelling.

Labels, data and formulas

Just as a reminder, here are the basics of spreadsheets.

The concept of rows, columns, cells and cell references

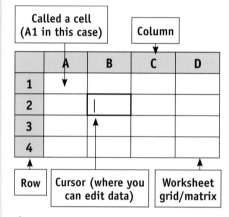

▲ Rows, columns, cells and cell references.

Labels

Labels are used for titles, headings, names, and for identifying *columns* or *rows* of data. You should never have values on a spreadsheet without labels, as a user will be left wondering what they represent.

Data

Data are the values (text or numbers) that you enter into the spreadsheet. It is the data that will be used for calculations or for producing graphs and charts.

Formulas

Formulas are used to perform calculations on the cell contents.

In order to distinguish between text and formulas a symbol, =, needs to be typed in first, like this =B3+B4.

Here are some calculations and what they do. Notice that you can use upper or lower case letters (i.e. capital or small letters).

=C3+C4 (adds the numbers in cells C3 and C4 together)

=A1*B4 (multiplies the numbers in cells A1 and B4 together)

=3*G4 (multiplies the number in cell G4 by 3)

=sum(b3:b10) (adds up all the cells from b3 to b10 inclusive)

=C4/D1 (divides the number in cell C4 by the number in cell D1)

=30/100*A2 (finds 30% of the number in cell A2)

Formulas and functions

A function is a specialized calculation that the spreadsheet software has memorized. There are many of these functions, some of which are very specialized.

A function must start with an equals sign (=) and it must have a range of cells to which it applies in brackets after it.

Average: For example, to find the average of the numbers in a range of cells from A3 to A10 you would use: =AVERAGE(A3:A10)

Maximum: =MAX(D3:J3) displays the largest number in all the cells from D3 to J3 inclusive.

Minimum: =MIN(D3:J3) displays the smallest number in all the cells from D3 to J3 inclusive.

Mode: =MODE(A3:A15) displays the mode (i.e., the most frequent number) in the cells from A3 to A15 inclusive.

Median: =MEDIAN(B2:W2) displays the median of the cells from cells B2 to W2 inclusive.

Sum: =SUM(E3:P3) displays the total of all the cells from cells E3 to P3 inclusive.

COUNT: Suppose we want to count the number of numeric entries in the range C3 to C30.

We can use =COUNT(C3:C30). Any blank lines or text entries in the range will not be counted.

COUNTA: To count a number of items or names of people we need to be able to count text entries. To do this we can use =COUNTA(C3:C30).

You need to make sure that headings are not included in the range so that they are not counted as well. Again blank lines are not counted.

IF: The IF function is called a logical function because it makes the decision to do one of two things based on the value it is testing. The IF function is very useful because you can use it to test a condition and then choose between two actions based on whether the condition is true or false.

The IF function makes use of something called relational operators. You may have come across these in your mathematics lessons but it is worth going through what they mean.

Relational operators
(=, <, >, <>, <=, >=)

Symbol	Meaning	Examples
=	equals	5 + 5 = 10
>	greater than	5*3 > 2*3
<	less than	-6 < -1 or 100 < 200
<>	not equal to	"Red" <> "White" or 20/4 <> 6*4
<=	less than or equal to	"Adam" <= "Eve"
>=	greater than or equal to	400 >= 200

▲ Relational operators.

Here are some examples of the use of a single IF function:

=IF(B3>=50,"Pass","Fail")

This function tests to see if the number in cell B3 is greater than or equal to 50. If the answer is true, Pass is displayed and if the answer is false, Fail is displayed.

=IF(A2>=500,A2*0.5,A2)

This tests to see if the number in cell A2 is greater than or equal to 500. If true, the number in cell A2 will be multiplied by 0.5 and the answer displayed (i.e. 250 will be displayed). If false, the number in cell A2 will be displayed.

Absolute and relative cell referencing

There are two ways in which you can make a reference to another cell and it is important to know the difference if you want to copy or move cells. An absolute reference always refers to the same cell. The other type of reference, called a relative reference, refers to a cell that is a certain number of rows and columns away. When the current cell is copied or moved to a new position, the cell to which the reference is made will also change position.

	A	B	C	D	E
1					
2					
3					
4		=A1			
5					
6					

▲ Relative cell referencing.

KEY WORDS

Absolute reference a reference to a cell used in a formula where, when the formula is copied to a new address, the cell address does not change.

Relative reference when a cell is used in a formula and the formula is copied to a new address, the cell address changes to take account of the formula's new position.

To understand the difference we will look at two examples. The first example shows relative referencing with cell B4 containing a relative reference to cell A1. This reference tells the spreadsheet that the cell to which it refers is 3 cells up and one cell to the left of cell B4. If cell B4 is copied to another position, say E5, then the reference will still be to the same number of cells up and to the left, so the reference will now be to cell D2.

	A	B	C	D	E
1					
2					
3					
4		=A1			
5					
6					

▲ Absolute cell referencing.

With absolute cell referencing, if cell B4 contains a reference to cell A1, then if the contents of B4 are copied to a new position, then the reference will not be adjusted and it will still refer to cell A1.

In most cases we will want to use relative cell references and the spreadsheet will assume that ordinary cell references are relative cell references. Sometimes we want to refer to the same cell, even when the formula referring to the cell is copied to a new position. We therefore need to make sure that the formula contains an absolute cell reference. To do this, a dollar sign is placed in front of the column and row number.

Cell B6 is a relative cell reference. To change it to an absolute cell reference we would add the dollar signs like this: B6.

Replication

Replicating a formula means copying a formula down a column or across a row whilst changing the formula slightly to take into account the changed position of the cells where the data is.

Data handling software: spreadsheet software *continued*

Formatting cells to match data types

There are many different types of data and some of these are shown in the following table:

Type of data	Example of data
Date	12/12/10
Integer (a whole number)	34
Decimal number	3.14
Percentage	4%
Currency	£3.45
Text	Jenny Hayter

If the general number format is used (which it will be unless you tell the software otherwise) the numbers will be shown with up to eleven digits (including all the numbers up to and after the decimal point). A cell that has a formula typed in will show the results of the formula rather than the formula itself.

Cells need to be able to hold the data you want to put into them. The spreadsheet will interpret the data you put into the cell. What is displayed in a cell depends on the cell format.

Although each cell is set to the general number format, it can change automatically depending on the data you type in. If you type in a pound sign followed by a number, the spreadsheet will assume that you are dealing with currency and will format the cell to currency automatically. It will only show the currency to two decimal places, so if you typed in £1.349, '£1.35' would be shown.

For large numbers you often use a comma to make them easier to read (e.g. 3,000,000). As soon as such a number is entered with the commas, the spreadsheet will apply the number format with the thousands separator and use a maximum of two decimal places.

If a number is entered ending in a % sign (e.g. 4%), then the spreadsheet will set the cell automatically to the percent format with two decimal places.

Cell presentation formats

Data can be presented in cells in a variety of different ways. We will look at these in this section.

Aligning cells

When you enter data into a cell, the spreadsheet automatically aligns (i.e. positions) the cells according to the following:

- Numbers are aligned to the right.
- Text is aligned to the left.

Do not put any spaces in front of numbers in order to align them as this will make it impossible for the spreadsheet to use the numbers in calculations.

If you want to align the data differently, you can use the special buttons for alignment on the formatting toolbar. Using this method, you can align them to the left, right or centre.

▲ Text alignment buttons.

Formatting text to make it stand out

Text can be made to stand out by formatting it in a number of ways:

- Font type – changes the shapes of letters and numbers.
- Font size – used to make headings, subheadings, etc., stand out.
- Bold, Italics, Underline – used to draw attention to text.

Borders and rotating text

Using borders you can: put a border around cells or groups of cells, shade in certain cells or groups of cells.

Rotating text is useful when you want a narrow column but the column heading is wide.

Adding colour

Colour may be added to:

- text
- borders
- background colours for cells.

Cell merging

Sometimes a label may be too big to fit into a single cell and when this happens it can be made to overflow into the other cells. This is called cell merging.

The benefits of using spreadsheet software

There are lots of benefits in using spreadsheet software such as:

- You can perform 'what if' investigations – you can make changes to the spreadsheet values to see what happens. For example, you may set up a spreadsheet to manage your money. You could see the effect on your finances of getting a part-time job paying £80 per week.
- Automatic recalculation – when an item of data changes, all those cells that are connected to the changed cell by a formula will also change.

▶ Formatting toolbar.

- Accurate calculation – provided the formulas are all correct, the calculations on the numbers will always be correct.
- It is easy to produce graphs and charts – once the data has been entered, it is very easy for the spreadsheet to produce graphs and charts based on it.

Layout of worksheets and linked sheets

When creating a worksheet from scratch it is best to plan it on paper first. Do a sketch in pencil to show where on the worksheet you are going to position everything. Do a few designs and choose the best one. It is a good idea to show your design to other people to get their opinion before making your choice.

It is possible to have two completely different worksheets that use each other's data. There needs to be a link between the worksheets for this. Linking worksheets is useful if a single worksheet starts to become very large. Instead of the one large spreadsheet you can split it into two with a link between the two.

KEY WORDS

Border lines, patterns, pictures that can be placed around a group of cells or a page.

Cell merging combining cells together so as to accommodate longer text.

Worksheet the document that is created using spreadsheet software.

What if? asking a question of a spreadsheet by supplying input to see what happens. For example, entering your monthly income and expenses to see what would happen if you had a car loan which cost £200 per month.

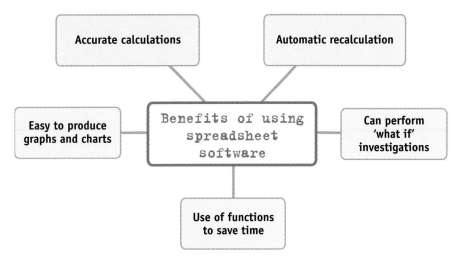

The benefits of using spreadsheet software.

Questions C

1 Cells can contain labels, data or formulas.
   (a) Explain what is meant by labels. *(1 mark)*
   (b) Explain what is meant by data. *(1 mark)*
   (c) Explain what is meant by a formula. *(1 mark)*

2 There are **two** different types of cell reference. Give the names of both of them. *(2 marks)*

3 Give the names of **two** functions that can be used in a spreadsheet. *(2 marks)*

4 Here are some statements concerning the reasons for putting formulas into spreadsheets.
   Put a tick next to those reasons that are correct. *(1 mark)*

Reason	Tick if reason is correct
If a cell changes, then all those cells that depend on the cell will change	☐
A more accurate answer is produced than with a calculator	☐
It improves the appearance of the spreadsheet	☐
The formulas in the spreadsheet need to be kept secret	☐

5 Describe **two** different ways a cell can be formatted to make it stand out. *(2 marks)*

Data handling software: spreadsheet software *continued*

Graph and chart creation

Lists of figures can be hard to understand, so it is easier to show them as a picture using graphs and charts. Creating graphs/charts makes it easy to:

- spot any inconsistencies in the data
- spot trends such as profits increasing or decreasing
- see the biggest or smallest reading.

There are lots of different graphs and charts to choose from so it is important to pick the one that is most suitable.

Pie charts

These are good for displaying the proportion that each group is of the whole.

For example, you could show a class's crisp preferences using a pie chart.

Bar charts

Good for displaying the frequency of different categories. Here is a bar chart to investigate the types of vehicle using a certain road as a shortcut.

Scattergrams/scattergraphs

To see how closely, if at all, one quantity depends on another. This is called correlation.

For example, you might start with the hypothesis that someone who is tall will have bigger feet. You would then collect height and shoe size data and then plot the pairs of values. A line of best fit can be added to the diagram like the one shown here.

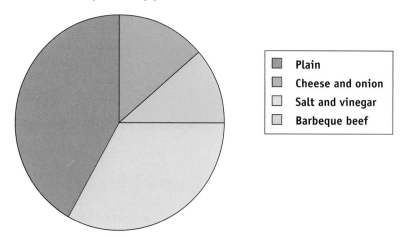

Group 7A's crisp preferences

- Plain
- Cheese and onion
- Salt and vinegar
- Barbeque beef

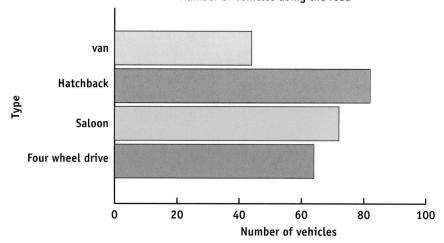

Number of vehicles using the road

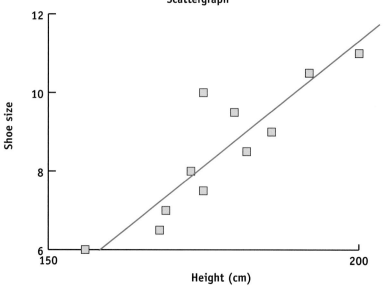

Scattergraph

Graph to show depreciation of a car

(line graph: Value (£) on y-axis from 2000 to 12000, Year on x-axis from 1 to 5; values decreasing from 12000 at year 1 to about 3000 at year 5)

Graphs and charts can be the output from a computer model.

Line graphs

These can be used to show trends. The graph shows how the value of a car falls over the years. This is called depreciation.

Things to remember to include when producing graphs/charts

- Use scales on those axes that have numbers on them. The computer usually sorts these out for you or you can change them to suit.
- Always include a title for the graph/chart.
- Always include a title for each axis (i.e., vertical (y) and horizontal (x)) to show what each axis represents.
- Use a legend where applicable. The legend is used with pie charts and can be used to say what the points on a graph show.

Modelling

Modelling means producing a series of mathematical equations that can be used to simulate a real situation. For example, it might predict the likely sales for a new product that is being developed or you could use it for showing the likely flow of money in and out of your bank account when you start work. For a personal finances model this could be: Can I afford to buy and run a car? Will I be able to afford a holiday in the summer if I do three hours overtime a week? All these questions are examples of 'what if' questions and you will see how useful spreadsheets are to be able to answer these questions.

The components of a simple model

Models consist of the following components:

Input values

These are the values that are not preset within the model. Input values are usually entered by the user using keyboard entry. It is important that these input values are validated so that only valid data is processed.

Variables

Variables are those items of data that we are likely to change in the model. For example, in a model to show the effect of inflation on someone's savings, the amount they have saved, the interest rate they are getting and the rate of inflation are all variables. Variables should never be put directly into formulas, since for a user to change their value they would have to understand formulas.

Constants

These are those numbers that do not change or that you want to keep the same. Be careful with constants because many quantities stay constant over a short period but not a longer period.

Constraints

A constraint is something that is imposed on a model. For example, you could have a credit limit imposed on you by the bank and your spending cannot go over it.

Rules (i.e. calculations and other operators)

Once data has been entered it can be subject to a range of operators:

Arithmetic (+, −, ÷, √, etc.)
Relational (=, <, >)
Logical (IF, AND, OR, NOT).

Sometimes these calculations and logical operators are referred to as rules.

Data handling software: spreadsheet software *continued*

Activity

1 Setting up a simple model

A university student is living away from home for the first time and they want to make sure that they budget the limited amount of money they will have. They are going to create a spreadsheet model. You are going to follow their steps.

1 Load the spreadsheet software Excel.

2 Enter the details shown on the following spreadsheet exactly as they appear on the right.

   Note: You will need to format the text in some of the cells. You will need to format cells D3 and D10 so that the text is wrapped in the cell. (This keeps the cell width the same by moving text so that it fits the width.)

3 In cell D4 enter the following formula to work out the amount the student gets per week from the student loan.
   =b4/c4

4 In cell D5 enter the following formula to work out the amount of money the student gets each week from their part-time job.
   =b5/c5

5 In cell D7 enter the formula =d4+d5
   This works out the total weekly income.

6 Enter a formula that will work out the weekly spending on rent and put the answer in cell D11.

7 Copy the formula you have entered in D11 relatively down the column as far as cell D16.

8 Put a formula in cell D18 to add up the spending from cells D11 to D16.

9 Enter a formula in cell D20 that will subtract the total spending from the total income.

10 Your completed spreadsheet should now look like that on the right.

11 Save your spreadsheet using the filename 'Budget model'.

First spreadsheet (cell G25 selected):

	A	B	C	D
1	**Weekly budget**			
2				
3	**Income**	**Amount**	**Weeks**	**Income per week**
4	Student loan (per term)	£2,250	12	
5	Weekly wage from part-time job	£105	1	
6				
7	**Total income per week**			
8				
9				
10	**Spending**	**Amount**	**Weeks**	**Spending per week**
11	Monthly rent	£250	4	
12	Books (per term)	£210	12	
13	Food (per term)	£280	4	
14	Clothes (per term)	£240	12	
15	Entertainment (per term)	£50	1	
16	Travel (per term)	£145	12	
17				
18	**Total spending per week**			

Second spreadsheet (cell F22 selected):

	A	B	C	D
1	**Weekly budget**			
2				
3	**Income**	**Amount**	**Weeks**	**Income per week**
4	Student loan (per term)	£2,250	12	£187.50
5	Weekly wage from part-time job	£105	1	£105
6				
7	**Total income per week**			£292.50
8				
9				
10	**Spending**	**Amount**	**Weeks**	**Spending per week**
11	Monthly rent	£250	4	£62.50
12	Books (per term)	£210	12	£17.50
13	Food (per term)	£280	4	£70.00
14	Clothes (per term)	£240	12	£20.00
15	Entertainment (per term)	£50	1	£50.00
16	Travel (per term)	£145	12	£12.08
17				
18	**Total spending per week**			£232.08

2 Using the spreadsheet model to find the answers to 'what if' questions

1   Load the spreadsheet called 'Budget model' if it is not already loaded.

2   You are going to make some changes to the spreadsheet. It is important that you do **not** save any of these changes.

3   The monthly rent has been increased to £275 per month and his employers have reduced his hours for the part-time job, which means he now only earns £50 per week. Will he now be spending more money than he receives? Make these alterations to the spreadsheet to find out. How much does he have left at the end of the week?

4   His grandparents decide they can give him £50 per week to help him.
    Add this amount to the spreadsheet in a suitable place and using a suitable label. Make any necessary changes to formulas. How much does he now have at the end of the month?

5   Save your spreadsheet using the filename 'Revised budget model'.

6   Print a copy of this spreadsheet on a single page.

7   Print a copy of this spreadsheet showing all the formulas used.

3 Improving the appearance of the model

You are now free to develop this model to improve its appearance.
    Here are some of the things you might consider:

• Using cell borders and shading to bring attention to the information in the main cells.
• Can you use an IF function to display different messages depending on whether there is a balance left or owed at the end of the week?
• Save the model using the filename 'Final budget model'.

4 Producing graphs and charts

For this activity you have to use the data from the spreadsheet 'Final budget model' to produce a couple of graphs/charts to show relevant data in the spreadsheet. It is up to you to produce the most appropriate graph/chart.
    Ensure that your graphs/charts have:

• a title
• each axis clearly marked or a legend used.

Questions D

1   Many computer models are created using spreadsheet software.
    (a) Explain what is meant by a computer model. *(3 marks)*
    (b) Describe a model you have used that has been created using spreadsheet software. *(2 marks)*

2   A spreadsheet model is used to show the money coming into and going out of a personal bank account.
    (a) Give **two** advantages in using a spreadsheet model to help model personal finances. *(2 marks)*
    (b) Give **one** disadvantage in using a spreadsheet model to help model personal finances. *(2 marks)*

3   Here is a formula that performs a calculation in a spreadsheet:
    =B7*B3
    The above formula contains two cell references. Cell references may be either absolute or relative.
    (a) Write down the relative cell reference in the above formula. *(1 mark)*
    (b) Write down the absolute cell reference in the above formula. *(1 mark)*

The formula is used in the following worksheet:

	A	B	C	D
1	**Ace Computer Supplies**			
2				
3	Rate of VAT	17.50%		
4				
5				
6	**Item**	**Price excluding VAT**	**VAT**	**Price including VAT**
7	16GB Pen drive	£24.99		
8	XD Media card (4GB)	£16.99		
9	SD Media card (8GB)	£32.99		
10	DVD-RW (6 pack)	£10.99		
11	DVD-R (6 pack)	£8.99		
12				

(c) The formula =B7*B3 is entered into cell C7. It is then copied down column C from cells C7 to C11.
    Explain with reference to this spreadsheet why the formula contains both absolute and relative cell references. *(2 marks)*
(d) Write down the formula that would need to be entered into cell D7 in order to work out the price including VAT. *(1 mark)*

Data handling software: database software

You will find out

▷ **About the features of database software**

▷ **About producing reports**

Data handling software is used to put data into a certain structure. Once the data is put into this structure it can be manipulated and output in lots of different ways. Data handling software can mean specialist database software but it is possible to create a simple database using spreadsheet software. In this section you will learn about the structure of a database and how the database structure enables control of the way information can be obtained.

Fields, records and files

An organized store of data on a computer is called a database.

Choosing the software to create a database structure

There are two types of software you could use to produce a database:

- spreadsheet software
- database software.

You can build a simple database by organizing the data in rows and columns in a table. In the database to the right the columns represent each of the fields and the rows are the records.

Fields, records and files: what do they all mean?

There are some database terms you will need to familiarize yourselves with. These are:

Data: These are facts about a specific person, place or thing.

Information: Information is data that has been processed into a form that is useful to the user.

Field: A field is an item of data. In other words it is a fact. A Surname would be an example of a field.

Record: The detail relating to a single thing or person is called a record. A record consists of fields.

File: A collection of related records is called a file. The group of records for all the pupils in the school is called the pupil file. Often a simple file holding a single database is called a table.

Table: In databases a table is used to store data with each row in the table being a record and the whole table being a file. When only one table is used, it is a very simple database and it is called a flat file database.

For more complex databases created using specialist database software, lots of tables can be used and such a database is called a relational database.

Key fields/primary key

A Key field/primary key is a field in an information handling system that is unique to a particular record. For example, in a file of all the children in a school a record would be the details about a particular pupil. The Key field/primary key would be Pupil Number, which would be a number set up so that each pupil is allocated a different number when they join the school. No two pupils would have the same number. Surname would not be unique and so is unsuitable for a Key field/primary key. It is possible to have more than one Key field/primary key in a record.

Searching for information

There are a number of ways that information can be searched for. Here are some of them.

Each column represents a field of the database

Sex	Year	Favourite sport
M	7	Football
M	7	Golf
F	8	Hockey
F	7	Football
M	7	Tennis
F	8	Tennis

Each row is a record of the database

Note:

RECORDS are always ROWS
FIELDS are always COLUMNS

⬆ **The structure of a database.**

Search engines

Search engines

Search engines are used to find information on the Internet but they can also be used to search for information on an organization's intranet (a type of internal network that uses the same technology as the Internet).

Key word searches

All information stores provide ways of searching for information using key word searches. When information is sought, the person searching for the information may not know such things as the Key field/primary key and they have to use several key words.

Typical tasks for which data handling software can be used

Organizing data

Data handling software is used to organize the data into a structure that allows it to be extracted to produce information in a flexible way.

Collecting data

Data from questionnaires, application forms, order forms, etc., can be put into a database structure. You have already come across the various ways (e.g., keyboarding, OMR, OCR, etc.) that the data can be captured by the computer.

Amending existing data

Amending existing data means that the data already stored in the database is being altered. Amending can include updating and deleting:

Updating: means bringing data up-to-date because of changes that have occurred since the data was originally input. Reasons for updating include: a woman changing her surname when she gets married, a person changing their credit card (i.e., different credit card company, different credit card number, different start and expiry dates), changing address, etc.

Deleting redundant data: means removing some of the data that is no longer needed from a data handling system. There are lots of reasons why data needs to be deleted, such as: where personal information is wrong and a data subject has asked for it to be deleted, when a person dies, when a customer has not placed an order for a long time, etc.

Searching/selecting/filtering records

In order to narrow down information we can restrict it by asking only for data satisfying certain criteria. For example, in a list of all the pupils in a school, we might only want a list of boys. This is classed as searching using a single criterion. The single search criterion could be: Sex = Boys. Searches can also be performed using multiple criteria. This means that data is being searched for using more than one criterion. For example, we could search for all the boys in a school born before a certain date. The search criteria might be set up something like this:

> Sex = Boys AND Date of Birth < 01/09/99

Sorting

Data can be sorted into ascending or descending order and it can be sorted on one or more fields.

Ascending order: in the case of numbers the smallest number is first and the largest number is last. In the case of text the letter A is first and the letter Z is last.

Descending order: in the case of numbers the largest number is first and the smallest number is last. In the case of text the letter Z is first and the letter A is last.

Reasons for sorting data include:

- If lists are printed, then it is easier to find a particular person if they are ordered according to surname.

- You can identify who your best customers are by the amount they have spent in a year. To do this you can sort them according to the total amount they have spent.

Merging data

Two database files can be merged together to form a single larger database file. For this to be done, the two databases must have an identical structure (i.e. the same fields, the same data type for the fields, etc.).

Report production

Reports are used to present the output from an information handling system. Reports are used to present the data in such a way that it is more suited to printing.

Here are some points about reports:

- Reports should have a relevant title.
- The report should contain a date. Information changes, so the person looking at the information needs to know that it is the latest version.
- Only data or information that is important should be included.
- The details of the report should be clearly laid out.
- The report should present the information in the clearest way possible (in some cases this will be using a graph or chart).
- The pages of the report should be suitably numbered (NB you can use headers and footers).

Creation and development of graphs/charts

Data from a database can be imported into the spreadsheet software for the production of graphs and charts. If the database is fairly simple, such as a database of the replies to a questionnaire, then it would make sense to use a flat file, in which case the data can be analysed using the software the data is already in.

Data handling software: database software *continued*

Questions E

1 (a) Explain what is meant by a validation check. *(2 marks)*
 (b) Give the names of **two** different validation checks that may be performed on data. *(2 marks)*

2 Explain the difference between sorting and searching data. *(2 marks)*

3 A luxury car rental firm keeps the details of the cars it rents out in a table. The structure and contents of this table are shown below.

Reg-number	Make	Model	Year
DB51 AML	Aston Martin	DB7	2009
CAB 360M	**Ferrari**	**360 Modena**	**2008**
P 762 GT	Ferrari	355 Spider	2000
MAS 12	Maserati	3200 GTA	2001
FG09 FRT	Porsche	911 Turbo	2009
M3 MMM	**BMW**	**M3 Conv**	**2010**
T433 YTH	Jaguar	XK8	2009

 (a) Give the names of **two** fields shown in the above table. *(2 marks)*
 (b) Give the name of the field that should be chosen as the key field. *(1 mark)*
 (c) Explain why the field you have chosen for your answer to part (b) should be chosen as the Key field. *(1 mark)*
 (d) The highlighted details are an example of which one of these? *(1 mark)*

> a record   a table
> a field   a file.

 (e) How many records are there in the above table? *(1 mark)*

4 Here is a sample of the data that is to be stored in an employee database. The data items shown are the employees' surname, initial, street, postcode and telephone number.

> Adams, V, 123 The High Street, L23 6DE, 0151-264-1112
> Dolan, N, 64 North Way, L9 8SS, 0151-267-0011
> Doyle, B, 12 Crosby Road, L23 2DF, 0151-264-1212
> Carrol, A, 15 Barkfield Drive, L23 7YH, 0151-261-0899
> Conway, T, 6 Windle Hey, L23 6ER, 0151-289-0899
> Harvey, J, 4 Empress Road, L22 7ED, 0151-340-9090
> Harvey, J, 4 Empress Road, L22 7ED, 0151-340-9090

 (a) A table is to be set up with five fields. Give names for the five fields that would be suitable for the above set of data items. *(5 marks)*
 (b) The person who is designing the database looks at the sample of data above and notices that there are two people with the same surnames and initial who live at the same address.
 (i) Explain why the surname would be an unsuitable key field. *(1 mark)*
 (ii) It is decided that each employee should be given a unique number. What would be a suitable field name for this field? *(1 mark)*
 (iii) Rather than have to keep remembering the last number used, it is decided that it would be better if this number were given automatically by the computer. What type of field should be given to this field from this list: Text, Numeric, AutoNumber or Boolean? *(1 mark)*

Data handling software: the use of relational databases and spreadsheets

In this section you will be looking at the two different types of database: the flat file database and the relational database.

Flat file and relational databases

Computerized databases may be divided into two types: the limited flat file database suitable for only a few applications, and the much more comprehensive and flexible relational database.

Flat file databases

Flat file databases for storing data are little more than a computerized card box file where a single card is used to store one record. A record is simply the complete information about a product, employee, student, order, etc. An item of information such as surname, date of birth, product number, product name, in a record is called a field.

Flat files only contain one table of data. This limits their use to simple data storage and retrieval systems such as storing a list of names, addresses, phone numbers, etc. Flat files are unsuited to business applications where much more flexibility is needed.

This flat file has been set up using spreadsheet software to analyse answers to questionnaires about recycling. Each row represents a record (i.e., the recycling details for one household, and the column headings (in bold) represent the field names with the data in columns below.

Simple flat files, which are the same as databases with only one table, can be set up in either specialist database or spreadsheet software. If the data needs a lot of further analysis, then it is easier to set it up using spreadsheet software.

The problems with flat file systems

Flat files store all the data in a single table. The disadvantages of using a flat file are:

- Data redundancy. There is often a lot of duplicate data needed in the table. Time is wasted re-typing the same data and more data is stored than needs to be, making the whole database larger.
- When a record is deleted a lot of data that is still useful, may be deleted.

	A	B	C	D	E	F	G	H	I	J	K	L	M	N	O	P
1	QNo	Title	Initial	Surname	Street	Postcode	No_in_house	Type	Garder	Paper	Bottles	Cans	Shoes	Carriers	Compost	Junk_mail
2	1	Mr	A	Ahmed	18 Rycroft Road	L12 5DR	1	S	S	Y	Y	Y	Y	Y	Y	10
3	2	Miss	R	Lee	1 Woodend Drive	L35 8RW	4	D	M	Y	Y	Y	N	N	Y	4
4	3	Mr	W	Johnson	42 Lawson Drive	L12 3SA	2	S	S	Y	Y	Y	N	N	Y	0
5	4	Mrs	D	Gower	12 Coronation Street	L13 8JH	3	T	Y	Y	N	N	N	N	N	9
6	5	Dr	E	Fodder	124 Inkerman Street	L13 5RT	5	T	Y	N	N	N	N	N	N	12
7	6	Miss	R	Fowler	109 Pagemoss Lane	L13 4ED	3	S	S	N	N	N	N	N	N	5
8	7	Ms	V	Green	34 Austin Close	L24 8UH	2	D	S	N	N	N	N	N	N	7
9	8	Mr	K	Power	66 Clough Road	L35 6GH	1	T	Y	Y	Y	Y	N	N	N	7
10	9	Mrs	M	Roth	43 Fort Avenue	L12 7YH	3	S	M	N	N	Y	N	N	N	7
11	10	Mrs	O	Crowther	111 Elmshouse Road	L24 7FT	3	S	M	Y	Y	Y	N	N	N	8
12	11	Mrs	O	Low	93 Aspes Road	L12 6FG	1	T	Y	Y	Y	Y	Y	N	N	11
13	12	Mrs	P	Crowley	98 Forgate Street	L12 6TY	5	T	Y	Y	Y	Y	N	N	N	15
14	13	Mr	J	Preston	123 Edgehill Road	L12 6TH	6	T	Y	Y	Y	N	N	N	N	2
15	14	Mr	J	Quirk	12 Leopold Drive	L24 6ER	4	S	M	Y	Y	N	N	N	Y	2
16	15	Mr	H	Etheridge	13 Cambridge Avenue	L12 5RE	2	S	L	Y	N	Y	N	N	Y	5
17	16	Miss	E	James	35 Speke Hall Road	L24 5VF	2	S	L	Y	N	Y	N	N	Y	5
18	17	Mrs	W	Jones	49 Abbeyfield Drive	L13 7FR	1	D	M	N	N	N	N	N	Y	5
19																

A flat file uses a single table of data set up like this.

Data handling software: the use of relational databases and spreadsheets *continued*

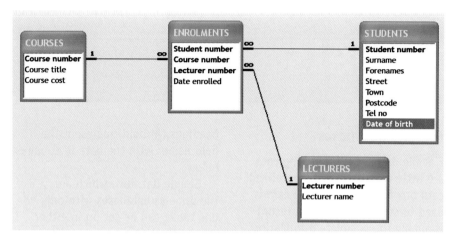

▲ This shows the way the data is stored in a relational database. There are four tables in this database (represented by the boxes) and the links (correctly called relationships) are drawn as lines between the tables.

Relational databases

In a relational database, we do not store all the data in a single file or table. Instead the data is stored in several tables with links between the tables to enable the data in the separate tables to be combined if needed.

To understand this look at the following example.

A tool hire business hires tools such as ladders, cement mixers, scaffolding, chain saws, etc., to tradesmen. The following would need to be stored:

• data about the tools
• data about the customers
• data about the rentals.

Three tables are needed to store this data and these can be called:

• Tools
• Customers
• Rentals

If the above were stored in a single table, in other words using a flat file, there would be a problem. As all the details of tools, customers and rentals are stored together there would be no record of a tool unless it had been hired by a customer. There would be no record of a customer unless they had hired a tool at the time.

In the flat file there would be data redundancy because customer address details are stored many times for each time they hire a tool. This means the same data appears more than once in the one table.

Hence there are serious limitations in using flat files and this is why data is best stored in a relational database where the data is held in several tables with links between the tables.

Tables consist of columns and rows organized in the following way:

• The rows apart from the first row represent the records in the database.
• The columns contain the database fields.
• The first row contains the field names.

Questions F

1 (a) What is meant by a flat file database? (*1 mark*)

(b) What is meant by a relational database? (*1 mark*)

(c) Describe an application where a flat file database would be suitable. (*2 marks*)

2 Databases are of two types: flat file and relational.

(a) Describe **two** differences between a flat file database and a relational database. (*2 marks*)

(b) A dress hire company needs to store details of dresses, customers and rentals. They want to store these details in a database.
Which type of database do you suggest and give **two** reasons for your answer. (*3 marks*)

Data handling software: emerging data handling applications

You will find out

▷ **About emerging data handling applications**

In this section you will be looking at emerging data handling applications. All these applications use large stores of data and/or modelling techniques to produce useful information.

Financial forecasting

Businesses often need to make predictions that will help them plan. Businesses create models that examine certain financial aspects of the business. For example, they can look at the model to check that they have enough money coming into the business each month to meet their expenses.

Here are some examples of financial models:

- sales analysis
- break-even analysis
- modelling the effects of inflation
- working out depreciation
- working out the value of a portfolio of investments
- profit and loss account
- cash flow forecast
- sales staff commissions
- breakdown of profit from each customer
- costings
- stock analysis.

Weather forecasting

Weather data such as wind speed, air temperature, ground temperature and humidity are logged continuously from remote weather stations throughout the world. The data collected from these stations are relayed back to the meteorological office. The data is then processed along with the data from satellite pictures to produce a weather forecast. The program that does this is a model. It uses the variables and lots of rules to try to predict what the weather is likely to be in the future.

Flight simulators

You can buy flight simulator software for your computer. Obviously you will not get the feel of a real plane but it will give you some idea what the controls are. Real flight simulators move in the same way as the plane, so you can get the feel of the plane accelerating along the runway, climbing and descending, etc.

As well as the rules that make up the models being used there are also some inputs needed into the system such as:

- type of weather (fine, snow, fog, thunderstorms, rain, etc.)
- the type of aircraft
- the total weight of the aircraft, as this will affect the plane's performance
- any problems with the aircraft (e.g., loss of power from an engine, undercarriage not coming down, etc.)
- the terrain (i.e., what the ground looks like from the plane)
- whether it is day or night
- the approach scenery to airport.

Expert systems for decision making

Expert systems are systems that behave in a similar way to a human expert in a certain field. Just like human experts, they can make decisions based on the vast amount of data they store. Like models, expert systems use rules and these rules are used with the set of data to make a decision.

Expert systems are used:

- for making medical diagnoses or giving medical advice
- finding where best to find minerals such as metal ore based on geological data
- for giving tax and financial advice to companies.

Questions G

1 (a) Explain what is meant by an expert system. (*1 mark*)

(b) Name **two** jobs that are likely to use an expert system. (*2 mark*)

(c) For **one** of the jobs mentioned in part (b) describe how the expert system would be used. (*1 mark*)

2 Flight simulators are used to train pilots.

(a) Explain what is meant by a flight simulator. (*2 marks*)

(b) Give **one** advantage in using a fight simulator to train pilots. (*1 marks*)

Questions

 Test yourself

The following notes summarize this topic. The notes are incomplete because they have words missing. Using the words in the list below, copy out and complete sentences A to O, underlining the words that you have inserted. Each word may be used more than once.

data type   validation   range   relational   presence

fields   key field   file   check digits   format

verification   record   expert   flat file

A A _____ is a field in a database that is unique to a particular record.

B The detail relating to a single thing or person in a database is called a _____ .

C A record consists of many _____.

D A collection of records is called a _____.

E A check performed by the software to make sure that the data being entered is allowable is called a _____ check.

F _____ means checking that the data being entered perfectly matches the source of the data.

G An important field that has been left blank and should have data entered into it can be detected using a _____ check.

H A validation check that would detect when letters of the alphabet had been entered into a field that was restricted to numbers would be a _____ check.

I Making sure that a number lies between an upper and lower value can be done using a _____ check.

J _____ checks are used on codes such as item code so as to make sure that the code being entered conforms to the correct combination of characters (i.e., letters and numbers).

K Double entry of data and proof reading are examples of _____.

L _____ are added to the end of account numbers or International Standard Book Numbers (ISBNs) to ensure that the original number has been entered correctly.

M A system that mimics a human expert and is used to help with decision making is called an _____ system.

N A simple database created using spreadsheet software and containing all the data in one table is called a _____ database.

O A database where the data is held in two or more tables with links between the tables is called a _____ database.

Examination style questions

1 When Year 7 students join the senior school, a form is filled in by their parents. The details on the form are then typed into a computer. The details are verified after typing.

Explain briefly, how the details may be verified. *(2 marks)*

2 A person's date of birth is entered into a database. State **three** things the validation program could check regarding this date as part of the validation. *(3 marks)*

3 When a new member joins a fitness club they are given a membership number. The membership number is made up in the following way:
> Customer date of birth as six numbers.
> The final two figures of the year in which the customer joins the fitness club.
> A letter which is either J or S depending on whether they are a junior or senior member.

(a) Write down the membership number for a junior member who joined the club in 2010 and was born on 21/05/98. *(1 mark)*

(b) When the membership number is entered into the database, it is validated.
Explain what is meant by data validation. *(2 marks)*

(c) Two examples of data validation are:
> range check
> format check.

Explain how these two methods could be used on the **membership number** field described above. *(2 marks)*

(d) It would be better if the membership number were unique to a particular member.
  (i) Explain why the method described might not result in a unique membership number. *(1 mark)*
  (ii) Explain **one** problem not having a unique membership number might cause. *(2 marks)*

4 The diagram shows a simple spreadsheet that a student uses to help budget her money.

	A	B	C	D	E
1					
2	Rent	£32.50			
3	Food	£13.00			
4	Electricity	£2.50			
5	Phone	£1.50			
6	Gas	£4.00			
7	Entertainment	£15.00			
8	Total				
9					
10					
11					
12					
13					

(a) Write down the contents of cell A4. *(1 mark)*
(b) Write down the contents of cell B7. *(1 mark)*
(c) Put a tick in the boxes next to those formulas that would correctly work out the total of her expenditure when placed in cell B8. *(2 marks)*

Formula	Tick if formula gives correct total
=B2+B3+B4+B5+B6+B7+B8	☐
+A2+A3+A4+A5+A6+A7	☐
=sum(B2:B7)	☐
=sum(A2:A7)	☐
=B2+B3+B4+B5+B6+B7	☐

5 The manager of a tool hire company wishes to use a relational database to help keep track of the business. The database stores the data in three tables, called: Tools, Customers and Rentals.

(a) Explain what a relational database is and what its main features are. *(5 marks)*

(b) What are the main advantages to **this** manager in storing the data in a relational database rather than a flat file database? *(3 marks)*

Questions *continued*

	A	B	C	D	E	F	G
1	Forename	Surname	Exam 1	Exam 2	Exam 3	Exam 4	Total
2	Amy	Hughes	56	34	67	78	
3	Jack	Danniels	56	58	45	56	
4	John	Harris	77	89	77	89	
5	Asif	Khan	57	79	75	78	
6	Ian	Handley	33	75	85	88	
7	Daisy	Doyle	74	45	88	90	
8	Jane	Adams	90	89	55	87	
9	Danielle	Prescott	87	90	77	77	
10	Harry	Sumner	99	100	88	90	
11	Jane	Hughes	45	56	65	66	
12	Adam	Jackson	55	50	45	54	
13							
14							
15	Average mark for all pupils						

6 A teacher has produced the spreadsheet above that records the marks in four examinations and works out the total mark.

   (a) Which of the following formulas would correctly give the total in cell G2? *(1 mark)*

   A =SUM(C2:C12)

   B =C2+D2+E2+F2+G2

   C =SUM(C2:F2)

   D =SUM(C2*F2)

   (b) Give a suitable formula to put into cell D15 to calculate the average of the numbers in column G. *(1 mark)*

   (c) Which cell formatting feature has been used in column A? *(1 mark)*

   (d) The text 'Average mark for all pupils' has cell formatting applied to it. Give the name of the cell formatting used. *(1 mark)*

   (e) Give **two** advantages of using spreadsheet software rather than working out the totals using pen, paper and a calculator. *(2 marks)*

7 Most schools now use databases to store details about each pupil. The table shows some of the fieldnames and data types stored in one pupil database.

Fieldname	Data type
UniquePupilNumber	Number
Firstname	
Surname	Text
FirstLineAddress	Text
SecondLineAddress	Text
Postcode	
LandlineNo	Text
DateOfBirth	Date
FreeSchoolMeals(Y/N)	

   (a) Give the most appropriate data types for the fields:
   Firstname
   Postcode
   FreeSchoolMeals(Y/N) *(1 mark)*

   (b) Give the names of **three** other fields that are likely to be used in this database. *(3 marks)*

   (c) Explain which field is used as the key field in the database and why such a field is necessary. *(2 marks)*

   (d) It is important that the data contained in this database is accurate. Describe how **two** different errors could occur when data is entered into this database. *(2 marks)*

   (e) Explain how the errors you have mentioned in part (d) could be detected or prevented. *(2 marks)*

8 A store keeps details about their customers and their orders in an information handling system. Part of the data in this system is shown below:

Customer number	Name	Item code	Size	Cost	Delivery
2314	J. Hughes	464	Small	£290	N
9819	D. Wong	255	Large	£767	Y
1311	C. Khled	747	Small	£239	N
8276	K. Lee	299	Small	£200	Y
9223	F. Smith	108	Large	£823	Y

   (a) Give the names of **two** key fields used in the above table. *(2 marks)*

   (b) There is one 'Boolean' field in this database. Give the name of it. *(1 mark)*

   (c) Give the names of **two** other fields that could be sensibly used in this table other than customer name, customer address and customer telephone number. *(2 marks)*

   (d) Give the name of a suitable validation check that could be used for the Size field and describe how it can reduce errors. *(2 marks)*

   (e) The store offers free delivery on all items with a cost greater than £200.
   How many of the customers shown would qualify for the free delivery? *(1 mark)*

Exam support

Worked example 1

A school keeps details of all its students on a computer. Part of the data is shown below. The data is structured in fields, records and files.

Student_Number	Surname	Forename	Date of birth	Form
1211	Lee	Jaccck	12/11/99	11T
1225	Hughes	Amy	34/08/09	11G

(a) Explain the terms:

  (i) Field   (ii) Record   (iii) File   *(3 marks)*

(b) The data contained in the above structure contains two mistakes. One of these mistakes could have been discovered by a verification process and the other mistake by a validation process.

Complete a table as below by explaining what the mistake is and whether verification or validation could have detected the mistake and describe a method that could be used to prevent the error. *(6 marks)*

Description of mistake	Discovered by verification or validation?	Description of method that could have been used to prevent the mistake

---

Student answer 1

(a) **(i)** *The information about a thing or person.*   **(iii)** *The whole lot of information about a thing or person.*

  (ii) *A row in the table.*

(b)

Description of mistake	Discovered by verification or validation?	Description of method that could have been used to prevent the mistake
Wrong date of birth 34/08/09 is impossible as the days in August only go up to 31	*Validation*	*Range check on the days in the date to ensure it is equal to or less than 31*
Forename has wrong name entered – Jaccck should be spelt Jack	*Verification*	*Use a spellchecker to make sure that the name is spelt correctly*

▲ Examiner's comment

(a) **(i)** The student has defined a record here instead of a field. No marks.

  (ii) This answer is a bit brief but worth one mark. A more complete answer would be to say that it is the details about a person, thing or transaction. An example would be the detail about one student which is a row in the table.

  (iii) This statement is a bit vague so no mark is given. If they had given an example such as a collection of all the records about students in the school, then this would have been clearer.

(b) The first row of answers are all correct. The last answer about a range check is OK but if you allocate a data type of Date to a field then you cannot enter an impossible date.

The second row contains a typing error and it is not appropriate to use spellcheckers with the names of people. The first two answers are correct for a mark each but the last answer gains no marks.
(6 marks out of 9)

END-OF-TOPIC REVIEW

Exam support *continued*

Student answer 2

(a) (i) *A field is an item of data or a fact about a student. Date of birth is an example of a field.*

(ii) *A record is a collection of fields about a person or thing. Here it is information about a particular student.*

(iii) *A file is a complete collection of records and would be the complete records of every student in the school.*

(b)

Description of mistake	Discovered by verification or validation?	Description of method that could have been used to prevent the mistake
Incorrect date of birth 34/08/09 This is an impossible date	Validation	Use Date format for the field. Once this is set, the computer will not allow an incorrect date to be entered
Typing error Jaccck should be spelt Jack.	Verification	Use a visual check Check by reading the entered data on the screen and correct any mistakes

▲ Examiner's comment

(a) (i) This is a good answer and notice the way the student has referred to the data in the table as an example. One mark for this.

(ii) Another good answer gains another mark.

(iii) Again another mark.

(b) All the parts to this answer are clear and the student has used and understood the terminology. Full marks are given for this part.

(9 marks out of 9)

Examiner's answers

(a) (i) One mark for a definition such as:

A field is an item of data such as surname, date of birth, etc.

(ii) One mark for a definition such as:

A record is a collection of fields about a person or thing.

A line in the table about one particular student is a record.

(iii) One mark for a definition such as:

A file is a collection of records that forms the complete set of information about a thing or person.

The details of all the records of all the students in a school is a file.

(b) One mark for each correct answer in the table to a maximum of six marks.

Description of mistake	Discovered by verification or validation?	Description of method that could have been used to prevent the mistake
Invalid date/wrong number of days for the month/cannot have more than 31 days in a month	Validation	Use Date format/set data type to Date Use a range check/restrict day to 31 or less
Typing error/transcription error Jaccck should be Jack	Verification	Use a visual check/proof read/get person who is the data subject to check their record

Worked example 2

Yasmin has started work after leaving university and has to live away from home. She has recorded her wages and costs in a spreadsheet and this is shown here.

	A	B	C	D	E	F	G	H	I	J
1	Month	Wages	Electricity	Gas	Phone	Rent	Clothes	Food	Total costs	Money left over
2	Jan	£1,500	£60	£55	£62	£210	£40	£600	£1,027	£473
3	Feb	£1,520	£60	£55	£65	£210	£40	£600	£1,030	£490
4	Mar	£1,550	£60	£55	£64	£210	£40	£600	£1,029	£521
5	Apr	£1,550	£60	£55	£50	£210	£40	£600	£1,015	£535
6	May	£1,680	£60	£55	£47	£210	£40	£600	£1,012	£668
7	Jun	£1,690	£60	£55	£47	£210	£40	£600	£1,012	£678
8	Jul	£1,730	£60	£55	£53	£210	£40	£600	£1,018	£712
9	Aug	£1,742	£60	£55	£54	£210	£40	£600	£1,019	£723
10	Sep	£1,800	£60	£55	£62	£210	£40	£600	£1,027	£773
11	Oct	£1,800	£60	£55	£44	£210	£40	£600	£1,009	£791
12	Nov	£1,800	£60	£55	£39	£210	£40	£600	£1,004	£796
13	Dec	£1,745	£60	£55	£53	£210	£40	£600	£1,018	£727
14										

(a) Which one of the following formulas could be used to work out the **Total costs** in cell
    I2? *(1 mark)*

    A =SUM(I2:I13)
    B =I2+I3+I4+I6+I7+I8
    C =SUM(C2:H2)
    D =C2+D2+E2+F2+G2+H2+I2

(b) Give a suitable formula that could be entered into cell J2 to work out the money Yasmin has
    over at the end of the month. *(1 mark)*

(c) The cells apart from cells in column A and row 1 have been formatted.

    Which of the following types of cell formatting have been used for these cells? *(1 mark)*

    A Euros
    B Calculation
    C Currency
    D Right align

(d) Labels are important in spreadsheets. Give the cell reference of a cell containing a
    label. *(1 mark)*

(e) Give two advantages of Yasmin using a spreadsheet such as this to help her budget her
    money. *(2 marks)*

Exam support *continued*

Student answer 1

(a) D

(b) B2–I2

(c) C

(d) A1

(e) It is quicker

It is more efficient

◀ Examiner's comment

(a) When adding up cells you do not include the cell where the answer is to be put so this answer is wrong.

(b) The student has forgotten to put the equals sign in front of this formula (i.e. =B2-I2). This small point has cost this student a mark here.

(c) This is correct so one mark here.

(d) A label is any cell that describes data on the spreadsheet so this is correct and gains one mark.

(e) This is a typical answer given by a weak student. The student needs to say in what way is it quicker and in what way is it more efficient. No marks for either of these answers.

(2 marks out of 6)

Student answer 2

(a) C=SUM(C2:H2)

(b) =B2–I2

(c) C Currency

(d) Row 1

(e) Provided the calculations have been set up correctly and tested, the formulas will always produce a correct calculation.

When one of the numbers in the spreadsheet is changed, the cells that depend on the changed cell will recalculate automatically.

◀ Examiner's comment

(a) This is correct so one mark here.

(b) This is correct so one mark here.

(c) This is correct so one mark here.

(d) All the cells in row 1 do contain labels but the question asks for a cell reference so this is an incorrect answer so no marks.

(e) These are both very good answers and worth a mark each.

(5 marks out of 6)

Examiner's answers

(a) One mark for the letter, formula or both
(i.e. C = SUM(C2:H2))

(b) One mark for a correct formula which must include the equals sign

(i.e. =B2–I2)

(c) One mark for C Currency

(d) One mark for any cell reference in row 1 or column A. It must be a cell reference and not a column letter or row number.

(e) One mark for each of two advantages of a spreadsheet such as:

- If set up correctly, the formulas will always produce a correct calculation.
- Automatic recalculation when numbers are changed in the spreadsheet.
- Once the spreadsheet has been set up it can be reused for different years by putting in different data.
- The data can easily be represented pictorially by getting the spreadsheet to produce graphs and charts.
- You can change the information in the spreadsheet in order to make and test 'what if' scenarios.

END-OF-TOPIC REVIEW

Summary mind maps

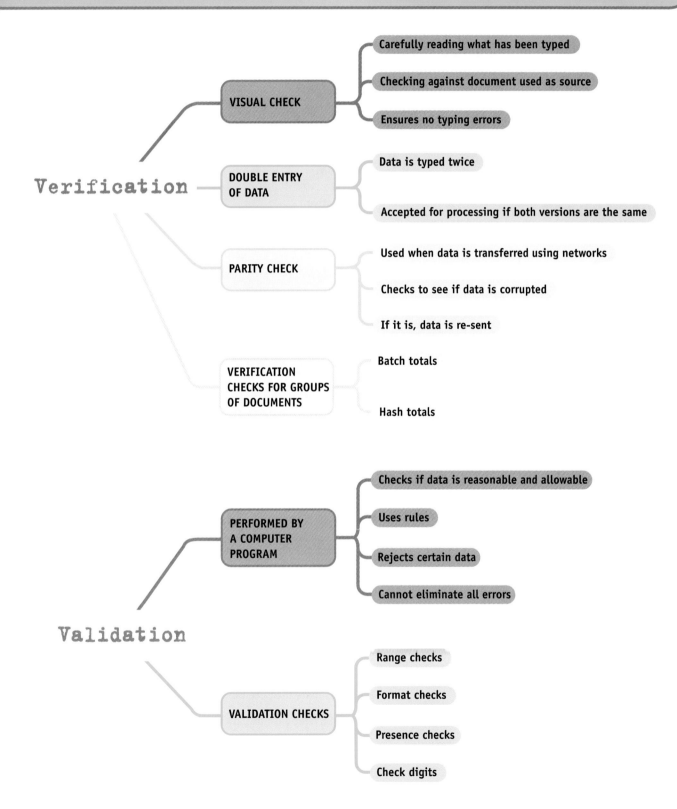

Verification

VISUAL CHECK
- Carefully reading what has been typed
- Checking against document used as source
- Ensures no typing errors

DOUBLE ENTRY OF DATA
- Data is typed twice
- Accepted for processing if both versions are the same

PARITY CHECK
- Used when data is transferred using networks
- Checks to see if data is corrupted
- If it is, data is re-sent

VERIFICATION CHECKS FOR GROUPS OF DOCUMENTS
- Batch totals
- Hash totals

Validation

PERFORMED BY A COMPUTER PROGRAM
- Checks if data is reasonable and allowable
- Uses rules
- Rejects certain data
- Cannot eliminate all errors

VALIDATION CHECKS
- Range checks
- Format checks
- Presence checks
- Check digits

Summary mind maps *continued*

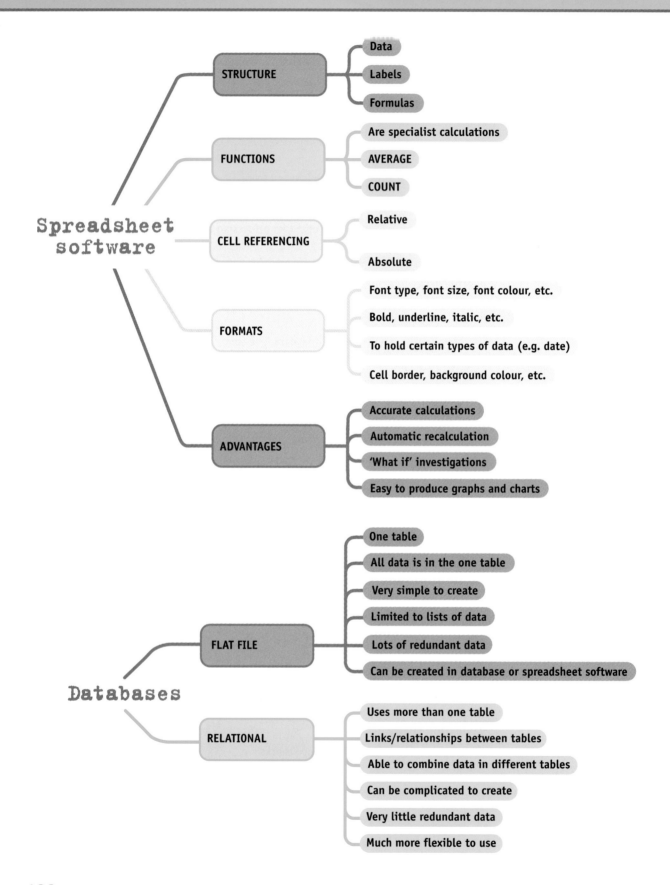

Topic 5

Keeping data safe and secure

The key concepts covered in this topic are:

- Backups and archiving

- Secure and safe practices in the use of ICT

- Appropriate user security methods and devices

- Malicious software and the damage it can cause

- The procedures users can take to minimize the risks of damage caused by malicious software

- How to avoid the loss/ disclosure of personal data to unauthorized users

- Data encryption and why it is used

There are many different ways in which data can be lost in an ICT system, so it is important that this data can be recovered. Backup copies of data should be kept.

In order to keep data secure, especially if it is personal data, special practices should be put in place. Malicious software is software that is designed to do damage to ICT systems and it is important that this software is prevented from entering systems.

In this topic you will be looking at all of these along with the methods that can be taken to prevent others from accessing any data that needs to be kept private.

Contents

Backups and archiving, secure and safe practices

You will find out

▷ **About backups and archiving**

▷ **About secure and safe practices in the use of ICT**

Data can be lost or destroyed in a number of ways. It can happen by accident, for example by a user saving an old version over the latest version of a file. Another accident could be a fire, flood, etc. Data can also be destroyed deliberately. An employee within the organization, or a hacker, could destroy data deliberately.

It is therefore necessary to keep copies of data for security purposes. These copies of data are called backup copies or backups for short. Old copies of files are also taken so that if they are needed they can be put onto the system. These old copies are called archive copies. In this section you will be looking at backups and archive copies.

Backups

ICT systems store huge amounts of data and this must be protected against loss. Backups are copies of the original data and programs that are kept for security purposes in case the original data or programs are damaged, destroyed or lost.

Backup copies of the data must be kept and procedures must be put in place to ensure that data can be easily recovered from the backups. Backup procedures are needed to:

- specify who is responsible for taking the backups
- specify how often the backups are taken (every hour, every day, etc.)
- state what media is used for storing backups
- specify where the backup copies are kept (e.g., fireproof safe, kept off-site, transferred using the Internet)
- specify how any data can be recovered from the backups.

Archiving

Backups are taken in case the original files are lost or become damaged. Archives are those files that are no longer needed in the short term but need to be kept for future reference.

▲ Backup procedures must specify the media used – in this case a CD.

Rather than clog the computer up with lots of files (which will make it slower), it is better to save those files you want to archive onto removable media such as CD or DVD and then store these in a safe place.

Keeping backups and archive copies safe

Backup and archive copies are kept safe by:

- using removable media
- placing them in a fireproof safe
- keeping them away from the computer because the thief may steal the backup copies as well as the computer
- removing them off site – this is in case there is a fire or the building is destroyed.

The use of backing storage media

Backups and archives need to be stored on removable media. By moving the media to another location, if the computer is stolen or destroyed by fire, earthquake, etc., then the backing store containing the backups can be used to re-create the data.

Backups and archive copies can be kept on the following media:

- portable magnetic hard disk drives
- optical media (e.g., recordable CD or DVD)
- magnetic tape/magnetic cartridge
- pen/flash drives, sometimes called memory sticks.

Secure and safe practices in the use of ICT

There are certain things you can do to minimize the likelihood of data being lost and these are outlined here.

Protecting data from accidental destruction

Accidents can happen in all sorts of ways. There are ways to protect the data from many of them and these include:

- User errors – untrained users may accidentally delete files or save old versions of files over new versions losing work in the process. Proper training will tell novice users about how to prevent this happening.
- Fire – use smoke alarms to detect fires early and minimize damage. Ensure wiring is checked for safety and do not overload sockets.
- Flood – with global warming this may be more likely to happen. If possible, computer systems should not be situated on the ground floor.
- Power loss – this can cause loss of data. Use an auxiliary power supply that comes on automatically should the mains power be lost.
- Any new software should be thoroughly tested to prevent program crashes, which can lose data.

▲ Natural disasters can destroy ICT systems.

Protecting data from deliberate damage

Deliberate damage can come from within or from outside the organization. For example, hackers may access a network via the Internet and cause damage to data.

There are a number of ways to protect data from deliberate damage:

- Ensure that unauthorized staff cannot access the data.
- Ensure that computers cannot be stolen (e.g., attach computers to the desk, use burglar alarms, use keypad or biometric methods to ensure unauthorized access to rooms does not take place, etc.).
- Use CCTV cameras to prevent theft and also to keep an eye on employees.
- Use latest virus checkers to prevent viruses entering the system and causing damage to data.
- Use firewalls to prevent hackers gaining access to data via the Internet and causing damage.
- Use user-IDs/usernames and passwords to prevent unauthorized access to computers.

- Use biometric methods (e.g., fingerprinting, retinal scanning, face recognition, etc.) to prevent unauthorized access to buildings, rooms and computers.
- Select staff that use computers carefully.
- Do not position computers where they can be seen by passers-by.

▲ It is best if computers cannot be seen through a ground floor window.

Questions A

1 The network manager for a school is in charge of the security of the network. They are responsible for taking regular backups.
   (a) Explain what is meant by backups. (*2 marks*)
   (b) Give **one** reason why it is essential to take regular backups. (*1 mark*)
   (c) Give **two** examples of backup media that can be used to store backups. (*1 mark*)

2 Damage to data can be accidental or deliberate.
   (a) Give **one** way in which data may be damaged accidentally. (*1 mark*)
   (b) Give **one** way in which data may be damaged deliberately. (*1 mark*)
   (c) It is better if backup copies of data are stored off-site. Explain what this means and explain why it is better to store them off-site. (*2 marks*)

Extension activity

A home computer user has lots of data that they would not want to lose permanently such as family photographs, their music collection, contact details for friends and family, etc.

Use the Internet to investigate the range of backing storage devices and media that can be used for backups. Produce a table showing details such as name, price, main advantages, etc.

Appropriate user security methods and devices

You will find out

▷ **About appropriate user security methods and devices**

In this section you will be looking at what can be done to prevent unauthorized access and how it is possible to restrict authorized users to only certain files. This section also covers how monitoring ICT is important in order to prevent and detect security breaches.

User security methods and devices

User-IDs/usernames: identifying the user to the system

A user-ID or username is series of characters that is used to identify a certain user to the network. The person who looks after the network will use this to allocate space on the network for the user. It is also used by the network to give the user access to certain files.

The network manager can also keep track of what files each user is accessing for security reasons.

Passwords: preventing unauthorized access to the system

A password is a string of characters (letters, numbers and punctuation marks) that the user selects. Only the user will know what the password is.

When the user enters the password, it will not be shown on the screen. Only on entry of the correct password will the user be allowed access to the network.

Encryption

If a computer or network is connected to the Internet then it could be hacked into. The hackers could simply intercept and read email or they could alter data or collect personal details and credit card numbers to commit fraud. Encryption is used to protect data from prying eyes by scrambling data as it travels over the Internet. Encryption is also used when saving personal data onto laptops or removable storage devices. If any of these gets lost or stolen then the data cannot be read.

Encryption should be used for:

- sending credit card details such as card numbers, etc., over the Internet
- online banking
- sending payment details (bank details such as sort code numbers, account numbers, etc.)
- confidential emails
- sending data between computers on a network where confidentiality is essential
- storing sensitive personal information on laptops and portable devices and media.

Restricting physical access

You can restrict a person from entering a building or room containing computers using keypads, magnetic strip card systems, electronic cards and biometric scanning systems. Biometric scanning systems can be used rather than usernames and passwords to allow

▲ Usernames and passwords are an essential part of network security.

▲ When encpyted data is sent to a person they need a key/password to read it.

access. Retinal scanning uses the unique pattern on the back of the eye to recognize a person, and fingerprint scanning uses the unique pattern on a person's finger to identify them.

▲ Keypads are used to prevent unauthorized access to rooms containing computers.

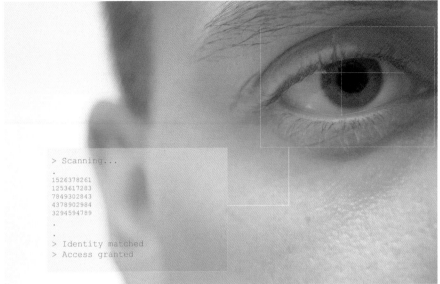

> Scanning...

1526378261
1253617283
7849302843
4378902984
3294594789

.
.
.
> Identity matched
> Access granted

▶ Magnetic strip cards can be used to restrict access to rooms and computers.

▲ Retinal scanning is used to restrict access to rooms.

▶ This fingerprint reader is used to prevent unauthorized access to computers.

Biometric methods have the main advantage in that there is nothing to remember such as a card or a code.

Restricting access to data

Keeping unauthorized people out of rooms containing computers will not always protect the data. Data can be accessed illegally by people who have legal access to the computer and only some of the data. Data can be accessed illegally by hackers who use the Internet to access the data.

Hierarchy of passwords

Access to certain files can be controlled at certain levels using a series of passwords. The higher up in the organization a person is, the more files they can gain access to and do things with. For example, a school secretary may access the files about teachers' names and addresses so that letters can be sent to them but they may not be allowed to alter the data. A head teacher would be allowed access to the files containing information about teachers' salaries for budgeting purposes but other staff may not be allowed access to this information.

Access rights

Access rights are given to staff by the network manager. These rights allow certain staff to access only certain files. For example, a member of staff who deals with customer orders can have access to those files such as the customer file needed to perform their job. This member of staff would not be given access rights to the personnel or payroll files.

In addition to this, access rights determine what you can do with the data in the files you have access to. For example:

- Read only access – you can only look at the data and not alter it.
- Read/write – you can view and alter data.
- Create – you can create new records.
- Delete – you can delete records.

Encryption

Should encrypted data be accessed by someone illegally or without proper permission to view it, the encrypted data will be meaningless.

Monitoring

Network software monitors the network for unusual activity. For example, if a user were trying to enter using lots of different passwords they would be locked out of the network.

Networks monitor unusual activity in accounts. For example, if a large credit card transaction were to take place on your account to pay for goods abroad, they may suspend the transaction until they have spoken to you.

107

Appropriate user security methods and devices *continued*

Transaction logs

When transactions (bits of business) are performed on the computer, there may not be any paperwork to go with the system. So that the system can be audited (i.e. checked), the software will have a function built in that provides an audit trail. The audit trail provides evidence of what has happened in the system. For example, if a record has been deleted, it will provide evidence of the record before the deletion along with the date and time and the name of the member of staff who performed the deletion and even the reason the record was deleted. Transaction logs are a deterrent to people who might be thinking of committing computer fraud, as they will know they are likely to be found out. It also provides evidence for the police to prosecute computer fraudsters.

Transaction logs deter computer fraudsters.

Questions B

1 Personal data held on computers is often encrypted.
   (a) Explain what encrypted means. (*2 marks*)
   (b) Give **one** reason why data is encrypted. (*1 mark*)

2 One method of protecting data against damage or loss is to restrict physical access to the computers.

   Describe **two** methods of controlling physical access to computers. (*2 marks*)

3 User-IDs and passwords are used to restrict access to data files held on networks.

   Explain the difference between a user-ID and a password. (*2 marks*)

4 Transaction logs are used to help prevent fraud.
   (a) Explain what is meant by a transaction log. (*2 marks*)
   (b) Describe **one** reason why a transaction log will help prevent fraud. (*1 mark*)

Extension activity 1

Produce a poster entitled 'Everything you need to know about passwords' that will alert users about the need to take certain precautions and actions when selecting and using passwords.

Extension activity 2

Identity theft is a real problem for all computer users. It puts off many people from banking online or buying goods and services over the Internet where they have to input their card details.

Perform some research using the Internet so you can write an article in your own words entitled 'What we can all do to protect ourselves from identity theft'.

You will need to mention the following in your article along with your own ideas of what you feel the readers need to know:

- What identity theft is
- The consequences of identity theft
- Phishing
- What you can do to ensure that you are not the next victim

Malicious software, damage and how to minimize risk of damage

▷ **About malicious software and the damage it can cause**

▷ **About the procedures users can take to minimize risk of damage caused by malicious software**

Certain software can be put on your computer without your permission or knowledge and it can do damage to your system. This software is called malicious software or malware for short. For example, it may erase programs or data, it may make your computer run slowly or crash or it may compromise the security of your computer and allow hackers to access your data.

In this section you will be looking at the different types of malicious software and the types of damage it can cause and also the steps you can take in order to minimize the risk of damage.

Viruses

Viruses pose a major threat to ICT systems. A virus is a program that replicates (i.e., copies) itself automatically and usually carries with it some payload that may cause damage. Once a computer or media has a virus copied onto it, it is said to be infected. Most viruses are designed to do something apart from copying themselves. For example, they can:

- display annoying messages on the screen
- delete programs or data
- use up resources, making your computer run more slowly
- spy on your online use – for example, they can collect usernames and passwords and card numbers used to make online purchases.

One of the main problems is that viruses are being created all the time and that when you get a virus infection, it is not always clear what a new virus will do to the ICT system. Apart from the dangerous payload many viruses carry, one of the problems with viruses is the amount of time that needs to be spent sorting out the problems that they create. All computers should be equipped with a virus checker/ scanner, which is a program that is able to detect and delete these viruses. These virus checkers need to be updated regularly, as new viruses are continually being developed and would not always be detected by older versions of virus checkers.

▲ Viruses pose a major threat to all computer systems.

To prevent a virus attack install virus checking software, do not open file attachments unless you know who they are from, train staff on the problems caused by viruses, do not allow staff to attach portable drives or memory sticks unless they are scanned first and do not allow employees to download games and other unauthorized software onto their computers.

Virus scanning software should be kept up-to-date and scans should be scheduled so that they are performed automatically on a regular basis.

Key logging software

Key logging software is put onto your computer without your permission. This software records your keystrokes and allows the person who put the software on your computer to see what you have typed. In this way your passwords, credit card details and banking details can be found. Someone would have enough information to steal your identity and commit fraud.

Malicious software, damage and how to minimize risk of damage *continued*

Other malware

Malware (malicious software) can do all sorts of things and includes the following:

- Programs that alter the browser software to redirect it to certain sites for advertising.
- Programs that make it easy to take over a computer system remotely.
- Programs that use your computer without your knowledge to send spam (i.e. unwanted emails) to other computers.
- Programs that make your computer slow.
- Programs that cause your computer to unexpectedly crash.

▲ Firewalls are used to protect networks from hackers.

The procedures to minimize risks of damage

Malicious software causes lots of problems to users. It is therefore important to use procedures to minimize the risk of damage caused by this software. In this section you will be looking at what a user can do to prevent malicious software infecting their computers.

Antivirus software

It is essential that all computers have antivirus software installed that will detect and destroy viruses and other malware. It is essential that this software:

- is kept up to date – usually updates are installed automatically using the Internet
- is used to scan the computer on a regular basis.

Firewalls

Firewalls are software, hardware or both used to filter out unauthorized requests from outside users to gain access to a network. This keeps hackers out. Firewalls also filter data so that only allowable data is allowed into the system. All networks and computers that have access to the Internet should have a firewall.

How to avoid the loss/ disclosure of personal data to unauthorized users

Personal data can be lost or disclosed by:

- hackers illegally gaining access to the computer

"I know a lot of highly-confidential company secrets, so my boss made me get a firewall installed."

KEY WORDS

Malware (malicious software) software such as viruses that are designed to do damage to a computer system or cause problems for the user.

Firewall a piece of software, hardware or both that is able to protect a network from hackers.

- the computer or media containing the data being stolen.

Passwords keep hackers out and for this reason they must be chosen carefully so that they are not easily guessed and they should be kept secret from others. There are a number of steps a user can take to minimize the risk of any of the above happening and these include:

- Use physical security such as locks on doors, locks on computers, biometric methods such as fingerprinting, etc., to prevent unauthorized access to buildings/computers.
- Do not leave a computer logged on while you are not sitting at it – others could come up and access the information.
- Change your password on a regular basis.
- Never write your password down.
- Passwords should include upper and lower case letters, numbers and punctuation marks.
- Passwords must be kept private and not be disclosed to others.
- Choose a password that is not easily guessed by others (e.g., the name of a pet, your favourite football team, etc.).
- Ensure that a firewall is installed to stop hackers.
- Encrypt personal data when it is stored on a computer or on portable media.
- Encrypt personal data as it is being transferred over a network.

"For security purposes, the information should make no sense at all to spies and hackers. We'll bring in someone later to figure out what you meant."

▼ **Physical security keeps people out of your computer.**

Questions C

1 A pupil information handling system is used to hold pupil details in a school. Some of this information is personal and needs to be protected and this is done by using passwords. Staff who use the system are given access rights.
  (a) Explain what is meant by a password. *(1 mark)*
  (b) Password protocols ensure that there is no unauthorized access to the personal data held. Describe **two** things that can be done concerning passwords that will help ensure that there is no unauthorized access to data. *(2 marks)*
  (c) Explain what is meant by 'access rights'. *(2 marks)*

2 Explain briefly how each one of the following helps improve the security of a network.
  (a) User-ID *(2 marks)*
  (b) Password *(2 marks)*
  (c) Encryption *(2 marks)*

Extension activity

Use the Internet to find out more about malware (including viruses) and the sorts of things it can do to an ICT system. Produce a short set of notes on what you have found.

END-OF-TOPIC REVIEW

Questions

 Test yourself

The following notes summarize this topic. The notes are incomplete because they have words missing. Using the words in the list below, copy out and complete the sentences A to H, underlining the words that you have inserted. Each word may be used more than once.

```
file attachments    training    passwords    checker
key logging    access rights    download    firewall
```

A _____ reduces the likelihood of users making mistakes such as copying an old file over a new file, deleting the wrong file, etc.

B To protect data from deliberate damage caused by hackers illegally gaining access to a computer network via the Internet, a _____ should be used.

C In order to prevent viruses entering an ICT system, a virus _____ should be used to search for and destroy viruses.

D Users should be told not to open _____ attached to emails unless they know who they are from.

E Users should also be told not to _____ music and games off the Internet as these are often infected with viruses.

F To protect the data stored in networks, user-IDs and _____ should be used to prevent unauthorized access.

G _____ software records your keystrokes and allows the person who put the software on your computer to see what you have typed.

H _____ allow some users to just view files whilst other users to both view and change their contents.

Examination style questions

1 A network manager is worried about hacking and computer viruses.
   (a) What is meant by a computer virus? (2 marks)
   (b) What is meant by hacking? (2 marks)

2 Computer users should always make backup copies of their data.
   (a) Give **two** ways in which a computer user might lose data. (2 marks)
   (b) Explain what is meant by a backup copy. (2 marks)
   (c) Give the names of **two** storage devices or media that a home user could use for taking backup copies. (2 marks)

3 For each of the following threats, outline **two** steps that an organization can take in order to reduce the seriousness of the threat.
   (a) Fire. (2 marks)
   (b) Theft of hardware. (2 marks)
   (c) Theft of data. (2 marks)

4 Data is often encrypted when being stored or sent over the Internet.
   (a) Give the names of **two** items of data a user may send over the Internet that are often encrypted. (2 marks)
   (b) What is meant by the term encryption? (2 marks)

5 One way to protect data from malicious or unauthorized access is to make use of usernames and passwords. These usernames and passwords are entered using the keyboard before the user is allowed access to the data and programs.
   (a) Give **one** purpose of a username. (1 mark)
   (b) Give **one** purpose of a password. (1 mark)
   (c) Users have to make up their own passwords. One guideline is that the password should be a minimum of 6 characters long.
   Write **three** additional guidelines for users when creating their own passwords. (3 marks)

END-OF-TOPIC REVIEW

Exam support

Worked example

Computer viruses are a threat to computer systems.

(a) Explain what is meant by a computer virus. *(2 marks)*

(b) Give **one** thing that a computer virus might do on a computer system. *(1 mark)*

(c) Give **one** way of preventing computer viruses entering a system. *(1 mark)*

Student answer 1

(a) A program that does damage.

(b) Destroy the computer.

(c) Use McAfee to stop viruses getting into your computer.

◀ Examiner's comment

(a) This is a bit vague because it is not specific about what it does damage to. Only one mark is given for this answer.

(b) This is a typical answer given by a weak pupil. Viruses can be removed and therefore cannot be said to 'destroy' the computer. No marks for this.

(c) Brand names should never be given. So instead of McAfee they should have said 'virus checking software or virus scanner'. No marks are given for this answer.

(1 mark out of 4)

Student answer 2

(a) A mischievous program that copies itself onto your computer and does harm by messing up settings or deleting data.

(b) It can start to make your computer run slow and can also cause it to crash unexpectedly.

(c) Use virus scanning software to scan for viruses and remove them if they are found.

◀ Examiner's comment

(a) A good answer which makes it clear that it is a program that copies itself so this answer is worth two marks.

(b) Again another good answer which gains one mark.

(c) This answer is correct and gains one mark.

(4 marks out of 4)

Examiner's answers

(a) Two marks allocated in the following way:
Program that copies itself automatically *(1)* and causes damage to data or causes the computer to run slowly *(1)*.

(b) One mark for an answer such as:
- Can erase files which means the operating system software cannot be loaded *(1)*.
- Can cause the deletion of data *(1)*.
- Can cause the computer to crash *(1)*.
- Can cause the changing of settings, which causes annoyance to the user *(1)*.
- Can copy passwords and usernames and transmit these to another person *(1)*.

(c) One mark for one of the following:
- Don't open file attachments unless you know who they are from.
- Install virus scanning/checking software.
- Keep virus scanning/checking software up-to-date.
- Don't download files from unknown sources.

Summary mind maps

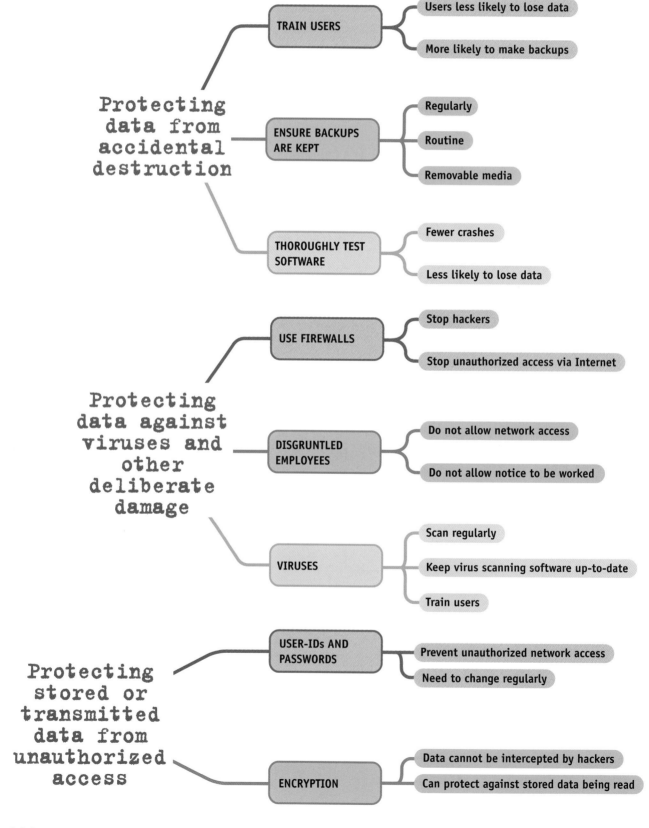

Protecting data from accidental destruction

- **TRAIN USERS**
  - Users less likely to lose data
  - More likely to make backups
- **ENSURE BACKUPS ARE KEPT**
  - Regularly
  - Routine
  - Removable media
- **THOROUGHLY TEST SOFTWARE**
  - Fewer crashes
  - Less likely to lose data

Protecting data against viruses and other deliberate damage

- **USE FIREWALLS**
  - Stop hackers
  - Stop unauthorized access via Internet
- **DISGRUNTLED EMPLOYEES**
  - Do not allow network access
  - Do not allow notice to be worked
- **VIRUSES**
  - Scan regularly
  - Keep virus scanning software up-to-date
  - Train users

Protecting stored or transmitted data from unauthorized access

- **USER-IDs AND PASSWORDS**
  - Prevent unauthorized network access
  - Need to change regularly
- **ENCRYPTION**
  - Data cannot be intercepted by hackers
  - Can protect against stored data being read

Legal, social, ethical and environmental issues when using ICT

The key concepts covered in this topic are:

- Legislation (laws) relating to the use of ICT
- Health and safety issues
- The need for good design of user interfaces
- How ICT can improve the quality of life for disabled people
- The environmental impact of digital devices
- The social and ethical implications of the electronic transmission of personal information

There are lots of legal requirements when working with ICT and you need to know about many of them. Some of these laws relate to what you can and cannot do using computers and software, while others are concerned with keeping you safe when using ICT.

In this topic you will be looking at the laws that relate to protecting data from misuse, the misuse of computers and copyright. You will also be looking at the health problems that can develop through the prolonged use of ICT equipment and what can be done to reduce the likelihood of them happening. There are also some safety issues, so in this topic you will look at the measures needed to avoid accidents.

You will also be looking at how the quality of life for people with disabilities can be improved by ICT, and the environmental impact of digital devices.

Contents

The Data Protection Act 1998

It is hard to keep information about yourself private. Everyone seems to want to store it and process it on ICT systems. Each time you fill in a form or complete a questionnaire you are supplying data about you that can then be processed by organizations. Finding out as much as they can about you enables companies to target their marketing. Privacy is a term used to describe keeping your personal details private.

▶ If personal information is wrong you could be refused a credit card or a loan.

The Data Protection Act (DPA) concerns personal data, which means data:

- about an identifiable person (i.e., the data must be about someone who can be identified by name, address, etc.)
- about someone who is living
- that is more personal than name and address (e.g., medical records, criminal record, credit history, religious or political beliefs, etc.).

There are a number of problems with organizations holding personal data:

- The personal data might be wrong, which means wrong decisions could be made.
- The organization may not take care of the personal data it holds, so others may find out about it.

Examples of the effect of wrong information:

- Your medical details could be wrong, meaning you get the wrong treatment – which could be life threatening.
- Wrong decisions might be made. For example, you could be refused a loan.
- Wrong exam results could affect you getting a job.

The provisions of the Data Protection Act 1998

ICT makes it easy for organizations and businesses to store and process information about individuals. This processing can build up a complete profile about someone. Much of this is done without the person being aware it is done.

To protect individuals against the misuse of personal data, in 1998 the government brought out a law called the Data Protection Act.

Rights of the data subject and the data holder

The person about whom the personal details are held is called the data subject by the Act. The person in the organization who is responsible for the personal data held is called the data holder.

The Data Protection Act 1998 protects individuals by placing obligations on the organizations who collect and process the data (i.e. the data holders) in the following ways.

Registration (also called notification)

It requires anyone who uses personal data to register with the Information Commissioner, who is the person who is in charge of the Act/Law. They must say what data they intend to hold and what they intend to do with it.

Individuals can see their own personal data

Anyone can apply to see the personal data held about them. Organizations have to show it and if there is any wrong information, then it must be corrected.

Data must be kept secure and up-to-date

Data subjects (the people the data is about) can sue an organization that does not keep their personal data secure.

The right for a person to claim compensation

If data is processed unlawfully by an organization then the person can take them to court and claim compensation.

The Data Protection Principles

The holder of the information has eight obligations (called Principles) placed on them by the Data Protection Act and these are summarized below.

The Data Protection Principles state that personal data should be:

1 processed fairly and lawfully
2 obtained only for specified purposes
3 adequate, relevant and not excessive
4 accurate and kept up-to-date
5 not kept any longer than is necessary
6 processed in accordance with the rights of the data subject
7 kept secure
8 not transferred to a country outside the EU unless they have a comparable data protection law.

> identity matched
> access granted

▲ Biometric methods, such as fingerprinting and retinal scanning, can be used to gain access to computer rooms.

Exemptions from the DPA

There are a number of exemptions:

- When the data is used for personal, family, household affairs or recreational use.
- Where the data is being used for preparing the text of documents (e.g., the writing of references using a word-processor).
- Where the data is used for producing accounts, wages and pensions.
- Where data is used for mail shots.
- Where the data is used by a sports or recreational club that is not a limited company.

- Where the data is used for the prevention or detection of crimes.
- Where the data is used for catching or prosecuting offenders.
- Collecting taxes or duty.
- Medical records or social worker reports.

KEY WORDS

Personal data data about a living identifiable person that is specific to that person.

Data Protection Act 1998 a law that restricts the way personal information is stored and processed on a computer.

Data holder/controller the person in the organization who is responsible for the personal data. They are responsible for making sure that the organization meets all the requirements of the Data Protection Act.

Data subject the person the personal data is about.

EXAM TIP

Many questions ask you about the Data Protection Principles, so you should try to remember them off by heart.

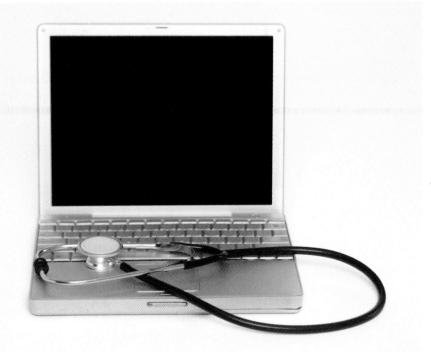

◀ You may be denied access to your medical records.

The Data Protection Act 1998 *continued*

Physical methods to prevent unauthorized access to computer systems

Physical security is all the sorts of security that prevent physical access by unauthorized people to the buildings, rooms the computers are in and the computers themselves. Good physical security will prevent theft of computers and data and some illegal access to computers.

Here are some things that can be considered:

- Locks – if entry to the building and computer rooms is restricted then it is much easier to secure the computers. Rooms should be locked with keypads, swipe cards and biometric methods (fingerprinting, retinal scanning and voice recognition).
- Clamps – these attach the computers to the desk. They will not stop a determined thief but will stop many others.
- Alarms – these include burglar alarms and alarms that are activated if a cable securing the computers is cut.
- Surveillance – CCTV cameras are positioned around the buildings and inside computer rooms to deter thieves and staff who might misuse computers.
- Location – it makes sense not to have lots of computers in public areas unless necessary. It also makes sense not to locate computer rooms on the ground floor where equipment can be seen by passers-by and easily stolen at night.

Questions A

1 Some people are not happy about organizations storing and processing personal information about them.
   (a) Explain, by giving **two** examples, what is meant by personal information. *(3 marks)*
   (b) Give **one** reason why a person might object to an organization storing personal information about them. *(2 marks)*

2 All schools use computer systems to store details about past and present students.
   Schools are required to notify the use of the personal data they hold under the terms of the Data Protection Act 1998.
   (a) Give **three** items of personal information the school is likely to store about their students. *(3 marks)*
   (b) Students in the school are given certain rights under the Data Protection Act.
   Explain **two** of these rights. *(2 marks)*
   (c) One student is worried that the personal information the school holds about them might be incorrect. Explain, with an example, how incorrect information could affect a student. *(2 marks)*

3 Physical security is needed to keep computers safe.
   (a) Explain what is meant by physical security. *(2 marks)*
   (b) Give **two** things an organization could do to ensure the physical security of its computers. *(2 marks)*

Extension activity

Find out more about the DPA by accessing the Information Commissioner's Office website at http://www.ico.gov.uk/

The Computer Misuse Act 1990 and other ICT legislation

There are a number of different misuses that arose as ICT systems became widespread. For example, hacking and the spreading of viruses became more of a problem. New laws such as the Computer Misuse Act 1990 and laws to deal with copyright theft needed to be introduced to deal with some of the misuses.

The purpose of the Computer Misuse Act 1990

The Computer Misuse Act 1990 was passed to deal with a number of misuses as the use of computers became widespread.

The Computer Misuse Act makes it an offence to:

- deliberately plant or transfer viruses to a computer system to cause damage to programs and data
- use an organization's computers to carry out unauthorized work
- hack into someone else's computer system with a view to seeing the information or altering it
- use computers to commit various frauds.

Hacking

Hacking is the process of deliberately attempting to or actually gaining access to an ICT system without permission. Most hackers use the Internet to gain illegal access to other computers connected to the Internet. Hacking could also be where an employee gains access to their manager's computer without their permission, for example to see a confidential job reference written about them.

Once a hacker has gained access to a system, they may:

- do nothing and be content that they have gained access
- gain access to sensitive or personal data
- use personal data to commit blackmail
- cause damage to data
- deliberately alter data to commit fraud.

Copyright law

Issues concerning copyright misuse

Many people spend a lot of time and money creating original work such as a piece of music, a picture, a piece of software, a photograph, a newspaper article, etc. Many of these people do it for a living, so it is only fair that their work should not be copied without permission.

The Copyright, Designs and Patents Act 1988 protects intellectual property from being copied such as:

- software
- text (e.g., books, magazine articles, etc.)
- a new innovative human–computer interface
- hardware (e.g., a flexible screen, the design of a power-saving chip, etc.)
- books and manuals
- images on websites.

Here are some actions that are illegal:

- copying software and music illegally
- copying images or text without permission
- copying sections of websites without permission
- sharing digital music illegally using peer-to-peer file sharing software
- running more copies of software than is allowed by the site licence.

The Computer Misuse Act 1990 and other ICT legislation *continued*

Avoiding plagiarism

Plagiarism is passing off someone else's work as your own. For example, cutting and pasting an article off the Internet and handing it in as an essay would be plagiarism.

In order to avoid plagiarism:

- Use several articles and put them into your own words.
- If you do use sections of someone else's work you must acknowledge them by stating the source of the material, the date and the name of the author.

The moral and ethical implications of illegal downloads and file sharing

You may think that illegal downloads and file sharing do not really hurt anyone as it is only the record companies, software companies and famous stars that have lots of money that are affected. The truth is it affects everyone and here is how:

- It is theft, as it deprives someone of some money and it is no different from shoplifting.
- The money from illegal copying is bad because much of the money is used to fund other illegal activities such as drug dealing, people trafficking, etc.

- Not everyone who produces copyright material is wealthy and many rely on this income for their everyday living expenses.
- Companies will not invest in new music, software, etc., if they think they will lose most of the income from illegal file sharing and copying.

ISP (Internet service provider) denying service

If you are caught illegally downloading music, video and other files then your Internet service provider (ISP) could deny you the facility of connecting to the Internet. The aim of this is to prevent persistent offenders from gaining Internet access.

Other legislation that applies to the use of ICT

The Freedom of Information Act 2000 – gives the right of access to information held by public authorities. Using this Act an individual can access information such as emails, meeting minutes, research reports, etc., held by local authorities. Usually this information would be about how public authorities carry out their duties, how they make their decisions and how they spend public money.

The Electronic Communications Act 2000 – deals with two things: it regulates the use of cryptographic services (i.e., services that allow data to be encrypted, such as services for sending credit/debit card details to make online purchases). It also makes digital signatures legally binding in the same way that handwritten signatures are legally binding. Both of these are important when conducting business electronically.

The Regulation of Investigatory Powers Act 2000 – concerned with the regulation of public bodies such as the police, MI5, etc., to carry out surveillance and investigation in order to detect and prevent terrorism and crime. The Act allows police, MI5, councils and other government departments to read your emails, listen to your private phone calls, view your text messages and monitor all your searches made on the Internet.

KEY WORD

Digital signature a way of ensuring that an email or document sent electronically is authentic. It can be used to detect a forged document.

Questions B

1. Give the name of the Act that is designed to allow organizations to prosecute anyone accessing their ICT systems illegally. *(1 mark)*

2. Explain, by giving an example, what is covered by the Computer Misuse Act 1990. *(2 marks)*

3. Passwords are one method used to protect against unauthorized access to ICT systems. Give **one** other way in which unauthorized access can be prevented. *(2 marks)*

4. Briefly explain the term software piracy. *(2 marks)*

Extension activity

Someone has said to you that as many people copy software and music illegally, it is morally OK even though it is illegal. Produce a word-processed magazine article putting both sides of the argument.

Health and safety issues at work

You will find out

▷ **About the potential health hazards when using computers**

▷ **About the methods of preventing or reducing the risks of health hazards**

As there are potential hazards when using computers and other ICT equipment, you need to be aware of what the hazards are. You also need to be aware of the symptoms of the medical conditions they cause. In this section you will be looking at both of these aspects.

As you will be using computers throughout your life, you need to ensure that you do as much as possible to avoid health problems. In this topic you will looking at the causes of the health problems and what you can do to prevent or reduce the risk of them occurring.

The potential health hazards when using computers

The main health hazards are:

- Repetitive strain injury (RSI) – this is caused by typing at high speed or using a mouse over a long period of time. RSI is a painful illness that causes swelling of the joints and is similar to arthritis. It can get so bad that many sufferers are unable to use their hands.
- Eye strain – looking at the screen all day can give you eye strain. Many of the people who use computer screens for long periods have to wear glasses or contact lenses. The symptoms of eye strain include blurred vision and headaches.
- Back ache – is a painful condition that prevents you from sleeping properly and doing many activities such as playing sport.
- Stress – computers can cause situations that are very stressful, such as losing your work, getting a virus, being unable to connect to the Internet and so on. All these things tend to go wrong at the worst possible time; for example, when you have an important piece of work to hand in. Stress is also caused by too much work to complete in too little time. Stress can produce headaches and can affect a person's behaviour towards others. Stress can cause depression and mental illness.

Methods of preventing or reducing the risks of health hazards

Back ache

The following can cause back ache:

- Not sitting up straight in your chair (i.e. incorrect posture).
- Using a laptop on your knee for long periods.
- Working in cramped conditions.

KEY WORD

RSI repetitive strain injury. A painful muscular condition caused by repeatedly using certain muscles in the same way.

▲ Back ache is a common ailment in computer users.

To help prevent back problems:

- Use an adjustable chair (NB in workplaces this is a legal requirement but you need to ensure that the chair you use at home is adjustable).
- Always check the adjustment of the chair to make sure it is suitable for your height. Use a foot support, called a footrest, if necessary.
- Sit up straight on the chair with your feet flat on the floor.
- Make sure the screen is lined up and tilted at an appropriate angle.

121

Health and safety issues at work *continued*

Repetitive strain injury (RSI)

The following can cause RSI:

- Typing at high speed.
- Using a mouse for long periods.
- Not adopting correct posture for use of mouse and keyboard.
- Not having properly arranged equipment (e.g., keyboard, mouse, screen, etc.).

To help prevent RSI:

- Adjust your chair to the correct seating position for you.
- Make sure there is enough space to work comfortably.
- Use a document holder.
- Use an ergonomic keyboard/mouse.
- Use a wrist rest.
- Keep your wrists straight when keying in.
- Position the mouse so that it can be used keeping the wrist straight.
- Learn how to type properly – two finger typing has been found to be much worse for RSI.

Eye strain

The following can cause eye strain:

- Using the screen for long periods.
- Working without the best lighting conditions.
- Glare on the screen.
- Dirt on the screen.

To help avoid eye strain:

- Keep the screen clean, so it is easy to see characters on the screen.
- Use appropriate lighting (fluorescent tubes with diffusers).
- Use blinds to avoid glare.
- Give your eyes a rest by focusing on distant objects.
- Have regular eye-tests (NB if you use a screen in your work, then your employer is required by law to pay for regular eye-tests and glasses if they are needed).

Stress

The following can cause stress:

- The pace of work (e.g., too much to do in too little time).
- Worry about using the new technology – older people may feel they cannot cope.
- Software that is frustrating to use because it has not been designed properly.
- Losing work, problems with viruses and technical problems.

To help prevent stress:

- Have a help-desk to help with user problems.
- Train users fully in all the ICT systems they use so they do not get stuck.
- Ensure that all software is thoroughly tested so that it does not crash.
- Design the software so that it is easy to use.
- Ensure that users do not have an unreasonable workload.
- Take regular breaks to avoid stress.

Safety issues

There are a number of other safety issues related to using computers and these include the following:

- Excessive heat/temperatures – computers give out large amounts of heat and rooms containing them can become unbearably hot in the summer. It is for this reason that most computer rooms are air conditioned.

▼ Air conditioning allows you to adjust the temperature in a room.

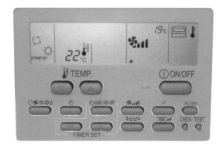

- Management of electrical systems/ computers – computers need lots of power sockets. Computer equipment uses a lot of power and if multi sockets are used then it is easy to overload the mains circuit. This is dangerous and could cause a fire. Computer rooms should be wired specially.

▲ Electrical circuits should not be overloaded as it can cause fires.

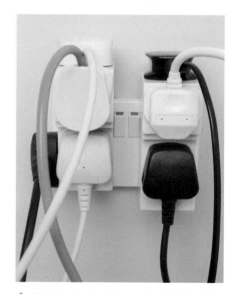

▲ Circuits should not be overloaded like this.

- The cables need to be managed. The cables are of two types: electrical, which carry the power to the components of computer systems, and the cables such as network cables, that carry the data around. There should be no trailing wires that are likely to cause a tripping hazard.

- Any malfunctioning equipment must not be used and should be reported to the technician.
- Lighting is important in computer rooms. There needs to be sufficient light, yet the light should not be so powerful that it produces glare on the screen. Normally lights in computer rooms have diffusers that throw the light out evenly and prevent reflections on the screen.
- Sunlight can be a problem. Apart from heating up the room, it makes the screens difficult to see. Computer rooms should have adjustable blinds to control the amount of light. Screens should also be positioned so they are not in full sun.
- Fire prevention is important. Fire extinguishers should be provided and many large organizations use sprinkler systems that activate automatically. Smoke detectors should also be used.
- Food and drink should be kept away from computers. A drink spill over a computer or keyboard is very dangerous.
- UPS (uninterruptible power supplies) and surge protectors should be used. A power failure can be dangerous. Apart from the damage it can cause to the computers, all the lights go out, which is dangerous. A UPS is used to ensure the power is switched over to a generator or battery supply if the mains fails.
- Surges in power are also dangerous and a surge protector prevents this happening.

▲ **A spacious office with diffused lighting.**

Activity

Investigating the equipment available to reduce health risks in using ICT

Computer equipment manufacturers and office equipment manufacturers produce many different pieces of equipment to minimize health risks in using ICT.

For this activity you have to produce a handout on the equipment available and how it reduces certain health risks. In this handout you will need to:

- find pictures of the piece of equipment/furniture
- identify which health problem(s) the piece of equipment reduces
- explain how it reduces the health problem
- list the web address(es) where you found the picture and information.

KEY WORD

Ergonomics an applied science concerned with designing and arranging things people use so that the people and things interact most efficiently and safely.

Extension activity

The Health and Safety Executive (HSE) is a government body responsible for enforcing health and safety in the workplace. Further information about health and safety aspects of using computer screens can be found at:

- http://www.hse.gov.uk/pubns/indg36.pdf

Use this site and any other you can find for information in order to produce a short leaflet (you decide which software to use), outlining the health and safety issues, to be given to Year 7 students when they start senior school.

Health and safety issues at work *continued*

Questions C

1 The use of ICT systems has been associated with a number of health problems.
   (a) State **three** health problems that have been associated with the prolonged use of ICT systems. *(3 marks)*
   (b) In order to avoid computer-related health problems certain preventative actions can be taken. Describe **six** such preventative actions that can be taken to alleviate the health problems you have identified in part (a). *(6 marks)*

2 An employee who spends much of their time at a keyboard typing in orders at high speed is worried about RSI.
   (a) What do the initials RSI stand for? *(1 mark)*
   (b) Give **one** of the symptoms of RSI. *(1 mark)*
   (c) Write down two precautions that the employee can take to minimize the chance of contracting RSI. *(2 marks)*

3 Copy the table and tick (✓) the correct column to show whether each of the following statements about health risks in using ICT is true or false. *(5 marks)*

	True	False
The continual use of keyboards over a long period can give rise to aches and pains in the hands, arms and wrists	☐	☐
RSI stands for repeated stress injury	☐	☐
Wrist rests and ergonomic keyboards can help prevent RSI	☐	☐
Back ache can be caused by slouching in your chair when using a computer	☐	☐
Glare on the screen can cause RSI	☐	☐

4 A computer worker said that using computers can be stressful. Describe **one** situation in which using a computer is stressful. *(1 mark)*

EXAM TIP

Always be guided by the mark scheme to decide how much to write. For example, if you are asked to describe an advantage or disadvantage for one mark, then just a brief statement would be enough. If two marks were allocated, then you would be required to supplement this with further detail or an appropriate example.

Always think out your answer before you start writing it. You need to ensure you make your answer clear, so you need a little time to think about it.

Advantages (sometimes called benefits) and disadvantages are very popular questions. When covering a topic for revision, it is a good idea to list advantages and disadvantages where appropriate.

You need to be clear about the health problems (i.e., what they are called), the symptoms (i.e., how they affect your body) and what can be done to help to prevent them.

Extension activity

Repetitive strain injury (RSI) has become a major worry for those people who use computers continually throughout their working day.

You are required to use the Internet to find out more about this condition. You need to find out:

- What are the symptoms?
- Can you make it better?
- What is the likelihood of getting it?
- What can you do to prevent it?

Design of user interfaces, ICT systems and quality of life for the disabled

You will find out

▷ **About how ICT systems can affect the quality of life experienced by persons with disabilities**

▷ **About the need for good design of user interfaces**

In order to reap the benefits of ICT systems, the ICT systems need to be accessible to everyone. People with disabilities are able to use ICT to help them communicate and keep their independence. For example, people with limited mobility can shop from home and access information and education using ICT systems. They can also gain employment making use of the fact that teleworking (i.e., working from home using ICT) is now possible. In order that disabled people can use ICT they need specially designed hardware such as Braille keyboards.

User interfaces need to be as easy to use as possible and they should not cause health problems. They also need to be capable of being adjusted so disabled people can use them.

How ICT systems can affect the quality of life experienced by people with disabilities

ICT developments have helped people with disabilities gain employment and do many of the things they could not do without the use of ICT. Above all ICT has allowed people with disabilities to remain independent.

In this section you will be looking at devices to support disabilities. There are a number of ways ICT can help people with disabilities and these are outlined below.

The use of specialist input devices

There is a huge range of specialist input devices that can be used by people with disabilities to help them perform day-to-day tasks.

▲ A Braille keyboard.

▲ This keyboard can be used by sighted or sight-impaired people.

Braille keyboards are used to enter text into a computer and are used by blind or partially sighted people. Voice recognition systems can be used that enable people to issue commands and use speech to enter data into a word-processing document.

Customizable interfaces that allow ICT to be used by people with disabilities

When interfaces are being designed, it is important to realize that people with a range of disabilities will also be using them.

People who are visually impaired (i.e., blind or partially sighted) can be helped by using an interface that can be customized by the user. Interfaces are customized in the following ways:

- a facility to speak words on the screen
- a facility to zoom in so that the page is magnified
- allow a user to increase the font size
- allow a user to choose those font types that are easy to read
- using plenty of contrast between the text and the background
- allow the user to change the colour scheme.

People who have a hearing impairment (i.e., completely or partially deaf) can be helped by:

- using visual warnings rather than sound warnings
- using typed versions of any speech used
- using subtitles for any video used.

Design of user interfaces, ICT systems and quality of life for the disabled *continued*

Examples of Improvements in the user interface

Here are some examples of improvements in user interfaces:

▲ Touch screens on mobile devices avoid having to use tiny keyboards and screens.

▲ Most software has graphical user interfaces that are similar to each other and this makes new software easy to learn and use.

Communication and control devices

Things that people without disabilities take for granted such as turning devices on or off, closing blinds or curtains, opening and closing the front door, etc., can be very difficult for someone who has limited mobility. Devices can be controlled using a keypad or computer and this gives a disabled person more independence.

Text to voice systems allow someone who cannot speak to communicate with others. They can type in words that are then converted to speech. In some cases the devices can be operated with a blink of an eye or by blowing down a pipe.

▲ Use of voice/speech recognition rather than the use of a keyboard for entering text means the user is less likely to contract RSI.

▲ Online help means users get instant help thus avoiding stress.

Questions D

1 Explain how voice recognition can be used by someone who is unable to use their hands to type. (*2 marks*)

2 Most software and websites are customizable so that people with disabilities are able to use them effectively.
   (a) Explain what customizable means. (*1 mark*)
   (b) Give **two** examples of ways that a user interface can be customized. (*2 marks*)

3 Describe **one** piece of computer hardware that has specifically been created for someone who is disabled. (*2 marks*)

Extension activity

Software usually provides features that enable disabled people to use them more easily.

For this extension activity you have to use a few pieces of software (e.g., operating system software, application software such as word-processor, etc.) and find out what options there are to make them easier for disabled people to use. One way you could find out is to use the online help that is provided as part of the software.

Write a brief set of notes on how each piece of software can be customized.

Environmental impact, social and ethical implications for personal information

You will find out

▷ **About the environmental impact of digital devices**

▷ **About the social and ethical implications of the electronic transmission of personal information**

The use of digital devices has both positive and negative environmental impacts and in this section you will learn about them. The use of ICT raises a lot of social and ethical issues and in this topic you will be looking at issues such as the introduction of national databases and the problems they can create. Many people are worried that there is far too much state involvement in people's lives and that there is too much monitoring and surveillance.

The environmental impact of digital devices

Digital devices have an impact on the environment, some positive and some negative.

The use of digital services

Using ICT can reduce the environmental impact in a number of ways.

Positive ways

- It can reduce journeys to banks, shops, meetings and to work and therefore cut down on pollution.
- Use of GPS prevents people getting lost and using more fuel than necessary.
- Videoconferencing reduces travel, which causes a lot of pollution.
- Digital music means you do not have to produce CDs, packaging, etc.
- Digital media reduces the need for paper-based newspapers, books, etc.
- Traffic management systems in towns and cities keep traffic moving and reduce pollution.

Negative ways

- People tend to replace technology very quickly and this is wasteful.
- Huge amounts of fuel and raw material are used to manufacture digital devices.
- Computers use huge amounts of electricity.
- Printouts waste huge quantities of paper.

Recycling and disposal

The production of ICT equipment produces lots of carbon dioxide and the use of the equipment produces lots as well. Carbon dioxide is a greenhouse gas and causes global warming, which is bad for all of us.

In order to help the environment there are a number of actions we can all take:

- Recycle hardware, as this reduces the greenhouses gases.
- Reduce the amount of printouts you make. Use print preview so you only print your final copy.
- Recycle paper – printouts and other paper documents should not be thrown away with general rubbish. Instead it should be collected for recycling.
- Switch off computer equipment rather than leaving it on stand-by.
- Teleworking or working from home – this will reduce congestion and pollution and cut down on greenhouse gas emissions.
- Recycle printer cartridges by having them re-filled with ink.
- Recycle mobile phones as your old phone can be someone's new phone.
- Computer hardware should be separated from the general rubbish for recycling rather than put in landfill sites.

▲ Redundant hardware ready for recycling.

Environmental impact, social and ethical implications for personal information *continued*

The purposes of national databases

There are many large national databases that have been set up by organizations such as the police, NHS, etc. Here are some of the main ones:

National DNA database – DNA uniquely identifies a particular person. It is used by police forces in the fight against crime. Anyone who is arrested will have details of their DNA added to the database. The main concern people have is that the samples are taken after arrest, so if the person is not charged then their DNA details are not deleted from the database. Some people argue that everyone's DNA details should be put on this database as this would make fighting crime much easier.

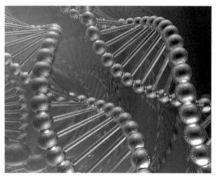

▲ **Everybody has a unique DNA structure.**

The Police National Computer (PNC) – this is a national police system that can be accessed by anyone who has authority to access it. It contains details of crimes and criminals. It allows the police to search on criminals and vehicles when they only have a small amount of information. For example, they could search for all the Ford Mondeos with a registration YY04 _ _ T, where the dashes are unknown letters.

The Passport Agency – anyone who has a passport will be on their

database. The database is used to identify criminals who are entering or leaving the country. It can also prevent people entering the country using forged passports.

The NHS national database – this database contains medical details for everyone who is able to access NHS services. Keeping this data centrally, means that if you were involved in an accident away from home, the doctors at the hospital would have access to your medical details. These could include details of allergies to certain drugs and this information could be life saving.

The costing of national databases

Large national databases are complex projects that are very expensive. Many of these projects go wildly out of control because the costs start to rise and some projects get abandoned halfway through. Some of these databases and other ICT systems are political issues. For example, the Labour Party favour the introduction of identity cards but the Conservative Party said that they are not in favour of them.

National identity cards

Many countries in the world have a national identity card that everyone has to carry. The UK was supposed to have had such a scheme for everyone but at present only foreign nationals have to have one. At the moment as a UK citizen you do not have to have one but you can buy one if you want one for £30.

Many people object to these cards for everyone because of the cost and because they interfere with civil liberties and also they feel that they do nothing to prevent terrorism and illegal immigration.

The security of public data

One of the problems with national databases is that they are accessed by lots of different people from lots of different locations. Trying to ensure the privacy and the security of this data is not easy. Much of this information would be difficult to re-create. For example, if all the tax files for everyone who pays tax in the country were lost, then it would cause havoc because the government would not have the money coming in to pay for public services.

Here are some of the things that can be done to ensure the security of public data:

- Regular backups taken with the copies of the original data kept off site.
- Training of all personnel who use data on such topics as not leaving computers unattended whilst logged on, viruses, data protection, etc.
- Use of firewalls to prevent hackers accessing data.
- Virus checkers to prevent the introduction of viruses.
- Physical security (e.g., access restriction on rooms, access restrictions to computers, etc.).

Links between public and private databases

There are often links between information held by private companies and public organizations. Many people are concerned that some private organizations are using information that was given to councils and government departments.

Here are some of the links:

- Building societies and banks sending information about interest to HM Revenue and Customs (i.e., about tax that should be paid).

- Insurance companies sending data about car insurance so that people can tax their cars online.
- The police and MI5 can gain access to databases of Internet service providers (ISPs) who keep details of all their customers' Internet use (e.g., emails sent and received, searches made, etc.).

CCTV

CCTV stands for closed circuit television and these are the cameras you see just about everywhere. Some of these cameras can be used with sophisticated software to actually recognize a person and others can recognize a car registration plate and find the name and address of the registered owner.

Government access to personal data

Many people are worried about the government holding so much personal data about all of us. The government say that they need this information for planning purposes. For example, they need to know about the nation's health in order to plan for hospitals, old people's homes, etc. Some people are worried that their right to privacy is being eroded.

The surveillance society

More and more government departments and councils are undertaking surveillance. Some of the surveillance is done to detect and prosecute criminals and some is done to protect us against terrorist attacks. Most people would agree that this is a good thing but some people are worried that surveillance is being directed at ordinary people.

For example, a local authority used surveillance to check whether parents whose child attended a popular school actually lived in the catchment area or just said they did to gain their child's admission.

Some people think the Act is a 'snoopers' charter for public bodies to check up on us all. Under an act of parliament the police, MI5, councils and other government departments can:

- demand access to your emails, instant messages, etc., from your Internet service provider without you knowing
- listen in secret to phone calls and see all your text messages
- monitor all your searches made on the Internet.

Monitoring/detecting loss or corruption of information

Fraud is always a problem with ICT systems and there are several ways in which checks can be made to monitor and detect the loss or corruption of information:

- Transaction logs monitor the changes made to information and can show what the information was before and after the changes.
- Unusual changes in activity are often detected by ICT systems automatically. For example, high value transactions may need to be authorized by someone in authority.
- Parity checks are used to detect that data is not corrupted as it is transferred from one place to another.

Questions E

1. (a) Give the meaning of the term CCTV. *(1 mark)*
   (b) People are worried about the huge rise in the use of CCTV. Give **one** reason why they are worried. *(1 mark)*

2. Public organizations set up national databases and they store lots of personal information about individuals.
   (a) Give **two** reasons why an individual might worry about these huge stores of information about them. *(2 marks)*
   (b) Give **one** example of a national database that stores personal information and is set up by an organization run by the government. *(1 mark)*

3. There have been many stories in the press about government and local councils snooping. Snooping involves using surveillance to find out about people and what they are up to.
   (a) Describe **two** ways ICT can be used for surveillance. *(2 marks)*
   (b) Explain, by giving an example, why the government or council might want to conduct surveillance on a person. *(2 marks)*

4. As computer users we can play our part by minimizing the amount of energy we use.
   (a) Give **three** things applicable to the use of ICT that we can do to minimize the amount of energy we use when working with computers. *(3 marks)*
   (b) Describe **one** way in which the use of ICT can help the environment. *(2 marks)*

Extension activity

Producing a poster on recycling

For this activity you have to produce a poster that is applicable to the recycling of computer equipment/mobile phones, etc. The main aim of the poster is to alert people to the problems of manufacturing equipment from scratch and the energy it uses and the problems with the carbon dioxide emissions it produces.

Questions

Test yourself

The following notes summarize this topic. The notes are incomplete because they have words missing. Using the words in the list below, copy out and complete the sentences A to P, underlining the words that you have inserted. Each word may be used more than once.

headaches   eye-tests   RSI

Data Protection   blinds

private   viruses   deleted   hacking

identity cards   surveillance

security   Computer Misuse   CCTV   back ache

A _____ is caused by typing at high speed or using a mouse over a long period of time.

B The symptoms of eye strain include blurred vision and _____.

C Working in cramped conditions and not adopting the correct posture when using computer can lead to _____

D An adjustable chair should be used in order to prevent _____.

E Adjustable _____ should be used on windows to prevent glare on the screen and the screen should also be kept free from glare from lights.

F It is important to have regular _____ and use glasses or contact lenses when working with computers, if needed.

G The _____ Act 1998 was passed to protect individuals from the misuse of personal data.

H Anyone can apply to see the data held about them and if the information is wrong then they can have it corrected or _____.

I The Computer Misuse Act makes it an offence to deliberately plant or transfer _____ to a computer system to cause damage to programs and data.

J Unauthorized use of an ICT system with a view to seeing or altering the data is called _____.

K Hacking is made a criminal offence under the _____ Act.

L Because national databases are used by thousands of different people in thousands of different places, many people are worried about the _____ of their personal data.

M Many countries have _____ that their citizens must carry with them and the details on the card can be used to check that the person is who they say they are.

N Many public databases are linked to _____ databases and this allows the passage of information between the two.

O Government has been criticized for the amount of snooping on their citizens. This snooping is called _____.

P One method of surveillance makes use of _____ cameras.

Examination style questions

1 (a) What do the initials RSI stand for? *(1 mark)*
   (b) RSI is a health problem that may be caused by prolonged computer use.
        Write a sentence to show how RSI is caused. *(2 marks)*
   (c) Write down **one** precaution that a computer user can take to minimize the chance of contracting RSI. *(1 mark)*

2 Here is a list of health problems. Write down the names of those that can be caused by prolonged computer use: *(4 marks)*

   Back ache
   Toothache
   Stress
   Sprained ankle
   RSI
   Eye strain

3 People who work with computers for long periods may experience some health problems. These health problems include eye strain and RSI.
   (a) Give the names of **two** health problems other than eye strain and RSI that a user may experience. *(2 marks)*
   (b) Explain **two** things a user should do when sitting in a chair at a desk and using a computer in order to prevent future health problems. *(2 marks)*

4 The Data Protection Act 1998 protects people from having their personal data misused.

   There are eight Data Protection Principles, which are regulations that an organization must adhere to when collecting, storing and processing personal information.
   (a) State **three** of the Data Protection Principles. *(3 marks)*
   (b) Tick **two** boxes to show which of the following have partial exemption from the Data Protection Act 1998. *(2 marks)*

	Tick *two* boxes
Word-processed documents	☐
Insurance company data	☐
A database of friends' names and addresses	☐
A database of doctors' patients	☐
Files stored on paper	☐

   (c) The Data Protection Act 1998 gives certain rights to data subjects.
        (i) Explain what is meant by a data subject. *(2 marks)*
        (ii) Give **two** rights that are given to data subjects under the Act. *(2 marks)*

5 ICT equipment should be recycled rather than added to landfill sites.
   Explain **two** reasons for this. *(2 marks)*

6 In order to minimize the effect on the environment in using ICT there are a number of actions we can all take. Describe **three** actions we can take. *(3 marks)*

Case studies

Case study 1

Cyber warfare

Most developed countries are totally dependent on their ICT systems and the loss of such systems could do serious damage to the infrastructure of countries.

For example, could you imagine the loss of the Internet for a lengthy period or the loss of the entire mobile phone network. What about the erasure of all the health information on the NHS computers or the erasure of tax information, so that the government could not collect money to pay for schools, hospitals, the police, etc.

In many ways damage to ICT systems could do a lot more damage than a series of terrorist bombs or even a war using conventional weapons.

Many terrorist groups use the Internet for recruitment, propaganda and communication purposes. They may also conduct cyber attacks against their enemies.

Some countries have started to investigate the use of the Internet to cause damage to the infrastructure of other countries. Targets would typically involve key businesses, the national power grid (for electricity supply), financial markets and government departments. The government has decided to set up a new office for cyber security. This department will monitor, analyse and counter any cyber attacks.

It is interesting to note that as well as protecting against cyber warfare, Britain is investigating the potential of using cyber warfare itself should the need arise.

The government has turned to hackers who have the experience to know how to get past security methods and break into networks.

Cyber attacks from other countries have already occurred. For example, there was an attack on the Foreign Office's computer from China and also an attack on the House of Common's computer system that temporarily closed it down.

Questions

1 **(a)** Explain what hacking is and why it is so important to keep hackers out of key networks. *(3 marks)*

   (b) Networks can be protected using firewalls. Explain how a firewall can be used to prevent unauthorized access. *(2 marks)*

2 Give **two** examples of systems that could be hacked into and deliberately damaged as part of a cyber attack. *(2 marks)*

3 Some people think it is morally wrong to give good well-paid jobs to hackers who have deliberately broken the law. State, with reasons, whether you agree or disagree with this. *(2 marks)*

4 Hacking is made illegal under a law. Give the full name of the law. *(1 mark)*

5 Terrorists use encryption to ensure the privacy of communication and to avoid being detected and caught.

   (a) Explain what encryption is and how it ensures the privacy of communication. *(2 marks)*

   (b) Some countries are worried that encryption of data causes as many problems as it solves. Explain why a country might ban encryption. *(2 marks)*

Case study 2

Hackers destroy a flight simulation site

Many people are interested in flying a plane but do not have the money to do this in reality. Instead they fly the planes virtually using flight simulation software.

A very popular website that covered all aspects of flight simulation has been destroyed by hackers. The hackers took down the site's two servers. The problem was that there was no external backup system. This meant that each server was used to back up the files on the other server. This meant that because both servers were affected, all the data was lost.

The person who founded the site said that the site would be down for the foreseeable future and that it might not be possible to set the site up again. One user of the site was really annoyed and said, 'there's a special place in hell for hackers who pull stunts like this'.

Questions

1 (a) Explain what is meant by the word 'hacker'. *(2 marks)*

(b) There is a law that makes hacking illegal. Give the name of this law. *(1 mark)*

2 It is essential for security purposes that all files are properly backed up.

(a) Give the names of **two** different media on which files can be backed up. *(2 marks)*

(b) It is important that data is backed up off site. Give **one** reason why data should be kept off site. *(1 mark)*

3 One or more servers are used in networks. Explain the purpose of a server. *(2 marks)*

Case study 3

The NHS losing patient medical records

You would think that your personal medical details are safe in the hands of the NHS, but they are not. The Information Commissioner, the person who is in charge of the Data Protection Act, has been forced to take action against the NHS many times for breaching data protection regulations.

Here are some of the things they did:

• One GP downloaded a complete patient database containing medical histories of 10,000 patients onto an unsecured laptop. The laptop was then stolen and never recovered.

• A memory stick containing around 6000 patient details was lost. Although the details were encrypted, the password was written on a piece of paper attached to the memory stick.

The Assistant Information Commissioner said that procedures were laid out by the NHS but were not being followed. He also commented that 'medical history is very sensitive personal information which is likely to cause harm and distress'. He went on to say that 'the law dictates that they must keep this information confidential'.

◀ Medical details are personal data and need to be protected.

Questions

1 What could a person do who has suffered harm and distress when their medical details were revealed through negligence? *(1 mark)*

2 One data protection regulation (called Data Protection Principles in the Data Protection Act) is that 'Personal data shall be accurate, and where necessary, kept up-to-date'. Give another **two** of the Data Protection Principles. *(2 marks)*

3 The Deputy Information Commissioner mentioned 'sensitive personal information'.
Give **three** items of sensitive personal information that you might find as part of a medical record. *(3 marks)*

4 All disks containing personal information should be encrypted.

(a) Explain what is meant by encrypted. *(2 marks)*

(b) If a laptop is stolen and the laptop has stored personal information that is encrypted on its hard drive, explain how this protects the information. *(1 mark)*

(c) Describe **two** ways in which medical details could be misused. *(2 marks)*

Exam support

Worked example

There are a number of health hazards associated with the use of computers.

(a) Give the names of **three** health hazards, outlining the health problems they create. *(6 marks)*

(b) For each of the health hazards described in part (a) describe what a user can do to help reduce the risk of their occurrence. *(3 marks)*

Student answer 1

(a) *People who use computers a lot get fat and this can cause a heart attack.*

You can get eye strain when using computers.

You can get repetitive strain injury which causes aches in your hands and wrists.

(b) *Fatness – do not snack while you are using your computer.*

Eye strain – have regular eye-tests.

Repetitive strain injury – use a wrist rest when using a keyboard or mouse.

◄ Examiner's comment

(a) Getting fat is not really directly caused by computers because this is caused by overeating or lack of exercise so no mark is awarded here.

The second answer is OK but it fails to explain what the symptoms of eye strain are (i.e., headaches, tiredness, etc.). Only one mark for this.

The third answer is fine and both the health hazard and the symptoms are made clear. Three marks are given for part (a).

(b) The answer about 'Fatness' gains no marks but the other answers are good and gain full marks. Two marks for this part.

(5 marks out of 9)

Student answer 2

(a) *Back ache which causes aches and pain in the lower back meaning you cannot get a good night's sleep.*

Too much change in the workplace causing stress, meaning you cannot sleep because you are worried all the time.

Incorrect lighting causing headaches which give migraine and blurred vision.

(b) *Back ache – use an adjustable chair and make sure you adjust it to suit your height. You can use a footrest if there is one.*

Stress – make sure that users get good training so they are not stressed by the changes they have to cope with.

Headaches – make sure that fluorescent tubes are used with diffusers on them to spread out the light.

◄ Examiner's comment

(a) Here the hazard has been identified and it is clear what discomfort this causes the user. Full marks so six marks for this part.

(b) Again an excellent answer. Notice how it is clear which health hazard is being referred to. Full marks again for this section so three marks.

(9 marks out of 9)

Examiner's answers

(a) One mark for the health hazard and one mark for an explanation of how it affects the user.

- Eye strain – causing headaches, migraines, blurred vision.
- Back ache – pain in back or shoulders.
- Stress – loss of sleep, tiredness, changes in personality, etc.
- RSI – pains in fingers, hands, wrists, etc.
- Neck strain – unable to move head without it hurting.
- DVT (deep vein thrombosis) – can cause a stroke or heart attack.

(b) One mark for each prevention method. For the mark it should be clear which health problem the prevention refers to.

Here are some of the many possible answers:

- Eye strain – have regular eye-tests/focus on distant objects/keep screen clean/eliminate glare on screen.
- Back ache – use adjustable chair/sit upright using correct posture.
- Stress – employers to provide adequate training on new systems/have regular breaks/employers to give reasonable workload.
- RSI – use wrist rests or supports; use systems that minimize keyboard and mouse use; use an ergonomic keyboard.
- Neck strain – use a copy holder; ensure the screen is level with your eyes.
- DVT (deep vein thrombosis) – do not sit in the same position; get up and walk around every now and again.

EXAM TIP

The Data Protection Act is very important and you need to know it in detail. Make sure you understand the reasons for the Act and the rights it gives, particularly to the person the data is about (i.e., the data subject).

There are a number of exemptions to the Data Protection Act. Make sure you can remember them.

Under the Data Protection Act, organizations must ensure the privacy and security of the personal data held. Make sure you understand all the methods that can be used to prevent unauthorized access.

Summary mind maps

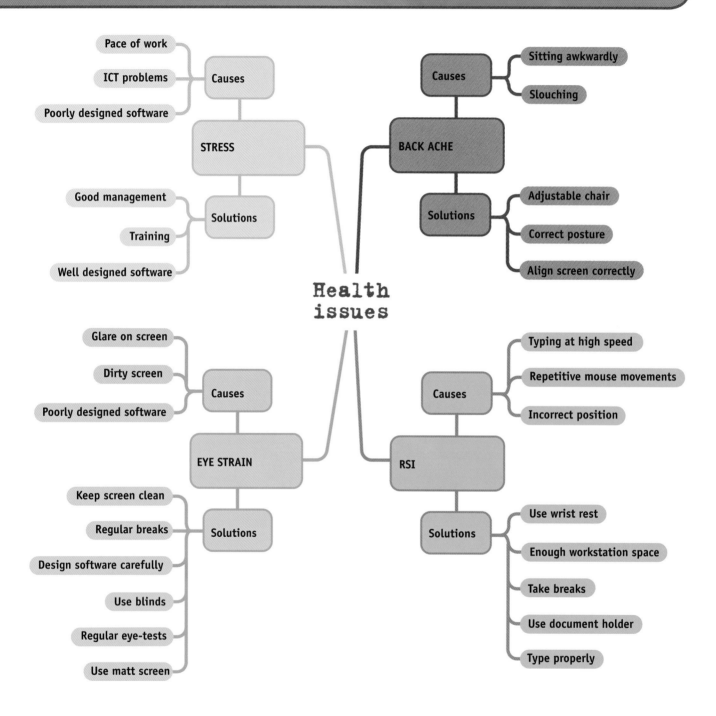

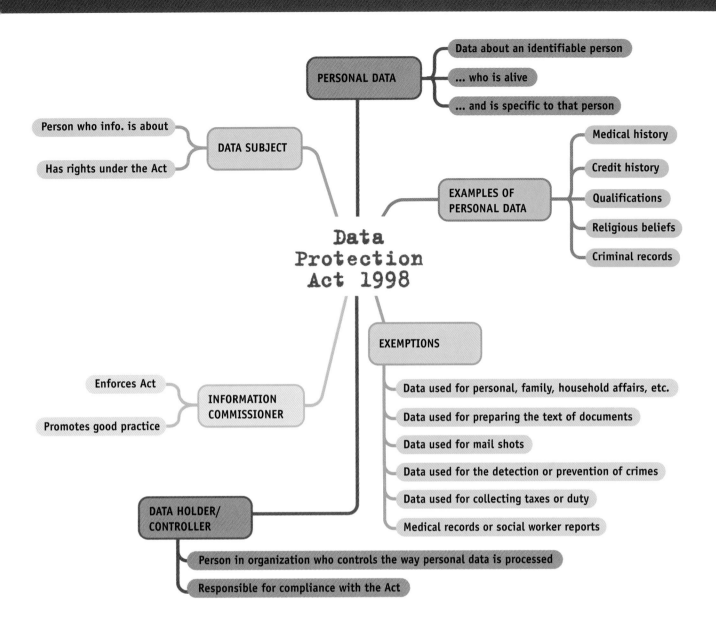

Data Protection Act 1998

PERSONAL DATA
- Data about an identifiable person
- ... who is alive
- ... and is specific to that person

DATA SUBJECT
- Person who info. is about
- Has rights under the Act

EXAMPLES OF PERSONAL DATA
- Medical history
- Credit history
- Qualifications
- Religious beliefs
- Criminal records

EXEMPTIONS
- Data used for personal, family, household affairs, etc.
- Data used for preparing the text of documents
- Data used for mail shots
- Data used for the detection or prevention of crimes
- Data used for collecting taxes or duty
- Medical records or social worker reports

INFORMATION COMMISSIONER
- Enforces Act
- Promotes good practice

DATA HOLDER/ CONTROLLER
- Person in organization who controls the way personal data is processed
- Responsible for compliance with the Act

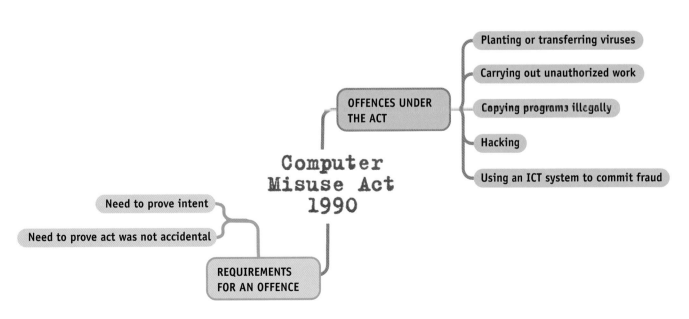

Computer Misuse Act 1990

OFFENCES UNDER THE ACT
- Planting or transferring viruses
- Carrying out unauthorized work
- Copying programs illegally
- Hacking
- Using an ICT system to commit fraud

REQUIREMENTS FOR AN OFFENCE
- Need to prove intent
- Need to prove act was not accidental

Summary mind maps *continued*

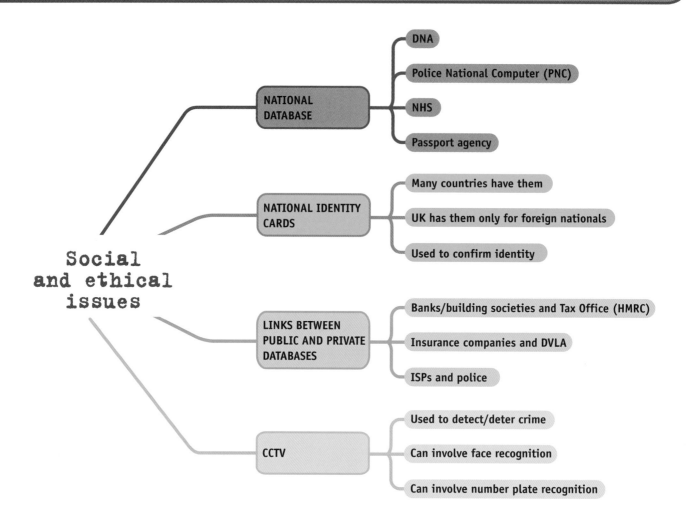

Topic 7

Using ICT systems

The key concepts covered in this topic are:

- Starting, accessing, exiting and shutting down ICT systems
- Adjusting system settings and user preferences
- Selection and use of user interfaces
- Management of folder structures and files
- Networking
- Troubleshooting

You will probably know quite a bit about this material already. After all, it is impossible to get much done on a computer without knowing a bit about folders and files. It is also important to know about the problems you have if you do not close programs and shut down your computer properly. This topic looks at these things and also the ways you can customize the user interface to suit the way you work. If computers are connected to the Internet they are networked. You therefore need to know about networks and this is particularly important as many people have more than one computer connected to the Internet in their homes. Also covered are the large numbers of ICT systems that we use in our lives.

Contents

Starting and stopping the computer, user interfaces, adjusting settings

You will find out

▷ **About the correct procedures to start, access, exit and shutdown ICT systems**

▷ **About the features of user interfaces**

▷ **About the selection and adjustment of system settings and user preferences**

In order to prevent problems with ICT systems it is important to shut down the computer properly when you have finished your work rather than simply turning the power off. When using networks, there are set procedures to follow to log-on to the network and to log-off from it. By adopting these procedures, the network facilities can be used by everyone who has permission to use them.

User interfaces enable humans to interact with the hardware and get jobs done. In this topic you will learn about what a user interface is and how settings can be adjusted to suit the way you work.

Starting the computer

As more than one person often uses the same computer, it is necessary for each user to have their own username and password. To start the computer you turn it on and then tell the computer which user you are from the list that has been created by the person who initially set up the computer. You are then asked for a password, which you then enter. On entering the correct password you are given access to the computer. You can only use the computer as a stand-alone computer as you will need to supply more details to log-on to a network.

Log-on and log-off (also called log-in and log-out)

In order to use a network you have to log-on/log-in. To do this you have to supply two things:

- your username or user-ID
- a password.

▽ Log-on/log-in means gaining access to the network after correctly giving your username and password.

The username or user-ID identifies you to the network. This means that the network will allocate storage space for you and allow you to use certain files. The password, which you should always keep private, ensures that you are who you say you are and not someone trying to access the network without permission.

Shutting down the computer properly

You should always shut your computer down properly otherwise the following can happen:

- You can lose data.
- Programs can be corrupted (i.e. damaged).

To exit the computer properly you should follow these instructions:

- Click on the start button (bottom left of your screen).
- From the menu that appears click on the arrow pointing to the right (bottom right menu item).
- Click on Shut Down.
- The computer has now been correctly shut down.

username: _____

password: _____

The selection and adjustment of system settings and user preferences

When you turn on your computer and the operating system loads, the first thing you will see is the user interface. The user interface provides the way for you to communicate with your computer. You can inform the computer what you want to do and the computer can tell you about any problems it has, such as not being able to find a certain file, or not being able to print out a document because the printer is not switched on. In this section you will be looking at user interfaces, what they consist of and how you can customize the interface to suit you.

Features of user interfaces

The three main types of user interface are as follows:

Command line/driven interface – this is where you have to type in precise instructions to get things done. These instructions or commands have to be issued very precisely and this makes it hard to use.

Menu-driven interface – here you are given a choice of things and you select the one you want – usually by typing a letter or number.

Graphical user interface (GUI) – the user interface used by Windows is a graphical user interface. It uses windows, icons, menus and pointers and makes use of a mouse. It is usually regarded as the easiest interface to use.

▲ The icons (small pictures) representing folders in a GUI.

Customizing the user interface

When you start to use a computer you often use it without making any changes to the user interface. However, if someone has used the computer before you and has made changes to the user interface, then this might prevent you working effectively. It is therefore important to know about the settings and how you can alter them for yourself.

If you use a networked computer, such as the ones at school, then the network will save any changes you make to the user interface. This means that the next time you log on using your username and password you will be presented with your own personalized user interface.

There are many ways you can customize the user interface and here are just some of them:

- You can alter the size of the icons.
- You can alter the way the mouse works.
- You can alter resolution, brightness and contrast on the computer screen.

Settings that can be changed in a user interface include the following: window size, mouse settings, icon size, screen resolution, etc.

A user interface normally consists of:

- icons
- folders
- windows
- menus
- help
- toolbars.

Making changes

There are many ways of making changes to the user interface and these include the following.

Adjusting window size – windows can be maximized, minimized and made any size in between.

- Maximizing a window makes the window occupy almost all the screen.
- Minimizing a window makes the window appear as just a title in the taskbar at the bottom of the screen.
- Re-sizing a window can be done by left clicking on one of the corners of the window and keeping the mouse button down, dragging the corner to the correct size.
- Restoring a window takes it back to its original size.

Mouse settings – you can change how the mouse buttons work, how the mouse pointer looks and how it works and alter the speed of the scroll wheel.

Icon size – if you right click the mouse button when on the desktop, you can adjust the size of the icons. You can have large, medium and classic (i.e., the smallest size). By making icons bigger you can improve the use for children and people with poor eyesight.

Screen resolution – this determines how sharp the icons, etc., appear on the screen. It also determines their size. Higher screen resolutions mean items on the screen are sharp but small. Screen resolution determines the number of pixels (i.e., dots of light) used on the screen (e.g., 1600 × 1200 pixels).

Desktop fonts – text and other items such as icons that appear on the screen can be made bigger or smaller. This can be done by increasing or decreasing the dpi (dots per inch).

Colour – you can change most of the colours used for the desktop. For example, you can change the colour of windows.

Position – you can alter the position of elements on the screen such as windows and toolbars.

Graphics – you can change the screensaver, background, customize icons and many other graphics elements.

Contrast – contrast determines the difference between the dark and light parts of the screen. Too much contrast can cause eye strain.

Volume – can be changed using the control panel. You can set the master volume and also change the volume for each of the programs you use.

Toolbars – these are the bars that appear across the top and sometimes the bottom of the interface you are using. There are many tools available and too many to put on the screen all in one go. You can customize toolbars by only adding those you require and you can add only those tools that you use regularly to the toolbar.

Set date and time – this can be done by double clicking on the time.

Starting and stopping the computer, user interfaces, adjusting settings *continued*

Activity

Customizing the user interface

1 Produce a document (use the help screens in Windows to help you) that will act as a reference manual for doing each of the following:
   • Adjusting the size of a window
   • Altering the position of a window
   • Adjusting mouse settings
   • Changing the size of icons displayed on the desktop
   • Altering the screen resolution
   • Changing the size of the desktop fonts
   • Changing the brightness and contrast of the screen
   • Changing the system volume.
2 Access the control panel by clicking on 'Start' and then clicking on 'Control Panel'. Investigate what options are available but do not alter any of the settings.
   Write a list of at least 20 things you can do using the Control Panel.
3 Using the online help provided by Windows, find out how to produce a shortcut to a program that you use regularly that does not have a shortcut at the moment.
   Create this shortcut.

Questions A

1 Operating systems allow the user to customize them.

   Give **two** ways a user can customize their operating system. (*2 marks*)

2 All computers need an operating system.
   (a) Explain what an operating system is. (*2 marks*)
   (b) List **three** different functions of an operating system. (*3 marks*)
   (c) Windows is one operating system. Give the name of **one** other operating system. (*1 mark*)

3 (a) Explain what is meant by screen resolution. (*1 mark*)
   (b) Give **one** reason why a user might want to change the screen resolution. (*1 mark*)

Extension activity 1

You have been asked to change the user interface for someone whose sight is poor. Use the Internet or the help provided in Windows to find out how the user interface can be customized to suit their needs.

Extension activity 2

Computers are still not that easy to use and the user interface could be improved considerably. For this extension activity you have to think about how you would like to communicate with your computer. See if you can produce a list of things that would improve the interface between you and your computer.

Folder structures and files, safe storage and retrieval, networking

Being organized is important when you are a computer user. You will have problems if you don't give your folders and files proper names that describe their contents. In this section you will be learning about how to organize files and folders.

As most computers are networked, it is important to know about the components that are needed to create a network. For example, networks need a medium through which the data signals travel from one computer to another. They also need devices to connect the networks together or can be used to connect one network to a different network. As well as hardware, special network software is needed to cope with the special security problems that arise when computers are connected together. In this section you will also be looking at the advantages and disadvantages of networking computers.

The management and organization of files and folders

Because of the large number of files you store on a computer over a period of time, you need to be organized in the way you maintain them. You need to think carefully about filenames that give you some idea of their contents. Files should always be put into folders so that they can be found quickly when needed.

In order for you to use ICT successfully you need to be able to do the following on files and folders:

- move
- delete
- copy
- rename.

Choosing sensible file names

Saving your word processed document files as doc1, doc2, etc., will not help you if you want to find a particular file. Always use sensible file names. The name should clearly indicate the content of the file.

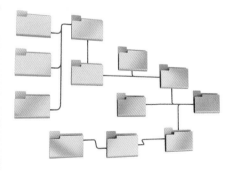

▲ It is important to create a folder structure.

Reasons for organizing folders and files

The reasons for organizing folders and files include:

- So you can find them easily – it will take you less time to find files, especially if it is a long time since you last used them.
- So they can be copied – for example, it is easier to copy a whole group of files in a single folder than files scattered in different places.
- So they are easily transferred – you may want to send them to others as file attachments using the Internet.

Networking

If more than one computer is used in the home or in a business, then it makes sense to network them. Networking means that devices such as printers and scanners can be shared between all the computers on the network. It also means that all the computers can share an Internet link that will allow all computers access at the same time. There is also the ability to share programs and data.

What is a network?

A network is two or more computers that are linked together so that they are able to share resources. These resources could be a printer, scanner, software or even a connection to the Internet. You can also share data using a network. For example, a pupil database in a school could be accessed from any of the computers connected to the network.

Folder structures and files, safe storage and retrieval, networking *continued*

Peer-to-peer and client–server networks

There are two ways of operating a network: peer-to-peer and client–server. Large organizations would use a client–server network because it is more powerful and can do a lot more. Peer-to-peer networking is fine for home networks or small businesses where a simple inexpensive network is all that is needed.

Whether an organization chooses peer-to-peer or client–server is mainly determined by the size of the network.

Peer-to-peer networks

Here are the main features of peer-to-peer networks:

- Each computer on the network has equal status.
- All computers can share each other's resources (e.g., data, an Internet connection, printers, scanners, etc.).
- They are only suitable for small networks with fewer than ten users.
- Only very basic knowledge is needed to set one up and use it.
- As more people use the network, the whole network slows down considerably.

Client–server networks

Here are the main features of client–server networks:

- One more powerful computer, called the server, is used to store the data and the programs needed by the whole network. The server is in control of the network.
- Software and data is stored on the server, so it can be accessed by all the computers on the network.
- The network is totally dependent on the server. If the server breaks down, the network cannot be used.
- They are the popular choice for networks that need lots of computers.

LAN (local area network)	WAN (wide area network)
Confined to a small area	Cover a wide geographical area (e.g., between cities, countries and even continents)
Usually located in a single building	In lots of different buildings, cities, countries, etc.
Uses cable, wireless, infrared and microwave links that are usually owned by the organization	Uses more expensive telecommunication links that are supplied by telecommunication companies
Cheap to build	Expensive to build
Cheap to run	Expensive to run

The main types of network: LAN and WAN

There are two types of network: a local area network (LAN) and a wide area network (WAN).

Basically a WAN is much bigger than a LAN and spread over a much wider area. The table above gives you the main features of each type of network.

The components of networks

This section looks at the hardware and software that are needed to create a network.

Data transfer media

Data transfer media are the material through which data travels from one computer to another in a network. For small, simple networks this is usually wire, but many networks work wirelessly. Wires add considerably to the cost of a network, especially the cost of installing them. The main forms of data transfer media are:

- metal wires
- fibre optic cable
- wireless.

The end of a fibre optic cable. Fibre optic cables can transmit data faster than metal cables.

Wireless Internet is available in many public places.

Metal wires can be used to transfer data.

Network cards

Before a computer can be connected to a network, it will need to have a network card. Most modern computers have one already installed when you buy the computer.

Hubs, switches and routers

All these devices allow the computers in a network to be joined so they are able to share files, resources and an Internet connection.

Hubs – are simple devices used to join computers in a network so they are able to share files and an Internet connection.

Switches – are like hubs in that they are used to join computers in a network but they are more intelligent. Switches look at each packet of data and then send it to the computer it was intended for. This reduces the amount of data travelling around the network and makes it work faster.

Routers – are devices that join several wired or wireless networks together. They are often used in the home to enable several computers to access the Internet using a single connection.

KEY WORDS

LAN (local area network) a network of computers on one site.

WAN (wide area network) a network where the terminals/computers are remote from each other and telecommunications are used to communicate between them.

Network a group of computers that are able to communicate with each other.

Networking software this is systems software that allows computers connected together to function as a network.

Network software

Small networks can be run using existing Windows software. For larger client–server networks, specialist network operating systems software is needed.

This software includes facilities to:

- keep track of the software being run on each computer
- keep all applications software up-to-date
- check that all computers have and are kept up-to-date with the latest virus checker
- check that a user has not loaded software illegally onto their computer
- check what hardware each computer has (e.g., processor, memory, size of hard drive, etc.).

Connecting networks together

Many networks are connected together. For example, you might have a couple of computers networked together in the home that share a connection to the Internet using a router. You therefore have a small network connected to the largest network in the world (i.e., the Internet).

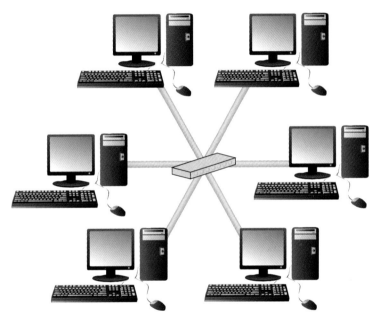

▲ A simple network makes use of a hub.

▼ A network card allows a connection to be made between the network cables and the computer.

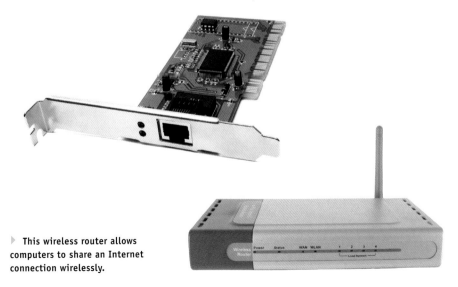

▷ This wireless router allows computers to share an Internet connection wirelessly.

Folder structures and files, safe storage and retrieval, networking *continued*

The advantages and disadvantages of using computer networks

Advantages

- You can share hardware – you can just have one printer and one scanner, as any of the computers connected to the network can use them.
- Software can be installed in one place – you do not need to install software on each computer. This makes it faster to install and easier to maintain. If the software needs to be upgraded, then this is much easier if only one copy is used.
- Improved security – work can be saved on the network. The network manager will make sure that the work is backed up. Passwords make sure that other people cannot access your work unless you want them to.
- Speed – it is very quick to copy and transfer files.
- Cost – when software is bought, the school can buy network versions. These are much cheaper than buying a copy for each stand-alone computer.
- Email facilities – any user of the network will be able to communicate using electronic mail. This will be much more efficient compared to paper-based documents such as memos, etc.
- Access to a central store of data – users will have access to centrally stored data.

Disadvantages

- A network manager will need to be employed – this can be quite expensive.
- Security problems – a virus could get onto the system and cause problems, or hackers may gain access to the data on the network.
- Breakdown problems – If the network breaks down, users will not have access to the important information held.
- Expensive – a server and cables and/or other communication devices will be needed. The installation costs of a network are also high.

KEY WORD

Stand-alone computer if a computer is used on its own without any connection (wireless or wire) to a network (including the Internet), then it is a stand-alone computer.

Questions B

1 Here are some of the things you can do with files. For each one explain clearly what is being done to the file. *(4 marks)*

      Copy   Move   Rename   Delete.

2 The organization of files into folders and subfolders is extremely important.
 (a) Explain the difference between a folder and a subfolder. *(2 marks)*
 (b) Give **two** reasons why file organization is important. *(2 marks)*

3 Write down what the abbreviation LAN stands for. *(1 mark)*

4 Describe what is meant by a computer network. *(1 mark)*

5 Most schools use networked computers to form a LAN rather than using stand-alone computers.
 (a) Explain the difference between computers in a LAN and stand-alone computers. *(2 marks)*
 (b) Describe **two** advantages to the students in using a LAN rather than using stand-alone computers. *(2 marks)*
 (c) Describe **two** disadvantages to the students in using a LAN rather than using stand-alone computers. *(2 marks)*

6 Give **three** advantages of a network over stand-alone computers. *(3 marks)*

7 Give the names of **three** devices whose resources may be shared using a network. *(3 marks)*

8 A school is thinking of installing a network system throughout the school. The school network is to be linked using metal wires. The school already owns all the computers they need. At the moment the computers are being used as stand-alone machines.
 (a) Give **two** other ways computers can be linked without the need for metal wires. *(2 marks)*
 (b) Explain what is meant by a stand-alone machine. *(1 mark)*
 (c) Give **two** items of hardware or software that the school will need in order to turn their computers into a network. *(2 marks)*

Troubleshooting

ICT systems are quite complex and therefore prone to problems. Luckily many of these problems are easy to identify and fix. In this section you will be looking at some of the common problems and you will find out how to troubleshoot problems with hardware and software. You will also learn about the difference between hardware problems and software problems and how they can be solved.

Identifying ICT problems and solving errors

ICT systems are complex and they can cause a lot of problems to the user. Users of computers need to know what to do when certain problems and errors occur.

Software freeze

Have you met the problem where the software just freezes and you cannot do anything? When this happens you have to press Ctrl + Alt + Del keys together and this gets you to the Task Manager where you can end the program. When this happens you may lose any unsaved work.

Error dialogues/messages

Error dialogues/messages appear when something is wrong such as:

- The computer memory is running low.
- You need the batteries changing for your wireless mouse or keyboard.
- There is a printer jam.
- The printer ink or paper is running low.

Usually all you have to do is click on the OK button to acknowledge that you have seen the message and are doing something about it.

Storage full

When you try to save your work and the computer informs you that the storage media is full, there are a number of things you can do:

- Delete some old files and free up some space. Most people have a lot of files that they no longer need, which simply clog up space on the storage media.
- Save your files on a friend's storage media.

Paper jam

A paper jam occurs when printer paper gets stuck in the printer. In many cases it is because the printer paper has not been put into the paper tray properly. To remove a paper jam you may need to first turn the power off and then follow the instructions in the manual, which may be paper based or online.

▽ The blue screen all computer users dread – it means you have probably lost the work you have done since the last time it was saved.

▲ Error dialogues.

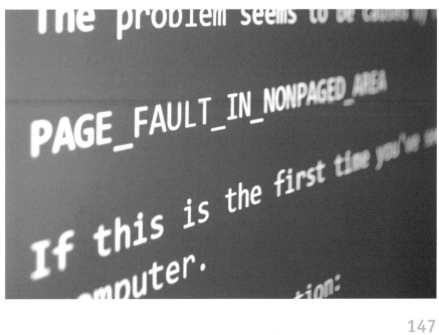

Troubleshooting *continued*

The control panel in Windows 7.

Uninstalling software

When you install new software on your computer there is a program that installs the software for you. If there is software on your computer that you no longer need, you can remove it to free up some space. Deleting the software is possible using 'delete' but the trouble is that it can leave parts of the program undeleted and this can cause future problems. The best way is to access the Control Panel. You can see under the heading 'Programs' that there is a program that will uninstall a program properly. To uninstall a program you simply click on this and then tell the computer which program you want to remove.

Getting help to fix problems

There are a number of ways to get help:

- For help with usernames, passwords and storage space on the network ask the network manager.
- For general advice about software – simply ask the person next to you. Many problems are solved like this.
- Use the online help provided by the software.
- Ask your teacher/lecturer.
- Access the help-desk of the supplier of the hardware/ software/communications service.
- This can be done using email or over the phone.

Troubleshooting activities

Hardware troubleshooting

Computer hardware is usually reliable and many of the problems are simple to solve once they have been identified. Hardware troubleshooting starts with simple things such as:

- Is the device switched on?
- Is the power getting to the device? Are the power indicator lights on?
- Are the data leads firmly in their sockets? If screens or computers have been moved then the leads may have worked loose.
- If the device is wireless (e.g., a mouse or a keyboard) then they contain batteries which may need replacing.

Troubleshooting hardware involves eliminating the simple problems. The manufacturer's website will probably have a 'frequently asked questions' section, which may solve the problem. You could also contact the help line for the manufacturer, who may be able to suggest a solution to the problem.

Wireless keyboards and mice have batteries that need to be replaced.

Software troubleshooting

Software problems are very common and like hardware you need to look at the simple things first. Sometimes switching off the computer and loading the operating system and then the application software is worth a try. Sometimes the only way to get software to work properly again is to reinstall the software. This can be done by using the original disks or downloading the software off the Internet.

▷ Most hardware and software manufacturers have a technical support department to help you solve computer problems.

Questions C

1 You are using some software when suddenly the software freezes, which prevents you doing anything with the computer.

Give the correct instructions that will enable you to start using the computer again. *(2 marks)*

2 A user is in a hurry to get out of the computer room and instead of logging off and shutting down their computer properly, they simply turn the power off. Give **one** reason why computers should be shut down properly. *(1 mark)*

3 A computer user is having a problem with a printer.
   (a) Explain **two** sources of help they could use to solve this problem. *(2 marks)*
   (b) Another user wants to remove a program and simply right clicks on the program name and selects 'delete'. Give **one** reason why doing this is not a good idea and explain how it should be done. *(2 marks)*

Extension activity 1

Use the online help provided by Windows to find out what to do in each of the following situations:

- software freeze
- when the screen resolution has been changed and you want to alter it to what you are used to.

Extension activity 2

A family of four all have their own computers. They would like to network these computers together. They have asked for your advice on what they need to do.

Write a list of the advantages of networking their computers together.

Write a list of the extra equipment they might need to create the network.

They would like to all share the same Internet connection and have asked how this might be done. Explain clearly what equipment is needed.

END-OF-TOPIC REVIEW

Questions

 Test yourself

The following notes summarize this topic. The notes are incomplete because they have words missing. Using the words in the list below, copy out and complete the sentences A to I, underlining the words that you have inserted. Each word may be used more than once.

folders   user-ID

customization   network   WANs

network cards   router   networking   LANs

A A group of computers linked together in order to share resources and files/ data is called a _____ .

B Networks confined to a single site or building are called _____ .

C Networks that use third party communication lines and are separated by a distance are called _____ .

D A device that joins several wired or wireless networks together is called a _____ .

E Files should always be put into _____ so that they can be quickly found when needed.

F Logging onto a computer usually involves supplying the system with two things: a _____ and a password.

G Making changes to a user interface in order to suit the way you like to work is called _____ .

H _____ software is systems software that allows computers connected together to function as a network.

I _____ provide a connection between a network cable and the computer and are an essential part of wired networks.

Examination style questions

1. People often have problems when using ICT. Explain how each of the following will affect a computer user and describe what can be done to remedy the situation:

   (a) Paper jam *(2 marks)*

   (b) Software freeze *(2 marks)*

   (c) Storage full *(2 marks)*

2. (a) Define computer hardware. *(1 mark)*

   (b) Define computer software. *(1 mark)*

   (c) The following table shows items of hardware and software.
   Classify each item by ticking the correct box. *(5 marks)*

Item	Hardware	Software
Printer	☐	☐
Operating system	☐	☐
Database	☐	☐
Microprocessor	☐	☐
Web browser	☐	☐

3. A user is having difficulty with a piece of hardware they have just bought.

   Describe **two** different ways they can get help with this problem. *(2 marks)*

4. A school uses a computer network.

   (a) Explain what is meant by a computer network. *(1 mark)*

   (b) The school decides to set up a LAN.

   (i) What is meant by the abbreviation LAN. *(1 mark)*

   (ii) Describe how a LAN differs from a WAN. *(2 marks)*

5. A school uses a LAN for its computers. The school is connected to the local authority's WAN.

   (a) Give the name of the device that is used to connect a LAN to a WAN. *(1 mark)*

   (b) Give two differences between a WAN and a LAN. *(2 marks)*

6. Networking computers brings many advantages to an organization.
   Describe the advantages of networking computers. *(8 marks)*

7. Computer users are able to customize their user interfaces.

   (a) Explain clearly what the above statement means and give **two** examples of customization. *(3 marks)*

   (b) Give **two** examples of customization for use by students in a school who have impaired eyesight. *(2 marks)*

Exam support

Worked example

A small solicitors' office has ten stand-alone computers. They have been told that it is much more effective if all the computers are formed into a network.

State **three** benefits that the organization would gain from networking their computers together. *(6 marks)*

Student answer 1

They would be able to access the Internet.

They would be able to send email to each other without using the Internet, which would be cheaper.

They could all use the same data.

◀ Examiner's comment

The first sentence is not strictly true. Stand-alone computers can of course access the Internet. What they probably meant to say is that by networking the computers together they could all share a single Internet connection. The examiner cannot read their mind and can only mark what appears, so this sentence is not worthy of a mark.

The second sentence is true and well explained because they could still send email to each other using the Internet but this can compromise the security of the data so organizations like to send email internally without using the Internet.

The last sentence is worth one mark.

The student should have looked at the mark scheme and realized that there are two marks for each benefit. So a brief benefit for one mark and further explanation of the benefit or an example should have been included for each.

(2 marks out of 6)

Student answer 2

Using a network they are able to share resources such as printers and scanners. This means that they need only buy one of each rather than one for each computer, which will be much cheaper.

Any computer will be able to access files stored on the server. This means it will not be necessary for data to be copied so that it can be transferred between the computers.

All the computers will be able to share a single Internet connection. This will be cheaper as all they need to buy is a router and they can then only pay for a single fast connection.

◀ Examiner's comment

This is a very well-structured and thought out answer. Notice the way they have sectioned their answer. The first sentence introduces the benefit and then extra sentences add further explanation.

This good examination technique has helped this student gain all the marks for this question.

(6 marks out of 6)

Examiner's answers

One mark each for a statement of the benefit and one mark for an explanation of the benefit x 3:

- Ability to share files *(1)* – no need to make copies of files as all the files can be accessed by all the computers on the network if needed *(1)*.
- Ability to share hardware resources *(1)* – no need to have a printer for each computer as any hardware device (e.g., printer, scanner, plotter, etc.) can be shared *(1)*.
- Ability to share software *(1)* – software can be shared, meaning that everyone will be using the same version. Maintaining software by keeping it up-to-date is made much easier *(1)*.
- Lower software costs *(1)* – it is cheaper to buy one network version with a licence for so many users compared to buying individual copies for each computer *(1)*.
- Improved security *(1)* – it is easier for network managers to control access to the Internet from computers *(1)*.
- Can share an Internet connection *(1)* – one connection can allow all users access *(1)*.
- Easier to back up files *(1)* – backing up is performed by the network manager rather than the individual users, which means backing up is taken seriously and users are less likely to lose data *(1)*.
- Improved communication *(1)* – networks have email facilities, which will improve communication between workers *(1)*.
- Central maintenance and support *(1)* – new upgrades to software need only to be added to the server and not to each computer *(1)*.

EXAM TIPS

If you are asked to explain something then giving a one word or a couple of words example is not sufficient. You must include a sentence.

If you are asked to 'give' an answer then one word or a couple of words is ok.

The word 'describe' means that you must give your answer in sentences. Be guided by the mark scheme as to how much you need to write. If there are two marks then the minimum you need is two clearly different points. It is important to note that you are never penalized for writing too much, although you may waste some time.

Be careful about being too creative in your English. You are always limited by the number of lines given for your answer on the paper. Most students get to the end of the number of lines and stop. You need to work out your answer and try to convey it with the minimum number of words. This gives you plenty of room for making more points.

Summary mind maps

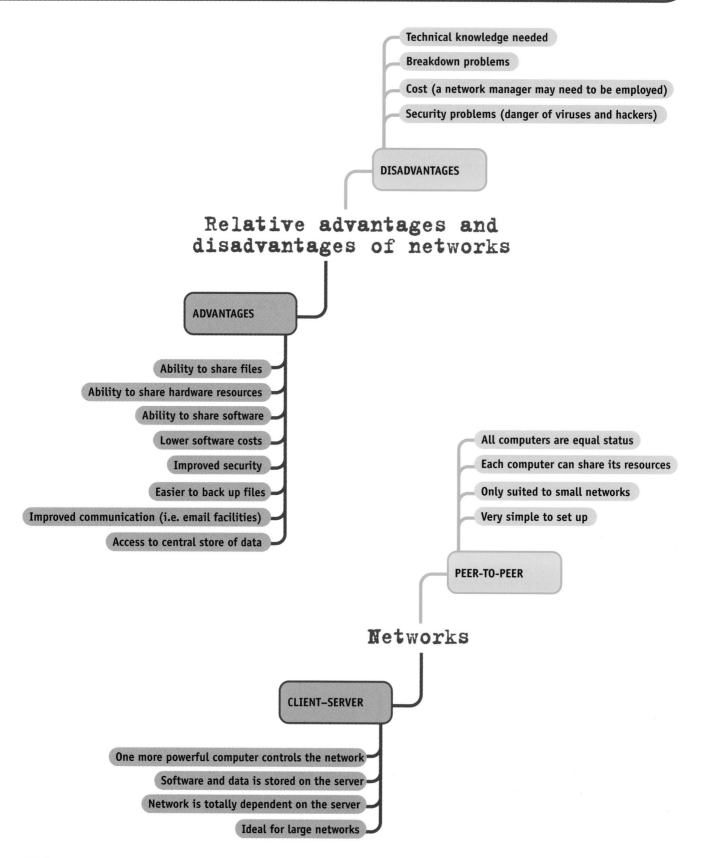

Technical knowledge needed

Breakdown problems

Cost (a network manager may need to be employed)

Security problems (danger of viruses and hackers)

DISADVANTAGES

Relative advantages and disadvantages of networks

ADVANTAGES

Ability to share files

Ability to share hardware resources

Ability to share software

Lower software costs

Improved security

Easier to back up files

Improved communication (i.e. email facilities)

Access to central store of data

All computers are equal status

Each computer can share its resources

Only suited to small networks

Very simple to set up

PEER–TO–PEER

Networks

CLIENT–SERVER

One more powerful computer controls the network

Software and data is stored on the server

Network is totally dependent on the server

Ideal for large networks

Monitoring, measurement and control technology

The key concepts covered in this topic are:

- Sensors and their uses
- Data logging and its advantages and disadvantages
- Controlling devices
- Monitoring and control in everyday life

Data logging involves collecting data automatically from sensors over a certain period of time, called the logging period. Data logging can be used in science lessons for monitoring temperature, light, force, etc. In geography lessons data logging can be used to record the weather. Data logging is used in society for monitoring traffic flow, monitoring pollution, keeping track of climate change, etc.

Data from sensors can be used to control devices. For example, the data from temperature sensors are used to turn heaters on or off to maintain a constant temperature. Most electronic devices you find in the home use some form of control, as you will see later in this topic.

Contents

Data logging

You will find out

▷ **About sensors**

▷ **About data logging**

▷ **About the advantages and disadvantages of data logging**

Data logging means taking measurements automatically using sensors that are able to measure physical quantities such as temperature, pressure, sound, etc.

In this section you will learn about the available sensors, data logging and the advantages and disadvantages data logging offers.

▲ This data logger contains built-in light sensor, sound sensor, temperature sensor, barometric pressure sensor and two inputs where you can attach a whole range of sensors.

Sensors

Sensors are used to detect and measure physical quantities. Here are some examples of sensors:

- Temperature/heat sensors – can be used in school experiments such as investigating the cooling of a hot drink in different thicknesses of cardboard cup. Heat sensors can be used to control a heating system in a home or classroom.
- Light sensors – detect the brightness of light. Can be used to see how light levels affect the growth of a plant. They can be used to control lights that come on automatically when it goes dark.
- Sound sensors – measure the loudness of a sound. Can be used in noise disputes.

- Pressure sensors – barometric pressure sensors measure air pressure; other pressure sensors measure depth of liquid or something pressing on them.
- Humidity sensors – these measure the moisture in the air.
- Passive infrared sensors (PIRs) – these are the sensors used in schools and homes to detect movement. They can be used in burglar alarms and also to turn lights on/off automatically in rooms when a person walks in/out.

Data logging

Data logging is where readings are taken regularly over a period of time using sensors.

The main features of data logging are:

- The readings are taken automatically – there is no need for a human to be present. This means that it is much cheaper than employing a person to do this.
- You can set the logging period – this is the total time over which the readings will be collected.

- You can set the logging rate (also called the logging interval) – this determines how often the readings are taken. For example, in an experiment to investigate the cooling of boiling water, you might decide to set the logging rate to be every minute.
- The sensors can be put in remote locations – you can put them anywhere in the world and the data can be sent back wirelessly and even using satellites.
- The data sent can be stored and processed by a computer.
- The data can be analysed (you can do calculations such as work on the mean, mode, median, range, etc.) and graphs and charts can be drawn. The data can be processed using a spreadsheet package.

Sending data to a computer

The data from a data logger can be sent to a computer. There are two ways to do this:

- Use wires to connect the data logger to the computer.
- Use wireless (usually Bluetooth).

Advantages and disadvantages of data logging

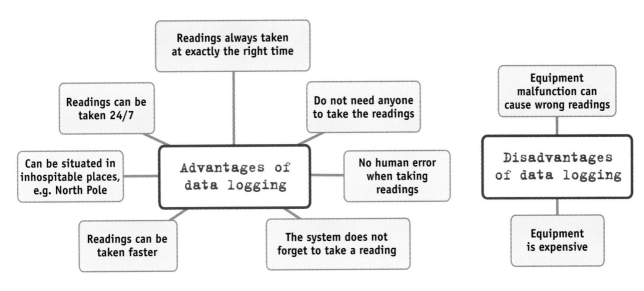

Advantages of data logging.

Disadvantages of data logging.

Activity

Which sensor?

A hot drink vending company wants to perform an experiment to see which cardboard cup is best at keeping hot drinks hot. They need to investigate how the temperature falls in each cup from the temperature at which the hot drinks are produced, which is about 90°C. They decide to use data logging for this.

1 Give the name of the sensor that is needed for this experiment. *(1 mark)*
2 A logging rate needs to be chosen for the data logger. Give the meaning of the term logging rate. *(2 marks)*
3 Out of the following, which logging rate should be chosen? Per second, per minute or per hour. *(1 mark)*
4 Explain what is meant by the logging period. *(2 marks)*
5 Out of the following, which logging period should be chosen? 30 seconds, 1 hour or 24 hours. *(1 mark)*
6 Explain your choice of answer for question 5. *(1 mark)*

KEY WORDS

Data logger a device that collects readings from one or more sensors. The time interval between each reading can be varied (called the logging rate) and the total time over which the data is logged (called the logging period) can also be varied.

Data logging the process of using an ICT system to collect data from sensors at a certain rate over a certain period of time. Remote weather stations use data logging.

Sensors devices that measure physical quantities such as temperature, pressure, humidity, etc.

Questions A

1 A sensor is used in a geography lesson to investigate how the outside temperature varies over the course of 24 hours. A data logger is used to collect the data from sensors.
  (a) What kind of sensor should be used with this system? *(1 mark)*
  (b) Explain why the sensor you have named in (a) is needed. *(1 mark)*
  (c) What is the logging period for this investigation? *(1 mark)*
  (d) Explain what is meant by a logging interval and suggest a suitable logging interval for this investigation. *(2 marks)*

2 Computer control is used to control growing conditions in a greenhouse. For example, a temperature sensor will turn on a heater if the temperature inside the greenhouse gets too cold.
  (a) Give the names of **two** other sensors that could be used in the greenhouse and for each one describe why it is needed. *(4 marks)*
  (b) Give **two** advantages in using ICT to monitor and control the growing conditions in the greenhouse. *(2 marks)*
  (c) Describe **one** disadvantage in using monitoring and control to control the growing conditions in the greenhouse. *(1 mark)*

Controlling devices

You will find out

▷ **About using a sequence of instructions to control a screen image or an external device**

▷ **About controlling a range of devices**

The data from sensors can be used to control devices such as lights, sirens, motors, etc. The data from the sensors is sent to a computer (in most cases a very simple one), where the computer decides what control signal to issue to an output device/actuator such as a light. In this section you will be looking at the way devices can be controlled by a computer.

Actuators

An actuator is a mechanism that causes a device to be turned on or off, adjusted or moved. An actuator therefore produces some form of movement according to a signal sent to it by the computer. Actuators are needed to turn taps on/off, alter valves, open windows by different amounts, etc.

Sensors and actuators for visible, tactile and audible and other physical signals

Tactile means related to the sense of touch. Some sensors are able to detect touch. The touch pad on a computer is one example. Many devices such as touch screens, touch switches on household devices such as microwaves contain touch/tactile sensors.

It is also possible to use an actuator that uses signals from a computer to respond in a similar way to a human hand. Robot arms, for example, can pick goods from a conveyer belt and pack them in boxes.

Visible sensors respond in a similar way to the human eye. Sensors in digital cameras (both still and video) and webcams contain sensors that sense images and then digitize them.

There are devices that are able to send an image as an electrical signal to sensors that have been implanted in a human brain and this has restored sight for some people.

Audible sensors respond to sound signals. The commonest audible sensor is the microphone.

Computers can control sound (bells, sirens, buzzers, beeps, etc.) and sound often acts as an indicator or warning. For example, when a washing machine or dishwasher has finished, it often makes a beep, or alarms sound when an intruder is sensed, etc.

Using a sequence of instructions to control devices

In control systems it is necessary to give a series of commands for the system to obey. For example, the following set of commands can be used to move an arrow on the screen of a computer. When the arrow moves, it leaves a line.

    FD distance
    LT angle
    RT angle

Hence, using the commands FD 5 would move the arrow forward 5 units and LT 90 would turn the arrow left through an angle of 90°.

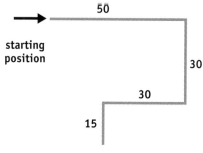

▲ Here is a shape that was drawn on the screen with the numbers representing the lengths of the lines.

The list of instructions that would draw this shape is as follows:

    FD 50
    RT 90
    FD 30
    RT 90
    FD 30
    LT 90
    FD 15

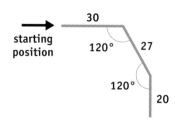

▲ Here is a more complex shape that makes use of angles other than right angles.

The set of instructions to draw this shape on the screen are:

    FD 30
    RT 60
    FD 27
    RT 60
    FD 20

▼ Most household electrical appliances use computer control.

The main components of a control system

The main components of a control system are:

- **Sensors –** which are the input devices that send data to the computer/processor.
- **Computer/processor** – uses a control program to decide what action to take when it receives data from the sensors. Once the decision has been made, a control signal is sent to the output device.
- **Output devices** – such as lights, heaters, motors, etc., that are controlled by the control signals.

Non-feedback control systems

If you are writing a simple program to control a robot arm by rotating it, you can issue instructions to a stepper motor. A stepper motor rotates in short steps and you can determine how many steps you need. This will determine the angle it moves through.

▲ Stepper motors turn through set angles. This makes them ideal output devices for turning a tap so as to control how much water is released.

The motor will rotate through an angle and then stop. This is a non-feedback system because there is no way of detecting whether it has actually moved through the correct angle. If there was an obstacle in the way of the arm, it may not have been able to move the correct angle. If another instruction was issued then it will simply move from its incorrect starting point.

▲ This security light system uses a PIR sensor to detect a person, so the security lights are turned on.

Simple control systems

Security light system – uses a PIR sensor to sense movement. As soon as the sensor detects movement the system turns the light on. After a period of time the system turns the light off.

A burglar alarm – works in a similar way to the security light using PIRs as the input into the system. This time the output device is a bell or siren that sounds when the alarm is on and movement is detected.

▲ PIR sensors are used to detect intruders and sound an alarm siren in a burglar alarm system.

Electronic toys and games

Many children's toys and games use computer control. Instructions are issued in the form of a stored program and the device then obeys them.

Automatic doors

Automatic doors use motion sensors to detect someone walking towards the door. A signal is sent to an actuator (electric motor) to open the door. The door will only close if the system detects that there is no-one in the vicinity.

▲ Automatic doors use motion sensors to detect people walking towards them.

Burglar alarms and security systems

Modern burglar alarms are quite complex. They use computer control to enable people to set up zones. For example, when they are sleeping upstairs in a house they may want the downstairs alarmed but not the upstairs. Burglar alarms use motion detectors in each room and other detectors on windows and doors to detect people trying to break in.

Car parking systems

Car park management systems provide a means of directing vehicles around a network to car parks with available spaces. Special signs indicating how many spaces are left are controlled by a central computer that uses data from how many cars have entered the car park and how many have left. Computer control is also used to control the barriers in a car park.

▲ A computer-controlled car park barrier – the system has to count the cars coming in and going out to know how many spaces are left.

Controlling devices *continued*

Traffic control systems

Traffic control systems are found in all towns and cities and they ensure that the traffic runs fairly smoothly during the morning and evening rush hours and at other times during the day.

The aims of the traffic control system are:

- To improve the traffic flow.
- To improve driver and pedestrian safety by reducing frustration.
- To make sure that any delays in a journey are kept to a minimum.
- To reduce the risk to the environment caused by fumes from waiting traffic.
- To reduce the use of fossil fuels.

Town traffic systems need to be able to cope with a huge increase in traffic flow from the suburbs into a town centre in the morning and the corresponding reversed flow during the early evening. Setting the traffic lights on a set sequence would not be able to cope with this and serious delays would be the result.

In a traffic control system, the traffic flow is assessed on the basis of the quantity of vehicles around the whole area. Using this information the system can detect in which direction the majority of the traffic is flowing. It can then make sure that cars on main routes into a town will be given more green lights than usual so that the traffic in this direction runs more smoothly. In the evening this situation will be reversed.

Data concerning the number of cars passing is measured using an underground detector cable set into the road surface before a junction.

▲ Traffic control systems help keep traffic moving thus reducing pollution.

▶ The sequence of traffic lights.

KEY WORD

Actuators devices such as motors that react according to signals given to them by the computers. An actuator can be used to open a window in a greenhouse.

Output devices controlled by control systems

The input signals from sensors are passed to the computer, where control signals are passed to output devices to control them. These output devices include the following:

- **Stepper motor** – a motor that turns in a series of small steps. The control signals tell the stepper motor how many steps and in which direction it should move. You can therefore control the angle through which the motor rotates. Stepper motors are found in robot arms.
- **Bells/sirens** – these are used in control systems where an alarm signal needs to be sounded. Burglar alarms use bells/sirens.
- **Heaters/coolers** – are used for controlling the temperature of an environment. Central heating/air conditioning systems use heaters/coolers as the output device.
- **Light** – floodlights or flashing lights are often used in control systems. For example, as well as sounding an alarm, a fire or burglar alarm system will also flash a warning light.

How control systems work

Input bits (0s or 1s) are detected by the sensors. For example, the input bit for a temperature sensor might be set to 1 if the temperature is too high. Otherwise it will be set to zero.

Output bits (0s and 1s) control the output devices. For example, if an output bit is set to 1, a heater could be turned on and if it is 0 it will be switched off.

The control program deals with the input bits and applies rules to it in order to set each of the output bits.

Example

In the heating system in a school, if the temperature gets too high, the heater is switched off and a fan is turned on. If it gets too cold, the fan turns off and the heater comes on.

The input bits and the output bits can be put into a table like this. The first row in the table shows the way the inputs and outputs are numbered.

Input bits	Output bits	
1	2	3
0	0	0

Input bit
    1 = a temperature sensor
Output bits
    2 = heater on/off control
    3 = fan on/off control

The bit pattern for the inputs and outputs is initially: 000

This means the temperature sensor records that the temperature is not too high and that the heater and fan are off.

Here are some bit patterns and what they mean:

1	2	3
0	1	0

The input temperature is 0, which means it is too cold, so this produces a 1 for bit 2 which means the heater is switched on. Bit 3, which is the bit for the fan, is 0 which means it is off.

If the temperature goes too high, bit 1 changes to a 1 and bit 2 (the heater) is switched off (i.e. it is a 0) and bit 3 (the fan) is turned on (i.e. it is a 1).

The bit pattern for this situation would be:

1	2	3
1	0	1

Robotics

Robots have been widely used in manufacturing for years, especially for painting and welding in car factories. Robots are also used for picking and packing goods in large warehouses.

Robots have been developed that will do some of the tasks humans hate to do such as mowing the lawn or vacuuming the floors.

▲ Robots have been developed for use on farms and these robots can perform a variety of farm tasks such as planting, weeding in-between crops, crop spraying and picking crops.

▲ Robots will eventually be seen in all homes. This vacuuming robot is already in the shops.

There are robots available for the home that will wash floors, clean gutters and clean swimming pools.

The robots that are available at the moment in the home are usually capable of performing one task. In the future you will probably buy a single multifunctional robot capable of carrying out a range of different tasks.

▲ Mowing the lawn is a chore for many people, so this robot lawnmower is a useful device.

Controlling devices *continued*

Questions B

1 A turtle that draws on paper uses the following instructions.

FORWARD *n*	Move *n* cm forward
BACKWARD *n*	Move *n* cm backwards
LEFT *t*	Turn left *t* degrees
RIGHT *t*	Turn right *t* degrees
PEN UP	Lift the pen off the paper
PEN DOWN	Place the pen on the paper

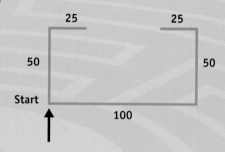

Write a set of instructions that makes the turtle draw the following shape.
Assume that the pen is down at the start.
(4 marks)

2 A particular control system controls the conditions in a greenhouse. Sensors for temperature, light, humidity and soil moisture send data to the computer.

If a sensor has detected that a value is too high, it sends a value of 1 to the computer otherwise it sends a 0.

The 4 bits (one for each sensor) are sent in the following order:

Temperature	Light	Humidity	Moisture (soil)

For each of the following, describe the conditions in the greenhouse when the following combination of bits are received *(4 marks)*

(a) 0000
(b) 1100
(c) 0011
(d) 1010

3 Give an example of how a digital pressure sensor could sensibly be used in a school. *(2 marks)*

Extension activity

Use the Internet to research examples of children's toys that use computer control.

Produce some notes explaining how the toys use control for their operation.

Control–feedback loop

You will find out

▷ **About the main components of the control–feedback loop**

▷ **About applications of control**

Control systems are all around us and we could hardly do without them. We have many control systems in the home controlling the heating, washing machines, dishwashers, showers, burglar alarms and so on. Once you are in a car the number of control systems shoots up. There are control systems to control the management of the engine, the braking system, the airbags and so on. You will also learn what feedback is and how it makes a control system more useful.

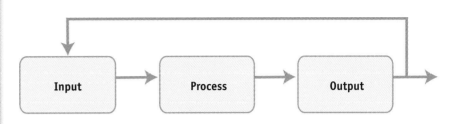

▲ Three stages of control; input, process and output with the feedback loop.

Control systems

Here you will be looking at control systems that incorporate something called feedback. Basically, having feedback makes the control system more intelligent and more useful.

Analogue to digital conversion

Analogue quantities are continuously variable, which means that they do not jump in steps from one value to another. Temperature is an analogue quantity because temperatures do not jump from one degree to the next as there are many values in between.

Digital quantities jump from one value to the next. Computers are nearly always digital devices and can only operate with digital values. If analogue values such as temperature readings need to be input into a computer, they first need to be converted to digital values using an analogue to digital converter.

The main components of the control–feedback loop

The above diagram shows the three stages of control: input, process and output. It also uses feedback.

Inputs to a control system can come in different ways. They can be:

- given by the user as an instruction (e.g., press a button)
- sensed by sensors that send signals to the computer (e.g., a light sensor senses that a person has walked through a door).

Input data is gathered by an input device and sent to the processor for processing. The processor works with the data and a stored program to work out what it needs to output. Some of the output is fed back to the input using the feedback loop.

The importance of feedback

A computer can be used to control a robot arm. If we want the robot arm to move through a certain angle, we can give an instruction to a special motor that moves small steps at a time. When the command has been issued, the arm will move to the required position. If there is an object in the way of the arm, it will stop. The problem is that if this happens, it will assume that it has reached its desired position. The computer can no longer be sure of its position.

What is needed is a way for the arm to relay its actual position back to the computer. It can do this by making use of sensors. The sensors continually send data about the position of the arm back to the computer. If the robot arm is not in the correct position then remedial action can be taken to put it in the correct position. Here, output from the system directly affects the input. Such a system is said to use 'feedback'.

KEY WORDS

Control getting the computer to operate devices automatically.

Control program the step-by-step instructions that control the output devices.

Feedback where the output from a system directly affects the input.

Control–feedback loop *continued*

Example of process control making use of feedback

Here is a simple example of process control.

In a chemical process a container is filled with water to a certain level and heated up to a temperature of 80°C.

1   The computer issues a control signal to the motorized tap instructing it to turn the tap on and let the water into the container.

2   As the water enters and the level rises, the water pressure is continually fed back to the computer.

3   As soon as the pressure reaches a certain value the water is up to the correct level. A control signal is sent back to the tap to turn the water off. At the same time a signal is fed back to the computer from the temperature sensor. If the temperature of the water is less than 80°C, a control signal is sent to the heater to turn it on.

4   The temperature is continually measured and sent back to the computer, which compares the temperature with its set level (i.e. 80°C). At soon as the temperature reaches this level, a control is issued to the heater to turn it off. At any time the temperature drops below 80°C, the heater is switched on again so that the temperature remains constant at 80°C.

In order to grow plants successfully they need perfect growing conditions. Computer control can be used to monitor the conditions and keep these conditions constant.

Greenhouses have sensors that collect data and this data is sent to the computer which controls the various output devices.

The sensors used to collect the input data include:

*   light
*   moisture
*   temperature.

The output devices that are controlled by the computer include:

*   lamps (to make the plants grow faster)
*   heater
*   motor to turn the sprinkler on/off to water the plants
*   motor to open or close the windows (to cool the greenhouse down if it gets too hot).

A control program is written that is used to control the outputs using the inputs it obtains from the sensors.

For example, the moisture sensor continually measures the amount of moisture in the soil. If the soil gets too dry, a signal is sent to the motor that turns the sprinkler on. Once the soil is wet enough, it is turned off.

▲   **Lamps, heaters, motors that open/close windows and sprinkler systems are controlled automatically by computers.**

Questions C

1   The following diagram shows the input devices and output devices used in a control system.

Write the names of **four** input devices and **three** output devices in the boxes. (7 marks)

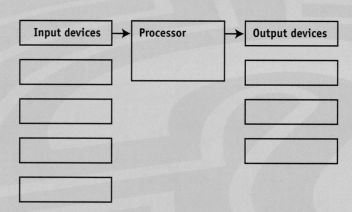

2   **(a)**   Many control systems make use of feedback. Explain what is meant by feedback. *(2 marks)*
     (b)   Explain how feedback is used to control a heater to keep the temperature of a room constant. *(4 marks)*

3   Give the names of **three** different output devices that can be controlled by a computer. *(3 marks)*

Questions

 Test yourself

The following notes summarize this topic. The notes are incomplete because they have words missing. Using the words in the list below, copy out and complete the sentences A to J, underlining the words that you have inserted. Each word may be used more than once.

> data logging   frequency   automatically   period   physical
>
> feedback   process control   sensors   humidity

A Data logging involves automatically collecting data from _____.

B The time over which the whole of the data is collected is called the logging _____.

C The process of using an ICT system to collect data from sensors at a certain rate over a certain period of time is called _____.

D In data logging, the logging rate, or logging interval, is the _____ at which the readings are taken.

E The main advantage with data logging is that the readings can be taken _____.

F A sensor that measures the amount of moisture in the air or soil is called a _____ sensor.

G Sensors are devices that measure _____ quantities such as temperature, pressure, etc.

H Control often makes use of _____ where the output has some influence on the input.

I The input to control systems is usually obtained from _____.

J Computers are often used to control a process in a factory. This is called _____.

Examination style questions

1 A home weather station consists of a base station that contains the processor and the display. Sensors are also included that are placed outside the house. Readings from the sensors are relayed back to the base station, which processes the data and produces weather information that is displayed on the screen.

   (a) Give the names of **two** different types of sensor that could be used with this system. *(2 marks)*

   (b) Describe **one** method by which the data can get from the remote sensors to the base unit that is situated inside the house. *(2 marks)*

   (c) Once the data has been sent to the base unit it is processed and the information is output. Describe **one** way that the weather information is output from the system. *(2 marks)*

2 (a) Give the name of a household device that uses a control system. *(1 mark)*

   (b) Explain how the control system controls the device you have named in part (a). *(3 marks)*

Exam support

Worked example

A cutter in a clothing manufacturing company is controlled by a computer. The cutter is used to cut various patterns in cloth automatically using the following instructions.

START   means start program

CU   means raise the cutter up

CD   means lower the cutter down

FD 10   means forward 10

BK 5   means backward 5

RT 90   means right turn 90 degrees

LT 45   means left turn 45 degrees

CS   means clear screen

END   means end program

The cutter always starts with the cutter up so that it does not start cutting. When the END command is used the cutter will automatically return to its starting position.

(a) Write a program using instructions similar to the above that will cut out the shape shown here. *(3 marks)*

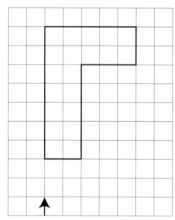

Starting postition
is at the tip of
the arow

(b) On the blank grid drawn below draw the shape that the cutter will cut out when carrying out the following program. *(2 marks)*

START

FD 6

CD

FD 3

RT 90

FD 7

RT 90

FD 7

RT 90

FD 2

RT 90

FD 4

LT 90

FD 5

CU

END

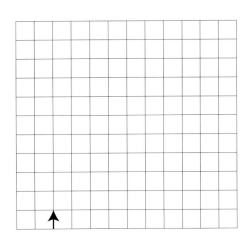

(c) Give **two** reasons why it would be difficult for the cutter to cut out a complex shape using only those commands given above. *(2 marks)*

Student answer 1

(a) FD 7

RT 90

FD 5

RT 90

FD 2

RT 90

FD 3

LT 90

FD 5

RT 90

FD 2

END

(b)

(c) *You can't go diagonally because the diagonal distances are more than one square.*

You can only go in straight lines.

▲ **Examiner's comment**

(a) There is no start command instructing the computer to start obeying the set of instructions. Also the student has started from where the shape starts and not from where the tip of the arrow is. There is also no instruction CD telling the cutter to go down and start cutting. The middle section of commands are correct but the student has failed to raise the cutter before the END command.

Only one mark is given for the middle section of correct commands.

(b) The student has drawn the correct shape for the instructions so full marks (i.e. 2 marks) are given.

(c) These are both valid reasons so two marks here.

(5 marks out of 7)

Exam support *continued*

Student answer 2

(a) FD 2

CD

RT 90

FD 2

LT 90

FD 5

RT 90

FD 3

LT 90

FD 2

LT 90

FD 5

LT 90

FD 7

CU

END

(b)

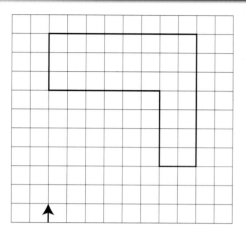

(c) You cannot give the instructions for curves.

Although you can move through angles it would be hard to know what distances to choose.

▲ **Examiner's comment**

(a) Most people would take a clockwise path around the shape but this student has decided to go anticlockwise. This is perfectly OK and these instructions will correctly cut the shape so three marks are given.

(b) The shape drawn on the gird is correct, so a full two marks here.

(c) Both reasons are correct so two marks are awarded.

(7 marks out of 7)

Examiner's answers

(a) One mark for all red steps correct.

One mark for all green steps correct.

One mark for all black steps correct.

NB This is only one of the many possible answers.

There is another correct answer given by a student in Student answer 2.

START

FD 2

CD

FD 7

RT 90

FD 5

RT 90

FD 2

RT 90

FD 3

LT 90

FD 5

RT 90

FD 2

CU

END

One mark for this section correctly drawn

START

FD 6

CD

FD 3

RT 90

FD 7

RT 90

One mark for this section correctly drawn

FD 7

RT 90

FD 2

RT 90

FD 4

LT 90

FD 5

CU

(c) One mark for each one to a maximum of two marks.

- The cutter can only travel in straight lines/You cannot cut a smooth curve
- The diagonal distances are not known so it is hard to move the cutter accurately through an angle

(b)

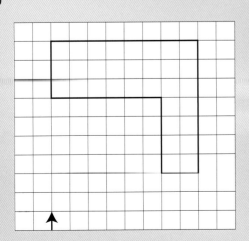

169

Summary mind map

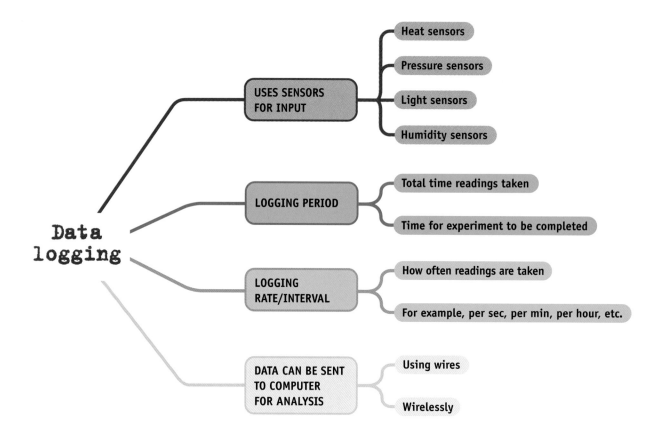

Data logging

USES SENSORS FOR INPUT
- Heat sensors
- Pressure sensors
- Light sensors
- Humidity sensors

LOGGING PERIOD
- Total time readings taken
- Time for experiment to be completed

LOGGING RATE/INTERVAL
- How often readings are taken
- For example, per sec, per min, per hour, etc.

DATA CAN BE SENT TO COMPUTER FOR ANALYSIS
- Using wires
- Wirelessly

ICT and modern living

The key concepts covered in this topic are:

- **How ICT systems have changed the way people go about their daily lives**
- **The impact of emerging technologies on organizations**

The use of ICT has changed life in most areas. For example, we no longer shop or learn in the way we used to. More and more aspects of our lives are conducted online.

We have become very dependent on communication systems such as mobile phones, the Internet and social networking sites. The way we entertain ourselves has changed with more time spent online than watching TV.

In this topic you will be looking at the way ICT has changed the way people go about their everyday lives and how emerging technologies are set to make a big impact on organizations.

Contents

How ICT systems have changed the way people go about their daily lives

You will find out

▷ **About how ICT systems have changed the way people go about their daily lives**

Most people have computers in their homes and access to the largest store of information in the world, the Internet. Using high speed broadband links they can access all sorts of multimedia material such as films, music, animation, etc.

This technology has changed the way people go about their daily lives and in this section you will be looking at the areas that have changed.

Communication

Years ago people kept in touch by telephone and letter but now there are lots of easier and faster ways to communicate including:

- SMS (simple message service) commonly called text messages
- email
- voice mail
- fax
- chat rooms
- instant messages
- social networking sites
- videoconferencing
- VoIP.

People can communicate very easily no matter where they are and this enables people to make changes to arrangements at the last minute, which they would have found impossible to do before. It is also very easy to communicate with people regardless of location. Many people have friends and family thousands of miles away but the use of VoIP and the Internet means they can communicate easily and even see each other while they are talking.

Improved communication has also meant that companies are easily able to set up branches around the world. Cheap phone calls abroad has meant that some jobs have been lost abroad owing to lower wage costs in some countries.

Online shopping

Online shopping means purchasing goods and services using the Internet. Most businesses have websites to show the products and services available. Lots of these websites allow customers to browse online catalogues and add goods to their virtual shopping basket/trolley just like in a real store. When they have selected the goods, they go to the checkout where they have to decide on the payment method. They also have to enter some details such as their name and address and other contact details. The payment is authorized and the ordering process is completed. All that is left is for the customer to wait for delivery of their goods.

No opening hours – goods/services can be bought 24/7

Goods are delivered to your home – ideal if people cannot get out because they are elderly or disabled

Goods/services are cheaper because of lower costs of Internet business

Advantages of online shopping to customers

Cost savings are passed to customers with cheaper goods

Wider range of goods to choose from

Worldwide marketplace – you can order goods from anywhere in the world

No travelling costs to go shopping

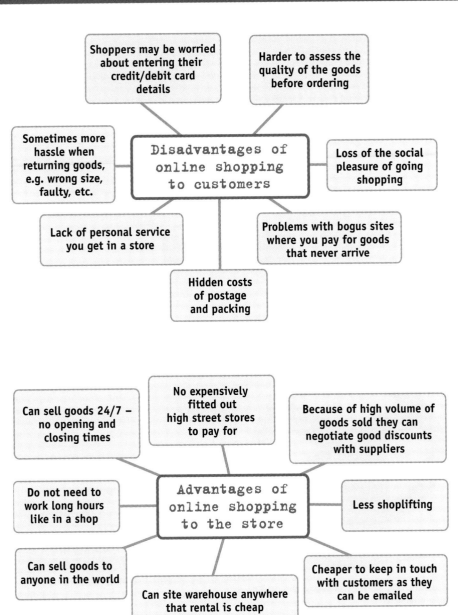

Disadvantages of online shopping to customers

- Shoppers may be worried about entering their credit/debit card details
- Harder to assess the quality of the goods before ordering
- Sometimes more hassle when returning goods, e.g. wrong size, faulty, etc.
- Loss of the social pleasure of going shopping
- Lack of personal service you get in a store
- Problems with bogus sites where you pay for goods that never arrive
- Hidden costs of postage and packing

Advantages of online shopping to the store

- Can sell goods 24/7 – no opening and closing times
- No expensively fitted out high street stores to pay for
- Because of high volume of goods sold they can negotiate good discounts with suppliers
- Do not need to work long hours like in a shop
- Less shoplifting
- Can sell goods to anyone in the world
- Can site warehouse anywhere that rental is cheap
- Cheaper to keep in touch with customers as they can be emailed

Disadvantages of online shopping to the store

- Specialist ICT knowledge is needed to set up the site
- Unemployment – staff in traditional shops lose their jobs so redundancy payments are made
- Business lost abroad if their goods are cheaper
- Virus attack could stop people being able to access the store
- Networks can fail and this means customers cannot access the store
- Not everyone has access to the Internet so you will lose some customers
- Personal data is kept about customers and this could be targeted by hackers
- Postage charges can put people off
- Danger of hackers accessing your banking/credit card details

KEY **WORD**

Online shopping is shopping over the Internet, as opposed to using traditional methods such as buying goods or services from shops or trading using the telephone.

△ Some of the components of an online shopping site.

△ Credit or debit cards are needed to make online purchases.

△ Card details are encrypted when paying for goods online.

How ICT systems have changed the way people go about their daily lives *continued*

Gaming

Many computers are used by all ages to play games, which vary from traditional games such as chess, cards, backgammon to flight/racing car simulations to fast-moving arcade-type games.

Games are important drivers in the computer industry and many home computers used to play games have more processing power than many computers used in a business setting.

For fast action computer games it is necessary to use:

- a fast processor
- a large screen
- a large amount of RAM
- a disk drive with plenty of storage capacity
- a high quality graphics card
- a high quality sound card
- large powerful speakers
- specialist input devices such as joysticks, game controllers, steering wheels, etc.

Input devices used in gaming:

▷ A games controller.

⏶ A steering wheels acts as an input device for a driving game.

◁ A joystick.

Advantages of computer games

- Young children can learn from them.
- They can make learning fun.
- Some games are played online as a team, so it encourages teamwork.
- They can lead to well-paid employment as a games designer, programmer, etc.

Disadvantages of computer games

- They can be addictive.
- They are often a sedentary activity where little physical activity takes place and this can lead to obesity.
- They can be very violent and some people think that this can cause teenagers to act violently.
- They waste time – schoolwork can suffer through the time spent playing games.
- Health problems – repeated use of input devices such as a joystick or mouse can lead to repetitive strain injury (RSI), also incorrect posture when sitting can lead to back ache.

Entertainment

Many people spend lots of time on their computers doing non-work-related tasks. There are all sorts of things that people can do to entertain themselves using a computer and these include:

- Digital photography/video photography – many people like to take pictures with a digital camera or phone. Some people have digital photography as a hobby.
- Online gambling – many people like to place bets, play bingo or other gambling games on the computer.
- Social networking – this is covered in its own section later.
- Online dating – people may find it hard to meet partners during their busy lives, so online dating is ideal for them.

- Watching TV programmes – you can watch some TV programmes you have missed using the i-players.
- Listening to the radio – you can listen to current and past radio programmes online.
- Listening to music – many people now store their music collection online and listen to the music using their computer or a portable device such as an MP3 player (which is often included as part of a mobile phone).
- Browsing the Internet – many people spend hours browsing the Internet looking for websites that are of interest to them.
- Reading online newspapers and magazines – all the popular newspapers and magazines have websites that are usually free.

Education and training

Education and training has benefited hugely through ICT and this is why you see so much ICT equipment in classrooms.

Here are some of the areas where ICT has helped:

- **Online tutorials** – use ICT to help you learn about a subject or topic. Online tutorials consist of content, simulations, animations, games and tests. They make use of multimedia and make learning fun. Learning can also be done away from the school/college premises.
- **Online assessment** – is where you take a test or an examination online. Online assessment is often provided as part of online tutorials, so once you feel you understand a topic or subject, you can take a test or assessment on it. The main advantages are that you can find out how you got on immediately and you can get an analysis of what you need to do more work on.
- **Virtual learning environment (VLE)** – is a software system that uses the Internet to support teaching and learning in a school, college or other educational institution. Using a VLE allows teachers to put on homework, students can communicate with each other and with their teachers, students can send their work electronically for marking and teachers can return it marked, etc.
- **Interactive whiteboards** – these are present in many classrooms and allow pupils to interact with material in a classroom situation. They can also be used for showing multimedia material such as presentations, animations and video.

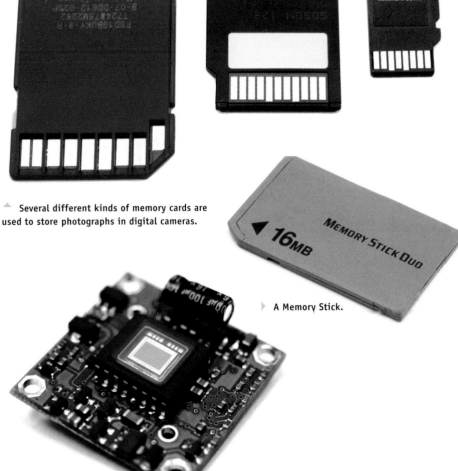

▲ Several different kinds of memory cards are used to store photographs in digital cameras.

▶ A Memory Stick.

▲ This is the image sensor in a camera.

How ICT systems have changed the way people go about their daily lives *continued*

Banking and financial

Online banking

Many of the tasks you would have gone to a bank branch to do, you can now perform at home using Internet or online banking. Using online banking you can:

- view bank statements
- transfer money between accounts
- make payments for bills
- apply for loans.

▲ When you access a secure link, the web address should start with https not just http.

Social networking

Social networking is a very popular use of computers connected to the Internet. Here are some of the main social networking sites and the services they offer.

"I'm updating the tragic story of Romeo and Juliet. In my version, they are destined to be apart forever because he's on Facebook and she's on MySpace."

Facebook

Facebook offers a way of keeping up-to-date with your friends online. You set up a profile of yourself and you then decide what about you is displayed if someone else also on Facebook types your name. You can see small pictures of other people in their profile along with a list of the people they are friends with. You can send alerts out to all your friends about what you are up to. For example, if you decide to go away to university then everyone can be notified easily.

Facebook offers a great way of getting in touch with people you have lost touch with.

MySpace

MySpace is a social networking site with a music connection holding the site together. Many bands and artists have chosen to have their own pages on the site along with the pages of millions of other ordinary people. MySpace has provided a way for artists to reach their audience. The site allows direct communication between famous artists and their fans. As well as musicians other celebrities have their own MySpace pages.

KEY WORD

Social networking site a website that is used to communicate with friends, family and to make new friends and contacts.

When you sign up for MySpace you have to design a Profile page by adding a picture, making a quote and giving some information about your favourite music. You can also add information about your hobbies, the films and books you like, who you would like to meet, and choose your top friends.

The site has a range of services such as:

- email
- bulletins
- blogs
- friend comments
- photographs
- groups
- videos
- music.

Many people put personal details up on this website and although some settings allow anyone to view them, you can set your profiles to private so you can select who sees them.

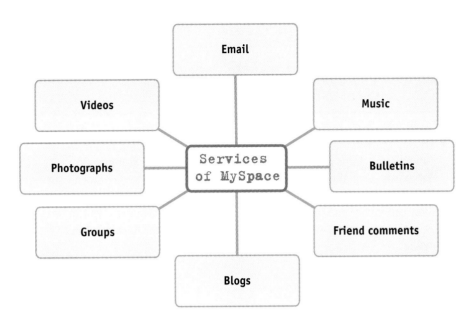

Services of MySpace
- Email
- Videos
- Photographs
- Groups
- Blogs
- Music
- Bulletins
- Friend comments

Bebo

Bebo is a popular social networking site with mainly younger users. There is a whiteboard feature where you can detail what your friends got up to the night before.

There are plans for users to be able to share and download their favourite tracks using the site.

Twitter

Twitter is the simplest of all the social networking sites. All it asks is 'what are you doing now?' and you can reply using your computer or your mobile phone. Twitter then sends your reply to all your friends, so they can then repeat the process the other way around. If you are interested in the minute detail of other people's lives then Twitter is the social networking site for you.

The above explanations of some of the main social networking sites give you some of the advantages of these sites but there are some disadvantages.

Disadvantages of social networking sites

- Many employers and schools ban their use because some people get addicted to them and spend too much time on them.
- Paedophiles have been known to surf networking site pages for their next victim.
- Many young people share too much information on these sites and they do not realize that their teachers, potential employers, etc., can view the information.
- There is a danger of identity theft.
- You have to be on all the sites your friends use if you want to take advantage of the services they offer.

Online/remote working

If you have an Internet connection then you can communicate easily with people all around the country or even the world. Many people who use computers for their work are able to do their work at home. Working from home using ICT equipment and telecommunications is called teleworking or online working.

There are many light, portable devices such as PDAs, tablet computers, laptops and netbooks. These mean that people can work on the move and from any location, as they can use a wireless connection to access the Internet.

The advantages of using ICT/ the Internet

The use of ICT is so popular because of the advantages it brings which include:

- Increased productivity – you can get more done in the same time by using ICT.
- Improved security – it is much easier to copy disks of data than a lot of paper.
- Allows people to communicate in different ways (e.g., SMS, VoIP, email, chat rooms, etc).
- Improved presentation of material – can use templates for word-processed documents, DTP documents, etc.
- Can search for information using search criteria in databases or by using search engines in the Internet.
- Can perform tasks it would be impossible to produce without computers (e.g., accurate weather forecasting).

"I do all of my tweeting on Twitter now."

177

How ICT systems have changed the way people go about their daily lives *continued*

The disadvantages of using ICT/the Internet

There are some disadvantages in using ICT including:

- Jobs can disappear abroad (e.g., call centres, IT jobs).
- Privacy is destroyed by surveillance, large public databases, exchange of personal data, etc.
- Data can easily be stolen. It is easy to copy data onto removable media.
- They can have a negative environmental impact.
- Systems can break down causing considerable disruption.
- You may become a victim of cyber crime (e.g., hacking, fraud, etc.).

Questions A

1. Many devices have revolutionized the way we work and play. Mobile phones are one such device.
   - (a) Other than mobile phones, describe how a device or system has changed the way people work or play. *(3 marks)*
   - (b) Briefly describe an emerging technology that is likely to change society. *(2 marks)*

2. (a) Discuss the developments in ICT that have enabled remote and mobile working. *(6 marks)*
   - (b) Despite advances in ICT there are still limitations in remote and mobile working. Describe **two** such limitations. *(2 marks)*

3. Many people have joined social networking sites. Explain what a social networking site is and give **two** things you might do using the site. *(4 marks)*

4. Social networking sites are not without their dangers. Give **two** dangers in using social networking sites. *(2 marks)*

5. When goods are ordered over the Internet, payment has to be made.
   - (a) Give **one** method of payment used over the Internet. *(1 mark)*
   - (b) Describe why some people may not want to put their payment details into a website. *(2 marks)*
   - (c) Describe **one** way the online store can make sure that payment details are safe. *(2 marks)*

6. E-commerce sites are very popular for the sale of music and software.
   - (a) Use the list below to complete the table showing the most suitable facility needed for each task. *(7 marks)*

   Email   Shopping basket   Encryption   Links

   Website   Dialup   Online database   Modem

   Broadband   Fastband   Virus protection   PDA

Task	Facility needed
To allow lots of items to be selected for purchase	
To allow customers to enter their payment details safely	
To allow customers to browse the e-commerce site at high speed	
To allow the details of customers and their orders to be kept by the e-commerce site	
To allow customers to view all the items for sale	
To allow customers to access other websites that may be of interest	
To communicate with customers about problems with their order	

   - (b) Music and software can be sent by post or it can be downloaded from the site.
     - (i) Explain what is meant by downloaded. *(1 mark)*
     - (ii) Give **one** advantage to the e-commerce store of downloads. *(1 mark)*
     - (iii) Give **one** advantage to the customer of being able to download their purchases rather than receive them by post. *(1 mark)*

7. Online shopping has changed the way that most people shop.
   - (a) Give **two** advantages of buying goods over the Internet. *(2 marks)*
   - (b) Give **two** disadvantages of buying goods over the Internet. *(2 marks)*
   - (c) Some organizations will benefit by the use of online shopping, whilst others will not.
     - (i) Give the names of **two** types of organization that would benefit by the use of online shopping.
     - (ii) Give the names of **two** organizations that would likely lose out by the use of online shopping. *(4 marks)*

The impact of emerging technologies on organizations

▷ **About the impact of emerging technologies on organizations**

ICT technology changes all the time and new applications are continually created to take advantage of the developments. In this section you will be looking at some of the emerging technologies and the impact they have on organizations.

Artificial intelligence

Artificial intelligence is the science of getting computers to learn in a similar way to the way the human brain learns new things. The aim of this is to make computers more intelligent and make them able to work things out for themselves.

Artificial intelligence is a reasoning process performed by computers that allows the computer to:

- draw deductions
- produce new information
- modify rules or write new rules.

KEY WORD

Artificial intelligence (AI) creating computer programs or computers that behave in a similar way to the human brain by learning from experience, etc.

The computer, just like a human, is able to learn as it stores more and more data.

Biometrics

Biometrics have been used to identify people by:

- fingerprints
- the pattern on their retina (i.e., the pattern of blood vessels at the back of the eye).

These have the following uses.

Fingerprint scanning:

- Used for recording attendance in school/college.
- Used for access to buildings and rooms.
- Used to restrict access to computers.

Retinal scanning:

- Used for access to buildings and rooms.

There are some new developments in biometrics:

- Face recognition systems – where a person can be identified by their face. Faces are stored on a database and the image from a CCTV camera is used to find a match.
- Walk recognition systems – people have a unique way of walking and this can be used to identify people from behind. This is used by the police.

▷ Retinal scanning makes use of the unique pattern of blood vessels in the retina.

Computer-assisted translation

Computer-assisted translation is a type of translation from one language into another where the person doing the translation uses computer software to help them with the translation. They usually include spellcheckers, grammar checkers, and databases of terminology. Some advanced computer-assisted translation programs will take the text in one language and turn it into the word-processed text in a different language automatically or with minimal human involvement.

Quantum cryptography

Quantum cryptography uses a special branch of physics to produce a very secure method of encryption. It allows a sender and receiver to communicate in private using a special key. If someone is trying to eavesdrop on the communication, the system is able to detect this and the system stops the communication. This method is used by the military to send orders to troops, and also for sending financial and banking details over networks.

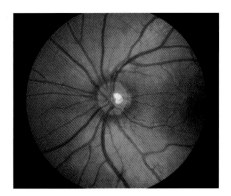

The impact of emerging technologies on organizations
continued

Vision enhancement

Vision enhancement uses special sensors (which are usually special cameras) that detect information from images that are outside the visible spectrum. This information is then put together with the ordinary image to make it clearer. Vision enhancement is used in some luxury cars to provide a screen that a driver can glance at when driving in poor visibility (e.g., fog, spray, lights from oncoming cars, rain and at night).

3D printing

A normal printer is a 2D printer. Basically it prints on paper that has length and width. A 3D printer is able to produce a 3rd dimension, which is height. It does this by printing a layer at a time, so by printing layers it is able to produce this varying height to produce a 3D shape. In actual fact it is not ink it prints. Instead the material being sprayed is polymer that builds up.

3D printing is used for:

- producing false teeth, crowns, veneers for dentists
- producing quick prototypes of products for designers
- producing 3D components that have been designed using CAD (computer-aided design) software.

▲ A 3D printer.

Virtual reality

Virtual reality is a simulation of the real world, or an imaginary world that is created using computers. Sometimes the image is displayed on a computer screen and sometimes it is displayed on a specially designed headset that you wear. In some cases users are able to interact with the virtual environment using a keyboard and mouse or by using a specially wired glove.

▶ A virtual reality headset being worn for a game.

Questions B

1. (a) Explain what is meant by virtual reality. (*2 marks*)
   (b) Give **one** example of an application where virtual reality would be used. (*1 mark*)

2. An engineering company produces designs of components using CAD (computer-aided design) software. The designs are then turned into prototypes of components using 3D printing.
   (a) Explain the difference between 2D (i.e. normal) printing and 3D printing. (*2 marks*)
   (b) Give **one** advantage in the engineering company using 3D printing. (*1 mark*)

3. One emerging technology is vision enhancement. Clearly explain what vision enhancement is and give **one** example of its use. (3 *marks*)

Extension activity

Use the Internet to research each of the following topics to find out about the latest applications:

- 3D printing
- Virtual reality
- Vision enhancement.

Write a short paragraph on each summarizing what you find out about each one.

Questions

 Test yourself

The following notes summarize this topic. The notes are incomplete because they have words missing. Using the words in the list below, copy out and complete the sentences A to H, underlining the words that you have inserted. Each word may be used more than once.

Internet   VLE   artificial intelligence

ATMs   virtual reality   abroad

wirelessly   social networking

A Online working usually involves working using a computer and the _____.

B Many Internet users on the move connect to the Internet _____ using their laptops, PDAs or other portable devices.

C Many people choose to visit _____ in order to get cash rather than wait in queues inside the branch.

D Many schools use a _____, which is a software system that uses the Internet to facilitate learning.

E _____ websites are websites that enable people to keep in touch with friends and family as well as make new friends.

F The simulation of a real or imaginary world using ICT is called _____.

G One disadvantage in the use of ICT is that with cheap and reliable communication methods many jobs can be lost _____.

H Getting computer programs to behave in a similar way to the way the human brain works is called _____.

Questions *continued*

Examination style questions

1 A new online store is being set up.
   Using the list below, choose the most suitable facility needed for each task
   listed. *(7 marks)*

   Database   Shopping cart   Broadband

   Encryption   Checkout   Customer reviews   Search

Task	Facility needed
Go straight to a product if you know a description	
A place to put items you want to buy	
A fast Internet connection that allows you to browse quickly	
The system to ensure the security of credit/debit card details	
You can see what others say before you buy	
The place where you pay for goods	
The basis of the online catalogue of goods for sale	

2 Many people are worried that with so many online sites, the high street will
   look completely different.

   Discuss the ways that online shopping changes the way we shop. *(5 marks)*

3 Discuss in detail the advantages to shoppers in shopping online. *(6 marks)*

4 Online banking is very popular with home users of ICT.
   (a) Give **three** services offered by online banking. *(3 marks)*
   (b) Some people are sceptical about online banking. Describe **two** worries
   that people might have with online banking. *(2 marks)*
   (c) Describe **one** way that the banks can address **one** of the worries you
   have described in part (b). *(1 mark)*

Exam support

Worked example

Discuss briefly **three** emerging technologies that are going to have an effect on home, school, business or commerce. For each of the technologies you describe, you need to say what their main benefit is. *(9 marks)*

Student answer 1

Robots will be able to do all the jobs around the house for you such as clean your bedroom, put all your magazines away, clean up the empty drinks bottles.

They will be able to do all sorts of stuff.

Social networking sites as you can find out about your friends and where they live.

You can also find out about the friends of your own friends and so on. It is great if you are a nosey parker like me!

You will be able to talk to your mobile phone like you talk to other people. You will be able to ask it to dial a certain number or play a certain music track for you. It will be great as you do not have to bother with those tiny keyboards that drive you mad.

◀ Examiner's comment

The specification says that students need to learn about emerging technologies. Some leeway either side is needed so technologies that are with us now and are slightly into the future are acceptable. Wildly futuristic prophecies are not what is required.

This means this student's idea of the capabilities of robots is way into the future, so this is not an acceptable answer. If the student had mentioned about robots vacuuming their bedroom floor, then this would have been an acceptable answer.

The section on social networking sites is a possible answer because some of these are relatively new and more are developed all the time. However, this chatty style of writing is not really appropriate in an examination and should be avoided.

The third part to the answer is better with clear benefits being explained.

If you look at the range of marks with their criteria in the Examiner's answers you will see it falls into the 4–6 mark range. The examiner considers it only worthy of the lower end of these marks.

(4 marks out of 9)

Student answer 2

Identifying people from behind will help businesses because there will be fewer robberies. People will not be able to put on a mask as when they walk away the database will look for someone with the same walk. Because this is distinctive, it can be used as evidence. The businesses insurance premiums will go down as robberies will decrease as they are more likely to be caught.

Flexible screens will be great. You don't have to look at tiny screens especially when you are surfing the Internet on your mobile phones.

I think there will be a huge increase in the use of voice recognition systems. You will be able to talk to your phone and instead of dialling numbers you will be able to just say 'ring Amy at home'. This will mean people will not have to struggle using tiny keyboards or keyboards on touch screens.

◀ Examiner's comment

The first part of the answer is of technology that is currently being used and they have explained it clearly.

The second answer is a little brief especially on the benefits. Students should always be specific in their answers.

The third part to this answer is very clearly explained.

(6 marks out of 9)

Exam support *continued*

Examiner's answers

The students can give answers that discuss any fairly new or developing technology for their answer. Wildly futuristic new uses for ICT should not be awarded marks as the technology must be recent or emerging.

Some of the following may be cited by students:

- The use of flexible screens
- The use of server technology (where programs and storage are not on the device itself)
- The use of portable devices with more power (i.e., greater storage, processing speed, etc.)
- The use of voice recognition
- Multifunctional devices (e.g., phones, digital TV, movie players, laptops all rolled into one)
- The use of robots
- The use of artificial intelligence
- The use of biometric methods (especially in schools).

Mark scheme

9–7 Candidates give a clear, coherent answer identifying three emerging technologies.
They use appropriate terminology and accurate spelling, punctuation and grammar.

4–6 Candidates identify some of the emerging technologies but their responses lack clarity.
There are a few errors in spelling, punctuation and grammar.

1–3 Candidates simply list a range of points or give a very brief explanation.
The response lacks clarity and there are significant errors in spelling, punctuation and grammar.

0 Response not worthy of credit.

EXAM TIPS

In longer questions, the mark you get will not only depend on the content of your answer (i.e., the number of correct points you make) but also on the way you write your answer. You will also be marked on your correct use of spelling, punctuation and grammar.

You will not have the ICT facilities such as an online thesaurus and spellchecker in the exam, so you will need to ensure that you use the correct words.

Proof reading (i.e. visual checking) is not just restricted to working on a computer. When you have completed your answer to a question, you need to read through the answer carefully to check that it makes sense and that you have used the correct spelling and punctuation.

Summary mind maps

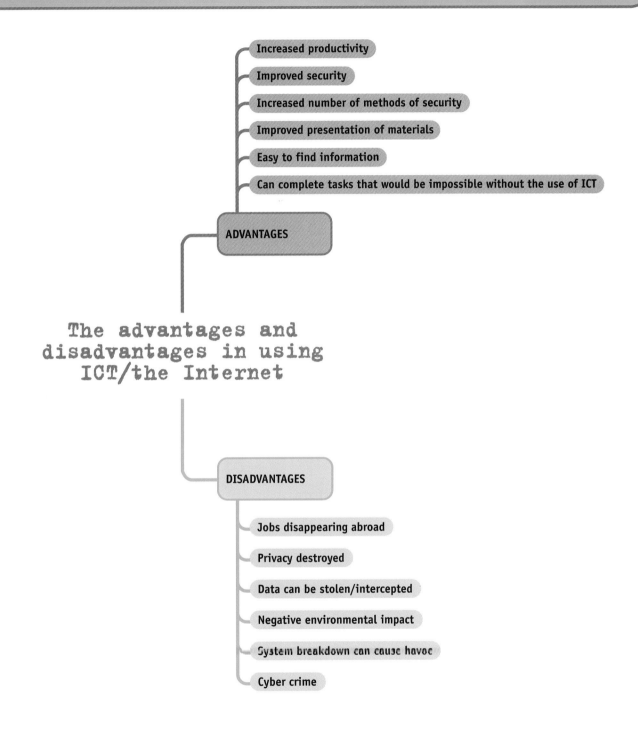

Increased productivity

Improved security

Increased number of methods of security

Improved presentation of materials

Easy to find information

Can complete tasks that would be impossible without the use of ICT

ADVANTAGES

The advantages and disadvantages in using ICT/the Internet

DISADVANTAGES

Jobs disappearing abroad

Privacy destroyed

Data can be stolen/intercepted

Negative environmental impact

System breakdown can cause havoc

Cyber crime

Summary mind maps *continued*

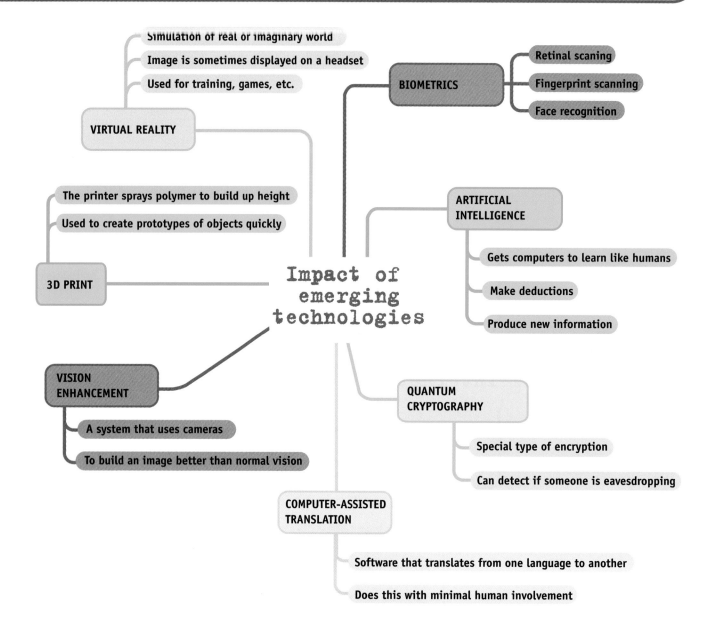

ICT systems

The key concepts covered in this topic are:

- Systems
- Hardware
- Software

You have already looked at ICT systems in Topic 1, where you looked at ICT systems used in the home, at school and in society. In Topic 10 you will be looking at ICT systems in a business or organizational context.

Contents

Systems

ICT systems consist of hardware, software and communications equipment. The type of ICT system used depends on the organization or business and the type of task that is being performed. Organizations and businesses perform a wide range of tasks and will often use lots of different hardware, software and communications equipment. In this section you will be looking at more specialist ICT systems.

Specialist equipment

Some computer equipment is used by almost everyone who uses ICT. An example of this would be a monitor/screen, mouse, keyboard, printer, etc. Some other pieces of equipment are not that common and are used in a narrow range of applications. An example of this would be a graphics tablet, which you are likely to see being used by engineers, kitchen/bedroom designers, fashion designers, etc. Some pieces of equipment, such as a Braille keyboard, are designed specifically for use by the disabled.

The use of microprocessor technology

In Topic 1 you were introduced to microprocessor technology. This technology is used for controlling devices and its use is common in the home. It can be found in devices such as washing machines, DVD players/recorders, cameras, central heating control systems, etc.

Microprocessor technology is also used for commercial applications, apart from their use in computers and mobile devices such as PDAs, smart mobile phones, etc. Here are some commercial applications for microprocessors:

Air conditioning systems – these keep offices at constant temperature throughout the year regardless of the outside temperature. This is very important in rooms containing computers, which can get very hot in the summer.

For controlling industrial processes – microprocessors are used to control temperatures in reaction vessels, to control pumps that pump liquids in and out, to control temperatures and so on. The applications for this include the production of food, drink and chemicals.

▲ Microprocessors are used to control industrial processors.

Access control to car parks, buildings and rooms – microprocessors are used to decide whether a person is allowed access according to inputs from keypads, magnetic strip cards, biometric information, etc.

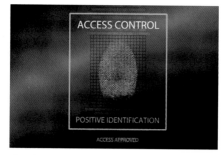
▲ Biometric access systems use microprocessors.

Operating systems and applications software

Computer hardware is useless without the software that supplies the instructions to tell it what to do. There are specialist operating systems and applications software that is used by commercial organizations

▶ Air conditioning systems use microprocessors for control.

and you will learn about them in the software section of this topic.

Mobile, portable and desktop ICT tools

Many people who work in businesses or organizations often spend time attending meetings and training courses or visiting customers. Organizations provide portable devices for these people to help them be more productive and keep in touch with others. Using these devices allows them to send and receive emails, access the Internet, access popular applications such as presentation and word-processing software, etc. They can usually use these devices to access as much information as they could whilst sitting at their desk in the office.

Differences between the technologies used, and the applications for these technologies

ICT systems have to use a technology that is appropriate for their use. For example, if a device is to be made very small so that it can be portable then it may mean that a touch screen has to be used rather than a keyboard. This would also affect the software being used, as the operating system would need to cope with touch screen input.

The requirements for portable devices would be as follows:

- Less powerful chips – so as not to consume as much power.
- Light – this means computers such as netbooks do not have large hard drives or CD/DVD drives.
- Small screen – the size of the screen limits the size of the device and also the weight.
- Less memory – people often want a cheap portable device so less memory is an economy.
- Long battery life – this is so they can be used away from the mains power supply.
- Trimmed down operating system – so that it runs at reasonable speed on a slower chip.

Questions A

1 The staff employed by a construction company use a range of different types of computer and portable equipment in the course of their work. Here is a list of the equipment available to the staff:

PDA
Desktop computer
Laptop computer
Mobile phone

State which piece of equipment in the list above would be most suitable for the tasks shown in the table: (4 marks)

Task	Type of equipment
Recording measurements on a site visit whilst standing up	
Making a phone call on a site visit	
Preparing a report using word-processing software whilst on train journey	
Using CAD software to design the building	

2 Discuss the differences in the technologies used in a powerful desktop computer compared to a small laptop computer that is designed primarily to be used whilst on the move. (4 marks)

Hardware

You will find out

▷ **About specialist input, output, storage and communication devices**

▷ **About the advantages and disadvantages of these devices in certain situations**

Hardware is the physical components of a computer system such as screen/monitor, keyboard, mouse, printer, modem, etc. Topic 1 introduced you to the popular pieces of hardware and in this topic you will be looking at those items of hardware that have more specific uses.

Specialist input devices

Specialist input devices are those input devices that are used by a fairly small number of people and the devices are limited to a very small numbers of applications.

Magnetic ink character recognition/readers (MICR)

You may have noticed the funny looking letters and numbers (called characters) on the bottom of bank cheques.

⌐:'⌐'⌐'⌐''⌐''⌐' 0123456789

▲ Characters written in magnetic ink at the bottom of a cheque.

▸ Numbers are marked by shading on a lottery ticket.

These characters:

- are printed in magnetic ink
- can be read at very high speed by a machine called a magnetic ink character reader
- are read with 100% accuracy
- are hard to forge.

They are used by the bank for reading bank account details and the value of the cheque in order to process cheques.

▲ MICR is used to read bank cheques.

Optical mark recognition/ readers (OMR)

Optical mark recognition works by the user shading in marks on a form. The forms are then batched together and read in one go very quickly by an optical mark reader.

Optical mark recognition can be used for:

- reading lottery tickets
- automatically marking multiple-choice answer sheets
- reading questionnaires and analysing the results
- recording student attendance in a school or college.

Optical character recognition/ reader (OCR)

A scanner is used to scan an image of the characters (i.e., letters, numbers and punctuation marks) on a document. The special OCR software is then able to recognize the shape of the individual characters. The text can then be used with software such as word-processing or database software. OCR has the advantage that it is a fast alternative to typing text provided that the text is already available in printed form. OCR is not good at recognizing people's handwriting.

Graphics tablets

A graphics tablet consists of a pen-like device that you use to draw or write on a tablet (it looks a bit like a flat board) and it then appears on the computer screen. You can use a graphics tablet to design your own graphics. Some graphics tablets contain special buttons to select shapes or special pictures.

▲ A graphics tablet.

Specialist output devices

Specialist output devices are those output devices used only in specialist applications. These devices are not normally in general use.

A3 printers

Most people print using printers that are able to print on paper up to a maximum of A4 size. A3 printers print on larger paper than A4. A3 is twice the size of A4. A3 printers are used for the following tasks:

- printing out spreads of pages for magazines, books, newsletters, etc.
- printing out posters.

A0 plotters

These use a pen to draw lines on the paper and are ideal for drawing accurate scale diagrams. A0 plotters are used for:

- printing out plans by architects, kitchen designers, garden planners, etc.
- printing out scale drawings of components designed using computer-aided design (CAD) software.

▲ A plotter used to produce accurate scale diagrams/plans.

3D printers

You came across 3D printers in Topic 9 on ICT and modern living. They are specialist printers that can produce products in three dimensions. They build up the third dimension by spraying plastic/polymer. They are suitable for the following tasks:

- producing a model of an engineering part in 3D
- producing a medical item like a false tooth, etc.
- producing a map of an area in 3D.

Specialist storage devices

Businesses and organizations are storing more and more information, so they need reliable, fast, high-capacity storage devices. Usually storage is provided as magnetic hard drives. Where the organization uses a network, then all the data for the organization will be stored on a server whose purpose is to store all the programs and data needed. Sometimes these drives consist of two disk drives with one mirroring what the other one does. If one of

the drives breaks down then the system still works as the data can be obtained from the other drive.

Storage devices are also needed to back up the data held on the computer. In most cases the media or the drive including the media is removable, which means it can be taken off the premises.

▲ There are many hard drives used here.

Computers and portable devices

Although many people use these devices, they are often used for very specific applications. For example, a PDA might be used by a parcel delivery company for recording deliveries and customer signatures. A laptop might be used by a conservatory salesperson for displaying images of conservatories.

Laptops

Laptop computers (often simply called laptops) are designed to be portable, i.e. carried and used in different places. They are smaller than desktop computers and have a built-in screen and are much lighter and are designed to be used away from the power source. Laptop computers contain a rechargeable battery that can limit their use.

▲ Laptops are light and have rechargeable batteries.

Netbooks

Netbooks are smaller, lighter and less expensive compared to laptop computers.

Here are the main features of netbooks:

- much lighter than laptops (smaller screen and no CD/DVD drive reduces the weight)
- smaller keyboard
- smaller magnetic hard drive
- longer battery life (owing to the use of less powerful devices such as low power chips)
- cheaper – because some of the more expensive components are left out
- suited for general computing and Internet access.

Notebooks

Notebook computers are generally smaller and lighter than laptop computers and are designed to fit into a briefcase. Like netbooks they sometimes have components missing such as CD/DVD drives in order to reduce the weight.

Palmtops

Palmtop computers are small hand-held computers that are used by occasional computer users to send and receive email, surf the Internet, record deliveries, record meter readings or record orders taken.

▼ Many mobile phones now have many of the features of palmtops.

Hardware *continued*

Desktop computers

A desktop computer (or PC as they are sometimes called) is the type of computer that you are most likely to encounter at home or at school and in most organizations. In many cases desktop computers are connected, either with wires/cables or wirelessly, to form networks.

Desktop computers are full-sized computers with a full-sized keyboard and screen and are designed to be used in one place.

▲ Desktop computers have full-sized keyboards and are designed to be used in one place.

Tablet computers

Tablet computers bridge the gap between a smart phone such as a Blackberry or Apple iPhone and a netbook. Smart phones are a bit too small for browsing the Internet or watching videos but netbooks are not small or light enough to put in your pocket or handbag. Tablet computers have a touch screen interface and are set to be cheaper than current netbooks.

▲ Tablet computers – bigger than a smart phone but smaller than a netbook – are set to become very popular.

PDAs and hand-helds

Personal digital assistants (PDAs) or hand-held computers as they are sometimes called are small hand-held computers that enable the user to:

- keep track of meetings, appointments, birthdays, etc.
- store details of names, addresses, telephone numbers, email addresses, etc.
- synchronize details with those stored on a desktop or laptop computer
- browse the Internet
- send and receive email.

WAP

Wireless application protocol (WAP) is a method that is used to allow users to communicate using a hand-held device such as a mobile phone, PDA, etc. Internet access is provided by smaller browsers that require less memory and smaller file sizes.

Smart mobile phones

Smart mobile phones are those mobile phones that offer a lot more than just phone calls and text messaging. All new mobile phones can be considered to be smart mobile phones.

New services for mobile phones are being thought up all the time and who knows what they might do in the future. When mobile phones were first developed they were the equivalent of a telephone that could be used on the move. Nowadays they offer all sorts of new services and have started to blur the difference between a computer or PDA and a mobile phone. Many mobile phones also act as portable MP3 players, enabling you to play your music on the move.

Here are some of the services available through mobile phones:

- send and receive text messages
- make phone calls
- take digital photographs
- take short video clips
- surf the internet
- watch live TV
- send and receive email
- download and listen to music
- download and play games
- send picture messages
- play videos
- GPS (use your mobile phone as a satellite navigation system).

Questions B

1 Besides making voice phone calls, describe **three** tasks a mobile phone can perform. *(3 marks)*

2 Explain **two** differences between a desktop computer and a laptop computer. *(2 marks)*

Extension activity

Research the features of the latest mobile phones using the Internet.

Produce a list of your three most desirable mobile phones and their features.

Software

You will find out

▷ **About specialist software and their uses with organizations**

▷ **About the advantages and disadvantages of software applications**

Software is the programs that instruct the hardware what to do. It is essential for any ICT system. In this section you will be looking at the more specialist software and their relative advantages and disadvantages.

Specialist software

Specialist software is likely to be used by only some organizations. It is not like word-processing software, which most organizations can use. There are lots of examples of specialist applications software and here are some of the main ones:

- **Computer-aided design (CAD) software** – used by architects, engineers, designers to design and plan buildings, components, products, etc.
- **Kitchen design software** – produces plans and 3D models of what the kitchen looks like from different views.
- **Payroll software** – used to calculate wages, take out tax and national insurance and other deductions and produce wage slips.

- **Stock control software** – keeps track of stock and orders stock automatically when running low. Some stock control software uses information from the point of sale terminal to record goods as they are sold so that more can be reordered.
- **Expert systems** – used to simulate a human expert and to enable decisions to be made based on the information given in reply to a series of questions.
- **Control software** – used to issue a series of commands in order to control a device such as a robot, motor, object on a screen, etc.

There is also a lot of different programming software, which is software that is used to write other programs. Here is a summary of some programming languages and their main uses:

- Java – used for web programming.
- BASIC – used for education (i.e., to teach people about programming).
- COBOL – used for creating business programs.
- Visual Basic – used for creating applications software that uses a graphical user interface.

The advantages and disadvantages of software applications

By the time you take your GCSE exams in ICT you will be experienced in using all sorts of different software. You will find that different pieces of software can be used for doing an identical task. For example, a simple database can be created using spreadsheet software or specialist database software.

You need to consider the advantages and disadvantages of each piece of software for doing the task you have to do.

▲ An example of an employee payslip produced using payroll software.

Software *continued*

Questions C

1 An architect uses specialist hardware and software to produce the designs and plans for their clients. They also produce scale models of buildings that they can show to their clients at meetings.

They use a range of software some of which is general software that most businesses could use and some specialist software.

(a) In the table below, tick the boxes to show which items are general software (i.e., found in any office) and which are specialist software. (*6 marks*)

Software	General software	Specialist software
Word-processing package	☐	☐
CAD software	☐	☐
Web browser software	☐	☐
3D modelling software	☐	☐
Virus checking software	☐	☐
Email software	☐	☐

(b) In the table below, tick the boxes to show which items are general hardware (i.e., found in any office) and which are specialist hardware. (*6 marks*)

Hardware	General hardware	Specialist hardware
A0 plotter	☐	☐
Laser printer	☐	☐
Mouse	☐	☐
Graphics tablet	☐	☐
3D printer	☐	☐
Monitor/screen	☐	☐

2 A poster is to be designed using either word-processing software or desktop publishing (DTP) software.
(a) Give **two** advantages of using word-processing software for this task. (*2 marks*)
(b) Give **two** advantages of using DTP software for this task. (*2 marks*)

Questions

 Test yourself

The following notes summarize this topic. The notes are incomplete because they have words missing. Using the words in the list below, copy out and complete the sentences A to N, underlining the words that you have inserted. Each word may be used more than once.

optical character recognition   prototype

larger   smart   CAD   netbook

application   specialist   programming

barriers   Java   microprocessors   embedded

A Special software can be used to recognize the individual letters in a scanned piece of text and this is called

_____.

B A _____ is a small, light and portable computer that is mainly used for accessing the Internet.

C An A0 plotter prints maps and plans accurately on paper that is _____ than the A4 size used by most printers.

D _____ are used to control air conditioning units in offices, which keep a computer room at a constant temperature whether it is hot or cold outside.

E 3D printers can be used to spray plastic to form a 3D structure such as a _____ for a new engineering component.

F Typical features you would find on a _____ mobile phone include email, web browsing, satellite navigation, ability to play MP3s, etc.

G WAP stands for wireless _____ protocol.

H Word-processing software is non-specialist software, whereas software such as payroll or stock control software is classed as _____ software.

I _____ software is used to modify existing programs or write completely new ones.

J C++ and _____ are examples of programming languages.

K Engineers and architects are likely to use _____ software for the production of scale drawings, plans and 3D diagrams.

L Microprocessors are often _____ in electronic circuits and are used to control access to rooms and buildings.

M Microprocessors are also used to control car park _____, which only allow authorized cars to enter the car park.

N CAD software is _____ software because it is used by a limited number of people for their specialist job.

Summary mind maps

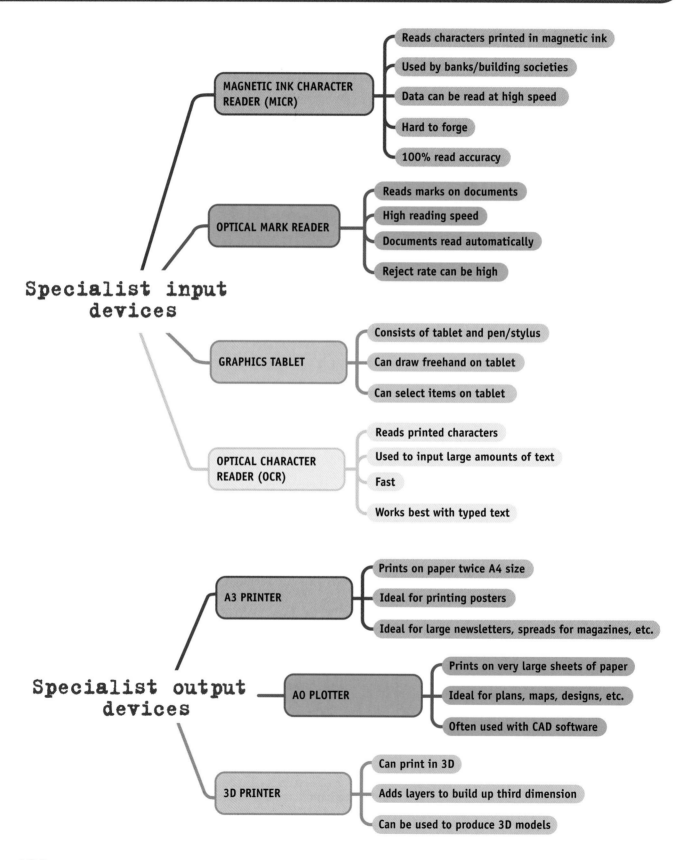

Specialist input devices

MAGNETIC INK CHARACTER READER (MICR)
- Reads characters printed in magnetic ink
- Used by banks/building societies
- Data can be read at high speed
- Hard to forge
- 100% read accuracy

OPTICAL MARK READER
- Reads marks on documents
- High reading speed
- Documents read automatically
- Reject rate can be high

GRAPHICS TABLET
- Consists of tablet and pen/stylus
- Can draw freehand on tablet
- Can select items on tablet

OPTICAL CHARACTER READER (OCR)
- Reads printed characters
- Used to input large amounts of text
- Fast
- Works best with typed text

Specialist output devices

A3 PRINTER
- Prints on paper twice A4 size
- Ideal for printing posters
- Ideal for large newsletters, spreads for magazines, etc.

A0 PLOTTER
- Prints on very large sheets of paper
- Ideal for plans, maps, designs, etc.
- Often used with CAD software

3D PRINTER
- Can print in 3D
- Adds layers to build up third dimension
- Can be used to produce 3D models

Topic 11

Networks

The key concepts covered in this topic are:

- What a network is and its components
- Network topologies
- The advantages and disadvantages of using computer networks (covered in Topic 7)
- The use of internal and external networks (covered in Topics 1 and 7)

Most computers are now connected to networks. For example, in the home your computer may be able to access the Internet, in which case it becomes part of a network. You may have a small network at home, which allows you to access the Internet on a desktop computer and a laptop at the same time. Networks provide so many more benefits compared to stand-alone computers (i.e., computers not connected to a network). In this topic you will be looking at the different types of network and the advantages that networking brings. The majority of content in this topic has been covered in other topics.

Contents

Networks and their components

▷ **About the main components of networks**

Networks consist of collections of computers that are able to send and receive data with other computers and also share resources such as an Internet connection and hardware such as scanners and printers. Networks need hardware and software to function. The type of hardware depends on the way the network is set up. In this section you will be looking at the main components of networks and their purpose.

The main components of networks

You covered the components of networks in Topic 1. Here is a summary of the main components.

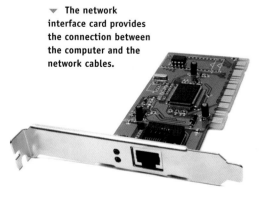

▼ The network interface card provides the connection between the computer and the network cables.

▲ Network cables are needed to connect computers and other devices such as routers, hubs and switches in wired networks.

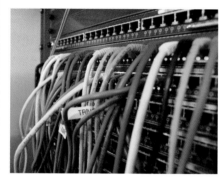

▲ A router is a networking device that routes and forwards information. It is used to connect two networks such as small internal networks and the Internet.

▲ Connecting a wireless router to the Internet. This will enable all the computers on the network to access the Internet wirelessly.

▲ A modem that provides a fast broadband connection to the Internet.

▲ The server controls the network on client–server networks.

▲ A network hub provides a connection point for connecting the wires in a network together so the computers in the network can communicate with each other.

Network software

Most operating systems are capable of running a small network such as the one you might have in a small office or in the home. Larger networks need specialist network operating systems.

Here is a summary of the software used with networks.

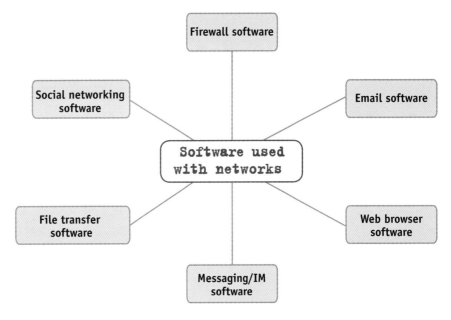

Network software.

Questions A

1 A company is thinking of installing a new network. They have the choice of a wired network, where cables are used to transmit the data, or a wireless network, where no cables are needed. Describe the relative advantages and disadvantages in using a wireless network. *(4 marks)*

2 Data may be transferred between the computers in a network in different ways.

Give the names of **three** ways of transferring the data between computers in a network. *(3 marks)*

3 Give the name of the device that is used so that several computers in a home can all share a single Internet connection. *(1 mark)*

4 Give the names of **two** pieces of software used with a network and for each one state the purpose of the software. *(4 marks)*

5 Explain the difference between a peer-to-peer network and a client–server network. *(2 marks)*

6 A small office uses a local area network. The telecommunications company supplies them with a cable into the building. They also supply them with a modem. They would like to set up a wireless network.
   (a) Give **one** reason they would like their network to be wireless. *(1 mark)*
   (b) A wireless router is bought. Give the purpose of a wireless router. *(1 mark)*
   (c) Explain why the network needs a modem. *(1 mark)*

7 A dentists' practice uses a local area network (LAN). The practice has five dentists and each dentist has a networked computer in their room and they use this to access patient records. Each networked computer has a printer attached and this printer is used to print out prescriptions, letters to hospitals, etc. The network is a client–server network and the server is located in the office.
   (a) Give **two** advantages of using this network instead of using stand-alone machines in each dentist's surgery. *(2 marks)*
   (b) The dentists would like to be able to access the Internet from their computers.
   Give the name of **one** extra piece of hardware that might be needed in order to access the Internet? *(1 mark)*
   (c) Explain **one** difference between a LAN and a WAN. *(1 mark)*
   (d) The LAN is a client–server network. Explain what this means. *(2 marks)*

Network topologies

▷ **About network topologies**

The computers and other devices in a network can be linked in different ways and in this section you will be looking at the different options. The method used to link computers is called a topology.

LAN (local area network)	WAN (wide area network)
Confined to a small area	Cover a wide geographical area (e.g., between cities, countries and even continents)
Usually located in a single building	In lots of different buildings, cities, countries, etc.
Uses cable, wireless, infrared and microwave links that are usually owned by the organization	Uses more expensive telecommunication links that are supplied by telecommunication companies
Cheap to build	Expensive to build
Cheap to run	Expensive to run

The two types of network: LAN and WAN

There are two types of network: a local area network (LAN) and a wide area network (WAN).

Basically a WAN is much bigger than a LAN and spread over a much wider area. The table above gives you the main features of each type of network.

Network topologies

The devices in a network may be arranged in different ways. Each way is called a topology.

It is important to note that in a wired network the topology would show how the wires are connected. However, many networks are now set up without wires, making use of radio, infrared or satellite links. The topologies in this case will show the communication links between the devices.

There are three main topologies:

- ring
- bus
- star.

The ring topology

This is a ring network that is also a peer-to-peer network because there is no server. With the ring topology:

- All the computers are arranged in a circle.
- Data sent by one computer passes around the ring until it reaches the correct computer.

Advantages of ring networks

- It is easy to add extra devices.
- Each computer has the same access as the others, so no one computer can 'hog' the network.

Disadvantages of ring networks

- If there is a break in the connection (wire or wireless), then the whole network fails.
- Faults are difficult to locate.
- It is impossible to keep the network running whilst equipment is added or removed because there is only one path for the data to follow.

The bus topology

With a bus topology:

- All the devices connected to the network are connected to a common shared cable called the backbone.
- Signals are passed in either direction along the backbone.

▲ **Ring topology.**

▲ **Bus topology.**

Advantages of bus topology networks

- They are cost effective because of the small amount of cable needed.
- Simple cable runs makes them easy to install.
- It is easy to add extra devices to the network.

Disadvantages of bus topology networks

- If more than about 12 devices are connected to the network, then the performance of the network is poor.
- If there is a break in the backbone cable, then the network cannot be used.

Star topology

The star topology uses a central connection point for all the devices on the network. The central connection point can be a server, or inexpensive devices called hubs, routers or switches.

▲ Star topology.

Advantages of star topology networks

- They are fault tolerant – if one of the cables fails, then the other computers can still be used.
- They are load tolerant – extra computers can be added without much loss in performance because all computers have their own path to the hub/router/switch/server.
- It is easy to add extra computers – extra computers can be added without disturbing the network.

KEY WORDS

LAN (local area network) a network of computers on one site.

Network a group of computers that are able to communicate with each other.

WAN (wide area network) a network where the terminals/computers are remote from each other and telecommunications are used to communicate between them.

Disadvantages of star topology networks

- Higher cost – the large amount of cabling needed makes it a more expensive topology.
- Dependence on the central hub/switch/router/server – if the device at the centre of the network fails, then the whole network will fail.

Example

The networks used by VistaWeb

VistaWeb are a poster design company who design posters for their clients. At the moment they use stand-alone computers but they would like to network the computers together. Networking the computers will mean:

- Expensive resources such as A0 plotters, colour laser printers, etc., can be shared.
- All the software can be stored on the server, which means it only needs to be installed once.
- At the moment staff have to back up their own work at the end of each day. Some staff have forgotten to do this and work has been lost. With a network all the files are in a central place so backing up is made easy.

There are a number of disadvantages and these include:

- They will need to appoint a network manager to be in charge of the network.
- Staff will need to be trained and the time to do this might put them behind with their work.
- Some older computers will need a network interface card to enable them to be connected to the network cable and there are other expenses such as the cables.

VistaWeb plan to use an internal network that uses Ethernet cables to connect the computers in the network together. The network is a client–server network in a star topology with the server as the central device. All the other computers on the network are connected to the server. Although there is more cabling with a star topology, the company wanted a network that can have more computers added without disturbing the network and one that is fault tolerant.

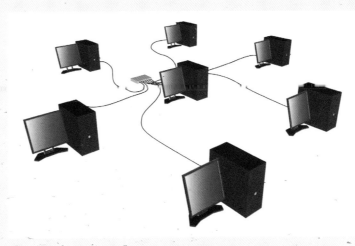

▲ A client–server network using a star topology.

Network topologies *continued*

Questions B

1 A firm of estate agents want to set up a small network in the one office. The network should be connected to the Internet so that they can communicate with their clients by email, send copies of adverts to local newspapers, browse the Internet for maps and so on.

  (a) Give **two** advantages in using a network rather than using stand-alone computers. *(2 marks)*

  (b) Give the names of **two** pieces of hardware, other than the computers themselves, that are essential for this network. *(2 marks)*

2 A café operates free Internet access while their customers have a drink. The system uses a wireless router.

  (a) Explain the purpose of a wireless router. *(1 mark)*

  (b) Describe why the use of the Internet can expose the user's computer to a number of threats compared to using the computer as a stand-alone computer. *(2 marks)*

3 The computers in a network are connected in a topology.

  (a) Explain what is meant by a network topology. *(2 marks)*

  (b) Give the names of **two** different network topologies. *(2 marks)*

4 **(a)** Explain the purpose of a broadband modem. *(2 marks)*

  (b) Give **one** advantage of a broadband modem compared to a dialup modem. *(1 mark)*

Extension activity 1

Produce a poster to be put up in the computer room entitled:

The advantages and disadvantages of networks

Use the Internet and information contained in the topic as your sources of information. You have to choose suitable software for this task and make it as eye-catching as you can.

Extension activity 2

Create diagrams using suitable software in order to produce a series of posters that show the following network topologies:

- Ring
- Bus
- Star

If there is space, and you have time, you could add the advantages and disadvantages of each topology to your posters.

END-OF-TOPIC REVIEW

Questions

 Test yourself

The following notes summarize this topic. The notes are incomplete because they have words missing. Using the words in the list below, copy out and complete the sentences A to N, underlining the words that you have inserted. Each word may be used more than once.

topology   client-server   bus   star   peer-to-peer

wireless router   hub   Internet   knowledge

ring   router   transfer   firewall   network

A A group of computers linked together in order to share resources and files/data is called a _____.

B A network where all the computers are of equal status is called a _____ network.

C A network where there is one powerful computer that takes charge of the network is called a _____ network.

D The method of connecting computers in a network is called the _____.

E The network where the computers are connected in a line is called a _____ topology.

F A network where the computers are connected in a circle is called a _____ network.

G A _____ topology is one where there is a computer or server at the centre and all the computers are connected to it.

H The _____ is the biggest network of computers in the world.

I The material through which the data travels in a network is called the data _____ medium.

J In order to create a wireless network a device called a _____ is needed.

K In order to protect an internal network from being accessed by hackers using the Internet a _____ is used.

L One disadvantage of a network is that _____ is needed to set one up.

M A connection device used to connect the cables in a network together is called a _____.

N A _____ can be used if several computers need to share the same Internet connection.

Summary mind maps

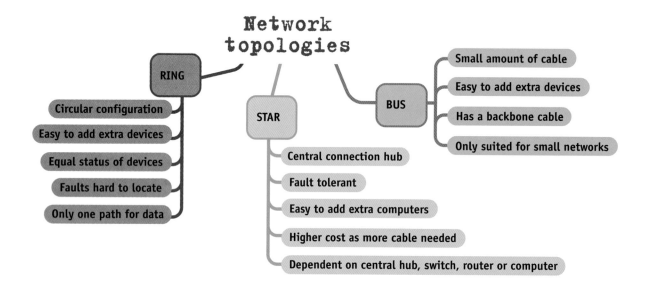

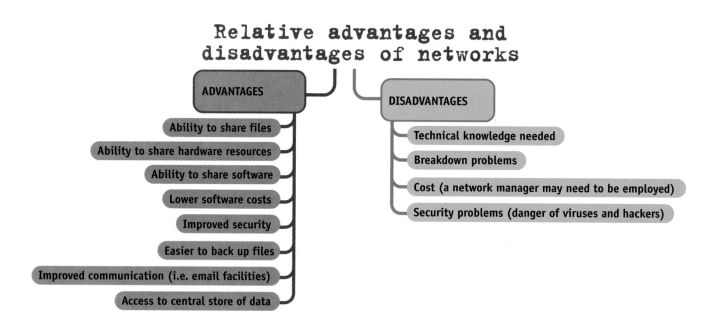

Information knowledge based systems (IKBS) and expert systems

The key concepts covered in this topic are:

- **The purpose of IKBS and expert systems**
- **How IKBS and expert systems are used for diagnostic work and decision making**

Artificial intelligence (AI) seeks to build computers so they can think and learn the way we do. As you can imagine, as the brain is so complex, building a computer that can think for itself is not going to be easy. We do have a range of computer systems that can appear intelligent and they have been developed to become experts in a certain area such as medicine. Such systems are able to mimic a human expert and are called expert systems or information knowledge based systems (IKBS). In this section you will be learning about IKBS/expert systems.

Contents

The purpose of IKBS and expert systems

You will find out

▷ **About the purpose of IKBS and expert systems**

▷ **About how IKBS and expert systems are used for diagnostic work and decision making**

IKBS or expert systems are computer systems that are designed to replace a human expert in a particular field such as medical diagnostics, the solving of computer problems, etc. You came across expert systems in Topic 4 and in this topic you will be looking more closely at these systems and their applications.

What is an expert system?

An expert system/IKBS is an ICT system that uses artificial intelligence to make decisions based on data supplied in the form of answers to questions. This means that the system is able to respond in the way that a human expert in the field would to come to a conclusion. A good expert system/IKBS is one that can match the performance of a human expert in the field.

KEY WORD

Expert system/IKBS an ICT system that mimics the decision-making ability of a human expert.

The three components of an expert system

Expert systems consist of the following components:

- **Knowledge base** – a huge organized set of knowledge about a particular subject. It contains facts and also judgemental knowledge, which gives it the ability to make a good guess, like a human expert.
- **Inference engine** – a set of rules on which to base decisions and most of these rules have the 'if-then' structure. It is the part of the expert system that does the reasoning by manipulating and using the knowledge in the knowledge base. There is usually a way of phrasing a question to the system or a way of searching for information using a search engine.
- **User interface** – the user interface presents questions and information to the operator and also receives answers from the operator.

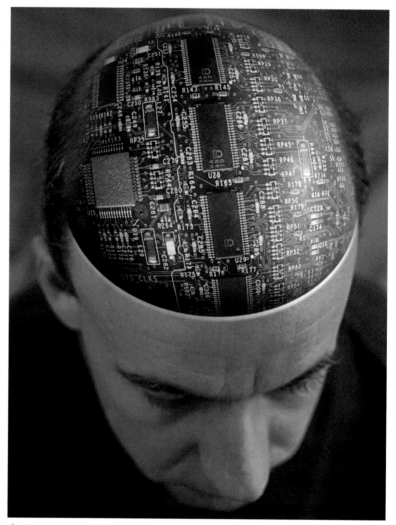

▲ Expert systems/IKBS are computer systems that behave like a human expert on a subject.

Examples of expert systems

Expert systems can be used for all sorts of applications and here are some of them.

Medical diagnosis

There are many different types of blood infections. If the correct antibiotic is given, the infection will clear up. The trouble is matching the correct antibiotic to the infection. This is where the expert system comes in. The expert system can be used by a less experienced doctor to make a correct diagnosis without having to waste time growing a culture, which could take several days, in which case the patient could be dead.

▲ Expert systems can enable doctors to make an expert diagnosis of a patient's illness.

▲ There are many examples of medical expert systems.

Designing buildings

If you want certain sized rooms in a building, then they can be put together in many different ways. Using an expert system will allow a builder to put the space together in the most economical way.

Prospecting for minerals and oil

Using geological information, an expert system can use the information to determine the most likely places to choose for further exploration. This reduces the cost of mineral or oil exploration.

▲ Expert systems can use geological data to predict where best to strike oil.

For giving tax advice to individuals and companies

Tax is complex and a lot of expertise is needed in order to give the correct advice. This is where expert systems come in. They are able to store a huge amount of data and they can ask the user a series of questions and come up with expert advice on how to pay less tax.

▲ Expert systems can give expert tax advice.

The purpose of IKBS and expert systems *continued*

Advantages and disadvantages of expert systems

There are a number of advantages and disadvantages of expert systems and these are outlined here.

Advantages of expert systems

- Fewer mistakes – human experts may forget but expert systems don't.
- Less time to train – it is easy to copy an expert system but it takes many years to train a human expert.
- Cheaper – it is cheaper to use an expert system rather than a human expert because human experts demand high wages.
- More expertise than a single expert – many experts can be used to create the data and the rules, so the expert system is a result of not one but many experts.
- Always asks a question a human expert may forget to ask.

Disadvantages of expert systems

- Lack common sense – humans have common sense, so they are able to decide whether an answer is sensible or ridiculous. Human experts can make judgements based on their life experiences, and not just on a limited set of rules as is the case with computer systems.
- Lack senses – the expert system can only react to information entered by the user. Human experts have many senses that they can use to make judgements. For example, a person describing a type of pain might use body language as well, which would not be detected by an expert system.
- The system relies on the rules being correct – mistakes could be made that make the system inaccurate.

Questions A

1. Expert systems are used in medicine to help diagnose illnesses.
   (a) Explain what is meant by an expert system. *(2 marks)*
   (b) An expert system consists of three components. Name **two** of these components. *(2 marks)*
   (c) Give **one** benefit to the patient in using an expert system. *(1 mark)*
   (d) Give **one** benefit to the doctor in using an expert system. *(1 mark)*
   (e) Give **one** possible disadvantage in using this type of expert system. *(1 mark)*

2. Expert systems can be used to help design buildings.
   (a) Give the **three** main parts of every expert system. *(3 marks)*
   (b) Describe, using examples, **two** advantages of using an expert system to plan and design a building. *(2 marks)*

3. Doctors and hospital consultants often make use of expert systems/IKBS in their work.
   (a) Give the meaning of the abbreviation IKBS. *(1 mark)*
   (b) Explain what is meant by an expert system/IKBS. *(2 marks)*
   (c) Describe **one** way in which a doctor or hospital consultant can make use of an expert system or IKBS. *(2 marks)*

4. Expert systems/IKBS are becoming popular uses for ICT.
   (a) Name **two** jobs that are likely to use an expert system/IKBS. *(2 marks)*
   (b) For each of the jobs you have named in part (a) explain how the expert system/IKBS would be used. *(2 marks)*

5. One example of where an expert system (IKBS) is used is to help doctors diagnose illnesses. Give **one** other use of an expert system. *(2 marks)*

6. Expert systems have many uses. For example one expert system called MYCIN is used by doctors to pinpoint the correct organism in blood that is responsible for a blood infection.
   (a) By referring to the above example give **one** advantage of using an expert system rather than a doctor. *(1 mark)*
   (b) By referring to the above example, give **one** disadvantage in using the expert system rather than a doctor. *(1 mark)*

Extension activity

Use the Internet to do some research on the uses of expert systems. For each use you find, write a short paragraph to explain how the expert system is used and what advantages it offers.

END-OF-TOPIC REVIEW

Questions

 Test yourself

The following notes summarize this topic. The notes are incomplete because they have words missing. Using the words in the list below, copy out and complete the sentences A to N, underlining the words that you have inserted. Each word may be used more than once.

knowledge base   IKBS   cheaper   tax   inference engine

diagnosis   decision   intelligence   experts   knowledge

user interface   expert   buildings   question

A Expert systems are sometimes called _____.

B Artificial _____ is a reasoning process performed by computers.

C An _____ system or IKBS is an ICT system that uses artificial intelligence to make decisions based on data supplied in the form of answers to questions.

D A _____ is a huge organized set of knowledge about a particular subject used by an expert system or IKBS.

E The set of rules on which to base decisions used by expert systems is called the _____.

F The part of the expert system where the user interacts with the system is called the _____.

G Expert systems have the advantage that they are usually built using the knowledge of many _____.

H Expert systems have the advantage that they will not forget to ask a _____ nor will they forget things.

I One application of expert systems is medical _____ where the expert system is used by a less experienced doctor to help make an expert and accurate diagnosis.

J Expert systems can be used for designing _____ where there are lots of possible designs to choose from.

K Expert systems have the advantage in that it is much _____ than consulting one or several human experts.

L Expert systems are used for _____ making. When there are a lot of possible decisions that could be made the expert system will point the user towards the best one.

M Expert systems can be used by accountants to give the best way of companies and individuals reducing the amount of _____ that they have to pay.

N IKBS stands for information _____ based system.

Summary mind map

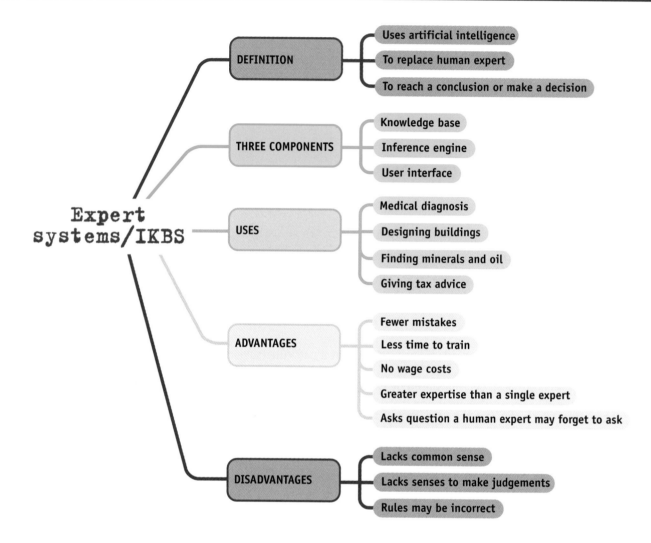

Expert systems/IKBS

DEFINITION
- Uses artificial intelligence
- To replace human expert
- To reach a conclusion or make a decision

THREE COMPONENTS
- Knowledge base
- Inference engine
- User interface

USES
- Medical diagnosis
- Designing buildings
- Finding minerals and oil
- Giving tax advice

ADVANTAGES
- Fewer mistakes
- Less time to train
- No wage costs
- Greater expertise than a single expert
- Asks question a human expert may forget to ask

DISADVANTAGES
- Lacks common sense
- Lacks senses to make judgements
- Rules may be incorrect

Topic 13
Project planning

The key concepts covered in this topic are:

- **The way ICT helps collaboration and teamwork**

- **The stages of the project management/ systems life cycle**

- **Systems investigation methods**

- **How ICT can be used to plan and manage projects**

- **Systems implementation strategies**

Many projects are too large to be completed by a single person. Also it is unlikely that a single person would have sufficient knowledge of all the areas of the project. It is therefore usually necessary to complete projects in a team. Each member of the team brings expertise in an area needed for the project.

Contents

Project planning

M any projects involve teams of people working together to get things done. The use of ICT makes this much easier. In this section you will be looking at collaborative working, what it is and what it involves.

The way ICT facilitates collaboration and teamwork

Collaboration means actively working together. In other words the people involved are working jointly together on a project. Collaboration is a recursive process.

This means that the work is continually refined and improved upon until everyone involved is satisfied with the results. Working as a team is ideal for this as they are able to review each other's work and suggest improvements.

Many tasks are completed by collaborative working. For example, a website may be created by several

▲ Collaboration involves teamwork.

different people, with each person completing a certain series of tasks. Matching the task to the person is important because all team members will have their strengths and weaknesses. For example, one person may have good knowledge of web design software, another might be very good at English and another might have an artistic streak.

ICT helps with this in the following ways:

- Work can be copied easily.
- Emails can be sent to groups of people.

- Shared storage areas can be set up so everyone can access files used for the project.
- An online diary (blog) can be set up to record project progress.
- Files can be attached to emails.
- People can chat about their work in chat rooms.
- Videoconferencing can be used for virtual meetings where project members work in different places.
- VoIP means team members can keep in touch by using cheap phone calls over the Internet.
- SMS messages and emails can be sent using mobile phones.
- Software can be used to produce Gantt charts, which are charts used to monitor and control project progress (more about these later).
- Mobile computing using portable devices such as laptops, netbooks, PDAs, etc., mean work can be completed away from the office or home and while travelling.

▲ Collaborative working enables a team to do things it would be impossible for them to do on their own. These ants have formed a bridge for other ants to walk across.

The main stages of the project management/systems life cycle

When developing new ICT systems, it is important that they are developed in a series of stages. The systems life cycle is the series of stages that are carried out in order to develop a new system or alter an existing system. In this section you will learn about the stages of the project management/systems life cycle and the sorts of things that are completed in each stage.

The following diagram shows the stages that are worked through when a new computer system is being developed. These stages are known as the systems life cycle.

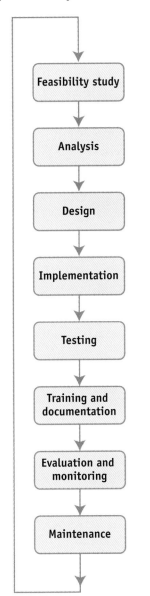

The eight stages involved in the development of a system.

Feasibility study

The feasibility study seeks to find out whether a new system can be developed at a reasonable cost and in a sensible amount of time. It looks to see if it is worth going to the effort of creating a new system. It checks that the benefits of the new system will outweigh the costs in producing it. At the end of the feasibility study a decision will be made whether or not to create the new system (or improve an old system).

Analysis

Analysis looks in detail at the current system or the requirements for a task that has never been performed before. The person performing the analysis is called a systems analyst, or just analyst for short. Analysis will normally involve the following:

- Identifying the problem that needs solving.
- Understanding the existing system.
- Understanding the proposed system, if there is no existing system.
- Identifying what the new system must be capable of doing.
- The feasibility study is often conducted as the first part of the analysis.

Design

During the design stage the systems analyst will take the desired outcomes and start to plan how best to create the system. Design will normally involve the following:

- Designing the system in line with the user requirements.
- Choosing methods for input, storage and output.
- Deciding on what processing needs to be performed on the data.
- Producing designs of input screens, output screens/reports, layouts of spreadsheets, databases, etc.
- Designing validation tests.
- Designing test plans.

Implementation

This is the stage where the system is actually built according to the design produced in the previous stage. All the different staff in the project team will bring their particular expertise to the project and work together to produce the working system.

Implementation will normally involve the following:

- Using the design produced in the previous stage to produce a working system.
- Programmers producing any programming code needed for the working solution.
- Producing the framework needed for databases.
- Using software tools to produce the working version.
- Modifying existing software.

Testing

Once the system has been implemented it should be thoroughly tested. The test plan that was created during the design stage is now used to test the system.

Testing may involve the following:

- Entering the test data as specified in the test plan created during the design stage.
- Comparing the results with what should have happened and making changes to validation checks if needed.
- If a website is being produced, testing it to ensure the content is correct, the links work and the navigation is easy to use.
- Comparing results of calculations with those produced manually.
- Checking that the validation checks work with typical, extreme and erroneous data.

User training and documentation

When new ICT systems are created, users need to be trained on how to use them. User documentation is documentation that the user can turn to for learning a new procedure or for dealing with a problem that has cropped up.

213

Project planning *continued*

Evaluation and monitoring

Evaluation and monitoring stage takes place soon after the implementation.

It is only then that the users and others involved in the development of the system will find out about any problems with the new system. Evaluation and monitoring normally involves the following:

- Checking that the original user requirements have been fully met by the new system.
- Assessment of how happy the clients are with the development of the new system.
- Setting up a review cycle so that the system is checked periodically to make sure that it is still meeting requirements.

Maintenance

Once they are developed, systems cannot be left until a new system is developed to replace them. Changes in the way the business or organization operates will need alterations in the system. Programs may need to be written or altered. For example, the rate of VAT could change, or changes in income tax could trigger the need for changes. Businesses change direction or get involved in new ventures.

Maintenance can involve:

- Setting up help-desk facilities to help users who experience problems with the new system.
- Extra functions that need to be added to the existing system are identified at the review meetings.
- Maintenance teams will alter existing programs or create additional ones.
- Any operational issues such as poor performance or software bugs will be identified at the review meeting and corrected by the appropriate staff.
- Any system crashes to be investigated to find out the reasons for their occurrence.

Questions A

1 Give the names of **three** ICT developments that help when teams of people who work remotely (i.e., in different parts of the country) work collaboratively on the same project. (*3 marks*)

2 Email is used to help people work together.
   (a) Give the names of **two** features of email that help people to work collaboratively. (*2 marks*)
   (b) Using **one** of your answers to part (a) describe how the feature would be used when working collaboratively. (*1 mark*)

3 Describe how each of the following ICT developments helps people work as part of a team: (*3 marks*)
   (a) An online diary/blog
   (b) Email
   (c) File attachments.

4 A firm of architects has branches all over the country. Sometimes people from different branches work on the same project together. They therefore need to communicate with each other.

   Explain **three** reasons why the firm of architects might choose to use videoconferencing to discuss a project they are all working on. (*6 marks*)

5 Here is a list of the steps that are stages of the systems life cycle. At present these are in the wrong order. Put the steps in the correct order. (*5 marks*)
   Evaluation
   Analysis
   Testing
   Implementation
   Design

6 Here are some of the steps that are stages in the systems life cycle.
   Testing
   Implementation
   Design
   Analysis
   Evaluation

   Write down the name of a step in the list above where the following tasks would be carried out:
   (a) Planning the construction of the new system. (*1 mark*)
   (b) Planning the testing of the new system. (*1 mark*)
   (c) Getting the user to answer a questionnaire to find out what is required from the new system. (*1 mark*)
   (d) Asking users what they think of the new system that has been developed. (*1 mark*)
   (e) Putting data into the computer to check if the output is what was expected. (*1 mark*)

Planning and managing projects

Before starting work on a project the team must plan the project by considering such things as who does what, establishing deadlines for tasks, planning how work will be reviewed, etc. They will also establish milestones, which are key points in the project where the progress of the project is assessed. Milestones are also stages where a particular part of the project is delivered.

▲ Meetings are an important part of managing a team of people collaborating on a project.

Project management

Someone has to be in charge of a project and take most of the responsibility for it and this person is called the project manager. A good project manager will ensure that:

- work is divided fairly among the team members
- each team member is given the most appropriate task for their skills and abilities
- conflicts/disagreements are sorted out
- the project does not go over budget
- the project's progress is reviewed regularly
- the work produced by team members is fit for purpose
- the deadlines are met.

ICT being used to manage projects

There are many examples where people work collaboratively using ICT and here are some examples:

The production of computer games – there are many people involved in the production of computer games from start to finish. There are designers who design the animations, there are programmers who create the programming code, there are people who advertise and market the game, there are people who design the covers, there are the people who produce all the DVDs, etc. All these people have to work together and pass work to each other for review and comments.

Business – most people in business work as a team. For example, insurance companies have to process claims made for accidents. Workflow software is used to ensure that the different people are given the information at the correct time in order to process the claim. For example, there will be claims forms to be processed, witness statements to be obtained, photographs and images to be processed, documentation from solicitors, quotes from garages for the repairs and so on. By all working together and the efficient use of ICT it means that the claims can be processed in the least amount of time.

Education – the production of a school magazine involves collaboration. Staff and students submit artwork and text for inclusion. Staff and student editors receive much of the material by email and they can then plan what material to include and a template. Different people can then work on their part of the magazine. Having a template means that the layout and design will be consistent. Staff and students will use email with file attachments to pass work to and from each other for comments. They will proof read each other's work and mark up any alterations needed. Refining of the work will take place until everyone is happy with the final result.

Cultural interaction – many schools have an exchange programme where students go to live in another country for a few weeks. It is a reciprocal arrangement and the other students come to live in this country for a few weeks at a later date. There is a lot of planning and organization needed and ICT is used to facilitate this.

Planning and managing projects *continued*

System investigation methods

System investigation involves finding out what people want from the new proposed system or looking at an existing system to find out how it works and might be improved. There are several ways that fact finding can be done.

Questionnaires – a questionnaire could be given to each user. The questions on the questionnaire should be about how the job is done now and not about the overall running of the business. It could also be about the information the new system needs to give them.

Interviews – interviews take longer than questionnaires, so this method is good if there are only a few users of the system. People at the different levels in the organization who will use the new system should be interviewed. At these interviews you can find out how the existing system works and what things are required from the new system.

Observation – here you sit with someone who is actually doing the job the new system is designed to do. You then see the problems encountered with the old system as well as chat to the user about what the new system must be able to do.

Inspection of records – this involves looking at any of the paperwork involved with the current system. This would include documents such as order forms, application forms, lists of stock and so on. You can also look at the records that are kept in filing cabinets.

> ▶ Questionnaires can be used to collect information about the new system from lots of people.

Systems implementation strategies

In order to change from one system to another it is necessary to have a way of doing this and this is called a systems implementation strategy. There are several methods used and these are outlined here:

Direct changeover – with direct changeover you simply stop using the old system one day and start using the new system the next day. The disadvantage of this method is that there is an element of risk particularly if the hardware and software are cutting edge. It the system fails then it can be disastrous to the business.

The advantage of this method is that it requires fewer resources (people, money, equipment) and is simple provided nothing goes wrong.

Parallel changeover – this method is used to minimize the risk in introducing a new ICT system. Basically, the old ICT system is run alongside the new ICT system for a period of time until all the people involved with the new system are happy it is working correctly. The old system is then abandoned and all the work is done entirely on the new system.

The disadvantages of this method are that it involves a lot of unnecessary work (as the work is being done twice) and is therefore expensive in people's time. It also adds to the amount of planning needed for the implementation.

Phased changeover – a module at a time can be converted to the new system in phases until the whole system is transferred. The advantage of this is that IT staff can deal with problems caused by a module before moving on to new modules. The disadvantage is that it is only suitable for systems consisting of separate modules.

Pilot changeover – this method is ideal for large organizations that have lots of locations or branches where the new system can be used by one branch and then transferred to other branches over time. The advantage of this method is that the implementation is on a much smaller and more manageable scale.

The disadvantage is that is takes longer to implement the system in all the branches.

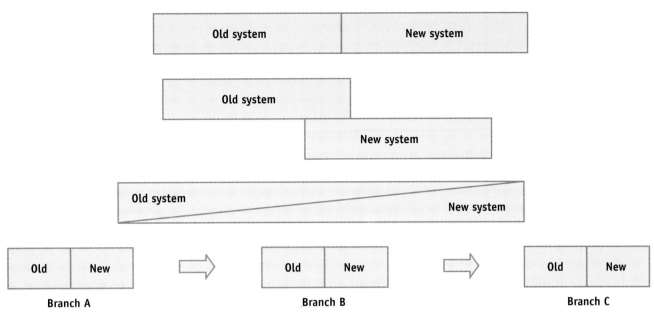

The four strategies for implementing systems: direct, parallel, phased and pilot.

Questions B

1 During the development of a new system it is important to find out how the existing system works if there is one. The usual way to do this is to perform a system investigation to collect facts about the existing system.

Name and describe **three** different ways of collecting facts about an existing system. (*6 marks*)

2 When one ICT system is being replaced by another there are a number of different ways of doing this. One way is direct changeover.

(a) Describe the system strategy for implementing systems called direct changeover. (*2 marks*)

(b) Give **one** advantage and **one** disadvantage of direct changeover. (*2 marks*)

3 Give the names of **three** different methods of conversion from one ICT system to another and discuss the relative merits of each method. (*6 marks*)

Activity

You have been asked to develop a database system for a small sports club with around 300 members. Using word-processing software, produce a questionnaire that could be sent to the club officials to enable you to get a better idea of what they require from the new system.

EXAM TIP

You may be asked to discuss the different implementation strategies for the organization in the scenario. Remember that you need to discuss this in relation to this organization and not a general discussion that could apply to any business. Also, remember that a 'discuss' question needs to be answered in complete sentences. When you do this, try to ensure that each sentence contains one or more points.

Extension activity

Produce a mind map (either hand drawn or produced using mind mapping software) that can be used to summarize what is involved in each of the systems implementation strategies shown here. Your mind map should also show the advantages and disadvantages for each method.

- Direct
- Parallel
- Phased
- Pilot

Questions

 Test yourself

The following notes summarize this topic. The notes are incomplete because they have words missing. Using the words in the list below, copy out and complete the sentences A to L, underlining the words that you have inserted. Each word may be used more than once.

collaborative   home working   collaboration   VoIP   distractions

family   direct   home   ICT   project   parallel

strategy   videoconferencing

A _____ means two or more parties working together in order to meet a common target or goal.

B _____ facilitates collaboration and teamwork using such facilities as email, blogs, chat rooms, videoconferencing, etc.

C Many people who work collaboratively are able to work from _____.

D Videoconferencing is an example of collaborative working because many people can discuss a _____ at a virtual meeting.

E _____ means working on a joint project from home by making use of computers and networking equipment.

F One big advantage with home working is that you are able to work around _____ commitments.

G A disadvantage of home working is that there are many _____ at home.

H _____ uses cameras and microphones in addition to computers and special software in order to conduct a virtual meeting.

I _____ is a cheap method of making phone calls over the Internet and many home workers make use of it.

J A systems implementation _____ is the way chosen to change from the old system to the new system.

K _____ changeover involves stopping using the old system one day and starting to use the new system the next day.

L _____ changeover involves the old ICT system being run alongside the new ICT system for a period of time until all the people involved with the new system are happy it is working correctly.

END-OF-TOPIC REVIEW

Summary mind maps

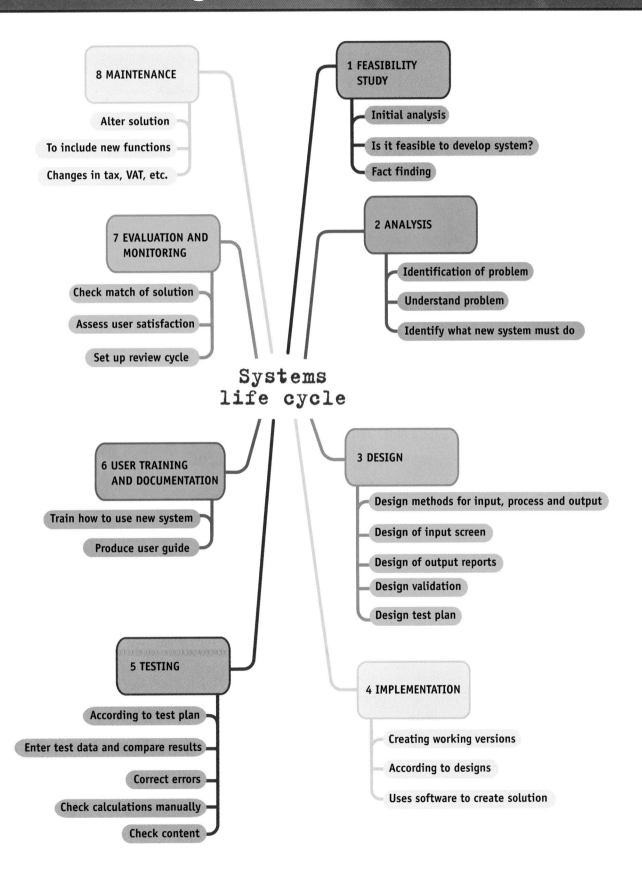

8 MAINTENANCE
- Alter solution
- To include new functions
- Changes in tax, VAT, etc.

7 EVALUATION AND MONITORING
- Check match of solution
- Assess user satisfaction
- Set up review cycle

6 USER TRAINING AND DOCUMENTATION
- Train how to use new system
- Produce user guide

5 TESTING
- According to test plan
- Enter test data and compare results
- Correct errors
- Check calculations manually
- Check content

Systems life cycle

1 FEASIBILITY STUDY
- Initial analysis
- Is it feasible to develop system?
- Fact finding

2 ANALYSIS
- Identification of problem
- Understand problem
- Identify what new system must do

3 DESIGN
- Design methods for input, process and output
- Design of input screen
- Design of output reports
- Design validation
- Design test plan

4 IMPLEMENTATION
- Creating working versions
- According to designs
- Uses software to create solution

Summary mind maps *continued*

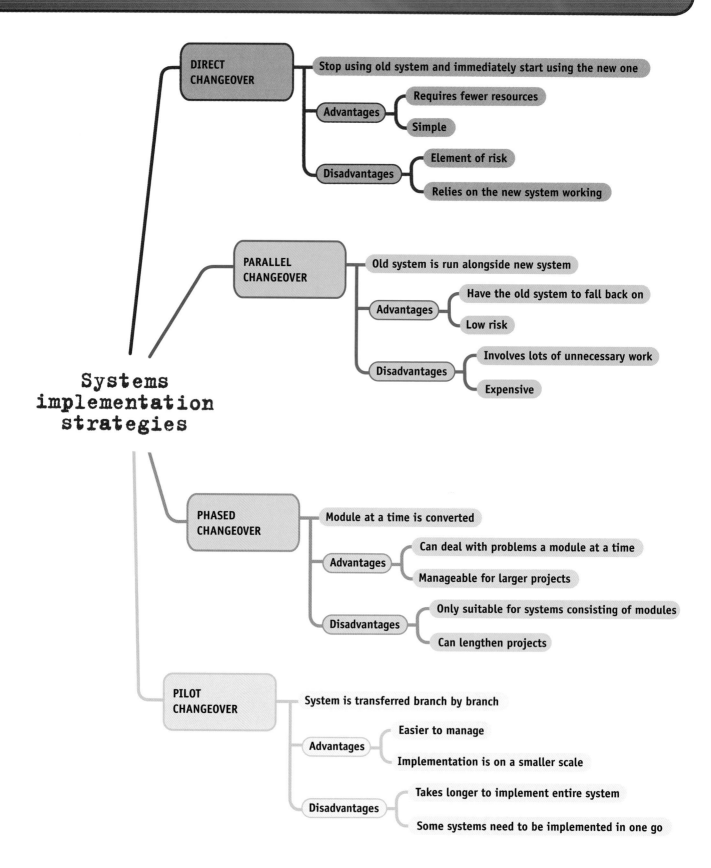

Topic 14

Exchanging information

The key concepts covered in this topic are:

- Communications
- Communication services

Organizations have to exchange information with their own employees and also with their customers, suppliers, government departments, etc. The use of networks is essential for the exchange of information. In this topic you will be looking at the services used by organizations for communication and the specialist hardware such as for videoconferencing that is used.

Contents

Communications and communication services

We all use communications and communication services in our everyday lives. Organizations and businesses also use these services to communicate with customers, clients, staff, other organizations, etc. In order to conduct their business efficiently, organizations and businesses use the latest communication systems. In this section you will be looking at communication services and the way an organization can use them. You may need to look back at Topic 2 for further explanation of some of the terminology and methods of communication discussed here.

Communications

In Topic 4 you came across the many types of communications available. All of these are used by different organizations to increase efficiency. For example:

- **Advertising** – many organizations use text (SMS) messages sent to mobile phones to let customers know about new offers/ promotions. Emails are sent to customers about offers with links to the advertiser's website.
- **Emails** – many organizations seek to reduce the cost of communicating with their staff, customers, trading partners, etc. It is so easy to send the same email to a group of people and you do not need paper, an envelope or a stamp.
- **Mobile phones** – their use means that people are immediately contactable wherever they are. SMS, email as well as traditional voice calls can be used.
- **Chat rooms** – many organizations such as colleges and universities set up chat rooms so that students can have virtual tutorials with their tutors.
- **Forums/message boards** – these are useful for posting and replying to messages. They are great for posting details of social occasions such as meals out, discos, barbeques, etc., in organizations.
- **VoIP** – means Voice over Internet Protocol and offers a way to use the Internet to make cheap phone calls to anywhere in the world. VoIP means that the cost of teleworking is reduced.
- **Videoconferencing** – allows people to meet virtually using ICT equipment even though they are in different places. Some educational institutions use videoconferencing for virtual lessons.

▼ This type of conference may be a thing of the past as more organizations turn to videoconferencing.

How organizations use the Internet

The use of the Internet is at the heart of most modern organizations. Many companies are wholly based on the Internet and could not function without it. The Internet bookstore Amazon is completely reliant on the Internet.

Web 2.0 applications

Web 2.0 means the latest services offered by the Internet. For example, Web 2.0 has the following features:

- **Blogs/web logs** – these are online diaries of events. Sometimes blogs are used so that everyone involved in a project can contribute to a blog about the progress of the project. On this blog they can discuss problems they had and how they were resolved.
- **Chat rooms** – chat rooms can be set up just to talk about the project being worked on. This is ideal for people who work in different places as they can arrange to meet in the chat room at a certain time to offer each other help and support.
- **Wikis** – this online encyclopaedia is ideal for researching certain facts about every subject imaginable.
- **Collaborative document publishing** – this allows people working together (i.e., collaboratively) and working remotely (i.e., not in the same place) to work on a joint document. This document could be a magazine, newspaper, newsletter, etc.
- **Video sharing** – this allows videos of work to be produced and shared with others for their comments.

Example

A fashion magazine making the most of communication

Bling, a new fashion magazine, brings the latest in fashion to its readers. There are two sides to the business: the editorial side and the business side.

The editorial side is where the freelance writers and journalists supply text for inclusion in the magazine and the freelance photographers and graphic designers produce the photographs and artwork.

The business side is where the sales staff visit the newsagents and other retailers to take orders for the magazine. There are also other sales staff who sell advertising space in the magazine. There are also staff who deal with invoices and accounts and these are based at the head office in London.

The following communication services are used in the business:

- SMS/texting – staff spend time with customers or in meetings and do not want to take phone calls during this time, so texting is a good way of contacting them.
- Fax – the editorial staff work together on the magazine. Faxing is good for sending from one place to another copies of designs drawn on paper.
- VoIP – phone calls are often made to other countries and the use of VoIP has reduced the costs of these calls along with calls made locally.
- Videoconferencing – meetings between freelance staff and staff employed at the head office are difficult as the freelance staff live all over the country and a few of them live abroad. Traditional meetings take up too much time and mean people have to spend time away from their families. Videoconferencing enables staff to do all the things they do at meetings electronically.
- Email – this communication is used the most. Communication can be short and to the point. The freelance staff can attach files to email. These attached files can contain text, photographs, graphics, etc.

All people who do work for the magazine can access the company network. This can be done remotely (i.e., away from the head office) using the Internet. In order to access the network they need to enter their user-ID and a password. This allows sales staff to enter the orders placed by newsagents directly from their PDAs. The advantage in doing this is that it avoids paperwork and fewer mistakes are made.

All computers (including laptops and PDAs) have the following software installed to aid communication:

- Web browser software – so that searches of the Internet can be made for ideas for designs, looking at competitor magazines, looking at high street fashions, etc.
- Email software – so that a user can send and receive email, attach files, send emails to groups of co-workers, etc.
- Messaging software – so that VoIP phone calls can be made using the Internet, texts can be sent and received and instant messaging can be used.

▼ Web 2.0 is the latest version of services for the Internet.

Questions A

1. **(a)** Give the name of the software used to view webpages. *(1 mark)*
   (b) Give the name of the software that is most often used for sending and receiving digital messages from one computer to another using the Internet. *(1 mark)*

2. When changing a password, explain why the user has to enter the password twice. *(2 marks)*

3. Describe **three** advantages in using emails rather than telephone calls in order to give some important information. *(3 marks)*

4. Explain the difference between a text message and an IM (instant message). *(2 marks)*

5. An online forum is set up by a group of people all working on a new magazine.
   Explain how the online forum would be useful to these people. *(3 marks)*

6. Videoconferencing is used by many organizations to conduct face-to-face meetings at a distance.
   (a) Explain **two** advantages of videoconferencing. *(2 marks)*
   (b) Explain **two** disadvantages of videoconferencing. *(2 marks)*

7. When people are working remotely using ICT, it can expose data to certain risks.
   (a) Give **two** methods by which you can ensure the security of the data held on the network. *(2 marks)*
   (b) There is a danger that when data is transferred using the Internet, it may be intercepted. Data is often encrypted when sent. Explain what encryption means and why it helps secure data. *(2 marks)*

END-OF-TOPIC REVIEW

Questions

 Test yourself

The following notes summarize this topic. The notes are incomplete because they have words missing. Using the words in the list below, copy out and complete sentences A to N, underlining the words that you have inserted. Each word may be used more than once.

videoconferencing   Internet   version   smart

forums   emails   Data Protection   conventions

VoIP   cyberbullying   web browser

group   wireless   ISP   address

A There has been a huge increase in the ways people can communicate with each other owing to the introduction of the _____.

B Use of the Internet means that cheap phone calls can be made to anywhere in the world by using a service called _____.

C Mobile communication has been made possible by the use of _____ mobile phones, which can be used to make phone calls, send texts, send _____ and browse the Internet.

D People who work remotely with other co-workers on the same project or task can keep in touch, and special _____ can be set up to allow them to post and respond to messages.

E Remote working is aided by _____, which allows people in different locations to attend 'virtual' meetings.

F When working collaboratively, people often have to use the same files, so it is important to use file naming _____.

G It is also important to ensure that the correct _____ of a file is used.

H If the project being worked on involves the use of personal data, then the _____ regulations will have to be adhered to.

I _____ communication is now very popular because you can work anywhere.

J Unfortunately some services are misused and there have been many cases of _____ where mobile phones or emails have been used to make threats.

K In order to connect to the Internet you need to use the services provided by an organization called an _____.

L In order to search for information on the Internet a piece of software called a _____ is needed.

M Using email you can send the same email to a _____ of people.

N Rather than type in an email address, you can select the person's email from the email _____ book.

END-OF-TOPIC REVIEW

Summary mind maps

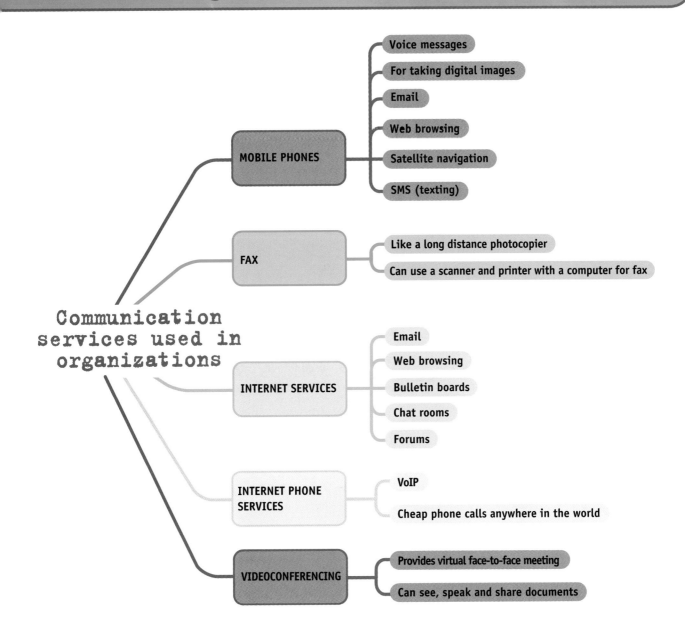

MOBILE PHONES
- Voice messages
- For taking digital images
- Email
- Web browsing
- Satellite navigation
- SMS (texting)

FAX
- Like a long distance photocopier
- Can use a scanner and printer with a computer for fax

Communication services used in organizations

INTERNET SERVICES
- Email
- Web browsing
- Bulletin boards
- Chat rooms
- Forums

INTERNET PHONE SERVICES
- VoIP
- Cheap phone calls anywhere in the world

VIDEOCONFERENCING
- Provides virtual face-to-face meeting
- Can see, speak and share documents

Summary mind maps *continued*

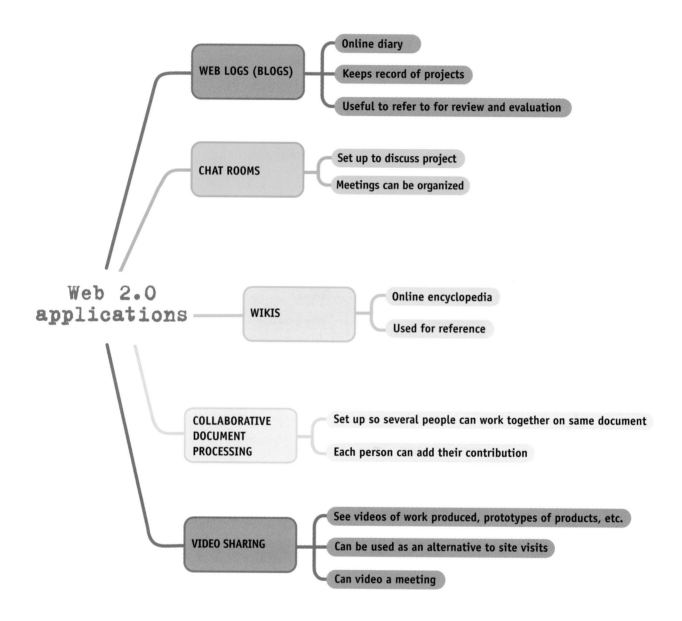

Web 2.0 applications

WEB LOGS (BLOGS)
- Online diary
- Keeps record of projects
- Useful to refer to for review and evaluation

CHAT ROOMS
- Set up to discuss project
- Meetings can be organized

WIKIS
- Online encyclopedia
- Used for reference

COLLABORATIVE DOCUMENT PROCESSING
- Set up so several people can work together on same document
- Each person can add their contribution

VIDEO SHARING
- See videos of work produced, prototypes of products, etc.
- Can be used as an alternative to site visits
- Can video a meeting

Topic 15
Presenting information

The key concepts covered in this topic are:

- The integration of applications to achieve outcomes
- The use of features of software used by organizations to present information

In order to present information it is usually necessary to use different applications software to create items, which are then combined. For example, you might be presenting information about a science experiment you have just completed. You may have produced a set of results collected using data logging equipment. You could import these results into spreadsheet software so that a line graph could be produced. You can then take this line graph and integrate it into a word-processed document.

This topic builds on what you learnt in Topic 3 and it assumes that you know and understand its content. It would be wise to revisit Topic 3 before starting this topic.

Remember that you will need to apply the content of this topic to the actual business or organization described in the pre-release material supplied by OCR.

Contents

Presenting information

▷ **About the integration of applications to achieve outcomes**

▷ **About the use and features of software used by organizations and other software used by businesses and organizations**

Organizations have to present information in the presentations they give to staff and customers and as written communications prepared using word-processing or desktop publishing software. Many organizations present information in their own websites.

In this section you will be looking at how material for documents, presentations and websites is created by using different software and how it is integrated into the software used to produce the final product.

The integration of applications to achieve outcomes

It is often necessary to use different applications to prepare a product such as a presentation, website, multimedia teaching package, etc. For example, web authoring software is used to integrate items that have been created using different software.

The following diagrams show what might be integrated into web authoring software:

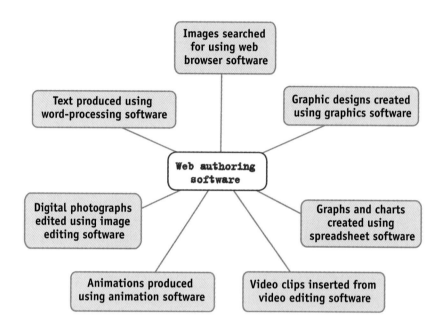

▲ Integrating items created, edited or obtained using other software into web authoring software.

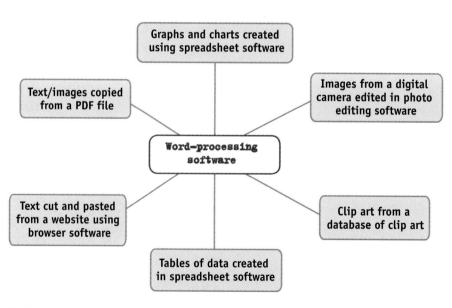

▲ Integrating items created, edited or obtained using other software into word-processing software.

The use of features of software used by organizations to present information

Software used to present information has many features that can be used to help make the information clearer. For example, you can alter the size of the font so that a reader can see the main headings and subheadings on the page. You can add bulleted points that give the reader a list of the important items.

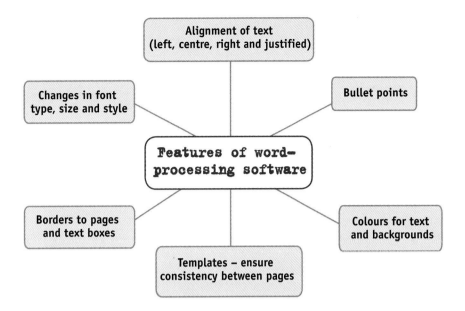

▲ Features of word-processing software that aid the presentation of information.

Questions A

1 A company produces and sells natural cosmetics. They are creating a website to promote their range of products such as natural shower gels, hair shampoo and conditioner.
  (a) Explain how each of the following can be used to present information about the products on the website: *(3 marks)*
    (i) Text
    (ii) Images
    (iii) Video
  (b) Besides using a website, give **two** other ways of presenting information about products to customers. *(2 marks)*

2 Choose the best of the following pieces of software to produce each of the following.
    Word-processing software
    Desktop publishing software
    Web authoring software
  (a) A paper-based catalogue of products. *(1 mark)*
  (b) A personalized letter to be sent to all customers about new products. *(1 mark)*
  (c) A website so that customers are able to place orders online. *(1 mark)*

3 The home page of a website for a company is being created using web authoring software. The home page contains the title of the company at the top of the page.

  Describe **three** ways that the name of the company could be made to stand out. *(3 marks)*

4 A poster for a concert is being designed using DTP software.
  (a) Give the meaning of the abbreviation DTP. *(1 mark)*
  (b) Explain **three** ways by which images can be incorporated into the poster. *(3 marks)*

5 A clothing company issues a paper-based catalogue to their customers from which they can place orders.
  (a) Photographs of models wearing the clothes are taken using a digital camera. Give **two** ways in which a photograph may need to be edited before it is suitable for inclusion in the catalogue. *(2 marks)*
  (b) Text is prepared using word-processing software. Explain why it is easier to do this rather than type the text straight into the document prepared using desktop publishing software. *(2 marks)*
  (c) Describe **two** features of DTP software that would make it better to produce the catalogue rather than using word-processing software. *(2 marks)*

Presenting information *continued*

Extension activity 1

You have been asked to produce a website for a new singer or band.

Think about the features of the web authoring software you can use to present the information on the band.

Write a list of each feature of the software and write a sentence to explain how it is used.

Extension activity 2

When a product such as a website is created it is important to know about who the intended audience for the material is.

A website is to be created for a young audience of ages 7–10.

Explain how you would ensure that the website you create is suitable for this audience.

Also explain what presentation features you would include and your reasons for including them.

Extension activity 3

For this extension activity you have been asked to produce a multimedia presentation or website to enable an outsider to get a feel of what it is like to live in your local community.

Here is what this presentation or website must contain:

1 A virtual tour of the area. You could use photographs for this or you could take video and import it into the software you are using to present the information.

2 Pages of content showing and explaining what it is like to live in your local community.

3 Interviews with people who live in the community. These can be text or you could use sound files.

Activity

Summarizing the features of software that aid the presentation of information

Websites and presentation software are both used to present information. There are features in these two pieces of software that can be used to present information. Organizations have to present information to staff, customers, trading partners, etc.

For this activity you need to use your knowledge of the following two pieces of software:

- Presentation software
- Web authoring software.

You need to create a diagram similar to the ones shown on pages 228–9 for the presentation features of word-processing software for each of these two pieces of software.

Your two diagrams should be produced using suitable software but you are free to choose which software you use to create these two diagrams.

END-OF-TOPIC REVIEW

Questions

 Test yourself

The following notes summarize this topic. The notes are incomplete because they have words missing. Using the words in the list below, copy out and complete the sentences A to K, underlining the words that you have inserted. Each word may be used more than once.

```
website    cut and paste    multimedia    import

     integrated    size    web authoring

 style    stand out    page layout    template
```

A A _____ can be used to present information to a much wider audience than with other methods.

B Websites are created using _____ software.

C Many components created in other software are _____ to complete a website.

D One way in which text or images viewed in one piece of software can be taken and inserted into another piece of software is by using _____.

E Most software used for the presentation of information can take a file created in one piece of software and _____ it into the software being used.

F Websites and presentations often make use of _____, which allows video, animations and sound to be shown as well as text and images.

G There are many ways in which the presentation of information can be improved. For example, important text on the page can be made to _____.

H This can be achieved by altering the font _____ by making it bigger.

I You can also alter the font _____ by using bold, underline, italics, etc.

J Before starting to produce a document you need to consider the _____.

K For multi-page documents, it is best to use a _____ to make the design consistent across all the pages.

Summary mind map

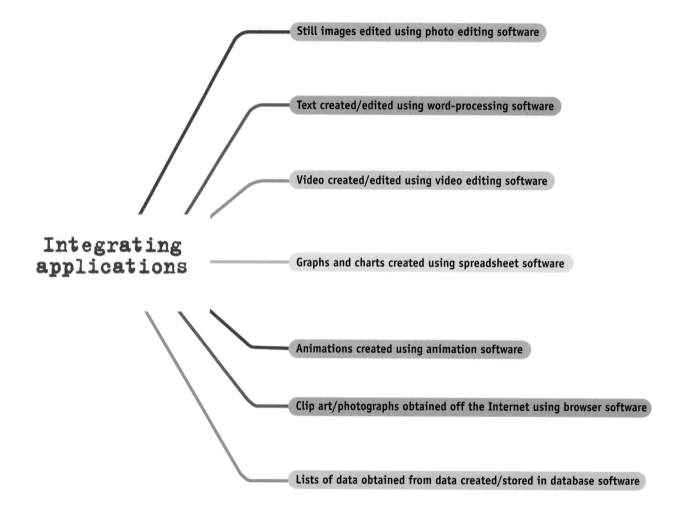

Still images edited using photo editing software

Text created/edited using word-processing software

Video created/edited using video editing software

Integrating applications

Graphs and charts created using spreadsheet software

Animations created using animation software

Clip art/photographs obtained off the Internet using browser software

Lists of data obtained from data created/stored in database software

Topic 16
Manipulating data

The key concepts covered in this topic are:

- **Data management**
- **Data handling software**

ICT systems process raw data to produce information. The manipulation of data involves taking the raw data and doing something with it such as putting it into a database structure so that meaningful information may be extracted from it. It could also involve putting the data into a computer model that applies formulas to the data to produce information on which decisions can be made.

You came across manipulating data in Topic 4, so you will probably need to look back at that topic. In this topic you will be looking at how businesses and organizations manipulate data.

Contents

Data management

You will find out

▷ **About the purpose and methods of data management used by commercial organizations**

▷ **About data management tools**

▷ **About the use of relational databases, spreadsheets and other software used by businesses and organizations**

Data management is the storage of the data in a form that makes it easy to manipulate the data in a way that gives the organization or business information. You need to remember that data is not simply confined to text and numbers; it can be photographs, videos, sounds, music, etc.

Data can be handled using spreadsheet software. Spreadsheet software is ideal if calculations need to be performed on the data. This is why spreadsheets are used to create models. Models can be used by businesses and organizations to provide breakdowns of costs. These models can be used to test various scenarios to see what happens.

In this section you will look at examples of how different organizations use data management to operate efficiently.

Example 1

A doctors' surgery

A doctors' surgery stores data in a relational database. The following tables are used:

- Doctors – holds details about each doctor.
- Patients – holds contact details on each patient.
- Patient medical history – holds the details of the patient's past medical history such as operations, drugs given, tests made, etc.
- Appointments – details of appointments made between each patient and the doctors.

A relational database was used because if they stored all the data in one big table there would be a lot of duplication of data. The practice manager is responsible for keeping this database up-to-date. They are also responsible for the extraction of information from the database. For example, one of the doctors wants to know how many patients received the flu jab last year so they can work out the costs of the vaccines for this year.

Data from the database is also used along with word-processing software to send mail merged letters to certain patients. For example, all those patients who are over 65 are sent letters to remind them about the flu jab.

The doctors run their own business, so they have to keep track of the money coming in from the NHS and the money going out on premises, costs of utilities (gas, electricity, phone, etc.), cost of staff (practice manager, nurses, etc.), the cost of equipment, and so on. The doctors use a spreadsheet to produce a model that shows these costs. They often use this spreadsheet to ask 'what if' questions. For example, they were thinking of employing an extra doctor and wanted to know if they could afford the wages. They used the spreadsheet model to help them make the decision.

The doctors also use an expert system to help them make a correct medical diagnosis when they are faced with a difficult set of symptoms. The medical expert system will ensure that the patient can be put on the correct antibiotics without delay.

▲ It is vital that patient medical records are accurate and kept up-to-date.

Example 2

A database of employees who work for a large company

The human resources department of a large company keep a database containing all their employees' details. When an employee joins the company they have to fill in an application form that contains their details such as name, address, date of birth, salary, department, etc. The details are entered into the database using an online form. The person who created the database included validation checks in order to trap any errors during the keying in of the data. Staff who input details into the database are trained to proof read (perform a visual check of) the data they have entered. They do this by carefully comparing what they have typed in with what is on the form.

When a new employee record is created, the database automatically generates an employee number that is used as the primary key. This number is unique for each employee. The employee number is used to distinguish between employees who have the same name.

The database needs to be kept up-to-date as:

- New staff join the company – they will need to have their details added to the database.
- Some staff leave – they will need their details archived and deleted.
- Staff may need some of their details to be changed – they may change their name, address, email, department, salary, etc.

Department managers and above are trained how to use the database. They are taught how to set up queries in order to extract required information such as:

- The salaries of all employees in their department so they can be given a rise.
- Details of all employees who have not received training on the Data Protection Act so that they can be sent on a course.
- Details of all employees who are approaching retirement age so that a decision can be made to offer them early retirement.

◀ Staff CVs are used as an information source for the human resources database.

In order to be able to extract the information required in the most flexible way the data is stored in a relational database. The relational database consists of six tables and there are links, called relationships, between the tables.

The use of a relational database reduces data redundancy which means that data is not unnecessarily duplicated. This reduces the amount of data staff have to enter.

The relational database software allows them to construct the queries and also to produce printed reports that are often asked for by department managers.

Data management *continued*

Example 3

Building a business model using spreadsheet software for a new business selling a new organic soap

Break-even analysis is used to determine how many of a particular product a company needs to sell in order to break even.

Naturasoap are a new company who are going to manufacture completely organic soap. They need to invest a lot of money up front and they would like to work out how many bars of soap they would need to sell in order to break even. They intend to set up this computer model using spreadsheet software. They chose spreadsheet software because it is the best software to deal with numerical information as there are lots of calculations that the spreadsheet can make automatically.

On starting the business, money has to be paid out for equipment, parts, premises, etc. This means that money is going out of the business but none is coming in. As Naturasoap start making and selling the bars of soap, the money starts coming back into the business. Eventually, when they have sold a certain number of bars of soap, they will break even.

This point, called the break-even point, occurs when the money coming in from the sale of the bars of soap balances the money that has been paid out. In other words, you are neither making a profit nor a loss. This point will be reached once a certain number of bars has been sold. Once past this point, the sale of the soap will start to produce a profit.

In order to produce the model for break-even analysis, Naturasoap need to work out the fixed costs and the variable costs. Fixed costs are those costs that do not depend on the number of bars of soap sold. Fixed costs would include rent of buildings, rates, salaries and finance costs.

Variable costs are the costs that depend on the number of bars of soap. So, the costs of the ingredients that make up the soap and the electricity used would be classed as variable costs.

Once they set up the model using spreadsheet software they can work out how many they need to sell to break even. They can then ask 'what if' questions such as 'if the price of the ingredients rose by 10%, how many more bars of soap will we need to sell in order to break even?'.

▲ **Naturasoap use a spreadsheet model to determine the number of bars of soap they need to sell to break even.**

Data handling software

You will find out

> **About commonly used features of data handling software and their purpose**

> **About how a data model may be used for project planning and costing**

Businesses and organizations generate and use a huge amount of data during the course of their business. This data can be used to answer questions such as:

- Who are our best customers?
- What percentage of our customers who first place an order place more orders?
- What form of advertising best attracts customers?
- How many orders are made each month?

In order to answer these questions the data needs to be stored in a database format. The database management software can then be used to extract the required information from the mass of data.

How a data model may be used for project planning and costing

Modelling is used in many business situations to mimic reality and to see the consequences of various courses of action as a mock up first. The people using the model can change the input values to see what happens to the output.

Project planning

For instance, project management software is used to allow a manager of a large project consisting of many tasks, performed by many different people, to create a model or simulation of the project. Most people are good at organizing a small number of tasks but once the number starts getting larger, the management of a project becomes very complicated. Using this model, the project manager can see the way that each of the tasks contributes to the time taken for completion of the whole project. The project manager could then alter the order of the tasks to see the effect this has on the duration of the whole project. The model could then be used to produce a series of graphs and charts that would enable the project manager to better understand the project.

Project costing

Models of the costs of a project can be created using spreadsheet software. The cost of the project will need to be estimated at the start. The cost of the project needs to be given to the people who have to make the decision on whether to go ahead with it or not.

As the project progresses, the costs may change. For example, if the project is running late, overtime may be offered to staff to help keep the project on track. Paying staff overtime will mean the costs of the project will rise. These can be added to the model to see if any cuts can be made to keep the final cost of the project within budget.

Other examples of modelling

Here are some examples of computer models being used in businesses.

▲ A model showing progress of a project can produce a chart like this, called a Gantt chart.

Using a model to work out what to do when the costs of ingredients or components of a product increase

A company that makes sweets might use a spreadsheet model to work out the costs in producing a certain type of sweet. If the price of any of the ingredients, such as sugar, or any of the other costs, such as rent or the price of fuel, were to rise then they could immediately see the effect that this would have on their profit. Knowing this, they could then decide whether to pass the increased cost on to the customer or whether to absorb it themselves and maybe put the price of the sweets up at a later date. The model enables the company to experiment with the costs and the management to make an informed decision.

Data handling software *continued*

Using a model to find out how many items you need to sell to make a profit

A company running coach tours around Scotland needs to know their break-even point, which would be the number of seats they would need to sell just to make zero profit, in other words to break even. Any company involved in selling either a product or a service will need to know the break-even position.

KEY WORD

Gantt chart A type of chart, with horizontal bars, used to plan and schedule jobs.

◀ If the price of cocoa goes up, then a sweet manufacturer may use a model to work out whether they should put up their prices.

Questions A

1 A computer dating company keep details of their members in a relational database. This database can be used by the staff to make suitable matches between people.

(a) Explain what is meant by a relational database. *(2 marks)*

(b) Give **two** features of a relational database. *(2 marks)*

(c) Give the name of the Act that covers the storage of personal data. *(1 mark)*

2 When a project is undertaken it is usually given a budget and a time by which it must be completed. Computer models can be created to help with both of these tasks.

(a) Explain what is meant by a computer model. *(2 marks)*

(b) Describe how a model created using spreadsheet software can be used to keep track of project costs. *(2 marks)*

(c) Give **one** advantage in using a computer model to help manage the costs. *(1 mark)*

3 Project management software is used to help ensure that projects are completed on time. A Gantt chart can be produced using this software. Explain what is meant by a Gantt chart. *(2 marks)*

4 A car hire company uses a computer to collect and store the details of customers who want to hire a car. The details are stored in a database. The company needs to store the customer details as well as details of their driving licence and driving experience.

(a) Write down **ten** suitable fields that should be included in this database. *(5 marks)*

(b) Here is a table that is used by the systems analyst to summarize the structure of the database. Using the ten fields in part (a), copy and complete this table. *(5 marks)*

	Field name	Field type (text, numeric, currency, date or logical) for a project
1		
2		
3		
4		
5		
6		
7		
8		
9		
10		

(c) It is important that data in the database is accurate, so it is necessary to verify and validate the data.

Explain the difference between data verification and data validation. *(2 marks)*

(d) It is important that the database has a field that is unique. What is the name given to this type of field? *(1 mark)*

(e) Give the names of **two** types of validation check that could be made on the data in the car hire database. *(2 marks)*

END-OF-TOPIC REVIEW

Questions

 Test yourself

The following notes summarize this topic. The notes are incomplete because they have words missing. Using the words in the list below, copy out and complete the sentences A to L, underlining the words that you have inserted. Each word may be used more than once.

```
Gantt    break-even    relational    report

extract    spreadsheet    calculations    form

database    name    query    presence check
```

A _____ databases are where data is stored in separate tables and the tables are related to each other.

B Relational database management software is used to create the structure of relational databases as well as manipulate and _____ the stored data.

C _____ charts are horizontal bar charts that are used for project planning to show when the tasks that make up the whole project start and finish.

D A request for specific information from a database is called a _____.

E _____ software is used primarily to hold data where _____ are performed on the data or the data is to be displayed using graphs and charts.

F Large organizations store all their data in a central _____ that everyone can access from networked computers.

G Printed information is usually extracted from a database in _____ format.

H Organizations include every cost (staff wages, software, hardware, training, etc.) in the cost of a project and these can be modelled using _____ software.

I _____ analysis is often performed as a computer model in businesses in order to determine the number of goods that must be sold just to make a profit.

J A screen used to enter data into a database or a document that is used to collect data is called a _____.

K In order to link two tables the linking field needs to have exactly the same _____ in both tables.

L Some fields in a database must always have data entered in them. A _____ checks to make sure that such a field has data entered into it.

Summary mind map

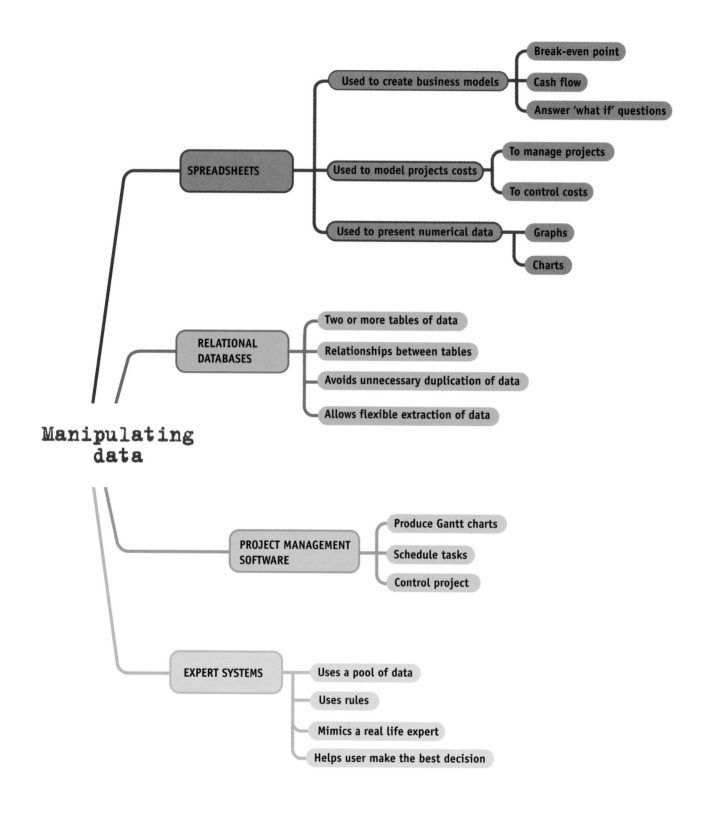

SPREADSHEETS
- Used to create business models
  - Break-even point
  - Cash flow
  - Answer 'what if' questions
- Used to model projects costs
  - To manage projects
  - To control costs
- Used to present numerical data
  - Graphs
  - Charts

RELATIONAL DATABASES
- Two or more tables of data
- Relationships between tables
- Avoids unnecessary duplication of data
- Allows flexible extraction of data

Manipulating data

PROJECT MANAGEMENT SOFTWARE
- Produce Gantt charts
- Schedule tasks
- Control project

EXPERT SYSTEMS
- Uses a pool of data
- Uses rules
- Mimics a real life expert
- Helps user make the best decision

Legal, social, ethical and environmental issues when using ICT in businesses and organizations

The key concepts covered in this topic are:

- **The main aspects of legislation relating to the use of ICT within businesses and organizations**

- **The changes in working practices due to the use of ICT in businesses and organizations**

- **The use of ICT for security, monitoring, surveillance and data security**

- **The environmental issues connected to the production, use and disposal of ICT systems**

- **The effect on natural resources of the creation and use of ICT systems**

In Topic 6 you looked generally at the legal, social and ethical issues. In this topic you will be looking at how the issues discussed in Topic 6 can be applied to businesses and organizations.

Contents

Legislation and changes in working practices due to the use of ICT

▷ **About the laws (legislation) that apply to the use of ICT in businesses and organizations**

▷ **About the changes in working practices due to the introduction of ICT**

In Topic 6 you covered the legislation that applies to the use of ICT. For this topic it is assumed that you have read and understood the content of Topic 6. If you are unsure, you should read through it again and keep referring back to it when reading this new section. This section also looks at the changes in working practices due to the use of ICT and in particular at home working.

The laws (legislation) that apply to the use of ICT in businesses and organizations

There are many different laws businesses and organizations must consider concerning the use of ICT and these are summarized here:

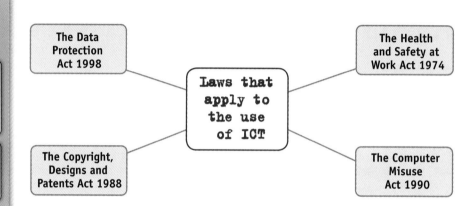

Laws that apply to the use of ICT.

The Data Protection Act 1998

The Health and Safety at Work Act 1974

Laws that apply to the use of ICT

The Copyright, Designs and Patents Act 1988

The Computer Misuse Act 1990

Examples of the Data Protection Act in use

Example 1

A school

A school stores personal information about staff and pupils on a computer system. This personal information is about health, qualifications, religion, salary (in the case of staff), etc.

As this is personal data, the school will need to comply with the Data Protection Act. To obey the terms of the Data Protection Act they will have to:

- register their use of personal data with the Information Commissioner
- allow people to see personal data stored about them if they ask
- keep the data safe and secure
- keep the data up-to-date
- correct or delete any data that is wrong.

Example 2

A doctors' surgery

A doctors' surgery stores patient records on a large database. Each doctor can access patient records using a computer connected to an internal network. The manager will have to:

- register their use of personal data with the Information Commissioner
- only allow patients to see their personal data if the doctor wants to show it, as this is one of the exemptions
- keep the data safe and secure using user-IDs, passwords and access rights
- ensure data is kept up-to-date
- correct or delete any data that is wrong.

They should ensure that the data is not easily copied. This can be done by:

- training staff to warn them about the consequences should this happen
- the use of locks so that unauthorized drives cannot be attached without permission
- encrypting the data so that even if the data is copied without permission it cannot be understood.

Example 3

Customer names and addresses and staff CVs

A firm uses a database of customer names and addresses for sending them regular mail shots. They also store CVs of their staff on the computer. These uses are exempt from the Data Protection Act and are listed in the exemptions in Topic 6.

The other laws being used

The other laws were also covered in Topic 6 so you will need to revisit the material in that topic when completing the following activities.

Activity

Health and Safety at Work Act

A new company is being set up and they are buying new office furniture and designing the office. As most of the staff will be using ICT, there are a number of things they need to consider in order to keep staff safe.

The manager has made the following notes as a reminder and you have to write what needs to be considered for each of them:

- chairs
- desks
- lighting
- blinds.

Activity

The Computer Misuse Act and the Copyright, Designs and Patents Act

A school is concerned about the behaviour of some of the students. It seems that they do not seem to understand how the Computer Misuse Act and the Copyright, Designs and Patents Act apply to them.

You have been asked to produce a pair of posters – one for each Act. The posters should spell out what they should not do. To give you an idea: the deliberate creation of computer viruses is forbidden under the Computer Misuse Act, so you need to make this clear.

Your poster should:

- be produced in colour
- be eye-catching
- contain only enough text to get the message across
- make it blatantly clear what they should not be doing.

Legislation and changes in working practices due to the use of ICT *continued*

Changes in working practices due to the use of ICT

The use of ICT has changed the way people can work. The main change is that it is possible for people to work together yet not be in the same place.

Collaborative working (i.e., people working together)

Many collaborative workers can work from home and keep in touch with each other using such ICT as that shown here:

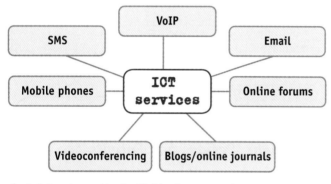

Collaborative working is aided by these ICT services.

Collaborative home working/teleworking

If you have an Internet connection then you can communicate easily with people all around the country or even the world. Many people who use computers for their work are able to do their work at home. Working from home using ICT equipment and telecommunications to do collaborative work is called home working or teleworking.

The advantages of teleworking to the employee:

There are a number of disadvantages of teleworking to the employee:

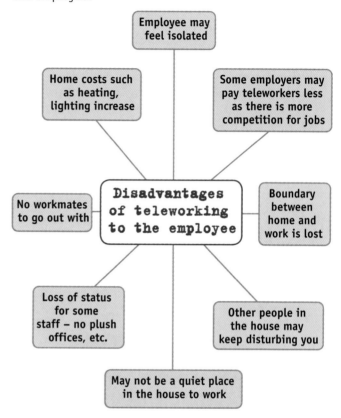

Why do employers allow staff to telework? You can see the advantages that teleworking offers to employers:

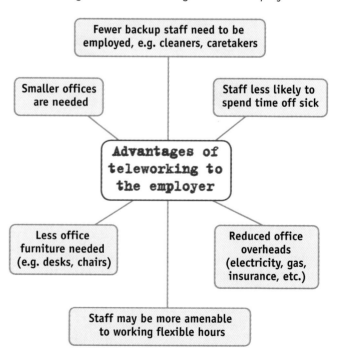

There are also a number of disadvantages of teleworking to employers:

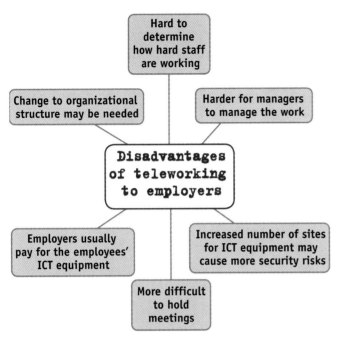

Hard to determine how hard staff are working

Change to organizational structure may be needed

Harder for managers to manage the work

Disadvantages of teleworking to employers

Employers usually pay for the employees' ICT equipment

Increased number of sites for ICT equipment may cause more security risks

More difficult to hold meetings

There are advantages to society in teleworking:

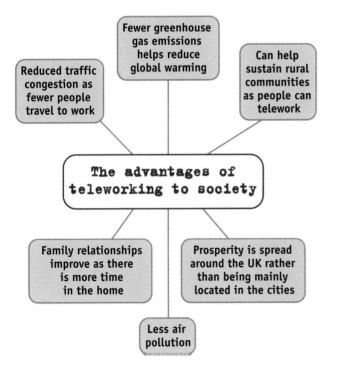

Fewer greenhouse gas emissions helps reduce global warming

Reduced traffic congestion as fewer people travel to work

Can help sustain rural communities as people can telework

The advantages of teleworking to society

Family relationships improve as there is more time in the home

Prosperity is spread around the UK rather than being mainly located in the cities

Less air pollution

EXAM TIPS

You may simply be asked about the advantages or disadvantages of teleworking. You can therefore give a mixture of answers that relate to the employer, employee or society as a whole.

When asked to give a certain number of advantages/disadvantages, always make sure that your answers are distinctly different.

Example

DC Designs

DC Designs are a graphic design company who produce eye-catching posters and adverts that are put on billboards around the country. They are a large organization and they expect their staff to use the Internet as part of their work.

The trouble is that some staff are not using this service responsibly. Employees are spending time:

- Doing their own work. In some cases employees were found doing paid work for another company using DC Designs' computers and software.
- Sending personal emails.
- Keeping in touch with their friends using social networking sites.
- Browsing the Internet for non-work-related information (e.g., music, jokes, information about holidays, etc.).

There have been some other problems such as:

- Computers with some important data stored on them have been stolen.
- There is little security and people can wander into the building and into computer rooms.
- Non-employees have been using the car park owned by DC Designs.

A meeting is held to discuss the issues and the following is decided:

- Training of staff will take place so staff know exactly what they can and can't do.
- Emails will be monitored – the network manager will read emails to check the email service is not being abused.
- The network manager will monitor the use of the Internet of each member of staff. This is so that any member of staff wasting time on non-work-related tasks can be identified.
- CCTV cameras will be set up in the offices – this is to deter thieves.
- Biometric methods will be used to limit access to the building and rooms.
- A car park barrier will be used in the car park so only authorized cars are allowed entry. It is hoped that a biometric method could be used.

Legislation and changes in working practices due to the use of ICT *continued*

Questions A

1. Grangeside Comprehensive School uses computers to store pupil and staff details. Much of the information stored is classed as personal data. All staff are to attend a training course to make them aware of the need to secure personal data.

   (a) Explain what is meant by personal data. (*1 mark*)

   (b) Give **one** reason why the school must protect the personal data about pupils from unauthorized access. (*1 mark*)

2. Give the names of **two** services making use of ICT that have made collaborative home working possible. (*2 marks*)

3. Many people now use ICT facilities to work from home. Home working is also called teleworking.

   (a) Describe **two** advantages to a worker in teleworking. (*2 marks*)

   (b) Describe **two** disadvantages to the worker in teleworking. (*2 marks*)

4. Home working/teleworking can benefit society. For example, family relationships can improve as more time is spent at home.

   Describe **two** other ways in which society benefits from home working/teleworking. (*2 marks*)

Extension activity 1

Use the Internet to find out about home working/teleworking. Find out about the types of job where home working/teleworking is appropriate. Also find out about how employees feel about home working/teleworking.

Produce a brief word-processed document explaining what you have found out.

Extension activity 2

An insurance company is thinking of allowing some of its staff to work from home by making use of ICT. Most of the staff who work from home will be helping clients process their house contents and buildings insurance claims.

Produce a mind map showing the devices and services that the insurance company could use that will allow staff to work from home.

You can use specialist mind map software or use the graphics capability of other software such as word-processing software.

The use of ICT for security, monitoring, surveillance and data security and environmental issues

▷ **About the use of ICT for security, monitoring, surveillance and data security**

▷ **About the environmental issues in using ICT**

You came across the use of ICT for security, monitoring, surveillance and data security in Topics 5 and 6. If you are unsure of what these terms mean and what is involved in each of them, then you should look back at these topics.

There are lots of ways ICT can be used for security. For example, you can use ICT to restrict access to buildings and rooms. ICT can also be used for monitoring, for example employers often monitor their staff using their ICT facilities in order to check they are not misusing them.

In this section you will also be revisiting environmental issues.

Security

There are a number of ways in which ICT can be used for security and these are summarized here:

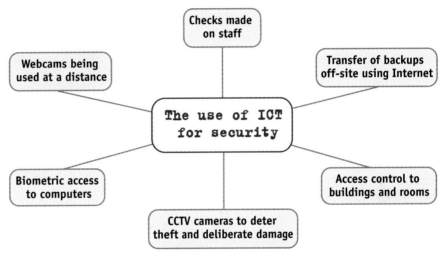

▲ The use of ICT for security.

Monitoring

There are a number of ways in which ICT can be used for monitoring and these are summarized here:

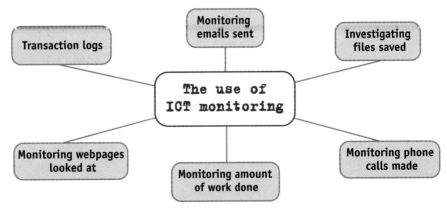

▲ The use of ICT monitoring.

247

The use of ICT for security, monitoring, surveillance and data security and environmental issues *continued*

Surveillance

There are a number of ways in which ICT can be used for surveillance and these are summarized here:

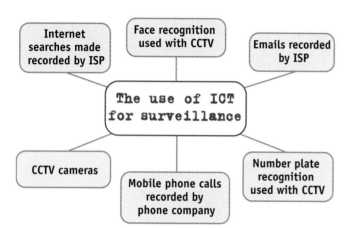

The use of ICT for surveillance.

Data security

There are a number of ways in which ICT can be used for data security and these are summarized here:

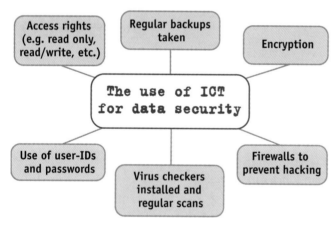

The use of ICT for data security.

Environmental issues and the effect on natural resources of the production and use of ICT systems

These issues were partially covered in Topic 6 and in this section you will be revising the issues as well as covering new ones and will see how they relate to organizations and businesses.

The production of ICT systems

To produce ICT systems requires both energy and resources:

- Energy – this is needed to produce and refine the metals used for circuits, to produce the plastics for cases, wires, etc.
- Resources – ores need to be refined to produce the metals that are turned into components. Oil is used to create plastics. All these need to be transported and this uses energy.

It uses a lot of energy to create metals from their ores.

The use of ICT systems

ICT systems use electrical power and the trouble is that many people leave then on standby when they are not being used rather than turning them off. Leaving them on standby uses almost as much energy as when the device is being used.

Switch devices off rather than leaving them on standby.

Rather than buy new computers, older computers should be upgraded by adding new chips, more memory, etc.

▲ Upgrading uses fewer resources and less power than buying a new computer.

The disposal of ICT systems

The main issues regarding the disposal of ICT systems are summarized in the following images:

▷ Empty ink-jet and toner cartridges should be recycled/refilled.

◁ Old computer equipment should be recycled.

▽ Computer equipment should not be thrown away with general rubbish as it will end up on a landfill site.

Example

Q&A Help Ltd

Q&A Help Ltd provide a call centre that provides help to users of computer hardware and software. They provide help both over the telephone and also online. They use ICT extensively and many of their staff are able to work from home.

They are a very environmentally aware company and they are conscious of the way their business affects the planet. All staff have attended or watched a virtual meeting conducted using videoconferencing about how the organization can reduce its effect on the environment.

▲ Q&A Help Ltd provide help to computer users.

Here is a summary of what was agreed at the meeting:

- More staff will be given the opportunity of working from home where possible so as to reduce journeys, improve the quality of life for staff, etc.
- Staff must reduce the number of printouts made and recycle any paper no longer needed.
- Wage slips will not be printed and posted as they will be sent electronically.
- ICT equipment must be switched off when not being used and not left on standby.
- Any new computers used must use low-power chips.
- Computers should be upgraded rather than replaced by new ones.
- Printer and toner cartridges must be sent to head office where they will be refilled and returned.
- Any old equipment must not be thrown out with general rubbish but instead recycled.
- A system of lighting will be introduced where the lights will go off automatically if motion is not detected by sensors in the room. This will help reduce the amount of electricity used and hence reduce carbon emissions.
- A heating system will be used where the temperature of each room can be adjusted individually and it will switch off the heating for a room when no-one is in the room.

Questions B

1 Give **two** ways in which an organization can reduce their carbon footprint. (2 marks)

2 A company is worried about their employees misusing their ICT systems.
 (a) Describe **two** ways in which an employee might misuse an ICT system. (2 marks)
 (b) Some companies monitor their employees' use of the systems. Describe **two** ways this monitoring could take place. (2 marks)

3 A suite of offices is being designed for a firm of solicitors. Some of the rooms are meeting rooms and are only occupied for part of the day.

 Describe **two** ways the organization can use ICT in order to reduce the environmental impact of the suite of offices. (4 marks)

The use of ICT for security, monitoring, surveillance and data security and environmental issues *continued*

Example

Whizz Logistics

Whizz Logistics are a parcel delivery company that works for a number of e-commerce businesses delivering parcels to homes throughout the country. Because of the high value of many of the parcels they deliver, security is very important at their depots. Many of the customers they deliver to have special delivery instructions. For example, if the person is at work there may be a delivery instruction to leave the parcel at the house next door. This information along with the addresses would be useful to burglars so it is important that this data is kept secure.

ICT is used in the depots to recognize the vans entering and leaving the depots. This uses a CCTV camera along with a computer with optical character recognition software installed. The image is taken using the camera and then the individual letters and numbers are recognized. The details of the vehicle and driver are obtained and the time out of the depot is recorded. CCTV cameras are also used at various places, such as the loading bays, where the parcels are loaded onto the vans. These CCTV cameras record the footage on hard drives that are archived on a regular basis onto magnetic tape. Biometric access control is used to gain access to the buildings. This biometric method uses fingerprinting as a means of giving access to authorized staff.

Whizz Logistics use a WAN and the servers are located at the head office. Each evening backups of the data are transferred to a data recovery centre. This is done automatically using a high speed broadband link. The data recovery centre provides a backup service to many different companies and its use means that Whizz Logistics do not have to worry about recovering their data should it ever be lost.

Whizz Logistics pay well and recruit well-motivated and hard-working staff. Careful checks are made on everyone who joins the company. In the past they had problems with a member of staff who was found selling lists of customer details and contract details to their competitors. It was also subsequently found that the same member of staff had a criminal record. They also found that some staff abused the ICT facilities by:

- Sending lots of private emails in the firm's time.
- Doing freelance paid work for other organizations while they were being paid by Whizz Logistics.

- Making lots of private calls in the firm's time. One person was found to be making one-hour calls to their girlfriend in Australia!
- Spending far too much time on social networking sites.
- Engaging in cyberbullying of other employees.
- Accessing unsavoury material on the Internet.

In order to prevent the above it was decided to conduct training sessions to outline what was acceptable use and what wasn't. Disciplinary procedures were outlined and staff were left in no doubt as to what would happen to them if it was found they were misusing the ICT systems.

It was decided that to detect misuse it was necessary to monitor staff use of ICT facilities. The network manager and their staff would:

- routinely read emails
- monitor phone calls and record them
- monitor webpages accessed and the time spent on them
- look for software/music/images stored in a user's area on the network.

In addition a transaction log would be kept of all alterations made to files. This log would record the type of change made to a file, the reason the changes were made, who made them and the date and time. This log would provide evidence in a court of law. All the staff would be made aware that this log was being kept and the management hoped that this would act as a deterrent to anyone who was thinking of committing a fraud.

As well as taking regular backups, there are a number of other ways Whizz Logistics protects its data:

- Personal and financial data is always encrypted when it is stored and when it is transferred across networks.
- Virus scanners are installed on all computers and these are kept up-to-date by regular and automatic updates.
- Firewalls are installed in order to prevent hackers accessing the network using the Internet.
- Any computer connected to the network will be logged off automatically after a certain period of inactivity.
- All staff will be given access rights, which will control the files that they can view and also whether they have rights to alter the information.
- User-IDs and passwords are used to restrict access.

END-OF-TOPIC REVIEW

Questions

 Test yourself

The following notes summarize this topic. The notes are incomplete because they have words missing. Using the words in the list below, copy out and complete the sentences A to N, underlining the words that you have inserted. Each word may be used more than once.

collaborative home working   collaboration   personal

resources   VoIP   carbon   subject

distractions   family   project   home

Data Protection Act   Copyright, Designs and Patents Act

videoconferencing   Computer Misuse Act

A Many businesses and organizations store _____ data about a living individual such as medical details, credit history, income, religious beliefs, etc.

B The law that covers the use of personal data is called the _____.

C The person whom personal data is about is called the data _____.

D Hacking is made illegal under the _____.

E Copying software, music, images and text without permission is made illegal under the _____.

F _____ means two or more parties working together in order to meet a common target or goal.

G Many people who work collaboratively are able to work from _____.

H Videoconferencing is an example of collaborative working because many people can discuss a _____ at a virtual meeting.

I _____ means working on a joint project from home by making use of computers and networking equipment.

J One big advantage with home working is that you are able to work around _____ commitments.

K A disadvantage of home working is that there are many _____ at home.

L _____ uses cameras and microphones in addition to computers and special software in order to conduct a virtual meeting.

M _____ is a cheap method of making phone calls over the Internet and many home workers make use of it.

N Recycling old computer equipment reduces the natural _____ needed for manufacture and also reduces the _____ emissions.

Summary mind map

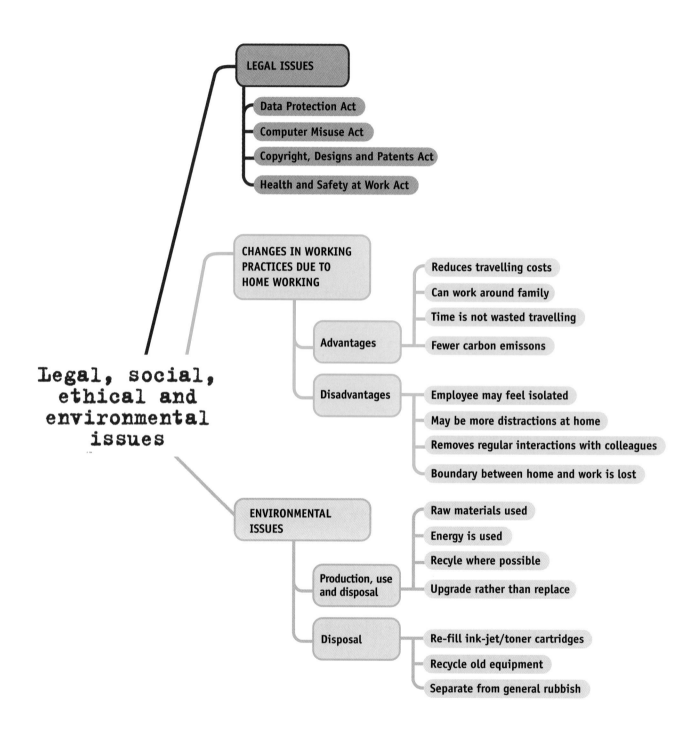

LEGAL ISSUES
- Data Protection Act
- Computer Misuse Act
- Copyright, Designs and Patents Act
- Health and Safety at Work Act

Legal, social, ethical and environmental issues

CHANGES IN WORKING PRACTICES DUE TO HOME WORKING

Advantages
- Reduces travelling costs
- Can work around family
- Time is not wasted travelling
- Fewer carbon emissons

Disadvantages
- Employee may feel isolated
- May be more distractions at home
- Removes regular interactions with colleagues
- Boundary between home and work is lost

ENVIRONMENTAL ISSUES

Production, use and disposal
- Raw materials used
- Energy is used
- Recyle where possible
- Upgrade rather than replace

Disposal
- Re-fill ink-jet/toner cartridges
- Recycle old equipment
- Separate from general rubbish

Topic 18

Managing data/keeping data safe and secure when using ICT

The key concepts covered in this topic are:

- **Appropriate methods that could be used to make backups and archives**

- **Secure and safe practices**

- **Appropriate user security methods and devices**

- **Procedures to minimize the risks of security breaches**

Organizations and businesses keep a huge amount of data. Without this data they could not function. Computer hardware and software can be replaced but if the data is lost then they may never recover from the loss and they could go out of business.

It is therefore extremely important that organizations and businesses take the security of their ICT resources seriously. Much of the theory for this topic has been covered in Topic 5, so you will probably need to look back at this to familiarize yourself before starting this topic.

Managing data/keeping data safe and secure when using ICT

You will find out

▷ **About appropriate methods that could be used to make backups and archives**

▷ **About secure and safe practices**

▷ **About appropriate user security methods and devices**

▷ **About procedures to minimize the risks of security breaches**

You should look back at Topic 5 before starting this topic. This topic looks at the safety and security of ICT systems and does this mainly by looking at an example.

You will have to answer questions in a context in Unit B063, so in the example given you will see how the theory is put into practice.

Backups and archives

Most large organizations operate 24/7, so their systems must be capable of running continuously. Here are the main points about backups:

- Backups are normally taken remotely (e.g., away from the main computer centre).
- Many systems use dual computer systems – so if one breaks down, the other one takes over.
- Uninterruptible power supplies are used to power the ICT systems, which means there should not be a problem with power cuts.

▶ Backups can be taken on removable media – but it is probably not a good idea to hold the disk like this!

Password protection

Access to files is restricted using usernames and passwords. The username allocates the user with certain access rights to data and the password ensures that the person using the system is who they say they are. Passwords protect against unauthorized access.

A password is a series of characters (usually letters, numbers and other characters on the keyboard) that is set up by the user and known only to them. They have to enter this each time they log-in to the network.

Example

A company with more than a few security problems

Student Rentals is a property company that rents accommodation to students in the main university cities. In each city there are two or three members of staff who work from home and manage all the houses in the area. These members of staff are given laptops for this work. The head office is where the main administration takes place. A network is used and it is possible for the members of staff in each of the cities to access data on this network.

There have been a number of security breaches such as:

- money going missing
- hackers gaining access to the network and altering some of the data on it
- students very worried about making online payments of rent using the Internet
- data being lost through backups not always being made
- virus attacks causing the loss of the use of the network for several days.

Student Rentals brought in a specialist ICT security company to give them advice on what they can do to make their ICT systems more secure and prevent security breaches. This company investigated the systems used and spoke to the staff and they came up with the following:

- Money is going missing because no transaction log is kept. This means members of staff can alter customer accounts and it is impossible to see what the account was before the alteration was made. Also details need to be kept of the member of staff who made the alteration and the time and the date.
- It seems that anyone who is in the building can walk up to a computer and start using it. Although passwords protect certain files, it was noticed that when staff were away from the computers (e.g., at lunch or at a meeting) they did not log-off. This meant anyone could access the data. Training is needed to teach staff the importance of logging off. The system should be altered so that it logs-off automatically after a certain period of inactivity.
- Some of the data stored is personal and it is therefore a requirement under the Data Protection Act that it is properly secured. They could be fined if it isn't. Data being stored on the laptops should be encrypted in case they are stolen. It might also be an idea to encrypt any personal data on the network. Any banking details being transferred should also be encrypted.
- Backups must be made regularly and a member of staff must be given responsibility. The backups should preferably be kept off site and the staff must make sure that the data can actually be recovered from the backups. They suggested the following methods:
  - Use removable media and take the backups home.
  - Use an online data recovery company who will supply software that will send the backup copies to them each night using the Internet.
- A firewall needs to be used. This is hardware, software or both that prevents hackers from accessing the internal network using the Internet.
- The problem with viruses can be reduced or eliminated by the use of a virus checker that should be kept up-to-date. Regular scans should be made.
- It was far too easy to gain access to computer rooms and computer equipment. It is suggested that the company should use some or all of the following:
  - Electronic passes/key pads/biometric entry systems to gain access to rooms containing computers.
  - Biometric methods such as fingerprints to access the computers.
  - Use of security cables to prevent theft of computers.

▲ Fingerprint recognition is a biometric method used to restrict access to computers.

▲ Virus checking software must be regularly updated.

255

Managing data/keeping data safe and secure when using ICT *continued*

Questions A

1 A company is having problems with computer viruses.
 (a) Explain what is meant by a computer virus. (*2 marks*)
 (b) Describe **two** things that can be done to reduce the likelihood of viruses causing damage to an ICT system. (*2 marks*)

2 A network manager is worried about hackers accessing the network.
 (a) Explain what is meant by hacking. (*2 marks*)
 (b) Explain what a network manager can do to prevent hackers accessing the network. (*2 marks*)

3 A school network stores data about past and present pupils. This data is contained in a database and any member of staff who has the access rights can view this data. Some staff are also allowed to edit the data.
 (a) Staff need to enter a password to gain access to the network. Explain how a hierarchy of passwords can be used to ensure the privacy of the personal data stored. (*2 marks*)
 (b) Each member of staff is given access rights to the files stored on the network. Explain, with reference to a school, why the access rights given to some staff may be different from those given to others. (*2 marks*)

4 In order to secure a network it is necessary to use methods that restrict physical access.
 (a) Give the names of **two** methods that can be used to restrict physical access. (*2 marks*)
 (b) Describe **one** way software can be used to restrict access. (*1 mark*)

5 An estate agent keeps all the details of the houses they have for sale on a computer. Backup copies of this data are taken each evening and are taken off-site.
 (a) Explain what is meant by a backup copy. (*2 marks*)
 (b) Give **two** types of media that can be used for taking backups. (*2 marks*)
 (c) Give **one** reason why backup copies should be taken off-site. (*1 mark*)

6 Transaction logs help prevent fraud by employees.
 (a) Describe what is meant by a transaction log. (*2 marks*)
 (b) Give **one** reason why a transaction log might deter employees from committing fraud. (*1 mark*)

Extension activity

Passwords are used to protect against hackers illegally accessing a computer using the Internet or accessing a computer directly. Some passwords people use are obvious and easily guessed, especially if the hacker knows the person who has created the password.

In order to understand hacking it is necessary to understand the techniques they use to try to gain access.

For this activity you have to find out about the sorts of things that hackers do in order to gain access to a password-protected computer system.

You will need to research using the Internet to find out about hacking.

After conducting your research, write a short paragraph explaining what you have found out.

Questions

 Test yourself

The following notes summarize this topic. The notes are incomplete because they have words missing. Using the words in the list below, copy out and complete the sentences A to N, underlining the words that you have inserted. Each word may be used more than once.

> backup   access   Protection Act   removable   encrypted
>
> rights   hackers   virus checking   biometric
>
> transaction   firewall   archive

A A school makes _____ copies of all its data for security purposes in case the original data is lost or damaged.

B Data that is no longer valid but may be needed sometime in the future is kept as an _____ copy.

C The school backs up its data onto _____ magnetic media which are taken off-site each evening.

D This means that if the building is destroyed by fire, the original data can be re-created using the _____ copies.

E The school takes security very seriously and staff and pupils use _____ methods to gain entry to the buildings and rooms.

F Fingerprinting was chosen as the biometric method used to control _____.

G Any personal data stored about pupils is _____, which means that should the data be stolen then it would be meaningless.

H Staff are given access _____ depending on their job.

I It is very important that the personal data of pupils is kept secure as it is a requirement under the Data _____.

J As the network containing the pupil details is connected to the Internet, it is important to protect the network from illegal access by _____.

K A _____ is used to prevent illegal access by hackers.

L Financial data such as banking and credit card details should always be _____ before sending over the Internet.

M _____ logs are kept that show which member of staff has accessed and changed a pupil record.

N In order to keep computer viruses out of the system the latest _____ software is installed and kept up-to-date with regular downloads from the Internet.

Summary mind maps

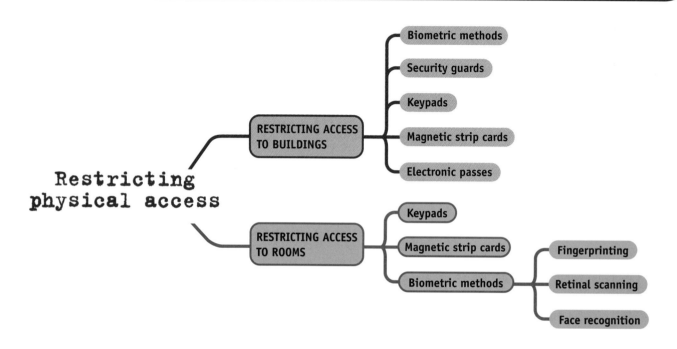

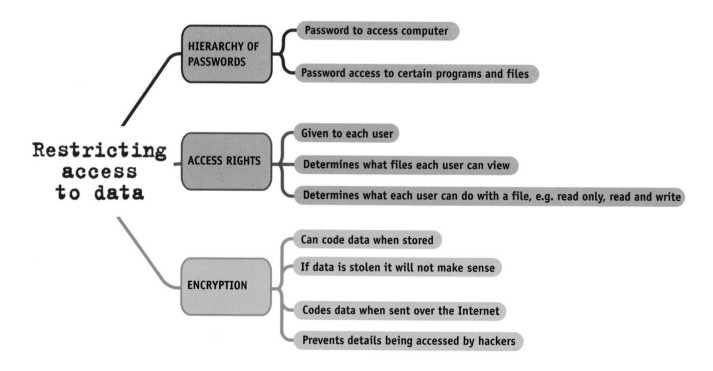

Topic 19

Current and emerging technologies

The key concepts covered in this topic are:

- Changes in everyday ICT use
- Evolving communication systems
- How emerging technologies affect the way companies and their staff operate and work together
- How new and emerging technologies could assist organizations

ICT developments shape the world we live in. Communication methods are likely to change as more and more devices are merged into one. For example, many mobile phones have functions of computers. In the future you are likely to see more integration of devices. For example, you would not need a satellite navigation system as well as a mobile phone or an MP3 player and a phone.

There are plans to use mobile phones to control certain devices in the home. For example, when you are away on holiday you can send a signal to the watering system to start watering your garden. You can control your lights in the house remotely and some systems will even open and close your curtains so that it looks as though someone is in.

Contents

Current and emerging technologies

You will find out

▷ **About changes in everyday ICT use**

▷ **About evolving communication systems**

▷ **About how emerging technologies affect the way companies and their staff operate and work together**

▷ **About how new and emerging technologies could assist organizations**

In this section you will be looking at developments in technology that are likely to change the way companies and organizations operate. Many of these changes affect communication devices that have limited use because the screen size needs to be kept small to make them portable.

© Randy Glasbergen.
www.glasbergen.com

"Stop using the tiny keyboard on your PDA and see if they grow back to normal."

Changes in everyday ICT use

The improvements in mobile devices

You will have noticed that mobile phones have many more functions than they used to have. They can be used to surf the Internet but their use is restricted by the size of the screen. Another factor is that if a keyboard is included, it becomes

harder to use. You can of course have a touch screen but even then the keys are not much bigger.

If people want to work and make calls they have to carry two devices: a laptop/PDA and a mobile phone.

The problems with laptops are:

- They are heavy (although notebooks are lighter).
- They have a short battery life.
- They are hard to use (small keys and screens that are hard to see).

Here are some emerging technologies that will help solve these problems:

- Low-power chips – these will not use the power up as fast.
- Longer life batteries – a whole day would be an ideal battery life.
- Able to use applications from the Internet – rather than have software on your computer, it would be stored on a server that you can access at high speed.

- Flexible screens – computer screens that fold out would mean devices could be portable yet still have a large screen.

Flexible screens

Flexible screens are set to make a huge impact on portable devices such as mobile phones, laptops, PDAs and notebooks.

What about these ideas based on flexible screens for the future:

- A 50-inch screen that you can unfold from your bag and use to give presentations.
- Electronic wallpaper. You can change the wallpaper at the press of a button.
- Reusable electronic newspapers that you can fold. They can update themselves from the Internet each day and even have interactive advertisements.

Nanotechnology

Nanotechnology is a scientific technology that is still in its infancy and is set to transform our lives like electricity or the internal combustion engine. New materials can be invented where standard-sized particles can be reduced to sizes as small as a nanometre. A nanometre is about one-hundred-thousandths the thickness of a human hair. At these sizes materials start to exhibit strange properties. For example, gold melts at room temperature and carbon is 100 times stronger than steel.

Nanotechnology will have the following uses in ICT:

- Personal computers with the power of today's computer centres.
- Chips containing films with over 1000 viewing hours.
- Miniaturized data storage systems with capacities equivalent to a whole library.
- Flexible display technologies and e-paper.
- Printable electronic circuits.

Evolving communications systems and how they affect the way people live

There are lots of ways evolving communications systems affect the way people live and here are some of them:

- It is much easier to arrange meetings at the last minute making use of videoconferencing equipment and chat rooms.
- It is easier to make changes to plans as people are contactable whilst on the move by mobile phone, email and SMS.
- Rather than carrying several devices such as sat nav, mobile phone, laptop, MP3 player, they can carry just one device.
- Greater use of digital communication rather than paper communication.
- Use of e-books and newspapers will enable news to be sent to a reader that can be used over and over again.

"It will never catch on. You can't train a puppy on an electronic newspaper!"

- Better user interfaces so that you can just tell a device to do or find something rather than have to use a keyboard or touch screen.

How emerging technologies affect the way companies and their staff operate and work together

The use of ICT has completely changed the way organizations work in a number of ways that include:

- Fewer staff can complete the same amount of work with the use of ICT.
- Smaller offices are needed as fewer staff are needed and storage is not needed for filing cabinets, etc., and also because more staff can work from home.
- Staff need regular training to use the new ICT systems. Staff need to work flexibly as customers

expect to place orders 24/7 and receive orders very quickly.
- More staff work from home using ICT equipment.
- Cheap phone calls mean many call centres have relocated abroad where the wage costs are lower.
- Teleworking/home working means staff spend no time commuting, have more time with their families and can work more flexibly. There is also less pollution as fewer journeys are made.
- Videoconferencing – means staff no longer need to spend time travelling to meetings and spend time away from their families.
- Remote working – people are able to work away from the office using ICT. They are able to access the company networks and it is easy to communicate with collaborative workers.

▶ New materials can be created with completely different properties.

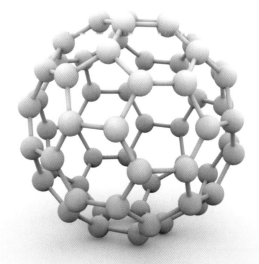

Current and emerging technologies *continued*

How new and emerging technologies could assist organizations

Businesses and other organizations are constantly looking at technology to see the possibilities to make the business more efficient. They are also looking at how they can minimize the effect of the their operations on the environment.

There are lots of ways new and emerging technologies could assist organizations and here are some of them:

- Increased use of robotics – reduces the costs of production, improves the quality of the product and means workers do not have to perform dangerous processes.
- Widespread use of the Internet – means that bills and credit card statements can be sent using email, which reduces costs and helps the environment.
- Smart meters – these will send the reading directly to the utility company (e.g., gas, electricity or water) and this will save having to send people out to read meters.
- Satellite navigation systems – delivery and parcel firms use this, which prevents them getting lost and using more fuel.
- More intelligent heating and lighting systems. For example, lights are switched off automatically if there is no-one in the room.

▶ **Satellite navigation systems help reduce fuel usage.**

Questions A

1 Many devices have revolutionized the way we work and play. Mobile phones are one such device.
  (a) Other than mobile phones, describe how a device or system has changed the way people work or play. *(3 marks)*
  (b) Briefly describe an emerging technology that is likely to change society. *(2 marks)*

2 (a) Discuss the developments in ICT that have enabled remote and mobile working. *(6 marks)*
  (b) Despite advances in ICT there are still limitations in remote and mobile working. Describe **two** such limitations. *(2 marks)*

3 Give **two** examples of tasks that are completed by robots. *(2 marks)*

4 Explain how emerging technology has enabled many more people to work whilst on the move. *(3 marks)*

Activity

Finding out about robots at home

Do some research using the Internet to find out about robots being used to perform tasks in the home.

Produce a mind map that summarizes what you have found out.

Extension activity

Finding out about the interesting world of nanotechnology

Nanotechnology is one of the newest and most interesting technologies and opens up lots of interesting and new ICT-based inventions.

You will cover nanotechnology in your GCSE Science lessons.

Look at the following site and pick out the parts that relate to ICT and write a couple of sentences about each development you think offers possibilities for the future.

http://www.nano.org.uk/news/newsarchive.htm

Questions

 Test yourself

The following notes summarize this topic. The notes are incomplete because they have words missing. Using the words in the list below, copy out and complete the sentences A to M, underlining the words that you have inserted. Each word may be used more than once.

packaging   storage   voice   paint   mobile

accidents   welding   flexible   flexibly   retraining

nanotechnology   battery   videoconferencing   home

A Robots are currently used in factories for the assembly and _____ of goods.

B Robots are also used in car factories for the _____ of panels on cars and also the spraying of _____.

C The use of _____ screens will mean we no longer have to struggle to see what is on the screen on portable devices.

D _____ is a new technology that uses materials with very small particles.

E This material can be used to make chips with huge _____ capacities.

F New interfaces such as _____ recognition will mean that devices can be controlled by human speech.

G Smart cars will be safer because they will be controlled by a computer in order to prevent _____.

H Flexible screens are an emerging technology that will make _____ devices easier to use.

I Low-power chips and longer _____ life will mean that portable devices remain working longer between charges.

J More widespread use of _____ will make it easier to conduct meetings.

K More staff are able to work from _____ by making use of ICT systems.

L This enables the staff to work _____ around their family and other commitments.

M Staff who use ICT in organizations will need regular _____ as new ICT systems are introduced.

Summary mind map

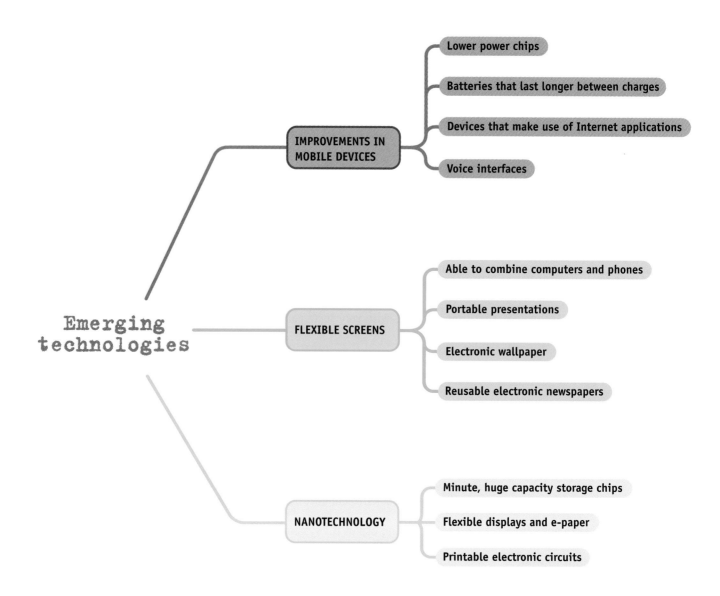

Emerging technologies

IMPROVEMENTS IN MOBILE DEVICES
- Lower power chips
- Batteries that last longer between charges
- Devices that make use of Internet applications
- Voice interfaces

FLEXIBLE SCREENS
- Able to combine computers and phones
- Portable presentations
- Electronic wallpaper
- Reusable electronic newspapers

NANOTECHNOLOGY
- Minute, huge capacity storage chips
- Flexible displays and e-paper
- Printable electronic circuits

The Examination for Unit B063: ICT in context

For the examination paper for Unit B063: ICT in context you will answer the questions in relation to a specific business(es) or organization(s).

You will be given pre-release material prior to the examination. You are expected to study this material carefully as the questions in the examination will refer to it. You will be able to prepare for the examination using this pre-release material by performing your own research, but you will not be able to take any notes or other material into the exam. Any preparation you do will have to be remembered. You will, however, be issued with a copy of the pre-release material in the examination that you will use for reference.

Tips on how to deal with the pre-release material

Here are some tips on how you can deal with the pre-release material in order to maximize your marks in the examination:

- Familiarize yourself with the material. You will need to know about the material and thoroughly understand it before taking the exam.
- There are lots of terminology and key words in ICT. Make sure you can define any terms that are used in the pre-release material.
- Go through the pre-release material and underline or highlight any key terms. These are words that you may need to research. For example, if the

pre-release material mentions 'specialist hardware' then you will need to find out about the specialist hardware used in that type of business or for the particular application.

- Think about if you were the examiner and you had to ask the questions based on the material. What questions would you ask? It is worth spending time writing some questions out and then answering them. Better still, why don't you pair up with others and swap questions and then mark each other's work?
- Use mind maps to summarize the main points made in the material. For example, if the pre-release material is based on a construction company, draw mind maps on the terms used or the concepts. Suppose the terms 'modelling

software' and 'expert systems software' had been used. You can do a bit of research using the Internet and produce a mind map/ diagram similar to that below.

Examples of pre-release material and sample examination questions

In order to give you an idea of the sorts of pre-release material you might be given, one is included here along with an example examination paper and also a set of answers. It is important to always answer these questions in the context of the pre-release material.

Also included is another example of pre-release material and questions for you to try yourself. The answers to this are provided in the Teacher's Resource Guide.

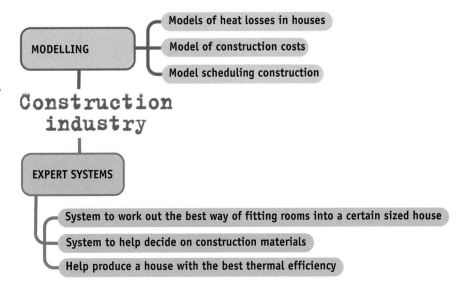

Specimen pre-release material 1

Scenario
KC Developments

KC Developments are a large company with branches throughout Britain who convert large houses into apartments. They work in conjunction with architects, who produce the plans, and builders and trades people, who supply bricklayers, plumbers, heating engineers, etc. They also have their own staff who project manage each development.

The Internet is used to find old properties that are suitable for conversion. The company also have a website that they use to advertise their apartments to prospective purchasers.

As most of the people work in offices throughout the country, communication is a problem. Some large projects are supervised and controlled by staff from different branches. These staff can do a large amount of travelling working on different projects.

Each member of staff is given a laptop computer with a range of non-specialist software and specialist software. They are also provided with a smart mobile phone. The laptop computers are used to store information about each project. Spreadsheet software is used for creating a budget for each building project.

There are regular meetings organized at the head office and the cost of meetings is high because travel expenses have to be paid and these frequently involve hotel accommodation costs. The owners of the company would like to look at ways to avoid everyone having to travel to meetings.

The company is very environmentally aware and would like to reduce the impact they have on the environment. They also use a computer model to minimize the heat losses from their conversions.

There is a network situated at the head office and each project manager is able to access the resources, such as files, stored on this network. As they are working remotely, they use the Internet to access this data. The owners of the company are concerned about the security of their network as they have heard all sorts of stories in the press.

As a building company they take health and safety of their staff very seriously. This applies to the use of ICT equipment.

KC Developments tie up large amounts of money in their projects and it is essential that all projects are completed on time and to a budget. They use software to help them ensure this.

Specimen pre-release material 1 *continued*

Sample examination questions

1 KC Developments use some specialist software. In the table below tick the boxes to show which software is specialist and which is general. *(5 marks)*

Software	Specialist (✓)	General (✓)
CAD package	☐	☐
Spreadsheet	☐	☐
Word-processing	☐	☐
Expert system	☐	☐
Web browser	☐	☐

2 KC Developments use some specialist hardware at their head office. Give **one** use for each of the following items of specialist hardware.
   (a) A0 plotter *(1 mark)*
   (b) 3D printer *(1 mark)*
   (c) Graphics tablet *(1 mark)*

3 KC Developments use a number of different methods to communicate.
   Draw a line joining the name of the chart with the type of information needed to be presented. *(4 marks)*

Gantt chart	Used to show the proportion of costs
Bar chart	Used to monitor project progress
Pie chart	Used to show the number of staff involved in a project over a year
Line graph	To show the trend of annual profit for KC Developments over the last 10 years

4 KC Developments need to send plans of the buildings that are being converted to trades people such as plumbers, plasterers, joiners, etc. These people use the plans to work out quotes for the work.
   (a) State **two** advantages in KC Developments sending the drawings to these people in digital form rather than on paper. *(2 marks)*
   (b) State **one** disadvantage in KC Developments using digital drawings rather than drawings on paper. *(1 mark)*

5 KC Developments communicate with their suppliers electronically.
   (a) Give **two** different features of email software that will help them communicate with their suppliers. *(2 marks)*
   (b) Describe **one** advantage in them communicating with their suppliers in this way rather than by using paper. *(1 mark)*

6 The website KC Developments uses to communicate with its customers has been produced using web authoring software.
   (a) Give **two** examples of other software that would be needed in addition to the web authoring software in order to produce a website. *(2 marks)*
   (b) For each of the pieces of software you have named in part (a), explain why they are needed. *(2 marks)*

7 The health and safety manager of KC Developments is concerned that not all staff are aware of the health and safety problems when working with ICT systems. They decide to give a presentation to all staff.
   (a) Give the names of **two** health problems that can arise due to incorrect use of ICT equipment. *(2 marks)*
   (b) Describe **two** things the health and safety manager should tell staff to do in order to minimize the health risks when working with ICT systems. *(2 marks)*

8 The owner of the company is very concerned about the security of the internal network located at the head office.

    (a) Explain why connection of the internal network to the Internet can increase the security risk. *(2 marks)*

    (b) Describe **two** ways the network can be protected from unauthorized access. *(2 marks)*

9 The owner of the company has heard about videoconferencing and wonders how it might benefit KC Developments. Explain how videoconferencing would benefit the company. *(8 marks)*

The quality of written communication will be assessed in your answer to this question.

10 Explain how ICT can help the project managers ensure that their projects are completed on time and within the budget allocated. *(8 marks)*

Answers to Sample examination questions: Pre-release material 1

1 One mark for each correctly placed tick.

Software	Specialist (3)	General (3)
CAD package	✓	☐
Spreadsheet	☐	✓
Word-processing	☐	✓
Expert system	✓	☐
Web browser	☐	✓

2 (a) One mark for one similar answer to the following:

- Printing out scale drawings
- Printing out plans

(b) One mark for one answer similar to the following:

- Producing a model of each apartment
- Producing a model to show planners
- Producing a model to show neighbours

(c) One mark for one answer similar to the following:

- To enable pre-drawn shapes such as kitchen units/appliances to be added to a plan.
- To leave more room on the screen for the plan.
- To enable a freehand sketch to be drawn using a stylus.
- To enable special finishes such as brick/stone/slate to be added to 3D diagrams.

3 One mark for each correctly drawn line.

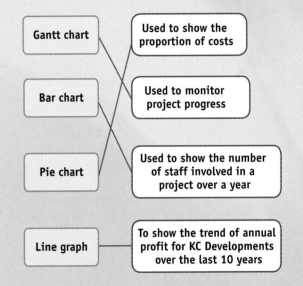

4 (a) Marks can only be awarded here if the answer clearly relates to KC Developments and addresses its needs.

One mark for each advantage similar to the following to a maximum of two marks.

- The drawings can be sent by email attachment, which is faster and cheaper than using post.
- The trades people can load the plans if they have suitable software and modify them rather than having to re-draw them.
- The plans can be stored more easily for future reference.
- It is much quicker to create a group and send all the people in the group the plans as file attachments.

Specimen pre-release material 1 *continued*

- It is easy to zoom in on any fine details in the plan.
- The plans can be copied to portable devices such as laptops and PDAs, which can be referred to during site visits.
- It is much cheaper to copy a file than have to copy a large sheet of paper with the plan on it.

(b) Marks can only be awarded here if the answer clearly relates to KC Developments and addresses its needs.

One mark for one disadvantage similar to the following:

- It is easier to refer to a plan on site than on a portable device, which tends to have a small screen.
- It is easier to draw amendments on a paper plan on site.
- It is easier for a group of people on site to view a plan on paper.
- Not all the trades people will have the knowledge of computers to be able to load the file KC Developments sends.

5 (a) One mark each for two features similar to the following:

- File attachments
- Sending the same email to a group
- Reply
- Forward

(b) One mark for one advantage such as:

- Faster as email is sent and received instantly.
- Lower cost as you do not need a stamp, paper and envelope.
- More environmentally friendly as fewer resources used.

6 (a) One mark for each of two examples such as:

- Graphics
- Word-processing
- Animation
- Photo/image editing

(b) One mark each for two reasons which must relate to the answer given in part (a) such as:

- Graphics – so that graphics can be designed and then integrated into the webpage.
- Word-processing – so that text can be typed in and edited before being imported/copied into the webpage.
- Animation – so that a moving graphic can be produced and added to a webpage.
- Photo/image editing – so that a photographic image can be edited before inclusion on the webpage.

7 (a) One mark each for two health problems similar to:

- Repetitive strain injury (RSI)
- Eye strain
- Back ache
- Stress

(b) One mark each for two answers such as:

- Adopt correct seating position/posture
- Use a document holder
- Use an ergonomic keyboard/mouse, etc.
- Learn how to type properly
- Use blinds to reduce glare on the screen
- Keep the screen clean
- Have regular eye-tests
- Have periodic rests/changes in activity

8 (a) One mark each for two points made similar to the following:

- There is a greater risk of viruses attached to emails, downloaded files, etc.
- Risk of hackers using the Internet to access the internal network.
- Malware might be installed, which copies passwords and account details.
- Danger of identity theft as financial details are sent over the Internet.

(b) One mark for each of two ways such as:

- Install the latest virus checking software
- Keep virus checking software up-to-date
- Install a firewall to repel hackers
- Change passwords regularly
- Use biometric methods (e.g., fingerprinting) to gain access to the computer.

9 This question is to be marked at levels of response:

Level 1 (0–3 marks)

- Only some aspects of the question have been addressed and basic benefits have been given.
- Answers may be simplistic with little or no relevance.
- There will be little or no use of specialist terms.
- There will be errors in grammar, punctuation and spelling.

Level 2 (4–6 marks)

- All aspects of the question have been addressed, although some of the advantages will be limited.
- There will be an attempt at a conclusion.
- For the most part, the information will be relevant and presented in a structured and coherent format.
- Specialist terms will be used appropriately and for the most part correctly.
- There may be occasional errors in grammar, punctuation and spelling.

Level 3 (7–8 marks)

- All aspects of the question will be addressed and all the advantages have been identified. The advantages will be well explained.
- There will be a reasoned conclusion.
- The student will have referenced the case study company and its needs.
- Information will be relevant, clear, organized and presented in a structured and coherent format.
- Specialist terms will be used correctly and appropriately.
- There will be few, if any, errors in grammar, punctuation and spelling.

The list below indicates the advantages that they should have identified in their research.

Points may include:

(One mark is given for a reason with one mark given for further detail or an example)

- Less stress for employees (*1 mark*) as they do not have to put up with train delays, bad weather, accidents, road-works, etc., as they travel to meetings (*1 mark*).
- Cheaper for KC Developments (*1 mark*) as they do not have to pay for travelling expenses or hotel accommodation (*1 mark*).
- A large number of people can take part in the meeting (*1 mark*), which may be prohibitive from an expense point of view for a real meeting (*1 mark*).

- Improved family life for their employees (*1 mark*) as they have to spend less time away from their families (*1 mark*).
- PowerPoint presentations and other visual aids can be shared between employees and others such as suppliers (*1 mark*), because you can attach the files to emails, which can be sent to a group (*1 mark*).
- Meetings can be called at very short notice (*1 mark*), which would be impossible to organize any other way (*1 mark*).
- It makes KC Developments 'greener' (*1 mark*) as there are no greenhouse gases emitted attending a virtual meeting (*1 mark*).
- Documents can be transferred electronically to each delegate's computer (*1 mark*), which means you don't need printouts which are wasteful (*1 mark*).

10 One mark for each of eight points similar to the following:

- An online diary (blog) can be set up to record project progress.
- Project managers can keep in touch with the project team to continually monitor progress.
- Regular project reports can be produced by the project manager and sent using file attachment and group email to the project team.
- Meetings can be held at the last minute to discuss problems and rather than everyone have to travel to KC Developments headquarters, they can use videoconferencing.
- Chat rooms can be set up where people can discuss the project and give each other help and support.
- Software can be used to produce Gantt charts that can be used to monitor progress.
- Project costs can be modelled using spreadsheet software.
- If the project goes over the budget, the project manager can economize by altering values in the model to see how the costs might be reduced.
- Project management software can be used to organize the best use of available resources such as money, people and equipment.
- Staff working on the project can work away from the headquarters using mobile computing.
- Staff can be instructed to send brief project reports by email each evening.
- Mobile phones can be used to contact staff when they are on site so that progress can be reviewed.

Specimen pre-release material 2

You should study the following pre-release material and do some research using the Internet, this book and other suitable sources on the ICT terms used and the types of systems covered. You main aim is to fully understand how the Council is using ICT and might use it in the future. You are free to prepare summaries, mind maps and notes but these can only be used to help you revise and you will not be able to take these into the examination with you.

Also included is a sample examination paper based on the pre-release material. The answers to this are included in the Teacher's Resource Guide, which your teacher should have a copy of.

Scenario
Midshires County Council

Midshires County Council is a public organization that is responsible for many services to the public, from collecting and disposing of household waste, keeping streets clean to monitoring and controlling traffic.

There is a traffic control centre at the council headquarters. It is the responsibility of this department to keep the traffic flowing around the busy areas. The council uses a computerized traffic control system to keep the traffic moving, particularly during the morning and evening rush hours.

The system uses a computer model to work out the best way to sequence the lights in the busy period. The inputs to the model are the details about the traffic obtained from sensors situated near busy junctions. These sensors send the real-time data back to the main computer. Once the computer has

processed the data the output from the model sends a signal back to the traffic lights to control them.

The Council are also responsible for parking enforcement and there is a team of Civil Enforcement Officers who are able to issue tickets for parking offences. They use a PDA to enter car registration details so they can work out which cars have parked for longer than they should have. People receive a parking ticket, which is written out by hand and placed on the vehicle windscreen. They are able to pay the fine on the council website using a credit or debit card. The payment site uses a secure server. If they do not pay the fine then the council is able to access the DVLA (Driver Vehicle Licensing Authority) database where the car registration number is entered and all the details about the keeper are displayed. They can then send a notice to their address saying they will be taken to court.

The council is also responsible for gritting the roads in winter. To use the minimum amount of grit but make the roads safe they need very accurate information about the weather. The traffic control centre also has several remote weather stations that collect data about the weather and then relay the data back to the centre using

modems and telephone lines. The data is used to predict the likelihood of black ice on the road surface. If this is likely, a notice is sent to the gritters to start gritting the road.

The council are also responsible for the fixed speed cameras and red light cameras in the area. Vehicle speeding systems consist of sensors to detect the vehicle speed and a camera that takes a picture of the speeding vehicle with the speed superimposed on the photograph. Using the registration number, information from the DVLA database is used to obtain the name and address of the registered keeper of the vehicle so that appropriate action can be taken.

Red light cameras detect and photograph those vehicles that have jumped the traffic lights and work in a similar way to the speed cameras.

The council also use a special type of ICT system called a Geographical Information System. Suppose a new bar is being planned and they have applied for planning permission from the council. The council have to write to local residents who live within a certain radius to see if they object. The GIS uses a map and the location of the proposed bar is marked. The computer then marks a circular area around the bar and produces a list of all the properties. They then word-process letters to the people living in the identified houses. The people who are affected are sent letters. They can object by letter or by filling in a form on the council's website.

The computers at the council are all networked and the main computer is situated in the council headquarters. There are many computers connected to the network and these are situated at the council headquarters and at other offices situated throughout the area.

The council are keen to investigate the possibility of home working or teleworking for certain staff.

There has been an increase in crime along a certain road that has lots of bars on it and they would also like to improve the security in this area. They would like to install CCTV cameras.

Specimen pre-release material 2 *continued*

Sample examination questions

1   Within the headquarters of the council, staff use specialist hardware and software. In the table below tick the boxes to show which items are general (found in any office) and which are specialist. *(5 marks)*

Equipment and software	General items	Specialist items
Word-processing software	☐	☐
Modem	☐	☐
Geographical Information System software	☐	☐
Web browser software	☐	☐
Email software	☐	☐

2   The council use a number of different methods to communicate.
Draw a line joining the name of the method of communication and the description of the information. *(3 marks)*

Email		Staff communicating internally with each other
Online forms		Weather data from remote weather station
Sensors		Public objections to planning applications

3   When people submit planning applications to the council they have to supply the council with a plan. This is usually sent to the council on paper. The council then digitize this so that it can be placed on the planning website.
(a)   Give the name of the piece of hardware that can be used to turn a paper plan into an image that can be stored and displayed on a computer. *(1 mark)*
(b)   Give **two** advantages to the council in turning a paper drawing into digital form. *(2 marks)*

4   The weather forecasting system uses several weather stations.
(a)   Give the names of **three** sensors that would likely be used in the weather stations. *(3 marks)*
(b)   The data is sent using a modem and a telephone line. Describe an alternative way of sending this data. *(2 marks)*

5   Staff are located at different offices, some of which are 30 miles from the council headquarters. This causes problems when meetings need to be organized.
Discuss the advantages and disadvantages of the council using videoconferencing. *(8 marks)*

The quality of written communication will be assessed in your answer to this question.

6   The council use lots of different software. State the type of software that would be most suited for each of the tasks shown in the following table. *(5 marks)*

Task	Type of software
To send letters to people who have not paid their parking fines	
To search for information about suppliers using the Internet	
To produce a pie chart showing the income from different fines	
To present data to staff at a meeting	
To calculate the costs involved in running a department in the council	

7   The council is thinking of using 'Web 2.0' applications as part of their online strategy. Describe **two** types of 'Web 2.0' applications that would be of use to the council. *(4 marks)*

8   People who receive fines for parking, speeding, etc., can pay their fines using a credit or debit card on the council's website.
    (a) Credit and debit card details are encrypted when they are transferred or stored. Explain what is meant by encryption and explain why it is needed. *(4 marks)*
    (b) It is important that only authorized council staff can access certain files. Describe **two** ways of restricting the access to computers to only authorized staff. *(2 marks)*

9   The council are responsible for collecting and recycling rubbish and other unwanted items. The council have to set a good example in the recycling of ICT systems.
    Give **three** things the council should do in order to minimize the effect of their ICT systems on the environment. *(3 marks)*

10 The traffic control system for Midshires County Council uses a computer model.
    (a) Explain the main components of a computer model. *(3 marks)*
    (b) Describe the inputs to this computer model. *(2 marks)*
    (c) Computer modelling could be used in other areas of the council's work. Other than traffic control, describe **two** situations in which a computer model could be used to aid the council. *(4 marks)*

11 The council is thinking of allowing some members of staff to work from home.
    Discuss the relative advantages of home working/teleworking for the council and its staff. *(8 marks)*

    The quality of written communication will be assessed in your answer to this question.

The controlled assessment units

Controlled assessment in ICT is coursework that you complete in a supervised environment. This is done to ensure that the work you produce is your own.

Here is what units you take for the two GCSE ICT courses:

- For the GCSE ICT Short course you will take one controlled assessment unit; Unit B062: Practical applications in ICT.
- For the GCSE ICT Full course you will take two controlled assessment units; Unit B062: Practical applications in ICT and either B064: Creative use of ICT or B065: Coding a solution.

It is important to note that the work you do for the controlled assessment unit will also use some of the work you do in the theory units of the course. You will need to refer back to the theory sections of this book to check on the meaning of certain things. For example, if you are asked to produce a model then you will need to check you understand what a model is by referring back to the section on modelling on page 85.

For each of the controlled assessment units you take, you will be given a scenario that outlines the task and also the mark scheme that shows how your teacher will mark your work. These are extremely important documents and you must read them carefully many times and refer to them continually when producing your solutions.

▶ Controlled assessment in ICT is undertaken in a supervised environment.

Unit B062: Practical applications in ICT

In this unit you will:

- Use common applications software to manipulate and process data and other information effectively and efficiently, and present information suitable for purpose and audience.

During your key stage 3 work and this GCSE course you will have used a variety of different applications software. This unit will test how well you can use the skills and the knowledge you have gained in order to complete a task.

For this unit, you will have to select one task from a range of tasks supplied by OCR that will test your practical ability in ICT. You will have to complete under controlled conditions work that demonstrates your practical ability in a number of areas and these are outlined in the following sections.

Investigating a need

You need to demonstrate a practical ability to:

- Research a given context documenting sources of information – this means you will have to look things up using the Internet, collect information such as text, artwork, sounds, etc. You will have to keep track of web addresses and other sources of information so that you can acknowledge where they came from and ensure you are not infringing copyright. You may need to conduct research to find out how to do something you are unfamiliar with. For example, you might have to produce details of profit and loss, so you should do some research on how this is done by other organizations.

- Analyse systematically the information requirements to solve the ICT problems – here you will need to think about the information you need and what you need to do with it to solve the problems you are given.
- Think creatively, logically and critically throughout the development process of a set ICT-based solution – you have to complete the task in a logical order and make sure that you give some thought to the best way of completing the task. It is always best to think about alternative designs, for example, and choose the best one. Any decisions you make should be justified by recording reasons.
- Find and select appropriate data and information that is fit for purpose, relevant and accurate – all the data and information you use should be appropriate for the task. Do not include any information that is not asked for or needed, and verify any information you use from the Internet. Just because it is published on a website does not mean it is correct.
- Work effectively with others to gain and share knowledge – this means you will have to work collaboratively for part of the task but the work you submit must be your own. For example, you can get fellow students to proof read your work and you can proof read theirs.
- Produce a design brief – this is a document that outlines the things that must be designed. For example, part of the design brief might be to use graphics software that conveys the right image for the organization.

- Produce a system specification with measurable success factors – here you need to list and explain what the system you are creating must be capable of doing. Think carefully here as you will have to produce what you have stated. You also need to identify a list of things that are measurable by which your system could be judged a success. For example, if you produced a mail merge to produce name details for delegates at a conference, you could say that this system would save a certain amount of time. If it did save this time then this aspect could be considered a success.

▲ You have to work with other people for part of this unit.

Unit B062: Practical applications in ICT *continued*

Practical use of software tools to produce a working solution

You need to demonstrate a practical ability to:

- Produce a fully working solution to a chosen set task – you must make sure that your solution works in the way expected.
- Select and use a range of ICT tools and techniques to develop effective solutions – you must make full use of the features of the software in order to produce the best possible solution.
- Understand software features and their use – you must gain the knowledge and skills in a variety of software so that you can pick appropriate software for the task. You must also identify the best techniques to use to save time and produce the results.
- Create sequences of instructions – when creating programs you have to create a list of correctly sequenced instructions. You also do this if you create a macro or a control program.
- Manipulate and process data and other information effectively and efficiently – here you have to use the best way to complete the task. For example, if you had to produce a large number of personalized letters, then you can use a mail merge.
- Integrate tools and techniques to work efficiently and to meet user needs – here you have to show how you have integrated material created or obtained from different software into the piece of software you are using. For example, in a mail merge, data created using spreadsheet or database software can be merged into a word-processed document using the mail merge tool of the word-processing software.

- Apply a wide range of tools and techniques across applications to produce ICT-based solutions – you need to show that you can use software correctly to produce a solution to the task given.
- Understand and adopt safe, secure and responsible working practices when using ICT – you need to show that you understand health and safety issues, are aware of security issues such as the taking of backups and do not engage in any of the misuses of ICT.

Important note

The software tools are the software and features of the software that you use to complete your task.

Practical use of file and data structure to produce a working solution

You need to demonstrate a practical ability to:

- Use software features – this means that you need to use lots of different features of software in order to complete the task.
- Model situations and data to explore and develop ideas – this means you have to model a certain situation. An example of this would be to model the cash coming into and going out of a small business using spreadsheet software. Another would be to model the data requirements of a school by creating a relational database containing data in a number of tables.
- Enter, develop and format data and information to suit processing purpose and audience – this is the part where you enter the data into the software you are using. You may have to format the data in some way. For example, you can format cells in spreadsheets to hold

certain types of data, or you can format text in a word-processed or DTP document by making it bold, changing the font type, etc.

- Apply creative and technical skills, knowledge and understanding of ICT tools and methods to import and export data – you will need to show here that you know how to import and export data from one software package to another.
- Check data accuracy and plausibility – you will need to show that you have used appropriate verification and validation checks in your solution to ensure as far as is possible that incorrect data is not processed. If you have used websites to gain information, you will need to check the accuracy of the information you have used.
- Create a suitable data structure for a task – here you will need to create structures to hold data such as tables for a database, a word-processed document with fields for variable information to be entered, a template for a presentation and so on.

Present your solution

You need to demonstrate a practical ability to:

- Use a range of ICT tools and media to communicate data and information effectively and in a form that demonstrates a clear sense of purpose and audience – you will need to use the full range of media (text, images, sound, animation, video, etc.) to communicate with the audience for your task.
- Understand how information should be interpreted and presented to suit purpose and audience – for example you may want to consider presenting information in a table or

graphically or as narration (spoken word). You need to think about how the audience would best take in the information given.

- Present information in ways that are fit for purpose and audience – all the material you use must be appropriate for your audience and their needs. The information must contain everything asked for and not contain things not asked for.

Evaluation

You need to demonstrate a practical ability to:

- Evaluate your own and others' contributions – there will be part of the task where you will have to work with others. Here you would need to consider how that went and what problems and successes you had.
- Test your solution – here you need to develop a test plan that will thoroughly test all parts of your solution. You may need to modify your solution in the light of these tests. Testing is a process that takes place throughout the development of the solution, so you need to learn to correct errors that you spot during the development. Testing is not simply restricted to you and you need to involve others in the testing process. For example, you are not the best person to decide whether the material you produce is easy to understand. Others will often spot mistakes in content, spelling or grammar.
- Create and review your own ICT-based solution – always be critical of your own work and continually think about how you could make things better. It is also important to consider your final solution and how that could have been made better.
- Review and modify work as it progresses to improve the quality of the ICT-based solution – you need to continually ask yourself or others whether the work being produced is good enough and if not, you need to see what you can do to improve it.

▲ Always be critical of your own work and continually think about how you could make things better.

- Identify strengths and weaknesses – you should be able to identify the strengths of your solution as well as its weaknesses.
- Identify areas to improve and recommend and justify appropriate changes that could be made – no matter how good a solution is, it can always be improved. It is important to be able to identify what could be done better if you had more time. Consider what you would do differently if you had a chance to complete the same task again.
- Present your evaluation in a relevant, clear, organized, structured and coherent format – ensure that you structure your evaluation carefully and that you include all the parts.

- Use specialist terms correctly and appropriately – you must use all the specialist ICT terminology that you have come across in the theory when you were learning about the software tools. Use the glossary at the back of this book to help you.

You will be allowed 20 hours under controlled conditions to complete the task. Up to 8 hours of this time should be spent on research/preparation and up to 12 hours should be spent completing the solution to the task.

The work that you produce will be internally assessed (i.e., assessed by your teacher) and externally moderated (i.e., checked by a person appointed by OCR).

Unit B064: Creative use of ICT

In this unit you will:

- Study a range of creative software in order to create a multimedia solution to a given problem

The task you will be given will require a solution that is made up of a number of different elements such as graphics, video, animation, sound clips, etc. The actual detail of what you have to do will be set by the OCR assessment board and you will need to provide evidence that you have performed the following steps in your solution:

- Analyse the problem
- Design the solution
- Develop the solution
- Test the solution
- Evaluate the solution.

You will also be expected to take part in group work and your contribution to the group will be assessed.

Analysis

This is where you have to analyse the problem so that you understand it and can identify what it is you have to do and determine the best approach to take.

During the analysis stage you will need to show the following:

- That you can identify and assess existing solutions to similar problems – for example, if you had to develop a certain website then it would make sense to take a look at similar websites and evaluate them so that you can understand what makes them good or bad.
- That you can produce a plan for the development of a multimedia solution – you covered project

planning in the theory and here you must use what you have learnt to plan your own project.

- That you specify the required hardware and software – here you need to say what hardware is needed for the system, i.e. what spec computer is needed, equipment such as printers, loudspeakers, flash memory, etc., what operating system is being used and which pieces of applications software (along with the versions) are needed.
- That you specify the user requirements – you will be given a copy of the controlled assessment materials that will tell you what the task is. From this you will need to identify as a list the things the user requires the system that you are developing to do.
- That you define the success criteria for a solution to a problem – here you need to write down a list of things that are important for the solution to be regarded as a success. For example, you might have as one of your success criteria that the system must be easy to use.

Design

Design is where you plan your designs for the solution. It is important to note that in the design stage you are not producing the solution.

During the design stage you will need to show the following:

- That you can explain how the proposed solution will be fit for purpose – you need to explain how what you are designing will do all that it is supposed to do.

- That you can design individual components of the solution – you need to show evidence of design. It is best to show examples of draft designs to show how you have reviewed and refined your designs.
- That you can design screen layouts – input screens, forms, spreadsheets, webpages, word-processing/DTP templates, etc., should be designed and evidenced.
- That you can design the overall solution incorporating navigational aids – you need to design the solution and remember that users of the system may not want to work through the product in the same way each time. In some systems, you will need to include navigational aids such as back and forward buttons, links, etc.
- That you design testing routines – this is where you decide what tests you need to perform and start to produce tables that include the tests, what happened and what remedial action was needed, if necessary.

Development

During the development stage you will need to show the following:

- That you can create new, or modify existing, components of a solution – this is where you use the software to create a working solution.
- That you can create screen layouts – you need to take your designs produced in the design stage and create them using the software.

- That you can create navigational aids – all the aids to navigation needed by the solution and which you identified in the design stage should be created using the software.
- That you can create a working solution – your solution must work, so time may need to be spent getting the system to work in the way you want it to work.
- That you have adhered to a prepared plan for your solution – in the analysis stage you produced a plan for the development of the system. You need to use this plan to help you complete the ICT system.

Testing

During the testing stage you will need to show the following:

- That you have tested the solution you have produced – here you take your test plan created in the design section and carry out the various tests on the system. Any remedial action needed to get the system to work properly should be taken.
- That you have used potential users of the system to test your solution – users will be able to identify errors you may have not spotted. They are also able to give an opinion about any aspects of the user interface that may need correcting.
- That you have tested solutions that other people have produced – you can test other class members' solutions and they can test yours. The more people involved in testing your solution, the better.

Evaluation

During the evaluation stage you will need to show the following:

- That you used the results of testing and identified the limitations of your solution – tests performed by others and yourself may reveal things that your solution does not supply.

The more people involved in testing your solution the better.

This is a limitation and you need to record these details in your evaluation.
- That you use the results of testing and recommend possible improvements to the solution – here you need to refer to the results of testing and explain how your solution could be improved upon.
- That you have evaluated the solution with regard to purpose – you need to record that your ICT system does everything that was identified as needing doing.
- That you have evaluated the solution with regard to the success criteria – here you need to take the list of the success criteria you produced in the analysis section and record whether they have been met. You should also make a comment on how well your solution matched the success criteria.
- Improve your solution – you need to comment on how you have continually improved your solution during development.

Working with others

During the development of the multimedia solution, you will need to show:

- That you have planned work with others and have identified objectives and clarified responsibilities – for some parts of the project, such as testing, you will have to work with other people in your class. In order to do this you need to identify the objectives (i.e., what and why the task is being done) and also made it clear who is responsible for which part of the task.
- That you have worked with others towards achieving given objectives, carrying out tasks to meet their responsibilities – the completed task you are working on together (e.g., testing, reviewing work, etc.) will provide the evidence for this.
- That you have recommended ways of improving work with others to achieve given objectives – you need to liaise with others to help you develop the best solution.

Unit B065: Coding a solution

Please note this is an alternative unit to Unit B064. If you are taking the GCSE Full course, you either do Unit B064 Creative use of ICT or this one Unit B065 Coding a solution, but not both of these units.

In this unit you will:

- Identify a potential coded solution to a problem by using basic programming techniques

If you take this 'Coding a solution' unit, your teacher/lecturer will teach you about the skills and techniques needed to produce program code.

For this unit you will be given an OCR set scenario where there will be outlined a problem for you for solve by creating program code. This will be given in general terms so that you can produce a solution that suits your abilities. In addition to the document outlining the task, you will also be given a mark scheme that will show you exactly how the marks will be allocated. These are both very important documents and you will need to continually refer to them to ensure you are doing exactly what is being asked for.

You will need to cover the following when creating your solution:

- Programming techniques
- Analysis
- Design
- Development
- Testing
- Evaluation.

Programming techniques

There are certain programming techniques that programmers use to help them solve problems.

For this section you will need to show the following:

- That you have identified and can use three basic programming constructs used to control the flow of a program: sequence, select and iterate – these are standard programming techniques that you will need to show.
- That you understand and can use suitable select statements – these statements can be used to select data (e.g., IF THEN, CASE, etc.).
- That you understand and use suitable loops including count and condition controlled loops – these are the standard way of repeating steps a certain number of times or until a value that changes reaches a certain number. This could include FOR NEXT, REPEAT, WHILE, etc.
- That you have used different data types, including Boolean, String, Integer and Real in an appropriate way in the solutions to the problems – this could include integers being used as counters, Boolean in IF THEN statements, etc.
- That you can use arrays as appropriate when solving problems – arrays can be used for storing simple data.

Analysis

In the analysis, you have to plan the development of a coded solution to a problem.

For this section you will need to show the following:

- Identify the information required to solve a problem – you need to read the problem carefully and think about what inputs, processing and outputs are needed.
- Produce a plan for the development of the solution – here you break what needs to be done into tasks and give an indication of timescales to complete each part. You could produce a Gantt chart to show this and continually monitor progress.

The first stage of analysis is to identify the information required to solve a problem.

- Specify the required hardware and software – this is an outline of what is needed in terms of hardware and software for your solution to work.
- Define the success criteria for later reference during evaluation – this is a list of things by which the coding solution can be regarded as a success.
- Participate in group work.

Design

For the design, you have to design a coded solution to a problem by developing suitable algorithms and test procedures.

For this section you will need to show the following:

- Describe how the proposed solution will be fit for purpose – how is the solution going to meet the requirements of users?

- Design individual components of the solution – here you design what you are going to do but not actually create the code as that is completed in the development section.
- Design input and output formats – here you can design input screens and design how the output from the system will appear.
- Design an overall solution using suitable algorithms – here you can use techniques such as pseudocode, flowcharts, etc.
- Design testing routines (i.e., create a test plan) – it is important to note that you are only doing the design here and not the actual testing.

Development

This is where you take your design and create a coded solution according to the design. In the development, you need to show how each sub-section is completed and how it forms part of the whole solution. You will need to annotate (add comments to) the code to explain its function.

For this section you will need to show that you can:

- Create a coded solution – here is where you show that you can follow your design to produce program code to solve the problem.
- Create systems for input to and output from the solution – there must be a system of obtaining the input to the system and also one to produce the output in the way desired by the user.
- Create navigational paths and methods – this will allow users to navigate the different parts of your solution.
- Create a working solution – here you will produce code and test and refine it until it works properly.
- Adhere to a prepared plan for your solution – you need to show here that you have followed the plan created in the analysis section and have used it during the development.

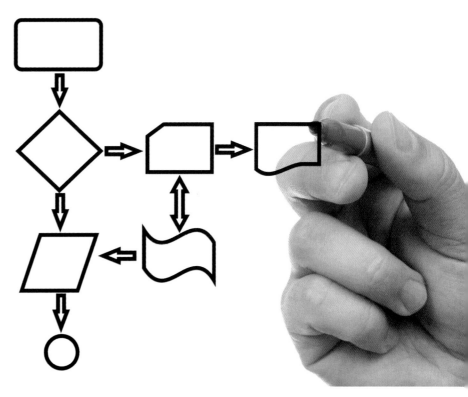

▲ Flowcharts are a useful tool for designing a coded solution.

Testing

Testing must be carried out on the solution to test that it works properly. It must do what it was supposed to do – this is called testing its functionality. It must also be tested to show that the solution matches the design criteria. You must show when the solution worked as expected.

For this section you will need to show that you can:

- Test the solution you have produced – here you need to use the test routines created in the design section and carry out the tests and record the results. Any remedial action needed should be taken and recorded.
- Allow the people who will potentially use the solution to test it to ensure it works properly – you can allow them to see if the solution works as expected. You can also get them to comment on ease of use.
- Test solutions that other people have produced – you can test other class members' solutions and they can test yours.

Evaluation

For an evaluation you reflect on the solution you have produced.

For this section you will need to show that you can:

- Use the results of testing and identify the limitations of your solution – did your solution work in the way you wanted it to or did you make compromises?
- Use the results of testing and recommend possible improvements to your solution – refer to your testing here. Did the users or other class members find things wrong and how could the solution be corrected or improved?
- Evaluate the solution with regard to purpose – did the solution do exactly what it was supposed to do?
- Evaluate the solution with regard to the success criteria – you can check to see how many of the success criteria have been met by the solution. You need to be honest here!
- Improve your solution – what changes could you make or additions could you add in order to improve the solution?

Aspects of the controlled assessment

There are some terms that are referred to in the controlled assessment. The following section will help you understand what is being described by these terms.

The system specification

The system specification is a list of the requirements of the system being created. Obviously system requirements are very different between websites, spreadsheet models, blogs, etc., but here are some examples of system requirements:

- It must be possible to sort the lists of students into ascending and descending order.
- The presentation must be interactive and the user must be able to choose what they do next rather than be presented with a list of slides in a set order.
- The webpages must include an animated logo positioned in the same place on each page.
- The system must record the personal details of all the members of the health club and these should be structured in a way that allows the data to be used for mail merges, reports, etc.
- The model must allow customers to change the interest rate, term of the mortgage and the amount borrowed so they can adjust these inputs to see what happens when one or more of them change.
- The system must be able to produce the results in a table or graphically according to the wishes of the user.
- The home page must be engaging to users so they want to follow the links to the other pages.

- Use a password to the system so that unauthorized access to personal data is prevented.
- Reduce the amount of typing needed so that users are less likely to contract health problems such as RSI.
- Make the user interface easy to use and therefore less stressful.

Success criteria

The success criteria are those criteria that if met would result in the solution being considered a success. For example, if one of the success criteria was that 'the system should incorporate a suitable security system to prevent unauthorized access' and you provided suitable access control using passwords, then this success criterion has been met by the solution.

Test plans

To make testing thorough, it is necessary to draw up a test plan. This outlines what testing will be done. The test plan is designed in part of the solution. The actual testing is performed in its own stage along with any remedial action. The tests are also referred to in the evaluation.

How should a test plan be structured?

Because ICT solutions to problems can be very different, you may need to modify a test plan to suit your own solution. Here are some tips:

- Number each test plan.
- Explain briefly what you are testing for.
- Explain briefly how that test is constructed.
- Give the test data that is to be used.

- Have a column for expected results – this is what should happen.
- Have a column for actual results – what actually happens.

Testing multimedia solutions

Testing multimedia solutions such as interactive presentations or websites is different from testing solutions created using software such as programming software, database software or spreadsheet software.

With a multimedia solution you would need to test that:

- The content is correct, engaging and conveys the right meaning – there should be no spelling or grammatical errors. You need to work together with others to do this.
- Every link works and goes to the correct page.
- All the interactive features work as intended – here you would need to check that buttons, hot spots, image maps, menu selections, etc., all work properly.
- The solution is robust and cannot be made to fail – make sure that there is nothing in the solution that will cause a computer to freeze.
- The product works properly with different browsers – with websites remember that users will use many different browsers to access your website. You need to check your site with a few different browsers.
- People are able to use the solution without help – make sure that you have developed a solution that is capable of being used by the majority of your users.
- The solution meets all user requirements – as always check that you have met all the user requirements with your solution.

Glossary

Absolute reference A reference to a cell used in a formula where, when the formula is copied to a new address, the cell address does not change.

Access rights Restrictions of a user's access to only those files they need in order to perform their job.

Address book The names and email addresses of all the people to whom you are likely to send email, stored as a file.

Application software Software designed to do a particular job.

Artificial intelligence (AI) Creating computer programs or computers that behave in a similar way to the human brain by learning from experience.

Bandwidth A measure of the amount of data that can be transferred per second over the Internet or other network.

Batch total A meaningful total that is used to check that the computer has input all the data.

Biometric A property of the human body such as fingerprints or pattern on the retina that can be used to identify a person.

Bitmap graphic A graphic or image that is stored as a map showing the position and colour of individual dots of light called pixels.

Blog A website that allows comments to be posted.

Bluetooth A method used to transfer data wirelessly over short distances from fixed and mobile devices.

Bullet point A block or paragraph of text that has a symbol placed in front to make the section of text stand out.

Character Any symbol (letter, number, punctuation mark, etc.) that you can type from the keyboard.

Check digit A decimal number (or alphanumeric character) added to a number for the purpose of detecting the sorts of errors humans normally make on data entry.

Client–server A network where several computers are connected to a more powerful computer that controls the operation of the network.

Compiler A program that converts program instructions written in a programming language into binary code that can be understood directly by the computer. It does this by converting all the instructions and then carrying them out in one go.

Compression Storing data in a format that requires less space. Bitmapped graphics such as photographs are usually compressed to a fraction of their normal file size.

Computer Misuse Act 1990 An Act that makes illegal a number of activities such as deliberately planting viruses, hacking, using ICT equipment for fraud, etc.

Content The actual text, images, etc.

Control total A meaningful total (e.g., the total of a batch of invoices) that is entered to check that all the data has been entered/processed.

Copyright, Designs and Patents Act 1988 A law making it a criminal offence to copy or steal software.

Data Raw facts and figures, e.g. readings from sensors, survey facts, etc.

Data capture Term for the various methods by which data can be entered into the computer so that it can be processed.

Data integrity The correctness of data stored.

Data logger A device that collects readings from one or more sensors. The time interval between each reading can be varied (called the logging rate) and the total time over which the data is logged (called the logging period) can also be varied.

Data logging The process of using an ICT system to collect data from sensors at a certain rate over a certain period of time. Remote weather stations use data logging.

Data Protection Act 1998 A law that restricts the way personal information is stored and processed on a computer.

Data redundancy Where the same data is stored more than once in a table or where the same data is stored in more than one table.

Digital camera A camera that stores a picture digitally.

Digital signature A way of ensuring that an email or document sent electronically is authentic. It can be used to detect a forged document.

Download To copy files from a distant computer to the one you are working on.

Encryption The process of coding files before they are sent over a network to protect them from hackers. Also the process of coding files stored on a computer/storage device so that if the computer/storage device is stolen, they cannot be read.

Ergonomics An applied science concerned with designing and arranging things people use, so that the people and things interact most efficiently and safely.

Expert system An ICT system that mimics the decision-making ability of a human expert.

Extranet An external network that can be used by the customers, suppliers and partners of an organization as well as the organization itself.

Favourites Storage area where the URL (i.e., the web address) of a website can be stored so that it can be accessed later using a link.

Feedback Where the output from the system directly affects the input.

Field A space in an information handling system or database used for inputting data. For instance, you could have fields for surname, date of birth, etc.

File attachment A file that is attached to an email.

Firewall A piece of software, hardware or both that is able to protect a network from hackers.

Footer Text placed at the bottom of a document.

Format checks Checks performed on codes to make sure that they conform to the correct combinations of characters.

Gantt chart A type of chart, with horizontal bars, used to plan and schedule jobs.

Gateway The device/software that translates between two different kinds of computer networks (e.g., between a WAN and a LAN).

GIGO Abbreviation for garbage in garbage out. It means that if you put rubbish into the computer then you get rubbish out.

GIS An ICT system used to capture, manage, analyse and display geographically referenced information.

GUI (graphical user interface) Interface that allows users to communicate with the computer using icons and pull-down menus.

Hackers People who try to break into a computer/computer network.

Hardware The physical components of a computer system.

Hash total Meaningless total of numbers such as order numbers used to check that all the data has been entered.

Header Text placed at the top of a document.

Hotspot An image or piece of text used as a link. When you click on the image or text, you are taken to another part of the same page, a different page or a different site, or it may open a new file or a new window.

Hub A hardware device used to join the cables in a network together.

Hyperlink A feature of a website that allows a user to jump to another webpage, to jump to part of the same webpage or to send an email message.

HyperText Markup Language (HTML) A computer programming language used to create documents on the World Wide Web. You use it to specify the structure and layout of a web document.

IKBS An alternative name for an expert system.

Image map An image that contains more than one hotspot.

Information Data that has been processed by the computer.

Information Commissioner The person responsible for enforcing the Data Protection Act. They also promote good practice and make everyone aware of the implications of the Act.

Input device The hardware device used to feed the input data into an ICT system such as a keyboard or a scanner.

Instant messaging (IM) A method of two people using real-time text to conduct a conversation.

Interactive Where there is a constant dialogue between the user and the computer.

Internet A huge group of networks joined together.

Internet service provider (ISP) A company that provides users with an Internet connection.

Interpreter A program that converts program instructions written in a programming language such as BASIC into binary code that can be understood directly by the computer. It does this by converting an instruction and carrying it out before moving to the next instruction where the process is repeated.

Intranet A private network used within an organization that makes use of Internet technology.

Kilobyte (KB) A measure (1024 bytes) of the storage capacity of disks and memory.

LAN (local area network) A network of computers on one site.

Magnetic ink character recognition (MICR) Input method making use of numbers printed onto a document, such as a cheque, in a special magnetic ink that can be read by the magnetic ink character reader at very high speed.

Mail merge Combining a list of names and addresses with a standard letter so that a series of letters is produced with each letter being addressed to a different person.

Malware Programs such as viruses which cause damage and security breaches to ICT systems.

Management information system (MIS) An ICT system that supplies information that helps give managers and others the information they need to make effective decisions.

Megabyte (MB) One million bytes.

Megapixel One million pixels (i.e. dots of light).

Memory cards Thin cards you see in digital cameras used to store photographs and can be used for other data.

Microprocessor The brain of the computer consisting of millions of tiny circuits on a silicon chip. It processes the input data to produce information.

MIDI (Musical Instrument Digital Interface) Used mainly to communicate between electronic keyboards, synthesizers and computers. MIDI files are compressed and the files are quite small.

Mind map A hierarchical diagram with a central idea or image at the centre of the map surrounded by branches that extend from the central idea.

MP3 Music file format that uses compression to reduce the file size considerably, which is why the MP3 file format is popular with portable music players such as iPods and mobile phones.

Multimedia Making use of many media such as text, images, sound, animation and video.

Network A group of computers that are able to communicate with each other.

Network interface card (NIC) A circuit board and a socket that enables the network cable (e.g., Ethernet cable) to be connected to the computer.

Networking software This is systems software that allows computers connected together to function as a network.

Notification The process of letting the Information Commissioner's Office know that an organization is storing and processing personal data.

OCR (optical character recognition) This is a combination of software and a scanner that is able to read characters into the computer.

OMR (optical mark reader/recognition) Reader that detects marks on a piece of paper. Shaded areas are detected and the computer can understand the information contained in them.

Online shopping Shopping over the Internet, as opposed to using traditional methods such as buying goods or services from shops or trading using the telephone.

Online tutorial Using ICT to help in the learning process.

Operating system The software that controls the hardware and also runs the programs.

Operating system software Software that controls the hardware of a computer and is used to run the applications software. Operating systems control the handling of input, output, etc.

Optical mark recognition (OMR) The process of reading marks (usually shaded boxes) made on a specially prepared document. The marks are read using an optical mark reader.

Output The results from processing data.

Parity check Check to make sure that the data sent is the same as that received when data is transmitted from one computer to another.

Password A series of characters chosen by the user that are used to check the identity of the user when they require access to an ICT system.

PDA (personal digital assistant) A small hand-held computer.

Peer-to-peer network Arrangement where each computer is of equal status.

Personal data Data about a living identifiable person that is specific to that person.

Piracy The process of illegally copying software.

Pixel A single point in a graphics element or the smallest dot of light that can appear on a computer screen.

Podcasts (Personal on demand broadcast) Digital media files that can be audio or video that are released in episodes so that you can be fed them automatically when you connect to the service.

Print server A computer in a network that controls one or more printers.

Process Any operation that transfers data into information.

Processing Performing calculations or arranging the data into a meaningful order.

Program The set of step-by-step instructions that tell the computer hardware what to do.

Range check Data validation technique that checks that the data input to a computer is within a certain range.

Real-time processing Type of processing where data received by the system is processed immediately without any delay.

Relational database A database where the data is held in two or more tables with relationships (links) established between them. The software is used to set up and hold the data as well as to extract and manipulate the stored data.

Relationship The way tables are related to or linked to each other. Relationships can be one-to-one, one-to-many or many-to-many.

Relative reference When a cell is used in a formula and the formula is copied to a new address, the cell address changes to take account of the formula's new position.

Report The output from a database in which the results are presented in a way that is controlled by the user.

RFID (radio frequency identification) Obtains data stored on a tag (a small chip) using radio signals, which means that the reading device and tag do not have to come into contact with each other.

Rollover button/image A button/image that changes its appearance when a cursor is moved over it.

Router Hardware device that is able to make the decision about the path that an individual packet of data should take so that it arrives in the shortest possible time.

RSI (repetitive strain injury) A painful muscular condition caused by repeatedly using certain muscles in the same way.

Sensors Devices that measure physical quantities such as temperature, pressure, humidity, etc.

SMS (short messaging service) (texting) Allows short low cost messages to be sent between phones. It is also possible to send text messages to phones using a computer or mobile device such as a PDA or palmtop.

Social networking site A website that is used to communicate with friends and family and to make new friends and contacts.

Software The programs used by computers.

Spellchecker Program usually found with a word-processor and most packages that make use of text, that checks the spelling in a document and suggests correct spellings.

Stand-alone computer If a computer is used on its own without any connection (wireless or wire) to a network, then it is a stand-alone computer.

Style sheets A document that sets out fonts and font sizes for headings and subheadings, etc., in a document. Changes to a heading need only be made in the style sheet and all the changes to headings in the document will be made automatically.

Swipe card Plastic card containing data stored in a magnetic strip on the card.

Templates Electronic files that hold standardized document layouts.

Thesaurus Software that suggests words with similar meanings to the word highlighted in a document.

Touch screen A special type of screen that is sensitive to touch. A selection is made from a menu on the screen by touching part of it.

Transaction A piece of business, e.g. an order, purchase, return, delivery, transfer of money, etc.

Transaction log A record kept of the changes that are made to the contents of a file and also the date, time and person who made them. This is done for security reasons.

Transcription error Error made when typing data in using a document as the source of the data.

Transposition error Error made when characters are swapped around so they are in the wrong order.

Update The process of changing information in a file that has become out of date.

URL (uniform resource locator) A web address.

User A person who uses a computer.

Username or User-ID A name or number that is used to identify a certain user of the network or system.

Validation checks Checks a developer of a solution sets/creates, using the software, in order to restrict the data that a user can enter so as to reduce errors.

Vector graphic A graphic that is expressed mathematically as an equation and can be resized without loss in quality.

Verification Checking that the data being entered into the ICT system perfectly matches the source of the data.

Videoconferencing ICT system that allows face-to-face meetings to be conducted without the participants being in the same room or even the same geographical area.

Virus A program that copies itself automatically and can cause damage to data or cause the computer to run slowly.

Voice recognition The ability of a computer to 'understand' spoken words by comparing them with stored data.

VoIP (Voice over Internet Protocol) Enables cheap international phone calls to be made using the Internet.

WAN (wide area network) A network where the terminals/computers are remote from each other and telecommunications are used to communicate between them.

WAP (wireless application protocol) Offers a way for users of mobile phones and other mobile devices to access the Internet.

Web browser Software program you use to access the Internet. Microsoft Internet Explorer is an example of a web browser.

Webcam A digital camera that is used to capture still images and video images (i.e. moving images).

Web logs (blogs) Websites that are created by an individual with information about events in their life, videos, photographs, etc.

Wi-Fi A trademark for the certification of products that meet certain standards for transmitting data over wireless networks.

WIMP (Windows Icons Menus Pointing devices) The graphical user interface (GUI) way of using a computer rather than typing in commands at the command line.

Index

Acknowledgements

The publisher and author would like to thank the following for their permission to reproduce photographs and other copyright material:

Background – Coloured swirls © Bocos Benedict/Fotolia
Background – Question mark © Stephen Coburn/Fotolia

p.2 © Parrus/Fotolia; p.2 © Dasha Kalashnikova/Fotolia; p.2 © Harris Shiffman/Fotolia; p.2 © Tinka/Fotolia; p.2 © Big Daddy/Fotolia; p.3 © Tan Kian Khoon/Fotolia; p.4 © Petr Ivanov/Fotolia; p.4 © Dmitriy Syechin/Fotolia; p.5 © almagami/Fotolia; p.5 © Inclusive Technology; p.5 © Inclusive Technology; p.6 © sasha/Fotolia; p.6 © Digital Photique/Fotolia; p.6 © Albo/Fotolia; p.7 © Glasbergen; p.7 © IKO/Fotolia; p.7 © Andres Rodrigo Gonzalez Buzzio/Fotolia; p.7 © Marek Tihelka/Fotolia; p.7 © GLUE STOCK/Fotolia; p.8 © io/Fotolia; p.8 © GR Digital User/Fotolia; p.8 © www.chipandpin.co.uk; p.9 © GreenGate Publishing Services; p.9 © Vieloryb/Fotolia; p.9 © Anatoly Vartanov/Fotolia; p.10 © JackF/Fotolia; p.11 © Alysta/Fotolia; p.12 © Andrzej Tokarski/Fotolia; p.12 © Amy Walters/Fotolia; p.13 © Nikolai Sorokin/Fotolia; p.13 © Glenn Jenkinson/Fotolia; p.15 © OrdinaryLight/Fotolia; p.15 © amorphis/Fotolia; p.16 © Marc Dietrich/Fotolia; p.16 © ussatlantis/Fotolia; p.17 © virtua73/Fotolia; p.17 © Viktor Gmyria/Fotolia; p.18 © Andrea Danti/Fotolia; p.19 © Kirsty Pargeter/Fotolia; p.20 © ann triling/Fotolia; p.22 © Ann Triling/Fotolia; p.23 © Jovan Nikolic/Fotolia; p.36 © Glasbergen; p.37 © Glasbergen; p.37 © Konstantin Shevtsov/Fotolia; p.38 © tetrex/Fotolia; p.40 © grandaded/Fotolia; p.40 © Glasbergen; p.41 © rmarinello/Fotolia; p.43 © Scott Maxwell/Fotolia; p.43 © daboost/Fotolia; p.45 © Stephen Finn/Fotolia; p.45 © Christopher Dodge/Fotolia; p.46 © Metin Tolun/Fotolia; p.47 © ta_samaya/Fotolia; p.47 © Petar Atanasov/Fotolia; p.47 © The AA; p.48 © Alex White/Fotolia; p.54 © M.Tomczak/Fotolia; p.58 © snoopdoug/Fotolia; p.59 © Vanessa/Fotolia; p.73 © kmit/Fotolia; p.73 © GreenGate Publishing Services; p.73 © GreenGate Publishing Services; p.74 © Thomson; p.75 © Photosani/Fotolia; p.75 © Kirill Roslyakov/Shutterstock; p.76 © Albert Lozano/Fotolia; p.78 © BlueMiniu/Fotolia; p.79 © Monkey Business/Fotolia; p.85 © Chad McDermott/Fotolia; p.104 © Nikolai Sorokin/Fotolia; p.105 © Mark Rasmussen/Fotolia; p.105 © Gina Sanders; p.106 © Helder Almeida/Fotolia; p.106 © Photosani/Fotolia; p.107 © Ossile/Fotolia; p.107 © Miqul/Fotolia; p.107 © Graça Victoria/Fotolia; p.107 © Andrew Brown/Fotolia; p.108 © Christopher Walker/Fotolia; p.109 © Martina Taylor/Fotolia; p.110 © Helder Almeida/Fotolia; p.110 © Glasbergen; p.111 © Glasbergen; p.111 © Yanik Chauvin/Fotolia; p.116 © Alex Kalmbach/Fotolia; p.117 © doug Olson/Fotolia; p.117 © Paul Hill/Fotolia; p.121 © Gina Sanders/Fotolia; p.122 © daseaford/Fotolia; p.122 © Vladimir Popovic/Fotolia; p.122 © Monkey Business/Fotolia; p.123 © victor zastol'skiy/Fotolia; p.125 © Techno-Vision Systems Ltd; p.125 © Hooleon Corporation; p.126 © Andres Rodrigo Gonzalez Buzzio/Fotolia; p.126 © Yuri Arcurs/Fotolia; p.126 © Jonny McCullagh/Fotolia; p.126 © auremar/Fotolia; p.127 © Jayziac/Fotolia; p.128 © Dmitry Sunagatov/Fotolia; p.133 © Sean Gladwell/Fotolia; p.133 © Sorin Popa/Fotolia; p.140 © androfroll/Fotolia; p.141 © Sean Gladwell/Fotolia; p.143 © Maxim_Kazmin/Fotolia; p.144 © Georgios Alexandris/Fotolia; p.144 © EW CHEE GUAN/Fotolia; p.144 © RTimages/Fotolia; p.145 © Marc Dietrich/Fotolia; p.145 © Sean MacLeay/Fotolia; p.147 © Arpad Nagy-Bagoly/Fotolia; p.147 © Jens Ochlich/Fotolia; p.148 © Viktor Gmyria/Fotolia; p.149 © JJAVA/Fotolia; p.156 © Data Harvest; p.158 © Iglira/Fotolia; p.159 © Nivellen77/Fotolia; p.159 © Arvind Balaraman/Fotolia; p.159 © kapp/Fotolia; p.159 © Arthur Eugene Preston/Shutterstock; p.159 © Michael Fritzen/Fotolia; p.160 © wrangler/Fotolia; p.160 © Andrey Khritin/Fotolia; p.161 © www.hortibot.dk; p.161 © Baloncici/Shutterstock; p.161 © www.mowbot.co.uk; p.164 © Pierre Emmanuel Turcotte/Istock, p.173 © treenabeena/Fotolia; p.173 © Edvard Kirbus/Fotolia; p.173 © Joerg Habermeier/Fotolia; p.174 © Viktor Gmyria/Fotolia; p.174 © Nikolai Sorokin/Fotolia; p.174 © ilumin8/Fotolia; p.175 © Clifford Farrugia/Fotolia; p.175 © Aleksandr Ugorenkov/Fotolia; p.175 © Denis Dryashkin/Fotolia; p.176 © OneO2/Fotolia; p.176 © xdominant7/Fotolia; p.176 © Glasbergen; p.177 © Glasbergen; p.179 © LightScribe/Fotolia; p.180 © Objet p.180 © Leah-Anne Thompson/Fotolia; p.188 © Red Rice Media/Fotolia; p.188 © Ina Van Hateren/Fotolia; p.188 © Henry Bonn/Fotolia; p.190 © Paul Morley/Fotolia; p.190 © kmit/Fotolia; p.190 © Ronald V/Fotolia; p.191 © Gejsi Marku/Fotolia; p.191 © B@rmaley/Fotolia; p.191 © pressmaster/Fotolia; p.191 © Rafa Irusta/Fotolia; p.192 © 300dpi/Fotolia; p.192 © Archos; p.193 © Katie Nesling/Fotolia; p.198 © Marc Dietrich/Fotolia; p.198 © Sabine/Fotolia; p.198 © Daniel Proll/Fotolia; p.198 © amorphis/Fotolia; p.198 © OrdinaryLight/Fotolia; p.198 © Orlando Florin Rosu/Fotolia; p.198 © Tan Kian Khoon/Fotolia; p.206 © DX/Fotolia; p.207 © Marcin Balcerzak/Shutterstock; p.207 © Denis Pepin/Fotolia; p.207 © TebNad/Fotolia; p.207 © Alexander Raths/Fotolia; p.212 © michanolimit/Fotolia; p.212 © che/Fotolia; p.215 © Kelly Young/Fotolia; p.216 © Ewa Walicka/Fotolia; p.222 © Pavel Losevsky/Fotolia; p.223 © kentoh/Fotolia; p.234 © idrutu/Fotolia; p.235 © Marzky Ragsac Jr./Fotolia; p.236 © Liv Friis-larsen/Fotolia; p.237 © Fernando Batista/Fotolia; p.238 © Monika Adamczyk/Fotolia; p.242 © Catherine Yeulet/Istock; p.243 © nyu/Fotolia; p.248 © mark huls/Fotolia p.248 © Midani/Fotolia p.249 © Alex Hinds/Fotolia; p.249 © bluehoon/Fotolia; p.249 © SS /Fotolia; p.249 © Waring D/Fotolia; p.249 © treenabeena/Fotolia; p.254 © Tobias Kaltenbach/Fotolia; p.255 © Kirill.R/Shutterstock; p.255 © Pixel/Fotolia; p.260 © Glasbergen; p.261 © Glasbergen; p.261 © Pawel Szczesny/Fotolia; p.262 © Floris70/Fotolia; p.266 © green308/Fotolia p.267 © pressmaster/Foltolia p.267 © endostock/Fotolia p.272 © Chris M/Fotolia p.272 © Stephen Finn/Fotolia p.273 © Harvey Hudson/Fotolia p.273 © Darryl Sleath/Fotolia p.273 © Jeff Greenberg/Alamy p.276 © picsfive/Fotolia; p.277 © Yuri Arcurs/Fotolia; p.279 © Yuri Arcurs/Fotolia; p.281 © Monkey Business Images/Fotolia; p.282 © Leo Blanchette/Fotolia; p.283 © Tombaky/Fotolia

Adobe product screen shots reprinted with permission from Adobe Systems Incorporated.

Microsoft product screenshots reprinted with permission from Microsoft Corporation.

Although we have made every effort to trace and contact all copyright holders before publication this has not been possible in all cases. If notified, the publisher will rectify any errors or omissions at the earliest opportunity.